Greek

lonely planet

phrasebooks
and
Thanasis Spilias

Greek phrasebook
4th edition – March 2010

Published by
Lonely Planet Publications Pty Ltd ABN 36 005 607 983
90 Maribyrnong St, Footscray, Victoria 3011, Australia

Lonely Planet Offices
Australia Locked Bag 1, Footscray, Victoria 3011
USA 150 Linden St, Oakland CA 94607
UK 2nd Floor, 186 City Rd, London ECV1 2NT

Cover illustration
by Yuki Kamimura

ISBN 978 1 74104 708 0

text © Lonely Planet Publications Pty Ltd 2010
cover illustration © Lonely Planet Publications Pty Ltd 2010

10 9 8 7 6 5 4 3 2 1

Printed by China Translation and Printing Service Ltd
Printed in China

Mixed Sources
Product group from well-managed
forests and other controlled sources
www.fsc.org Cert no. SGS-COC-005002
© 1996 Forest Stewardship Council

acknowledgments

Editor Meladel Mistica would like to acknowledge the following people for their contributions to this phrasebook:

Dr Thanasis Spilias for his translations. Thanasis studied in Greece (University of Thessaloniki) and Australia (The University of Melbourne, La Trobe University and The University of New England). He has taught Greek language and culture at Deakin and La Trobe Universities and worked as the State Consultant for Greek Language (Victoria, Australia). He is presently a Research Associate at La Trobe University. His main research interests are in Greek language and literature, Greek–Australian literature and literary translation. He has published articles in both Greece and Australia, and has co-edited *Reflections: Selected Works from Greek Australian Literature*. With G. Betts and S. Gauntlett, he has translated Vitsentzos Kornaros' *Erotokritos* into English.

Yukiyoshi Kamimura for the inside illustrations.

Lonely Planet Language Products

Publishing Manager: Chris Rennie

Commissioning Editor: Ben Handicott

Editor: Meladel Mistica

Assisting Editors: Branislava Vladisavljevic, Vanessa Battersby, Jodie Martire & Francesca Coles

Layout Designers: Margie Jung & David Kemp

Cartographer: Wayne Murphy

Project Manager & Managing Editor: Annelies Mertens

Managing Layout Designer: Sally Darmody

Layout Manager: Adriana Mammarella

Series Designer: Yukiyoshi Kamimura

Production Manager: Jo Vraca

make the most of this phrasebook ...

Anyone can speak another language! It's all about confidence. Don't worry if you can't remember your school language lessons or if you've never learnt a language before. Even if you learn the very basics (on the inside covers of this book), your travel experience will be the better for it. You have nothing to lose and everything to gain when the locals hear you making an effort.

finding things in this book

For easy navigation, this book is in sections. The Tools chapters are the ones you'll thumb through time and again. The Practical section covers basic travel situations like catching transport and finding a bed. The Social section gives you conversational phrases, pick-up lines, the ability to express opinions – so you can get to know people. Food has a section all of its own: gourmets and vegetarians are covered and local dishes feature. Safe Travel equips you with health and police phrases, just in case. Remember the colours of each section and you'll find everything easily; or use the comprehensive Index. Otherwise, check the two-way traveller's Dictionary for the word you need.

being understood

Throughout this book you'll see coloured phrases on each page. They're phonetic guides to help you pronounce the language. You don't even need to look at the language itself, but you'll get used to the way we've represented particular sounds. The pronunciation chapter in Tools will explain more, but you can feel confident that if you read the coloured phrase slowly, you'll be understood.

communication tips

Body language, ways of doing things, sense of humour – all have a role to play in every culture. 'Local talk' boxes show you common ways of saying things, or everyday language to drop into conversation. 'Listen for ...' boxes supply the phrases you may hear. They start with the Greek translation (so a Greek speaker can look up the phrase they want to say to you) and then lead in to the pronunciation guide and the English translation.

introduction 8

map 8   introduction 9

tools 11

pronunciation **11**
  vowel sounds........................11
  consonant sounds................12
  word stress............................13
  intonation.............................13
  reading & writing 14
a–z phrasebuilder **15**
  contents.................................15
  adjectives & adverbs 17
  articles...................................17
  be...18
  case..19
  demonstratives....................20
  gender....................................21
  have..21
  negatives...............................22
  personal pronouns...............23
  plurals....................................24
  possessives...........................25
  prepositions..........................26

  questions...............................27
  requests.................................29
  verbs......................................29
  word order.............................31
  glossary.................................32
language difficulties **33**
numbers & amounts **35**
  cardinal numbers.................35
  ordinal numbers...................36
  fractions.................................37
  useful amounts.....................37
time & dates **39**
  telling the time....................39
  the calendar..........................40
  present...................................41
  past..41
  future.....................................42
  during the day......................42
money....................................**43**

practical 45

transport **45**
  getting around 45
  tickets....................................46
  luggage..................................49
  plane......................................50
  bus, trolley bus & coach 50
  train & metro 51
  boat..52
  taxi...54
  car & motorbike...................55
  bicycle....................................59
border crossing....................**61**
  border crossing....................61
  at customs.............................62

directions **63**
accommodation....................**65**
  finding accommodation 65
  booking ahead &
    checking in........................66
  requests & queries...............68
  complaints.............................70
  checking out.........................71
  camping.................................72
  renting...................................73
  staying with locals..............74
shopping **75**
  looking for.............................75
  making a purchase...............76

CONTENTS

5

bargaining...............................77
books & reading.....................78
clothes.....................................79
electronic goods....................79
hairdressing............................81
music & DVD............................81
video & photography............81
repairs......................................83
communications 85
post office................................85
phone..87
mobile/cell phone.................89
the internet.............................90

banking 91
sightseeing..........................93
getting in.................................95
tours..96
business...............................97
doing business.......................97
looking for a job....................99
**senior & disabled
travellers 101**
children 103
travelling with children.....103
talking with children..........105
talking about children........106

social 107

meeting people.................. 107
basics......................................107
greetings & goodbyes.......107
addressing people..............109
making conversation..........110
nationalities..........................111
age...112
occupations & studies........113
family......................................114
farewells.................................115
interests.............................117
common interests................117
music.......................................118
cinema & theatre.................119
feelings & opinions.........121
feelings...................................121
opinions..................................122
politics & social issues........123
the environment...................125
going out...........................127
where to go...........................127
invitations..............................128
responding to invitations..129
arranging to meet...............129
drugs.......................................130
romance..............................131
asking someone out...........131

pick-up lines.........................131
rejections...............................132
getting closer........................133
sex..134
love..135
problems.................................136
leaving....................................136
**beliefs & cultural
differences 137**
religion....................................137
cultural differences.............138
art..139
sport......................................141
sporting interests................141
going to a game...................142
playing sport.........................143
fishing.....................................146
horse riding...........................147
soccer/football.....................148
tennis & table tennis..........149
water sports..........................150
outdoors............................151
hiking......................................151
beach.......................................153
weather...................................154
flora & fauna.........................155

food 157

eating out 157
  basics...157
  finding a place to eat 158
  at the restaurant 160
  at the table............................164
  talking food 165
  methods of preparation.... 165
  nonalcoholic drinks 166

  alcoholic drinks 167
  in the bar 169
  drinking up 170
self-catering 171
vegetarian & special meals..173
  ordering food.......................173
  special diets & allergies 174
culinary reader....................175

safe travel...191

essentials............................191
  emergencies..........................191
  police 192
health....................................195
  doctor 195
  symptoms & conditions 198

  women's health...................201
  allergies...................................202
  parts of the body 203
  alternative treatments.......204
  pharmacist 204
  dentist.....................................206

dictionaries 207

english–greek
  dictionary 207

greek–english
  dictionary 239

index 251

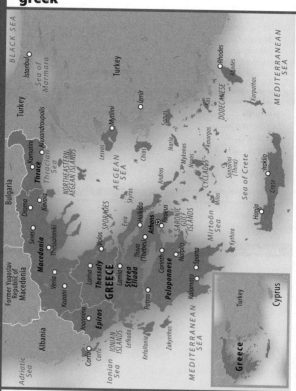

■ official language

For more details, see the **introduction**.

Aristotle, Homer, Plato, Sappho, Herodotus and Alexander the Great can't all be wrong in their choice of language – if you've ever come across arcane concepts such as 'democracy', exotic disciplines like 'trigonometry' or a little-known neurosis termed 'the Oedipus complex', then you'll have some inkling of the widespread influence of Greek language and culture. With just a little Modern Greek under your belt, you'll have a richer understanding of this language's impact on contemporary Western culture.

Greek is the official language of Greece and a co-official language of Cyprus, in addition to being spoken by emigrant communities in Turkey, Australia, Canada, Germany and the United States. In total, there are over 13 million Greek speakers worldwide.

Modern Greek constitutes a separate branch of the Indo-European language family, with Ancient Greek its only (extinct) relative. The first records of written Ancient Greek were found in the fragmentary Linear B tablets, dating from the 14th to the 12th centuries BC. By the 9th century BC, the Greeks had adapted the Phoenician alphabet to include vowels – the first alphabet to do so – and the script in use today came to its final form some time in the 5th century BC. The Greek script was the foundation for the Cyrillic script (used in Slavic languages) and the Latin alphabet (used in English and other European languages).

Although written Greek may have been remarkably stable

at a glance ...

language name: Greek

name in language:
Ελληνικά e·li·ni·ka,
Νέα Ελληνικά ne·a e·li·ni·ka
(Greek, Modern Greek)

language family:
Indo-European
(Hellenic branch)

key countries:
Greece, Cyprus

approximate number of speakers:
13 million worldwide

close relatives:
Ancient Greek

donations to English:
anarchy, astronomy, cosmos, democracy, drama, logic, politics ...

introduction

over the millennia, the spoken language has evolved considerably. In the 5th century, the dialect spoken around Athens (known as 'Attic') became the dominant speech as a result of the city-state's cultural and political prestige. Attic gained even greater influence as the medium of administration for the vast empire of Alexander the Great, and remained the official language of the Eastern Roman Empire and the Orthodox Church after the demise of the Hellenistic world. Once the Ottoman Turks took Constantinople in 1453, the Attic dialect lost its official function. In the meantime, the common language – known as *Koine* (Κοινή ki·*ni*) – continued to evolve. It developed a rich history of popular songs (δημοτικά τραγούδια thi·mo·ti·*ka* tra·*ghu*·thia) and absorbed vocabulary from Turkish, Italian, Albanian and other Balkan languages.

When an independent Greece returned to the world stage in 1832, it needed to choose a national language. Purists advocated a slightly modernised version of Attic known as *Καθαρεύουσα* ka·tha·*re*·vu·sa (from the Greek word for 'clean'), which no longer resembled the spoken language. *Koine*, or *laiki* as it was also known (λαϊκή la·*i*·ki means 'popular'), had strong support as it was spoken and understood by the majority of Greeks – in the end, this was the language which gained official recognition. By the mid-20th century, *Koine/laiki* was known as 'demotic' and continued in daily use. It was banned during Greece's military dictatorship (1967-74) but then reinstated as the official language of the Hellenic Republic.

This book gives you the practical phrases you need to get by in Greek, as well as all the fun, spontaneous phrases that can lead to a better understanding of Greeks and their culture. Once you've got the hang of how to pronounce Greek words, the rest is just a matter of confidence. Local knowledge, new relationships and a sense of satisfaction are on the tip of your tongue. So don't just stand there, say something!

abbreviations used in this book

a	adjective	n	neuter (after Greek)
acc	accusative	n	noun (after English)
f	feminine	nom	nominative
gen	genitive	pl	plural
inf	informal	pol	polite
lit	literal	sg	singular
m	masculine	v	verb

The pronunciation of Greek is easy to master, as most of the sounds correspond to those found in English. Use the coloured pronunciation guides to become familiar with them, and then read directly from the Greek when you feel more confident.

vowel sounds

Greek vowels are pronounced separately even when they're written in sequence, eg ζώο *zo·o* (animal). You'll see though in the table below that some letter combinations correspond to a single sound – ουρά (queue) is pronounced *u·ra*.

When a word ending in a vowel is followed by another word that starts with the same or a similar vowel sound, one vowel is usually omitted and the two words are pronounced as if they were one – Σε ευχαριστώ se ef·kha·ris·to becomes Σ' ευχαριστώ sef·kha·ris·to (Thank you). Note that the apostrophe (') is used to show that two words have been joined together.

symbol	english equivalent	greek example	transliteration
a	car	αλλά	a·*la*
e	bet	πλένομαι	*ple*·no·me
i	lid	πίσω, πόλη, υποφέρω, είδος, οικογένεια, υιός	*pi*·so, *po*·li, i·po·*fe*·ro, *i*·thos, i·ko·ye·*ni*·a, *i*·os
o	lot	πόνος, πίσω	*po*·nos, *pi*·so
u	put	ουρά	u·*ra*
ia	nostalgia	ζητιάνος	zi·*tia*·nos
io	ratio	πιο	pio

consonant sounds

Most Greek consonant sounds are also found in English – only the guttural gh and kh might need a bit of practice. Double consonants are only pronounced once – άλλος *a*·los (other).

symbol	english equivalent	greek example	trans-literation
b	bed	μπαρ	bar
d	dog	ντομάτα	do·*ma*·ta
dz	adds	τζαμί	dza·mi
f	fit	φως, αυτή	fos, af·ti
g	gap	γκαρσόν	gar·son
gh	guttural sound, between goat and loch	γάτα	gha·ta
h	heat	χέρι	he·ri
k	kit	καλά	ka·la
kh	loch (guttural sound)	χαλί	kha·li
l	let	λάδι	la·thi
m	mat	μαζί	ma·zi
n	not	ναός	na·os
ng	singer	ελέγχω	e·leng·kho
p	pin	πάνω	pa·no
ps	lapse	ψάρι	psa·ri
r	red (trilled)	ράβω	ra·vo
s	sad	στυλό	sti·lo
t	top	τι	ti
th	theatre	θέα	the·a
țh	the	δεν	țhen
ts	hats	τσέπη	tse·pi
v	vase	βίζα, αύριο	vi·za, av·ri·o
y	yes	γέρος	ye·ros
z	zoo	ζέστη	ze·sti

word stress

Most Greek words have only one stressed syllable, but some have two. Stress can fall on any of the last three syllables. In our pronunciation guides, the stressed syllable is always in italics, but in written Greek, the stressed syllable is always indicated by an accent over the vowel, eg καλά ka·*la*.

If a vowel is represented by two letters, it's written on the second letter, eg ζητιάνος zi·*tia*·nos (beggar). If the accent is marked on the first of these two letters, they should be read separately, like in Μάιος *ma*·i·os (May). Where two vowels occur together but are not stressed, a diaeresis (¨) is used to indicate that they should be pronounced separately, eg λαϊκός la·i·*kos* (popular). When stress falls on a capitalised vowel (like in Έχασα *e*·ha·sa (I lost)), the accent is written to the left of the letter.

intonation

Intonation in mainland Greece is rather flat, except in questions, when the voice is raised at the end of the sentence. Many island dialects have a more 'singing' intonation.

pronunciation

reading & writing

The Greek writing system was simplified in 1982, when the old stress symbols and aspiration marks (ie an accent indicating that a sound is pronounced with a puff of air before it) were abolished, although they may still be found in old books.

The modern Greek alphabet consists of 24 letters. Their pronunciation is shown in the box below for spelling purposes, eg when you need to spell your name to book into a hotel. Many of the letters of the Greek alphabet are also used in the Roman alphabet. Some letters, however, are a little misleading – they look like English letters but are pronounced very differently. For more information, see the consonant table on page 12 and the box on page 34.

Greek punctuation uses the same symbols as in English, except for the question mark – this is written as a semicolon (;).

greek alphabet			
A α *al·*pha	B β *vi·*ta	Γ γ *gha·*ma	Δ δ *ṭhel·*ta
E ε *ep·si·lon*	Z ζ *zi·*ta	H η *i·*ta	Θ θ *thi·*ta
I ι *yio·*ta	K κ *ka·*pa	Λ λ *lam·ṭha*	M μ mi
N ν ni	Ξ ξ ksi	O o *o·mi·kron*	Π π pi
P ρ ro	Σ σ/ς* *sigh·*ma	T τ taf	Y υ *ip·si·lon*
Φ φ fi	X χ hi	Ψ ψ psi	Ω ω *o·me·gha*

* The letter Σ has two forms for the lower case – σ and ς. The second one is used at the end of words.

TOOLS

contents

The index below shows the grammatical structures you can use to say what you want. Look under each function – in alphabetical order – for information on how to build your own phrases. For example, to tell the taxi driver where your hotel is, look for **giving instructions** and you'll be directed to information on **negatives**, **prepositions** and **requests**. A glossary of grammatical terms is included at the end of this chapter to help you.

Abbreviations like nom and acc in the literal translations for each example refer the case of the noun or pronoun – this is explained in the glossary and in **case**.

asking questions

questions	27	word order	31

describing people/things

adjectives & adverbs	17

doing things

case	19	personal pronouns	23
verbs	29		

giving instructions

negatives	22	prepositions	26
requests	29		

indicating location

case	19	demonstratives	20
prepositions	26		

making statements
be	18	personal pronouns	23
word order	31		

naming people/things
articles	17	case	19
demonstratives	20	gender	21
plurals	24		

negating
negatives	22	word order	31

pointing things out
demonstratives	20	prepositions	26

possessing
case	19	have	21
possessives	25		

TOOLS

16

adjectives & adverbs

Adjectives in Greek normally come before the noun, just like in English. They take different endings to agree with the noun they qualify (see **case**, **gender** and **plurals**) – we've given their standard forms below. Adjectives are shown in the nominative form in lists throughout this book and in the **dictionary** – these forms won't always be strictly correct within a sentence, but you'll still be understood. To find out more, see **case**.

	masculine	feminine	neuter
singular	καλός δρόμος ka·*los* thro·mos good road	καλή τύχη ka·*li* ti·hi good fortune	καλό ποτό ka·*lo* po·to good drink
plural	καλοί δρόμοι ka·*li* thro·mi good roads	καλές τύχες ka·*les* ti·hes good fortunes	καλά ποτά ka·*la* po·ta good drinks

Adverbs normally end with the sound a (eg καλά ka·*la* 'well').

He filled in the form quickly.

Συμπλήρωσε το έντυπο	si·*bli*·ro·se to *e*·di·po
γρήγορα.	*ghri*·gho·ra

(lit: filled-in the-acc form-acc quickly)

articles

The Greek words for 'a' and 'an' change form to agree in gender and case with the noun they refer to.

		masculine	feminine	neuter
indefinite article (a/an)	**nom**	ένας *e*·nas	μια mia	ένα *e*·na
	acc	ένα(ν) *e*·na(n)	μια mia	ένα *e*·na
	gen	ενός *e*·nos	μιας *mi*·as	ενός *e*·nos

The Greek equivalents of 'the' also change form according to the noun – see also **case**, **gender** and **plurals**.

			masculine		feminine		neuter	
definite article (the)	nom	sg	o	o	η	i	το	to
		pl	οι	i	οι	i	τα	ta
	acc	sg	το(ν)	to(n)	τη(ν)	ti(n)	το	to
		pl	τους	tus	τις	tis	τα	ta
	gen	sg	του	tu	της	tis	του	tu
		pl	των	ton	των	ton	των	ton

Articles alway come before the noun:

a road	**ένας** δρόμος	*e·nas thro·mos*
the road	**ο** δρόμος	*o thro·mos*

be

making statements

The verb είμαι *i·me* (be) changes depending on who or what is the subject (doer) of the sentence. These are the forms for the present and past tenses.

present			past		
I am	είμαι	*i·me*	I was	ήμουν	*i·mun*
you are sg inf	είσαι	*i·se*	you were sg inf	ήσουν	*i·sun*
you are sg pol	είστε	*i·ste*	you were sg pol	ήσαστε	*i·sa·ste*
he/she/it is	είναι	*i·ne*	he/she/it was	ήταν	*i·tan*
we are	είμαστε	*i·ma·ste*	we were	ήμαστε	*i·ma·ste*
you are pl	είστε	*i·ste*	you were pl	ήσαστε	*i·sa·ste*
they are	είναι	*i·ne*	they were	ήταν	*i·tan*

TOOLS

18

The future tense is formed by placing the word θα tha (will) in front of the present tense forms.

I'll be there tomorrow.
Θα είμαι εκεί αύριο.   tha *i*·me e·*ki* av·ri·o
(lit: will be there tomorrow)

case

**doing things · indicating location ·
naming people/things · possessing**

Greek uses four different cases, usually shown by word endings, to indicate a noun's role and its relationship to other words in the sentence. Adjectives, articles, demonstratives and pronouns also change their form to agree with the noun they go with.

nominative **nom** – shows the subject of a sentence

The car won't start.
Το αυτοκίνητο δεν αρχίζει.   to af·to·*ki*·ni·to then ar·*hi*·zi
(lit: the-**nom** car-**nom** not starts)

accusative **acc** – shows the direct object of a sentence

Please bring the menu.
Παρακαλώ φέρε το μενού.   pa·ra·ka·*lo fe*·re to me·*nu*
(lit: please bring the-**acc** menu-**acc**)

genitive **gen** – shows possession or the indirect object of a sentence

What's the address of the hotel?
Ποια είναι η διεύθυνση του   pia *i*·ne i *thi*·ef·thin·si tu
ξενοδοχείου;   kse·no·tho·*hi*·u
(lit: which is the-**nom** address-**nom** the-**gen** hotel-**gen**)

vocative **voc** – to address someone directly

Officer, I think there's been a mistake.
Κύριε, νομίζω ότι έχει γίνει   *ki*·ri·e ni·*mi*·zo o·ti *e*·xi *yi*·ni
κάποιο λάθος   *ka*·pio *la*·thos
(lit: sir-**voc** I-think that has been some-**nom** mistake-**nom**)

Greek nouns in the **dictionaries**, the **culinary reader** and word lists in this book are given in the nominative case. You can use this form as a default and, although this won't always be grammatically correct within sentences, you'll still be understood.

demonstratives

indicating location • naming people/things • pointing things out

The words for 'this' and 'that' in Greek change their endings depending on the form of the noun they determine (see **case**, **gender** and **plurals**). We've only given the nominative forms here – in most cases you'll be understood just fine.

		masculine		feminine		neuter	
this	sg	αυτός	af·tos	αυτή	af·ti	αυτό	af·to
	pl	αυτοί	af·ti	αυτές	af·tes	αυτά	af·ta
that	sg	εκείνος	e·ki·nos	εκείνη	e·ki·ni	εκείνο	e·ki·no
	pl	εκείνοι	e·ki·ni	εκείνες	e·ki·nes	εκείνα	e·ki·na

Does this train go to Lamia?
Πηγαίνει αυτό το τρένο   pi·ye·ni af·to to tre·no
στη Λαμία;   sti la·mi·a
(lit: goes this-nom the-nom train-nom to Lamia-acc)

That bag is mine.
Εκείνη η τσάντα είναι   e·ki·ni i tsa·da i·ne
δική μου.   thi·ki mu
(lit: that-nom the-nom bag-nom is mine)

This is my bag.
Αυτή η σάκα είναι δική μου.   af·ti i sa·ka i·ne thi·ki mu
(lit: this-nom the-nom bag-nom is mine)

gender

Greek nouns have gender – masculine **m**, feminine **f** or neuter **n**. You need to learn the grammatical gender for each noun as you go, but you can often identify it by the noun's ending as shown in the table below. Adjectives, articles and pronouns take the same gender to agree with the noun they qualify.

common noun endings				
masculine	sg	**-ας** πατέρας pa·te·ras father	**-ης** ναύτης naf·tis sailor	**-ος** δρόμος thro·mos road
	pl	**-ες** πατέρες pa·te·res fathers	**-ες** ναύτες naf·tes sailors	**-οι** δρόμοι thro·mi roads
feminine	sg	**-α** πόρτα por·ta door	**-η** τύχη ti·hi fortune	
	pl	**-ες** πόρτες por·tes doors	**-ες** τύχες ti·hes fortunes	
neuter	sg	**-μα** όνομα o·no·ma name	**-ι** αγόρι a·gho·ri boy	**-ο** ποτό po·to drink
	pl	**-τα** ονόματα o·no·ma·ta names	**-α** αγόρια a·gho·ria boys	**-α** ποτά po·ta drinks

have

The verb έχω *e·kho* (have) only changes form according to who or what is the subject (doer) of the sentence. To form the future tense (as in the example on page 22), just place the word θα tha (will) in front of the present tense forms.

present			past		
I have	έχω	e·kho	I had	είχα	i·kha
you have sg inf	έχεις	e·his	you had sg inf	είχες	i·hes
you have sg pol	έχετε	e·he·te	you had sg pol	είχατε	i·kha·te
he/she/it has	έχει	e·hi	he/she/it had	είχε	i·he
we have	έχουμε	e·khu·me	we had	είχαμε	i·kha·me
you have pl	έχετε	e·he·te	you had pl	είχατε	i·kha·te
they have	έχουν	e·khun	they had	είχαν	i·khan

I'll have no money by the end of my trip!

Δεν θα έχω χρήματα με
το τέλος του ταξιδιού!
(lit: not will I-have money-acc with
the-acc end-acc the-gen trip-gen)

ţhen tha e·kho khri·ma·ta me
to te·los tu tak·si·ţhiu

negatives

giving instructions • negating

To make a statement negative, add the word δεν ţhen (not)
before the verb:

I speak Greek.

Μιλώ Ελληνικά.
(lit: speak Greek)

mi·lo e·li·ni·ka

I don't speak Greek.

Δεν μιλώ Ελληνικά.
(lit: not speak Greek)

ţhen mi·lo e·li·ni·ka

In commands, use the word μην min (not) instead:

Don't swim here.

Μην κολυμπάς εδώ.
(lit: not swim here)

min ko·li·bas e·ţho

Note that, unlike English, Greek has double negatives:

I don't want anything.
Δεν θέλω τίποτε.   then the·lo ti·po·te
(lit: not want nothing)

personal pronouns

doing things • making statements

In Greek, there are two words for 'you' – an informal one, εσύ
e·si (used with friends, younger people or family members),
and a formal one, εσείς e·sis (used when addressing strangers,
authority figures or older people). In this phrasebook we've
used the form of 'you' (and the verb form) appropriate for each
situation.

	subject nom	
I	εγώ	e·gho
you sg inf	εσύ	e·si
you sg pol	εσείς	e·sis
he/she/it	αυτός/αυτή/αυτό	af·tos/af·ti/af·to
we	εμείς	e·mis
you pl	εσείς	e·sis
they m/f/n	αυτοί/αυτές/αυτά	af·ti/af·tes/af·ta

	direct object acc		indirect object gen	
me	με	me	μου	mu
you sg inf	σε	se	σου	su
you sg pol	σας	sas	σας	sas
him/her/it	τον/την/το	ton/tin/to	του/της/του	tu/tis/tu
us	μας	mas	μας	mas
you pl	σας	sas	σας	sas
them m/f/n	τους/τις/τα	tus/tis/ta	τους	tus

Greek pronouns vary according to case – the subject or doer of an action is in the nominative case while the object is in the accusative or genitive case.

Both direct and indirect object pronouns are placed before the verb. If you have both in a sentence, the indirect pronoun comes first. In commands, they come after the verb.

I gave my passport to him.

Του έδωσα το
διαβατήριό μου.
   tu e·tho·sa to
   thia·va·ti·ri·o mu
(lit: him-**gen** I-gave the-**acc** passport-**acc** my)

I gave it to him.

Του το έδωσα.
   tu to e·tho·sa
(lit: him-**gen** it-**acc** I-gave)

It's not necessary to use a subject pronoun in Greek, as verb endings show who the subject is. A subject pronoun can be used for emphasis or when there's no verb in the sentence.

I go to school everyday.

Πηγαίνω στο σχολείο
κάθε μέρα.
   pi·ye·no sto skho·li·o
   ka·the me·ra
(lit: go-I to school-**acc** every day)

I **did it.**

Εγώ το έκανα.
   e·gho to e·ka·na
(lit: I-**nom** it-**acc** did)

plurals

naming people/things

Plural nouns take different endings depending on gender – see the table under **gender** for the most common ones. Adjectives, articles, demonstratives and pronouns also have plural forms to agree with the plural noun.

possessives

Possession can be expressed not only with the verb 'have' but with possessive pronouns and adjectives as well.

The possessive adjectives (my, your, his etc) are placed after the noun, with the definite article before the noun (also see **articles**). They don't change for case, gender or number.

possessive adjectives		
my	μου	mu
your sg inf	σου	su
your sg pol	σας	sas
his/her/its	του/της/του	tu/tis/tu
our	μας	mas
your pl	σας	sas
their	τους	tus

I've lost my car keys.

Έχασα τα κλειδιά   *e·*kha·sa ta kli·*thia*
του αυτοκινήτου μου.   tu af·to·ki·*ni·*tu mu
(lit: lost the-**acc** keys-**acc** the-**gen** car-**gen** my)

Possessive pronouns (mine, yours etc) are formed by adding the word δικός/δική/δικό thi·*kos*/thi·*ki*/thi·*ko* **m/f/n** in front of the possessive adjective. This word agrees in gender and case with the noun it refers to – endings are the same as those the adjectives take (see **adjectives & adverbs**). To keep things simple we've only given the nominative case in the next table.

possessive pronouns			
	masculine	**feminine**	**neuter**
mine	δικός μου ţhi·*kos* mu	δική μου ţhi·*ki* mu	δικό μου ţhi·*ko* mu
yours sg inf	δικός σου ţhi·*kos* su	δική σου ţhi·*ki* su	δικό σου ţhi·*ko* su
yours sg pol	δικός σας ţhi·*kos* sas	δική σας ţhi·*ki* sas	δικό σας ţhi·*ko* sas
his/hers/its	δικός του/της/του ţhi·*kos* tu/tis/tu	δική του/της/του ţhi·*ki* tu/tis/tu	δικό του/της/του ţhi·*ko* tu/tis/tu
ours	δικός μας ţhi·*kos* mas	δική μας ţhi·*ki* mas	δικό μας ţhi·*ko* mas
yours pl	δικός σας ţhi·*kos* sas	δική σας ţhi·*ki* sas	δικό σας ţhi·*ko* sas
theirs	δικός τους ţhi·*kos* tus	δική τους ţhi·*ki* tus	δικό τους ţhi·*ko* tus

Those bags are ours.

Εκείνες οι τσάντες είναι   e·*ki*·nes i *tsa*·des *i*·ne
δικές μας.   ţhi·*kes* mas
(lit: those-**nom** the-**nom** bags-**nom** are ours)

prepositions

Many prepositions require the noun used after them to be in a
particular case (see **case**) – σε se (to/at/in), από a·*po* (from), με
me (with), για yia (for), προς pros (towards), κάτω από ka·to a·*po*
(under), πάνω σε *pa*·no se (on) are all followed by the accusative. The genitive is used after μεταξύ me·tak·*si* (between).

I'd like to book a seat to Athens.

Θα ήθελα να κρατήσω   tha *i*·the·la na kra·*ti*·so
μια θέση για την Αθήνα.   mia *the*·si yia tin a·*thi*·na
(lit: I-would like to book
a seat-acc for the-acc Athens-acc)

What's the difference between 1st and 2nd class?

Ποια είναι η διαφορά μεταξύ   pia *i*·ne i thia·fo·*ra* me·tak·*si*
πρώτης και δεύτερης θέσης;   *pro*·tis ke *thef*·te·ris *the*·sis
(lit: which is the-nom difference-nom between
first-gen and second-gen class-gen)

questions

To ask a yes/no question, just raise the intonation at the end
of a sentence. Note that Greek uses a semicolon (;) instead of
a question mark.

The bus stop is over there.

Η στάση του λεωφορείου   i *sta*·si tu le·o·fo·*ri*·u
είναι εκεί πέρα.   *i*·ne e·*ki pe*·ra
(lit: the-nom stop-nom the-gen bus-gen is there over)

Is the bus stop over there?

Η στάση του λεωφορείου   i *sta*·si tu le·o·fo·*ri*·u
είναι εκεί πέρα;   *i*·ne e·*ki pe*·ra
(lit: the-nom stop-nom the-gen bus-gen is there over)

The subject and the verb are often reversed in questions (see
word order). You can also start a question with a question
word – the verb comes in the second place, just like in English.
The table on the next page lists the main question words.

question words		
How?	Πώς;	pos
How many?	Πόσοι/Πόσες/Πόσα; m/f/n pl	po·si/po·ses/po·sa
How much?	Πόσος/Πόση/Πόσο; m/f/n	po·sos/po·si/po·so
What?	Τι;	ti
When?	Πότε;	po·te
Where?	Πού;	pu
Who?	Ποιος/Ποια/Ποιο; m/f/n sg	pios/pia/pio
	Ποιοι/Ποιες/Ποια; m/f/n pl	pii/pies/pia
Which?	Ποιος/Ποια/Ποιο; m/f/n sg	pios/pia/pio
	Ποιοι/Ποιες/Ποια; m/f/n pl	pii/pies/pia
Why?	Γιατί;	yi·a·ti

How do you pronounce this?
Πώς προφέρεις αυτό;   pos pro·fe·ris af·to
(lit: how you-pronounce this-acc)

How much is it?
Πόσο κάνει;   po·so ka·ni
(lit: how-much makes)

When's the first bus?
Πότε είναι το πρώτο   po·te i·ne to pro·to
λεωφορείο;   le·o·fo·ri·o
(lit: when is the-nom first-nom bus-nom)

Who is that?
Ποιος είναι εκείνος;   pios i·ne e·ki·nos
(lit: who-nom is that-nom)

Why can't I board this train?
Γιατί δεν μπορώ να ανεβώ   yia·ti then bo·ro na a·ne·vo
σ'αυτό το τρένο;   saf·to to tre·no
(lit: why not can to board to-this-acc the-acc train-acc)

requests

A simple and polite way to make a request is to use the verb as found in the table on page 30, in its second-person present form, followed by παρακαλώ pa·ra·ka·*lo* ('please'). Use the informal (singular) form with people you know well, and the polite (plural) form with others.

Would you please open the window?

ανοίγεις το παράθυρο,	a·*ni*·yis to pa·*ra*·thi·ro
παρακαλώ; sg inf	pa·ra·ka·*lo*

(lit: open the window please)

Would you please open the window?

ανοίγετε το παράθυρο,	a·*ni*·ye·te to pa·*ra*·thi·ro
παρακαλώ; pl pol	pa·ra·ka·*lo*

(lit: open the window please)

For the negative form, see **negatives**.

verbs

The dictionary form of all Greek verbs ends in -ω ·o or -ομαι o·me, which is the present tense form of the first person singular (like in 'I eat'). The ending -ω represents 'active' verbs (which show someone actively doing something – πηγαίνω pi·*ye*·no 'go'), while -ομαι is for 'stative' verbs (which show a state or condition, and don't require movement – κάθομαι *ka*·tho·me 'sit'). These endings change according to the subject of the sentence. Sometimes changes in the verb stem (the form of the verb before the ending) occur, but if you use the endings shown on the next page, you'll be understood just fine.

present

Active and stative verbs have different sets of endings.

	active verb eg 'write'		stative verb eg 'think'	
dictionary form	γράφω	ghra·fo	σκέφτομαι	skef·to·me
I	γράφ**ω**	ghra·fo	σκέφτομαι	skef·to·me
you sg inf	γράφ**εις**	ghra·fis	σκέφτεσαι	skef·te·se
you sg pol	γράφ**ετε**	ghra·fe·te	σκέφτεστε	skef·tes·te
he/she/it	γράφ**ει**	ghra·fi	σκέφτεται	skef·te·te
we	γράφ**ουμε**	ghra·fu·me	σκεφτόμαστε	skef·to·ma·ste
you pl	γράφ**ετε**	ghra·fe·te	σκέφτεστε	skef·tes·te
they	γράφ**ουν**	ghra·fun	σκέφτονται	skef·ton·de

past

The past tense endings for all verbs are provided below. There are some irregularities, however – as the stress in the verb moves back to the third syllable from the end, the prefix ε e· (augment) is added to the verb when there are less than three syllables. Also, the final letter before the ending sometimes changes.

	all verbs eg 'write'	
I	έγραψα	e·ghra·psa
you sg inf	έγραψες	e·ghra·pses
you sg pol	γράψατε	ghra·psa·te
he/she/it	έγραψε	e·ghra·pse
we	γράψαμε	ghra·psa·me
you pl	γράψατε	ghra·psa·te
they	έγραψαν	e·ghra·psan

future

The easiest way to express an action in the future is by using the present tense forms and adding the word θα tha (will) in front of them.

I'll send you a postcard everyday.

Θα σου στέλνω μία   tha su *stel*·no mia
κάρτα κάθε μέρα.   *kar*·ta *ka*·the *me*·ra
(lit: will you-**gen** send a-**acc** postcard-**acc** every day)

word order

asking questions • making statements • negating

While the sentence order of subject–verb–object is most common in Greek, all other combinations are correct too – the word order is relatively free as Greek uses case (meaning that different word endings express the role of a word in the sentence). You might notice, however, that emphasised words are usually at the beginning of the sentence (see also **negatives** and **questions**).

The cashier didn't give me the correct change.

Ο ταμίας δεν μου έδωσε   o ta·*mi*·as then mu *e*·tho·se
τα σωστά ρέστα.   ta so·*sta re*·sta
(lit: the-**nom** cashier-**nom** not me-**gen** gave
the-**acc** correct-**acc** change-**acc**)

The cashier didn't give me the correct change.

Δεν μου έδωσε τα σωστά   then mu *e*·tho·se ta so·*sta*
ρέστα ο ταμίας.   *re*·sta o ta·*mi*·as
(lit: not me-**gen** gave the-**acc** correct-**acc**
change-**acc** the-**nom** cashier-**nom**)

Note that the indirect object comes before the direct object.

glossary

active verb	a verb that involves someone actively doing something – 'he **travelled** for many moons'
adjective	a word that describes something – '**ancient** hero'
adverb	a word that explains how an action was done – 'he **heroically** set out to find his father'
article	the words 'a', 'an' and 'the'
case (marking)	word ending that shows the role of the thing or person in the sentence
demonstrative	a word that means 'this' or 'that'
gender	Greek nouns can be masculine, feminine or neuter
imperative	a command – '**prove** to me that you are Odysseus'
noun	a thing, person or idea – 'an odyssey'
number	whether a word is singular or plural – 'journey' or 'journeys'
object (direct)	the thing or person that's directly affected by the action – 'Penelope offered **dinner** to her suitors'
object (indirect)	the person in the sentence that benefits from an action – 'Penelope offered **them** dinner'
personal pronoun	a word that means 'I', 'you', etc
possessive pronoun	a word that means 'mine', 'yours', etc
preposition	a word like 'for' or 'before' in English
stative verb	a verb that doesn't require movement – 'Penelope **missed** her husband very much'
subject	the thing or person that does the action – '**the suitors** took advantage of her hospitality'
tense	marking on the verb that tells you whether the action is in the present, past or future – 'travelled'
verb	the word that tells you what action happened – 'Odysseus **disguises** himself as a beggar'
verb stem	the part of a verb which does not change – like 'charm' in 'charmed' and 'charming'

Do you speak (English)?
Μιλάς (Αγγλικά);   mi·*las* (ang·gli·*ka*)

Does anyone speak (English)?
Μιλάει κανείς (Αγγλικά);   mi·*la*·i ka·*nis* (ang·gli·*ka*)

Do you understand?
Καταλαβαίνεις;   ka·ta·la·*ve*·nis

Yes, I understand.
Ναι, καταλαβαίνω.   ne ka·ta·la·*ve*·no

No, I don't understand.
Όχι, δεν καταλαβαίνω.   *o*·hi ţhen ka·ta·la·*ve*·no

I (don't) understand.
(Δεν) καταλαβαίνω.   (ţhen) ka·ta·la·*ve*·no

Pardon?
Συγνώμη;   sigh·*no*·mi

I speak (English).
Μιλώ (Αγγλικά).   mi·*lo* (ang·gli·*ka*)

I don't speak Greek.
Δεν μιλώ Ελληνικά.   ţhen mi·*lo* e·li·ni·*ka*

I speak a little.
Μιλώ λίγο.   mi·*lo li*·gho

Let's speak Greek.
Ας μιλήσουμε Ελληνικά.   as mi·*li*·su·me e·li·ni·*ka*

---

tongue-tied

If you're after a challenge, try this tongue twister for size.

Ο παπάς ο παχύς έφαγε παχιά φακή.
Γιατί, παπά παχύ, έφαγες παχιά φακή;
o pa·*pas* o pa·*his* e·fa·ye pa·*hia* fa·*ki*
yia·*ti* pa·*pa* pa·*hi* e·fa·yes pa·*hia* fa·*ki*
(The fat priest ate thick lentil soup.
Why, fat priest, did you eat thick lentil soup?)

I would like to practise Greek.

Θα ήθελα να εξασκήσω
τα Ελληνικά μου.

tha *i*·the·la na ek·sa·*ski*·so
ta e·li·ni·*ka* mu

What does (μώλος) mean?

Τι σημαίνει (μώλος);

ti si·*me*·ni (*mo*·los)

How do you …?   Πώς …;   pos …
  pronounce this   προφέρεις αυτό   pro·*fe*·ris af·to
  write 'Madhuri' γράψεις   *ghrap*·sis
        'Μαδουρή'   ma·thu·*ri*

Could you   Θα μπορούσες   tha bo·*ru*·ses
please …?   παρακαλώ να …;   pa·ra·ka·*lo* na …
  repeat that   το επαναλάβεις   to e·pa·na·*la*·vis
  speak more   μιλάς πιο αργά   mi·*las* pio ar·*gha*
  slowly
  write it down   το γράψεις   to *ghrap*·sis

---

alphabet soup

Some Greek letters might look like English ones, but they're pronounced quite differently.

upper case	lower case	pronunciation
Β	β	v
Η	η	i
Ρ	ρ	r
Υ	υ	i
Χ	χ	h
Ν	ν	n
Ξ	ξ	ks
Σ	σ/ς	s
Ω	ω	o

See the box on page 14 for the full Greek alphabet.

TOOLS

34

cardinal numbers

In Greek, some numbers (one, three, four, and numbers linked to them like 21 and 13) change according to gender – that is, they have different forms when the noun they're associated with is masculine m, feminine f or neuter n. When simply counting, you use the neuter form.

1	ένας/μία/ένα m/f/n	e·nas/mi·a/e·na
2	δύο	thi·o
3	τρεις/τρία m&f/n	tris/tri·a
4	τέσσερις m&f	te·se·ris
	τέσσερα n	te·se·ra
5	πέντε	pe·de
6	έξι	ek·si
7	εφτά	ef·ta
8	οχτώ	okh·to
9	εννέα	e·ne·a
10	δέκα	the·ka
11	έντεκα	e·de·ka
12	δώδεκα	tho·the·ka
13	δεκατρείς m&f	the·ka·tris
	δεκατρία n	the·ka·tri·a
14	δεκατέσσερις m&f	the·ka·te·se·ris
	δεκατέσσερα n	the·ka·te·se·ra
15	δεκαπέντε	the·ka·pe·de
16	δεκαέξι	the·ka·ek·si
17	δεκαεφτά	the·ka·ef·ta
18	δεκαοχτώ	the·ka·okh·to
19	δεκαεννέα	the·ka·e·ne·a
20	είκοσι	i·ko·si
21	είκοσι ένας/μία m/f	i·ko·si e·nas/mi·a
	είκοσι ένα n	i·ko·si e·na

22	είκοσι δύο	*i*·ko·si *thi*·o
30	τριάντα	tri·*a*·da
40	σαράντα	sa·*ra*·da
50	πενήντα	pe·*ni*·da
60	εξήντα	ek·*si*·da
70	εβδομήντα	ev·*tho*·*mi*·da
80	ογδόντα	ogh·*tho*·da
90	ενενήντα	e·ne·*ni*·da
100	εκατό	e·ka·*to*
200	διακόσια	thia·*ko*·sia
1000	χίλια	*hi*·lia
1,000,000	ένα εκατομμύριο	*e*·na e·ka·to·*mi*·rio

ordinal numbers

τακτικοί αριθμοί

Ordinals agree in gender with the noun they're associated with.

1st	πρώτος/πρώτη m/f	*pro*·tos/*pro*·ti
	πρώτο n	*pro*·to
2nd	δεύτερος/δεύτερη m/f	*thef*·te·ros/*thef*·te·ri
	δεύτερο n	*thef*·te·ro
3rd	τρίτος/τρίτη/τρίτο m/f/n	*tri*·tos/*tri*·ti/*tri*·to
4th	τέταρτος/τέταρτη m/f	te·*tar*·tos/te·*tar*·ti
	τέταρτο n	te·*tar*·to
5th	πέμπτος/πέμπτη m/f	*pem*·tos/*pem*·ti
	πέμπτο n	*pem*·to
6th	έκτος/έκτη/έκτο m/f/n	*ek*·tos/*ek*·ti/*ek*·to
7th	έβδομος/έβδομη m/f	ev·*tho*·mos/ev·*tho*·mi
	έβδομο n	ev·*tho*·mo
8th	όγδοος/όγδοη m/f	ogh·*tho*·os/ogh·*tho*·i
	όγδοο n	ogh·*tho*·o
9th	ένατος/ένατη/ένατο m/f/n	e·na·tos/e·na·ti/e·na·to
10th	δέκατος/δέκατη m/f	*the*·ka·tos/*the*·ka·ti
	δέκατο n	*the*·ka·to

fractions

κλάσματα

a quarter	ένα τέταρτο n	*e*·na *te*·tar·to
a third	ένα τρίτο n	*e*·na *tri*·to
a half	μισό n	mi·*so*
three-quarters	τρία τέταρτα n pl	*tri*·a *te*·tar·ta
all	όλα n pl	*o*·la
none	τίποτε	*ti*·po·te

useful amounts

χρήσιμα ποσά

The words for 'How much?' and 'How many?' take different forms for the gender of the noun they refer to, as shown below.

How much?	Πόσος/Πόση m/f	po·sos/*po*·si
	Πόσο; n	po·so
How many?	Πόσοι/Πόσες m/f	po·si/*po*·ses
	Πόσα; n	po·sa
How much water?	Πόσο νερό; n	po·so ne·*ro*
How much sugar?	Πόση ζάχαρη; f	po·si *za*·kha·ri
How many men?	Πόσοι άντρες; m	po·si *a*·dres
How many women?	Πόσες γυναίκες; f	po·ses yi·*ne*·kes

I'd like (a) ...	Θα ήθελα ...	tha *i*·the·la ...
Please give	Παρακαλώ	pa·ra·ka·*lo*
me (a) ...	δώσε μου ...	*tho*·se mu ...
(100) grams	(εκατό)	(e·ka·*to*)
	γραμμάρια	ghra·*ma*·ria
half a dozen	μισή ντουζίνα	mi·*si* du·*zi*·na
dozen	μια ντουζίνα	mia du·*zi*·na
half a kilo	μισό κιλό	mi·*so* ki·*lo*
kilo	ένα κιλό	*e*·na ki·*lo*
bottle	ένα μπουκάλι	*e*·na bu·*ka*·li
jar	ένα βάζο	*e*·na *va*·zo
tin	ένα κουτί	*e*·na ku·*ti*
packet	ένα πακέτο	*e*·na pa·*ke*·to
slice	μια φέτα	mia *fe*·ta
few	λίγα	*li*·gha
less	λιγότερο	li·*gho*·te·ro
(just) a little	(μόνο) λιγάκι	(*mo*·no) li·*gha*·ki
lot	πολύ	po·*li*
many	πολλά	po·*la*
more	πιο πολύ	pio po·*li*
some ...	μερικά ...	me·ri·*ka* ...

To find out how to put these amounts to use, see **self-catering**, page 171.

---

what's in a name?

Although Greeks have moved around their own country and emigrated worldwide, you can sometimes tell from their surnames where they originally come from. People whose name ends in -ακης -a·kis are from Crete, -ατος -a·tos from Cephallonia, -ιδης -i·this from Macedonia, and -πουλος -pu·los from the Peloponnese.

telling the time

λέγοντας την ώρα

Telling the time in Greek is straightforward. For 'It's … o'clock' simply say είναι *i*·ne (lit: it-is) followed by the number, then η ώρα i *o*·ra (lit: the hour). Note that η ώρα is optional. To give times after the hour say the number of hours, then και ke (lit: and) and the number of minutes. For times before the hour say the number of hours, then παρά pa·*ra* (lit: minus) and the minutes. Instead of 30 or 15 minutes, say μισή mi·*si* (half) for the half hour and τέταρτο te·tar·to (quarter).

What time is it?
  Τι ώρα είναι;   ti *o*·ra *i*·ne

It's (ten) o'clock.
  Είναι (δέκα) η ώρα.   *i*·ne (*the*·ka) i *o*·ra

Five past (ten).
  (Δέκα) και πέντε.   (*the*·ka) ke *pe*·de

Quarter past (ten).
  (Δέκα) και τέταρτο.   (*the*·ka) ke te·tar·to

Half past (ten).
  (Δέκα) και μισή.   (*the*·ka) ke mi·*si*

Quarter to (ten).
  (Δέκα) παρά τέταρτο.   (*the*·ka) pa·*ra* te·tar·to

Twenty to (ten).
  (Δέκα) παρά είκοσι.   (*the*·ka) pa·*ra* *i*·ko·si

At what time …?
  Τι ώρα …;   ti *o*·ra …

At (ten).
  Στις (δέκα).   stis (*the*·ka)

At (7.57pm).
  Στις (7.57μ.μ.).   stis (ef·ta ke pe·*ni*·da ef·ta me·ta to me·si·*me*·ri)

the calendar

το ημερολόγιο

days

Monday	Δευτέρα	thef·*te*·ra
Tuesday	Τρίτη	*tri*·ti
Wednesday	Τετάρτη	te·*tar*·ti
Thursday	Πέμπτη	*pem*·ti
Friday	Παρασκευή	pa·ra·ske·*vi*
Saturday	Σάββατο	*sa*·va·to
Sunday	Κυριακή	ki·ria·*ki*

months

January	Ιανουάριος	i·a·nu·*a*·ri·os
February	Φεβρουάριος	fev·ru·*a*·ri·os
March	Μάρτιος	*mar*·ti·os
April	Απρίλιος	a·*pri*·li·os
May	Μάιος	*ma*·i·os
June	Ιούνιος	i·*u*·ni·os
July	Ιούλιος	i·*u*·li·os
August	Αύγουστος	*av*·ghu·stos
September	Σεπτέμβριος	sep·*tem*·vri·os
October	Οκτώβριος	ok·*tov*·ri·os
November	Νοέμβριος	no·*em*·vri·os
December	Δεκέμβριος	the·*kem*·vri·os

dates

What date is it today?

Τι ημερομηνία είναι σήμερα;   ti i·me·ro·mi·*ni*·a *i*·ne *si*·me·ra

It's (18 October).

Είναι (18 Οκτωβρίου).   *i*·ne (the·ka·okh·*to* ok·tov·*ri*·u)

seasons

spring	άνοιξη f	*a*·nik·si
summer	καλοκαίρι n	ka·lo·*ke*·ri
autumn	φθινόπωρο n	fthi·*no*·po·ro
winter	χειμώνας m	hi·*mo*·nas

present

παρόν

now	τώρα	*to*·ra
today	σήμερα	*si*·me·ra
tonight	το βράδι	to *vra*·thi
this week	αυτή την εβδομάδα	af·*ti* tin ev·tho·*ma*·tha
this ...	αυτό το ...	af·*to* to ...
morning	πρωί	pro·*i*
afternoon	απόγευμα	a·*po*·yev·ma
month	μήνα	*mi*·na
year	χρόνο	*khro*·no

past

παρελθόν

(three days) ago	(τρεις μέρες) πριν	(tris *me*·res) prin
day before yesterday	προχτές	prokh·*tes*
since (May)	από (το Μάιο)	a·*po* (to *ma*·i·o)
yesterday ...	χτες το ...	khtes to ...
morning	πρωί	pro·*i*
afternoon	απόγευμα	a·*po*·yev·ma
evening	βράδι	*vra*·thi

last night/week
την περασμένη νύχτα/εβδομάδα   tin pe·raz·*me*·ni *nikh*·ta/ev·tho·*ma*·tha

last month/year
τον περασμένο μήνα/χρόνο   ton pe·raz·*me*·no *mi*·na/*khro*·no

future

tomorrow ...	αύριο το ...	*av*·ri·o to ...
morning	πρωί	pro·*i*
afternoon	απόγευμα	a·*po*·yev·ma
evening	βράδι	*vra*·ţhi
tomorrow	αύριο	*av*·ri·o
day after tomorrow	μεθαύριο	me·*thav*·ri·o
next week	την επόμενη εβδομάδα	tin e·*po*·me·ni ev·ţho·*ma*·ţha
next month	τον επόμενο μήνα	ton e·*po*·me·no *mi*·na
next year	τον επόμενο χρόνο	ton e·*po*·me·no *khro*·no
in (six days)	σε (έξι μέρες)	se (*ek*·si *me*·res)
until (June)	μέχρι (τον Ιούνιο)	*meh*·ri (ton i·*u*·ni·o)

during the day

afternoon	απόγευμα n	a·*po*·yev·ma
dawn	αυγή f	av·*yi*
day	ημέρα f	i·*me*·ra
evening	βράδι n	*vra*·ţhi
midday	μεσημέρι n	me·si·*me*·ri
midnight	μεσάνυχτα n pl	me·*sa*·nikh·ta
morning	πρωί n	pro·*i*
night	νύχτα f	*nikh*·ta
sunrise	ανατολή του ήλιου f	a·na·to·*li* tu *i*·liu
sunset	δύση του ήλιου f	*ţhi*·si tu *i*·liu

but the most important time of day ...

... is probably the μεσημεριανή ανάπαυση me·si·*me*·ria·*ni* a·*na*·paf·si (siesta). Don't miss out!

How much is it?
Πόσο κάνει;   *po·so ka·ni*

It's (12) euros.
Κάνει (δώδεκα) ευρώ.   *ka·ni (tho·the·ka) ev·ro*

It's (12) Cyprus pounds.
Κάνει (δώδεκα) λίρες Κύπρου.   *ka·ni (tho·the·ka) li·res ki·pru*

It's free.
Είναι δωρεάν.   *i·ne tho·re·an*

Can you write down the price?
Μπορείς να γράψεις την τιμή;   *bo·ris na ghrap·sis tin ti·mi*

Do you accept ...?	Δέχεσαι ...;	*the·he·se ...*
credit cards	πιστωτικές κάρτες	*pi·sto·ti·kes kar·tes*
debit cards	χρεωτικές κάρτες	*khre·o·ti·kes kar·tes*
travellers cheques	ταξιδιωτικές επιταγές	*tak·si·thio·ti·kes e·pi·ta·yes*
Where's a/an ...?	Πού είναι ...;	*pu i·ne ...*
automated teller machine	μια αυτόματη μηχανή ανάληψης χρημάτων	*mia af·to·ma·ti mi·kha·ni a·na·lip·sis khri·ma·ton*
foreign exchange office	ένα γραφείο αλλαγής χρημάτων	*e·na ghra·fi·o a·la·yis khri·ma·ton*

The official currency in Greece is the ευρώ ev·ro (euro), which is made up of 100 λεπτά lep·ta (euro cents). Some vendors are also happy to take foreign currencies.

What's the …?	Πόσο είναι …;	po·so i·ne …
charge	το κόστος	to kos·tos
exchange rate	η τιμή	i ti·mi
	συναλλάγματος	si·na·lagh·ma·tos

I'd like to …	Θα ήθελα να …	tha i·the·la na …
cash a cheque	εξαργυρώσω	ek·sar·yi·ro·so
	μια επιταγή	mia e·pi·ta·yi
change money	αλλάξω χρήματα	a·lak·so khri·ma·ta
change a	αλλάξω μια	a·lak·so mia
travellers	ταξιδιωτική	tak·si·thio·ti·ki
cheque	επιταγή	e·pi·ta·yi
get a cash	κάμω μια	ka·mo mia
advance	ανάληψη	a·na·lip·si
	σε μετρητά	se me·tri·ta
withdraw	αποσύρω	a·po·si·ro
money	χρήματα	khri·ma·ta

I'd like …,	Θα ήθελα …,	tha i·the·la …
please.	παρακαλώ.	pa·ra·ka·lo
my change	τα ρέστα μου	ta re·sta mu
a refund	μια επιστροφή	mia e·pi·stro·fi
	χρημάτων	khri·ma·ton
to return this	να επιστρέψω αυτό	na e·pi·strep·so af·to

There's a mistake in the bill.

Υπάρχει κάποιο λάθος   i·par·hi ka·pio la·thos
στο λογαριασμό.   sto lo·gha·riaz·mo

Do I need to pay upfront?

Χρειάζεται να πληρώσω   khri·a·ze·te na pli·ro·so
από πριν;   a·po prin

I don't have that much money.

Δεν έχω τόσα πολλά   then e·kho to·sa po·la
χρήματα.   khri·ma·ta

getting around

κυκλοφορώντας

Which ... goes to (Athens)?	Ποιο ... πηγαίνει στην (Αθήνα);	pio ... pi·ye·ni stin (a·thi·na)
Is this the ... to (Athens)?	Είναι αυτό το ... για την (Αθήνα);	i·ne af·to to ... yia tin (a·thi·na)
boat	πλοίο	pli·o
bus	λεωφορείο	le·o·fo·ri·o
ferry	φέρυ	fe·ri
plane	αεροπλάνο	a·e·ro·pla·no
train	τρένο	tre·no
When's the ... (bus)?	Πότε είναι το ... (λεωφορείο);	po·te i·ne to ... (le·o·fo·ri·o)
first	πρώτο	pro·to
last	τελευταίο	te·lef·te·o
next	επόμενο	e·po·me·no

What time does it leave?
Τι ώρα φεύγει;   ti o·ra fev·yi

What time does it get to (Thessaloniki)?
Τι ώρα φτάνει στη   ti o·ra fta·ni sti
(Θεσσαλονίκη);   (the·sa·lo·ni·ki)

How long will it be delayed?
Πόση ώρα θα καθυστερήσει;   po·si o·ra tha ka·thi·ste·ri·si

Is this seat free?
Είναι αυτή η θέση ελεύθερη;   i·ne af·ti i the·si e·lef·the·ri

That's my seat.
Αυτή η θέση είναι δική μου.   af·ti i the·si i·ne thi·ki mu

Please tell me when we get to (Thessaloniki).

Παρακαλώ πέστε μου
όταν φτάσουμε στη
(Θεσσαλονίκη).

pa·ra·ka·lo pe·ste mu
o·tan fta·su·me sti
(the·sa·lo·ni·ki)

How long do we stop here?

Πόση ώρα θα
σταματήσουμε εδώ;

po·si o·ra tha
sta·ma·ti·su·me e·tho

Are you waiting for more people?

Περιμένεις για
περισσότερο κόσμο;

pe·ri·me·nis yia
pe·ri·so·te·ro koz·mo

Can you take us around the city, please?

Μπορείς να μας πάρεις
γύρω στην πόλη,
παρακαλώ;

bo·ris na mas pa·ris
yi·ro stin po·li
pa·ra·ka·lo

How many people can ride on this?

Πόσοι άνθρωποι μπορούν
να ανεβούν σ'αυτό;

po·si an·thro·pi bo·run
na a·ne·vun saf·to

Can you take me as well?

Μπορείς να πάρεις
και εμένα;

bo·ris na pa·ris
ke e·me·na

tickets

εισιτήρια

Where do I buy a ticket?

Πού αγοράζω εισιτήριο;

pu a·gho·ra·zo i·si·ti·ri·o

Do I need to book?

Χρειάζεται να κλείσω θέση;

khri·a·ze·te na kli·so the·si

A bunch of (10) tickets, please.

Μια δέσμη από (δέκα)
εισιτήρια, παρακαλώ.

mia thez·mi a·po (the·ka)
i·si·ti·ri·a pa·ra·ka·lo

Do you have a timetable (in English)?

Έχεις ένα πρόγραμμα
(στα αγγλικά);

e·his e·na pro·ghra·ma
(sta ang·gli·ka)

Can I get a tourist rail pass?

Μπορώ να έχω ένα τουριστικό πάσο για το τρένο;		bo·*ro* na *e*·kho *e*·na tu·ri·*sti*·ko pa·so yia to *tre*·no

A ... ticket to (Patras).	Ένα εισιτήριο ... για την (Πάτρα).	*e*·na i·si·*ti*·ri·o ... yia tin (*pa*·tra)
1st-class	πρώτη θέση	*pro*·ti *the*·si
2nd-class	δεύτερη θέση	*thef*·te·ri *the*·si
child's	παιδικό	pe·*thi*·ko
deck class (boat)	κατάστρωμα	ka·*ta*·stro·ma
one-way	απλό	a·*plo*
return	με επιστροφή	me e·pi·stro·*fi*
student's	μαθητικό	ma·thi·ti·*ko*
tourist class	τουριστική θέση	tu·ri·sti·*ki the*·si

I'd like a/an ... seat.	Θα ήθελα μια θέση ...	tha *i*·the·la mia *the*·si ...
aisle	στο διάδρομο	sto *thia*·thro·mo
(non)smoking	στους (μη) καπνίζοντες	stus (mi) kap·*ni*·zo·des
window	στο παράθυρο	sto pa·*ra*·thi·ro

listen for ...

Ακυρώστε το εισιτήριο.	a·ki·*ro*·ste to i·si·*ti*·rio	**Punch the ticket.**
ακυρώθηκε	a·ki·*ro*·thi·ke	**cancelled**
απεργία f	a·per·*yi*·a	**strike**
αυτό	af·*to*	**this one**
εκείνο	e·*ki*·no	**that one**
γεμάτο	ye·*ma*·to	**full**
καθυστέρησε	ka·thi·*ste*·ri·se	**delayed**
θυρίδα αγοράς εισιτηρίων f	thi·*ri*·tha a·gho·*ras* i·si·ti·*ri*·on	**ticket window**
πλατφόρμα f	plat·*for*·ma	**platform**
πρόγραμμα n	*pro*·ghra·ma	**timetable**
ταξιδιωτικός πράκτορας m	tak·si·thio·ti·*kos prak*·to·ras	**travel agent**

Is there (a) …?	Υπάρχει …;	i·par·hi …
air conditioning	έρκοντίσιον	e·kon·di·si·on
blanket	κουβέρτα	ku·ver·ta
sick bag	σακούλα εμετού	sa·ku·la e·me·tu
toilet	τουαλέτα	tu·a·le·ta

Can I get a sleeping berth?

Μπορώ να έχω μια θέση
με κρεβάτι;

bo·ro na e·kho mia the·si
me kre·va·ti

How much is it?

Πόσο κάνει;

po·so ka·ni

How long does the trip take?

Πόσο διαρκεί το ταξίδι;

po·so thi·ar·ki to tak·si·thi

Is it a direct route?

Πηγαίνει κατ'ευθείαν;

pi·ye·ni ka·tef·thi·an

Can I get a stand-by ticket?

Μπορώ να μπω στον
κατάλογο αναμονής
για εισιτήριο;

bo·ro na bo ston
ka·ta·lo·gho a·na·mo·nis
yia i·si·ti·ri·o

What time should I check in?

Τι ώρα να έρθω στον
έλεγχο;

ti o·ra na er·tho ston
e·leng·kho

I'd like to … my ticket, please.	Θα ήθελα να … το εισιτήριό μου παρακαλώ.	tha i·the·la na … to i·si·ti·ri·o mu pa·ra·ka·lo
cancel	ακυρώσω	a·ki·ro·so
change	αλλάξω	a·lak·so
confirm	επικυρώσω	e·pi·ki·ro·so

---

it's not roulette

If Athenian locals talk about μονά-ζυγά mo·na·zi·gha (odds-evens) and δακτύλιος thak·ti·lios (rings), they refer to traffic restrictions put in place in Athens to help minimise the notorious νέφος ne·fos (smog). The system is called 'odds-evens' because certain cars can enter the 'ring' (a restricted zone) on even or odd days of the month. The boundaries of the thak·ti·lios are marked with yellow hexagonal signs.

luggage

Where can I find a/the …?	Πού μπορώ να βρω …;	pu bo·ro na vro …
baggage claim	το χώρο αποσκευών	to kho·ro a·pos·ke·von
left-luggage office	φύλαξη αποσκευών	fi·lak·si a·pos·ke·von
luggage locker	τη φύλαξη αντικειμένων	ti fi·lak·si a·di·ki·me·non
trolley	ένα καροτσάκι	e·na ka·rot·sa·ki

My luggage has been …	Οι αποσκευές μου έχουν …	i a·pos·ke·ves mu e·khun …
damaged	πάθει ζημιά	pa·thi zi·mia
lost	χαθεί	kha·thi
stolen	κλαπεί	kla·pi

That's (not) mine.
Αυτό (δεν) είναι δικό μου.   af·to (then) i·ne thi·ko mu

Can I have some coins/tokens?
Μπορώ να έχω μερικά
κέρματα/κουπόνια;   bo·ro na e·kho me·ri·ka
ker·ma·ta/ku·po·nia

listen for …

αποσκευές χειρός f pl	a·pos·ke·ves hi·ros	carry-on baggage
διαβατήριο n	thia·va·ti·ri·o	passport
κάρτα επιβίβασης f	kar·ta e·pi·vi·va·sis	boarding pass
κουπόνι n	ku·po·ni	token
μεταβίβαση f	me·ta·vi·va·si	transfer
πτήση τσάρτερ f	pti·si tsar·ter	charter flight
τράνζιτ n	tran·zit	transit
υπέρβαρο n	i·per·va·ro	excess baggage

transport

49

plane

Where does flight (10) arrive/depart?
Πού προσγειώνεται/   pu pros·yi·o·ne·te/
απογειώνεται η πτήση (δέκα);   a·po·yi·o·ne·te i pti·si (*the*·ka)

Where's (the) …?	Πού είναι …;	pu *i*·ne …
airport shuttle	το λεωφορείο	to le·o·fo·*ri*·o
	του αεροδρομίου	tu a·e·ro·thro·*mi*·u
arrivals hall	η αίθουσα των	i *e*·thu·sa ton
	αφίξεων	a·*fik*·se·on
departures hall	η αίθουσα των	i *e*·thu·sa ton
	ανα χωρήσεων	*a*·na kho·*ri*·se·on
duty-free shops	τα αφορολόγητα	ta a·fo·ro·*lo*·yi·ta
gate (9)	η θύρα (εννέα)	i *thi*·ra (e·*ne*·a)

bus, trolley bus & coach

How often do buses come?
Κάθε πότε έρχονται τα   *ka*·the *po*·te er·kho·de ta
λεωφορεία;   le·o·fo·*ri*·a

Does it stop at (Iraklio)?
Σταματάει στο (Ηράκλειο);   sta·ma·*ta*·i sto (i·*ra*·kli·o)

What's the next stop?
Ποια είναι η επόμενη στάση;   pia *i*·ne i e·*po*·me·ni *sta*·si

I'd like to get off (at Iraklio).
Θα ήθελα να κατεβώ   tha *i*·the·la na ka·te·*vo*
(στο Ηράκλειο).   (sto i·*ra*·kli·o)

Where's the trolley bus stop?
Πού είναι η στάση του τρόλεϋ;   pu *i*·ne i *sta*·si tu *tro*·le·i

city a	αστικό	a·sti·*ko*
intercity a	υπεραστικό	i·pe·ra·sti·*ko*
local a	τοπικό	to·pi·*ko*

train & metro

Where's the nearest metro station?

Πού είναι ο πιο κοντινός   pu *i*·ne o pio ko·di·*nos*
σταθμός του μετρό;   stath·*mos* tu me·*tro*

Which line goes to (the port)?

Ποια γραμμή πηγαίνει   pia ghra·*mi* pi·ye·ni
(στο λιμάνι);   (sto li·*ma*·ni)

What station is this?

Ποιος σταθμός είναι αυτός;   pios stath·*mos* i·ne af·*tos*

What's the next station?

Ποιος είναι ο επόμενος   pios *i*·ne o e·*po*·me·nos
σταθμός;   stath·*mos*

Does it stop at (Kalamata)?

Σταματάει στην (Καλαμάτα);   sta·ma·*ta*·i stin (ka·la·*ma*·ta)

Do I need to change?

Χειάζεται να αλλάξω;   khri·*a*·ze·te na a·*lak*·so

Is it direct/express?

Είναι κατ'ευθείαν/εξπρές;   *i*·ne ka·tef·*thi*·an/eks·*pres*

Which carriage	Ποια άμαξα	pia *a*·mak·sa
is …?	είναι (για) …;	*i*·ne (yia) …
1st class	πρώτη θέση	*pro*·ti *the*·si
for dining	φαγητό	fa·yi·*to*
for (Kalamata)	την (Καλαμάτα)	tin (ka·la·*ma*·ta)

north & south

On Greek maps and road signs, 'N' stands for Νότια *no*·ti·a
(south) and 'B' stands for βόρια *vo*·ri·a (north).

boat

Where's the port/port police?
Πού είναι το λιμάνι/
λιμεναρχείο;
pu *i*·ne to li·*ma*·ni/
li·me·nar·*hi*·o

Can I have the ferry timetable?
Μπορώ να έχω το
πρόγραμμα του φέρι;
bo·*ro* na *e*·kho to
pro·ghra·ma tu *fe*·ri

Where does the boat to (Chios) leave from?
Από πού φεύγει το πλοίο
για τη (Χίο);
a·*po* pu *fev*·yi to *pli*·o
yia ti (*hi*·o)

When is the next boat for (Naxos)?
Πότε είναι το επόμενο
πλοίο για τη (Νάξο);
po·te *i*·ne to e·*po*·me·no
pli·o yia ti (*nak*·so)

Does this ferry go to (Rhodos)?
Πηγαίνει αυτό το φέρι
στη (Ρόδο);
pi·*ye*·ni af·*to* to *fe*·ri
sti (*ro*·tho)

How many hours is it to (Milos)?
Πόσες ώρες είναι για
τη (Μήλο);
*po·*ses *o·*res *i·*ne yia
ti (*mi·*lo)

How many stops does the boat make?
Πόσες στάσεις κάνει
το πλοίο;
*po·*ses *sta·*sis *ka·*ni
to *pli·*o

Where can I get a taxi boat?
Πού μπορώ να νοικιάσω
μια βάρκα με βαρκάρη;
pu bo·*ro* na ni·*kia·*so
mia *var·*ka me var·*ka·*ri

Where can we hire an uncrewed boat?
Πού μπορώ να νοικιάσω
μόνο μια βάρκα;
pu bo·*ro* na ni·*kia·*so
*mo·*no mia *var·*ka

I'd like a/an ...	Θα ήθελα ...	tha *i·*the·la ...
cabin for	μια καμπίνα για	mia ka·*bi·*na yia
one/two	ένα/δύο	e·na/*thi·*o
inside/outside	μια εσωτερική/	mia e·so·te·ri·*ki/*
cabin	εξωτερική καμπίνα	ek·so·te·ri·*ki* ka·*bi·*na

What's the sea like today?
Πώς είναι η θάλασσα
σήμερα;
pos *i·*ne i *tha·*la·sa
*si·*me·ra

Are there life jackets?
Υπάρχουν σωσίβια;
i·*par·*khun so·*si·*vi·a

What island is this?
Ποιο νησί είναι αυτό;
pio ni·*si* i·ne af·*to*

What beach is this?
Ποια παραλία είναι αυτή;
pia pa·ra·*li·*a *i·*ne af·*ti*

I feel seasick.
Αισθάνομαι ναυτία.
es·*tha·*no·me naf·*ti·*a

cabin	καμπίνα f	ka·bi·na
caïque (large fishing boat)	καΐκι n	ka·i·ki
captain	καπετάνιος m	ka·pe·ta·nios
car deck	χώρος για αυτοκίνητο στο κατάστρωμα m	kho·ros yia af·to·ki·ni·to sto ka·ta·stro·ma
catamaran	σχεδία καταμαράν f	she·thi·a ka·ta·ma·ran
cruise	κρουαζέρα f	kru·a·ze·ra
deck	κατάστρωμα n	ka·ta·stro·ma
excursion boat	εκδρομική βάρκα f	ek·thro·mi·ki var·ka
ferry	φέρι n	fe·ri
hammock	αιώρα f	e·o·ra
hydrofoil	ιπτάμενο δελφίνι n	ip·ta·me·no thel·fi·ni
inter-island boat	πλοίο συγκοινωνίας μεταξύ νησιών n	pli·o si·gi·no·ni·as me·tak·si ni·sion
jolly roger	βάρκα πλοίου f	var·ka pli·u
lifeboat	ναυαγοσωστική λέμβος f	na·va·gho·so·sti·ki lem·vos
life jacket	σωσίβιο n	so·si·vi·o
muster station	χώρος συγκέντρωσης m	kho·ros si·ge·dro·sis
purser's office	γραφείο λογιστή n	ghra·fi·o lo·yi·sti
sailing boat	ιστιοφόρο n	i·sti·o·fo·ro
small fishing boat	μικρή βάρκα για ψάρεμα f	mi·kri var·ka yia psa·re·ma
yacht	γιωτ n	yiot

taxi

I'd like a taxi …	Θα ήθελα ένα ταξί …	tha i·the·la e·na tak·si …
at (9am)	στις (εννέα π.μ.)	stis (e·ne·a prin to me·si·me·ri)
now	τώρα	to·ra
tomorrow	αύριο	av·ri·o

Where's the taxi rank?
Πού είναι η στάση για ταξί;   pu *i*·ne i *sta*·si yia tak·*si*

Is this taxi available?
Είναι αυτό το ταξί ελεύθερο;   *i*·ne af·*to* to tak·*si* e·*lef*·the·ro

Please put the meter on.
Παρακαλώ βάλε το   pa·ra·ka·*lo va*·le to
ταξίμετρο.   tak·*si*·me·tro

How much is it (to Petroupoli)?
Πόσο κάνει (για Πετρούπολη);   *po*·so *ka*·ni (yia pe·*tru*·po·li)

Please take me to (this address).
Παρακαλώ πάρε με σε   pa·ra·ka·*lo pa*·re me se
(αυτή τη διεύθυνση).   (af·*ti* ti ∂hi·*ef*·thin·si)

How much do you charge for the luggage?
Πόσο χρεώνεις για   *po*·so khre·o·nis yia
τις αποσκευές;   tis a·pos·ke·*ves*

Please …	Παρακλώ …	pa·ra·ka·*lo* …
slow down	πήγαινε πιο σιγά	*pi*·ye·ne pio si·*gha*
stop here	σταμάτα εδώ	sta·*ma*·ta e·*∂ho*
wait here	περίμενε εδώ	pe·*ri*·me·ne e·*∂ho*

car & motorbike

αυτοκίνητο και μοτοσακό

car & motorbike hire

I'd like to hire a/an …	Θα ήθελα να ενοικιάσω ένα …	tha *i*·the·la na e·ni·ki·*a*·so *e*·na …
4WD	4W ντράιβ	for·ghu·*il dra*·iv
automatic	αυτόματο	af·*to*·ma·to
car	αυτοκίνητο	af·to·*ki*·ni·to
manual	με ταχύτητες	me ta·*hi*·ti·tes
motorbike	μοτοσακό	mo·to·sa·*ko*
with …	με …	me …
air conditioning	έρκοντίσιον	e·kon·*di*·si·on
a driver	οδηγό	o·∂hi·*gho*

How much for daily/weekly hire?

Πόσο νοικιάζεται την
ημέρα/εβδομάδα;

po·so ni·*kia*·ze·te tin
i·*me*·ra/ev·tho·*ma*·tha

Does that include insurance/mileage?

Αυτό συμπεριλαμβάνει
ασφάλεια/χιλιόμετρα;

af·*to* si·be·ri·lam·*va*·ni
as·*fa*·li·a/hi·*lio*·me·tra

Can I take the car on a ferry?

Μπορώ να πάρω το
αυτοκίνητο στο φέρι;

bo·*ro* na *pa*·ro to
af·to·*ki*·ni·to sto *fe*·ri

Do you have a guide to the road rules in English?

Έχετε οδικό κώδικα
κυκλοφορίας στα Αγγλικά;

e·he·te o·thi·*ko* ko·thi·ka
ki·klo·fo·*ri*·as sta ang·gli·*ka*

Do you have a road map?

Έχετε οδικό χάρτη;

e·he·te o·thi·*ko* khar·ti

on the road

What's the speed limit?

Ποιο είναι το όριο ταχύτητας;

pio *i*·ne to *o*·ri·o ta·*hi*·ti·tas

Is this the road to (Lamia)?

Είναι αυτός ο δρόμος για
(τη Λαμία);

i·ne af·*tos* o *thro*·mos yia
(ti la·*mi*·a)

Where's a petrol station?

Πού είναι ένα πρατήριο
βενζίνας;

pu i·ne *e*·na pra·*ti*·ri·o
ven·*zi*·nas

Fill it up, please.

Γεμίστε το, παρακαλώ.

ye·*mis*·te to pa·ra·ka·*lo*

signs		
Απαγορεύεται η είσοδος	a·pa·gho·*re*·ve·te i *i*·so·thos	No Entry
Διόδια	thi·o·*thi*·a	Toll
Είσοδος	*i*·so·thos	Entrance (Freeway)
Έξοδος Εθνικής Οδού	*ek*·so·thos e·th·ni·*kis* o·*thu*	Exit Freeway
Προσοχή	pro·so·*hi*	Drive With Care
Μονόδρομος	mo·*no*·thro·mos	One-Way

listen for ...

άδεια οδήγησης f	a·thi·a o·thi·yi·sis	**drivers licence**
βενζίνα f	ven·zi·na	**petrol (gas)**
δωρεάν	tho·re·an	**free a**
επί τόπου	e·pi to·pu	**on-the-spot**
ασφάλεια f	as·fa·li·a	**insurance**
παρκόμετρο n	par·ko·me·tro	**parking meter**
Πράσινη κάρτα f	pra·si·ni kar·ta	**Green Card (international third-party insurance)**
χιλιόμετρα n pl	hi·lio·me·tra	**kilometres**

diesel	ντίζελ n	di·zel
leaded	μολυβδούχος f	mo·liv·thu·khos
LPG	υγραέριο n	igh·ra·e·ri·o
premium	σούπερ f	su·per
unleaded	αμόλυβδος f	a·mo·liv·thos
regular	απλή f	ap·li
unleaded	αμόλυβδος f	a·mo·liv·thos

Can you check the ...?	Μπορείς να κοιτάξεις ...;	bo·ris na ki·tak·sis ...
oil	το λάδι	to la·thi
tyre pressure	την πίεση των τροχών	tin pi·e·si ton tro·khon
water	το νερό	to ne·ro

(How long) Can I park here?

(Πόση ώρα) Μπορώ να παρκάρω εδώ;	(po·si o·ra) bo·ro na par·ka·ro e·tho

Do I have to pay?

Πρέπει να πληρώσω;	pre·pi na pli·ro·so

transport

57

problems

I need a mechanic.
Χρειάζομαι μηχανικό.
khri·*a*·zo·me mi·kha·ni·*ko*

I've had an accident.
Είχα ένα ατύχημα.
i·kha *e*·na a·*ti*·hi·ma

The car/motorbike has broken down (at Corinth).
Το αυτοκίνητο/μοτοσακό
χάλασε (στην Κόρινθο).
to af·to·*ki*·ni·to/mo·to·sa·*ko*
ha·la·se (stin *ko*·rin·tho)

The car/motorbike won't start.
Το αυτοκίνητο/μοτοσακό
δεν αρχίζει.
to af·to·*ki*·ni·to/mo·to·sa·*ko*
ţhen ar·*hi*·zi

I have a flat tyre.
Μ'έπιασε λάστιχο.
me·pia·se *la*·sti·kho

I've lost my car keys.
Έχασα τα κλειδιά του
αυτοκινήτου μου.
e·ha·sa ta kli·*ţhia* tu
af·to·ki·*ni*·tu mu

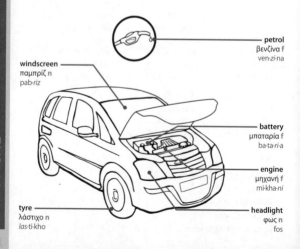

petrol
βενζίνα f
ven·*zi*·na

windscreen
παμπρίζ n
pab·*riz*

battery
μπαταρία f
ba·ta·*ri*·a

engine
μηχανή f
mi·kha·*ni*

tyre
λάστιχο n
las·ti·kho

headlight
φως n
fos

I've locked the keys inside.
Κλείδωσα τα κλειδιά μου
στο αυτοκίνητου.
*kli·*tho·sa ta kli·*thia* mu
sto af·to·*ki*·ni·to

I've run out of petrol.
Μου τελείωσε η βενζίνα.
mu te·*li*·o·se i ven·*zi*·na

Can you fix it (today)?
Μπορείς να το
επισκευάσεις (σήμερα);
bo·*ris* na to
e·pis·ke·*va*·sis (*si*·me·ra)

How long will it take?
Πόση ώρα θα κάμεις;
po·si *o*·ra tha *ka*·mi

bicycle

ποδήλατο

I'd like ...	Θα ήθελα ...	tha *i*·the·la ...
my bicycle repaired	να επισκευάσω το ποδήλατό μου	na e·pis·ke·*va*·so to po·*thi*·la·to mu
to buy a bicycle	να αγοράσω ένα ποδήλατο	na a·gho·*ra*·so e·na po·*thi*·la·to
to hire a bicycle	να νοικιάσω ένα ποδήλατο	na ni·*kia*·so e·na po·*thi*·la·to
I'd like a ... bike.	Θα ήθελα ένα ...	tha *i*·the·la e·na ...
mountain	ποδήλατο για βουνό	po·*thi*·la·to yia vu·*no*
racing	ποδήλατο κούρσας	po·*thi*·la·to *kur*·sas
second-hand	μεταχειρισμένο ποδήλατο	me·ta·hi·riz·*me*·no po·*thi*·la·to

How much is it per day?
Πόσο κοστίζει την ημέρα;
po·so ko·*sti*·zi tin i·*me*·ra

How much is it per hour?
Πόσο κοστίζει την ώρα;
po·so ko·*sti*·zi tin *o*·ra

Do I need a helmet?
Χρειάζομαι κράνος;　　　　khri·*a*·zo·me *kra*·nos

Is there a bicycle-path map?
Υπάρχει χάρτης για δρόμο　　i·*par*·hi *khar*·tis yia thro·mo
ποδηλάτου;　　　　　　　　po·thi·*la*·tu

Is this road OK for bicycles?
Είναι αυτός ο δρόμος　　　　*i*·ne af·*tos* o *thro*·mos
κατάλληλος για ποδήλατα;　　ka·*ta*·li·los yia po·*thi*·la·ta

I have a puncture.
Τρύπησε η ρόδα μου.　　　　*tri*·pi·se i *ro*·tha mu

---

gut feelings

Greeks tend to get pretty physical when they talk about their emotions:

I'm not impressed.
Δεν μου γεμίζει το μάτι.　　then mu ye·*mi*·zi to *ma*·ti
(lit: It doesn't fill my eye.)

I can't stand him/her.
Δεν τον/την χωνεύω.　　　then ton/tin tso·ne·*vo*
(lit: I can't digest him/her.)

I've had enough of you.
Μ'έπρηξες.　　　　　　　me·*prik*·ses
(lit: You've made me swollen.)

I regretted it.
Μου βγήκε από τη μύτη.　　mu *vyi*·ke a·*po* ti *mi*·ti
(lit: It came out of my nose.)

He/She put me under pressure.
Μου βαλε τα δυο πόδια　　*mu*·va·le ta thio po·*thia*
σ' ένα παπούτσι.　　　　　se·na pa·*put*·si
(lit: He/She put both my feet in one shoe.)

border crossing

περνώντας τα σύνορα

I'm ...	Είμαι ...	*i*·me ...
in transit	τράνζιτ	*tran*·zit
on business	για δουλειά	yia ţhu·*lia*
on holiday	σε διακοπές	se ţhia·ko·*pes*

I'm here for	Είμαι εδώ για	*i*·me e·*ţho* yia
(three) ...	(τρεις) ...	(tris) ...
days	μέρες	*me*·res
weeks	εβδομάδες	ev·ţho·*ma*·ţhes
months	μήνες	*mi*·nes

I'm going to (Limassol).
Πηγαίνω στη (Λεμεσό).   pi·*ye*·no sti (le·me·*so*)

I'm staying at (the Xenia).
Μένω στο (Ξενία).   *me*·no sto (kse·*ni*·a)

The children are on this passport.
Τα παιδιά είναι σ'αυτό   ta pe·*ţhia i*·ne saf·*to*
το βιαβατήριο.   to ţhia·va·*ti*·ri·o

listen for ...

άδεια f	*a*·ţhi·a	export permit
εξαγωγής	ek·sa·gho·*yis*	
βίζα f	*vi*·za	visa
διαβατήριο n	ţhia·va·*ti*·ri·o	passport
μόνος m	*mo*·nos	alone
οικογένεια f	i·ko·*ye*·ni·a	family
ομάδα f	o·*ma*·ţha	group
ταυτότητα f	taf·*to*·ti·ta	ID card

Can you stamp a separate paper instead of the passport?

Μπορείτε να σφραγίσετε
ένα χωριστό χαρτί αντί
για το διαβατήριο;

bo·*ri*·te na sfra·*yi*·se·te
e·na kho·ri·*sto* khar·*ti* a·*di*
yia to thia·va·*ti*·ri·o

Where can I get a travel permit for (Mt Athos)?

Πού μπορώ να πάρω μια
άδεια ταξιδιού για (το
Άγιο Όρος);

pu bo·*ro* na *pa*·ro mia
a·thi·a tak·si·*thiu* yia (to
a·yi·o *o*·ros)

at customs

στο τελωνείο

I have nothing to declare.

Δεν έχω τίποτε να δηλώσω.   then e·kho *ti*·po·te na thi·*lo*·so

I have something to declare.

Έχω κάτι να δηλώσω.   e·kho *ka*·ti na thi·*lo*·so

Do I have to declare this?

Πρέπει να το δηλώσω αυτό;   *pre*·pi na to thi·*lo*·so af·*to*

That's (not) mine.

Αυτό (δεν) είναι δικό μου.   af·*to* (then) *i*·ne thi·*ko* mu

I didn't know I had to declare it.

Δεν ήξερα πως έπρεπε να
το δηλώσω.

then *ik*·se·ra pos e·*pre*·pe na
to thi·*lo*·so

I have a doctor's certificate for this medication.

Έχω πιστοποιητικό γιατρού
για αυτό το φάρμακο.

e·kho pis·to·pi·i·*ti*·ko yia·*tru*
yia af·*to* to *far*·ma·ko

signs

Αφορολόγητα	a·fo·ro·*lo*·yi·ta	**Duty-Free**
Έλεγχος	*e*·len·ghos	**Passport Control**
Διαβατηρίων	thia·va·ti·*ri*·on	
Καραντίνα	ka·ran·*di*·na	**Quarantine**
Τελωνείο	te·lo·*ni*·o	**Customs**
Μετανάστευση	me·ta·*na*·stef·si	**Immigration**

directions
οδηγίες

Where's (the tourist office)?
Πού είναι (το τουριστικό γραφείο);
pu *i*·ne (to tu·ri·sti·*ko* ghra·*fi*·o)

What's the address?
Ποια είναι η διεύθυνση;
pia *i*·ne i thi·*ef*·thin·si

How far is it?
Πόσο μακριά είναι;
po·so ma·kri·*a i*·ne

How do I get there?
Πώς πηγαίνω εκεί;
pos pi·*ye*·no e·*ki*

What street is this?
Ποιος δρόμος είναι αυτός;
pios *thro*·mos *i*·ne af·*tos*

What village is this?
Ποιο χωριό είναι αυτό;
pio kho·*rio i*·ne af·*to*

Can you show me (on the map)?
Μπορείς να μου δείξεις (στο χάρτη);
bo·*ris* na mu thik·sis (sto *khar*·ti)

It's ...	Είναι ...	*i*·ne ...
close	κοντά	ko·*da*
behind ...	πίσω ...	*pi*·so ...
here	εδώ	e·*tho*
in front of ...	μπροστά από ...	bros·*ta* a·*po* ...
near ...	κοντά ...	ko·*da* ...
next to ...	δίπλα από ...	*thip*·la a·*po* ...
on the corner	στη γωνία	sti gho·*ni*·a
opposite ...	απέναντι ...	a·*pe*·na·di ...
straight ahead	κατ'ευθείαν	ka·tef·*thi*·an
there	εκεί	e·*ki*
north	βόρια	*vo*·ri·a
south	νότια	*no*·ti·a
east	ανατολικά	a·na·to·li·*ka*
west	δυτικά	thi·ti·*ka*

directions

63

χιλιόμετρα	hi·*lio*·me·tra	**kilometres**
λεπτά	lep·*ta*	**minutes**
μέτρα	*me*·tra	**metres**

avenue	λεωφόρος f	le·o·*fo*·ros
lane	πάροδος f	*pa*·ro·ṭhos
street	οδός f	o·*ṭhos*

| **by bus/taxi** | με λεωφορείο/ταξί | me le·o·fo·*ri*·o/tak·*si* |
| **on foot** | με πόδια | me *po*·ṭhia |

Turn ...	Στρίψε ...	*strip*·se ...
at the corner	στη γωνία	sti gho·*ni*·a
at the traffic lights	στα φανάρια	sta fa·*na*·ria
left	αριστερά	a·ris·te·*ra*
right	δεξιά	ṭhek·si·*a*

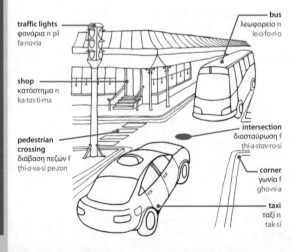

traffic lights
φανάρια n pl
fa·*na*·ria

shop
κατάστημα n
ka·*tas*·ti·ma

pedestrian crossing
διάβαση πεζών f
ṭhi·*a*·va·si pe·*zon*

bus
λεωφορείο n
le·o·fo·*ri*·o

intersection
διασταύρωση f
ṭhi·a·*stav*·ro·si

corner
γωνία f
gho·*ni*·a

taxi
ταξί n
tak·*si*

finding accommodation

βρίσκοντας κατάλυμα

Where's (a) ...?	Πού είναι ...;	pu *i*·ne ...
bed and breakfast	κατάλυμα με πρόγευμα	ka·*ta*·li·ma me *pro*·ghev·ma
camping ground	χώρος για κάμπινγκ	*kho*·ros yia *kam*·ping
guesthouse	ξενώνας	kse·*no*·nas
(3-star) hotel	ξενοδοχείο (τριών αστέρων)	kse·no·*tho*·hi·o (tri·*on* a·*ste*·ron)
mountain refuge	ορεινό καταφύγιο	o·ri·*no* ka·ta·*fi*·yi·o
pension	πανσιόν	pan·*sion*
room for rent	δωμάτιο για νοίκιασμα	*tho*·*ma*·ti·o yia *ni*·kiaz·ma
self-contained apartment	ξεχωριστό διαμέρισμα	kse·kho·ri·*sto* *thi*·a·*me*·riz·ma
some traditional accommodation	παραδοσιακό κατάλυμα	pa·ra·*tho*·si·a·*ko* ka·*ta*·li·ma
youth hostel	γιουθ χόστελ	yiuth *kho*·stel

---

local talk

dive	βουτιά f	vu·*tia*
rat-infested	γεμάτο ποντίκια	ye·*ma*·to po·*di*·kia
top spot	ωραιότατο σημείο n	o·re·*o*·ta·to si·*mi*·o

Can you	Μπορείτε να	bo·*ri*·te na
recommend	συστήσετε	si·*sti*·se·te
somewhere …?	κάπου …;	*ka*·pu …
cheap	φτηνό	fti·*no*
good	καλό	ka·*lo*
nearby	κοντινό	ko·di·*no*
romantic	ρομαντικό	ro·ma·di·*ko*

What's the address?

Ποια είναι η διεύθυνση;   pia *i*·ne i thi·*ef*·thin·si

For responses, see **directions**, page 63.

booking ahead & checking in

κλείσιμο θέσης από πριν και εγκατάσταση

I'd like to book a room, please.

Θα ήθελα να κλείσω ένα   tha *i*·the·la na *kli*·so *e*·na
δωμάτιο, παρακαλώ.   tho·*ma*·ti·o pa·ra·ka·*lo*

I have a reservation.

Έχω κάμει κάποια κράτηση.   *e*·kho *ka*·mi *ka*·pia *kra*·ti·si

My name's …

Με λένε …   me *le*·ne …

For (three) nights/weeks.

Για (τρεις) νύχτες/   yia (tris) *nikh*·tes/
εβδομάδες.   ev·tho·*ma*·thes

From (2 July) to (6 July).

Από (τις δύο Ιουλίου)   a·*po* (tis *thi*·o i·u·*li*·u)
μέχρι (τις έξι Ιουλίου).   *me*·khri (tis *ek*·si i·u·*li*·u)

listen for …		
Πόσες νύχτες;	*po*·ses *nikh*·tes	**How many nights?**
διαβατήριο n	thia·va·*ti*·ri·o	**passport**
γεμάτο	ye·*ma*·to	**full** a
κλειδί n	kli·*thi*	**key**
ρεσεψιόν f	re·sep·*sion*	**reception**

PRACTICAL

Do you have a ... room?	Έχετε ένα ... δωμάτιο	e-he-te *e*-na ... tho-*ma*-ti-o
single	μονό	mo-*no*
double	διπλό	thi-*plo*
twin	δίκλινο	*thi*-kli-no

How much is it per ...?	Πόσο είναι για κάθε ...;	*po*-so *i*-ne yia *ka*-the ...
night	νύχτα	*nikh*-ta
person	άτομο	*a*-to-mo
week	εβδομάδα	ev-tho-*ma*-tha

Can I see it?
Μπορώ να το δω; bo-*ro* na to tho

I'll take it.
Θα το πάρω. tha to *pa*-ro

Do I need to pay upfront?
Χρειάζεται να πληρώσω από πριν; khri-*a*-ze-te na pli-*ro*-so a-*po* prin

Can I pay by ...?	Μπορώ να πληρώσω με ...;	bo-*ro* na pli-*ro*-so me ...
credit card	πιστωτική κάρτα	pi-sto-ti-*ki kar*-ta
travellers cheque	ταξιδιωτική επιταγή	tak-si-thio-ti-*ki* e-pi-ta-*yi*

For other methods of payment, see **shopping**, page 77.

accommodation

67

requests & queries

When/Where is breakfast served?

Πότε/Πού σερβίρεται το πρόγευμα;

*po·*te/pu ser·*vi·*re·te to *pro·*yev·ma

Please wake me at (seven).

Παρακαλώ ξύπνησέ με στις (εφτά).

pa·ra·ka·*lo* ksip·ni·*se* me stis (ef·*ta*)

Do you ... here?	... εδώ;	... e·*tho*
arrange tours	Κανονίζετε ξεναγήσεις	ka·no·*ni·*ze·te kse·na·*yi·*sis
change money	Αλλάζετε χρήματα	a·*la·*ze·te *khri·*ma·ta

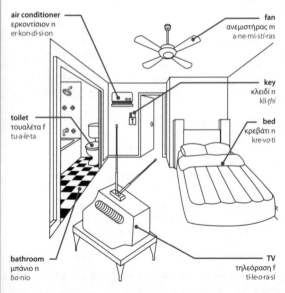

air conditioner
ερκοντίσιον n
er·kon·*di·*si·on

fan
ανεμιστήρας m
a·ne·mi·*sti·*ras

key
κλειδί n
kli·*thi*

toilet
τουαλέτα f
tu·a·*le·*ta

bed
κρεβάτι n
kre·*va·*ti

bathroom
μπάνιο n
*ba·*nio

TV
τηλεόραση f
ti·le·*o·*ra·si

Can I use the …?	Μπορώ να χρησιμοποιήσω …;	bo·ro na khri·si·mo·pi·i·so …
kitchen	την κουζίνα	tin ku·zi·na
laundry	το πλυντήριο	to pli·di·ri·o
telephone	το τηλέφωνο	to ti·le·fo·no
Do you have a/an …?	Έχετε …;	e·he·te …
elevator	ασανσέρ	a·san·ser
laundry service	υπηρεσία πλυντηρίου	i·pi·re·si·a pli·di·ri·u
message board	πίνακα μηνυμάτων	pi·na·ka mi·ni·ma·ton
safe	χρηματοκιβώτιο	khri·ma·to·ki·vo·ti·o
swimming pool	πισίνα	pi·si·na
Could I have (a/an) …, please?	Μπορώ να έχω …παρακαλώ;	bo·ro na e·kho … pa·ra·ka·lo
extra blanket	μια κουβέρτα ακόμη	mia ku·ver·ta a·ko·mi
my key	το κλειδί μου	to kli·thi mu
mosquito net	μια κουνουπιέρα	mia ku·nu·pie·ra
receipt	μια απόδειξη	mia a·po·thik·si

Is there hot water all day?
Υπάρχει ζεστό νερό όλη
την ημέρα;
i·par·hi ze·sto ne·ro o·li
tin i·me·ra

Is there a message for me?
Υπάρχει μήνυμα για μένα;
i·par·hi mi·ni·ma yia me·na

Can I leave a message for someone?
Μπορώ να αφήσω ένα
μήνυμα για κάποιον;
bo·ro na a·fi·so e·na
mi·ni·ma yia ka·pion

I'm locked out of my room.
Κλειδώθηκα έξω από το
δωμάτιό μου.
kli·tho·thi·ka ek·so a·po to
tho·ma·ti·o mu

accommodation

69

complaints

It's too ...	Είναι πάρα πολύ ...	*i*·ne *pa*·ra po·*li* ...
bright	φωτεινό	fo·ti·*no*
cold	κρύο	*kri*·o
dark	σκοτεινό	sko·ti·*no*
expensive	ακριβό	a·kri·*vo*
noisy	θορυβώδες	tho·ri·*vo*·ʈhes
small	μικρό	mi·*kro*

The ... doesn't work.	... δεν δουλεύει.	... ʈhen ʈhu·*le*·vi
air conditioner	Το ερκοντίσιον	to er·kon·*di*·si·on
fan	Ο ανεμιστήρας	o a·ne·mi·*sti*·ras
toilet	Η τουαλέτα	i tu·a·*le*·ta

Can I get another (blanket)?
Μπορώ να πάρω μια άλλη (κουβέρτα);
bo·*ro* na *pa*·ro mia *a*·li (ku·*ver*·ta)

This (pillow) isn't clean.
Αυτό (το μαξιλάρι) δεν είναι καθαρό.
af·*to* (to mak·si·*la*·ri) ʈhen *i*·ne ka·tha·*ro*

a knock at the door ...

Who is it?
Ποιος είναι;
pios *i*·ne

Just a moment.
Μια στιγμή.
mia stigh·*mi*

Come in.
Περάστε.
pe·*ra*·ste

Come back later, please.
Έλα αργότερα, παρακαλώ.
e·la ar·*gho*·te·ra pa·ra·ka·*lo*

70

checking out

What time is checkout?
Τι ώρα είναι η αναχώρηση; ti *o*·ra *i*·ne i a·na·*kho*·ri·si

Can I have a late checkout?
Μπορώ να φύγω αργά; bo·*ro* na *fi*·gho ar·*gha*

Can you call a taxi for me (for 11 o'clock)?
Μπορείτε να καλέσετε ένα bo·*ri*·te na ka·*le*·se·te *e*·na
ταξί (για τις έντεκα); tak·*si* (yia tis *e*·de·ka)

I'm leaving now.
Φεύγω τώρα. *fev*·gho *to*·ra

Can I leave my bags here?
Μπορώ να αφήσω τις bo·*ro* na a·*fi*·so tis
βαλίτσες μου εδώ; va·*lit*·ses mu e·*tho*

There's a mistake in the bill.
Υπάρχει κάποιο λάθος i·*par*·hi *ka*·pio *la*·thos
στο λογαριασμό. sto lo·gha·riaz·*mo*

Could I have my ..., please?	Μπορώ να έχω ... παρακλώ;	bo·*ro* na *e*·kho ... pa·ra·ka·*lo*
deposit	την προκατα- βολή μου	tin pro·ka·ta· vo·*li* mu
passport	το διαβατήριό μου	to thia·va·*ti*·rio mu
valuables	τα κοσμήματά μου	ta koz·*mi*·ma·*ta* mu

I'll be back ...	Θα επιστρέψω ...	tha e·pi·*strep*·so ...
in (three) days	σε (τρεις) μέρες	se (tris) *me*·res
on (Tuesday)	την (Τρίτη)	tin *tri*·ti

I had a great stay, thank you.
Είχα υπέροχη διαμονή, *i*·kha i·*pe*·ro·hi thi·a·mo·*ni*
ευχαριστώ. ef·kha·ri·*sto*

I'll recommend it to my friends.
Θα το συστήσω στους tha to si·*sti*·so stus
φίλους μου. *fi*·lus mu

camping

Do you have (a) …?	Έχετε …	e·he·te …
electricity	ηλεκτρισμό	i·lek·triz·mo
laundry	πλυντήριο	pli·di·ri·o
site	χώρο	kho·ro
shower	εγκαταστάσεις	e·ga·ta·sta·sis
facilities	για ντουζ	yia duz
tents for hire	τέντες για	te·des yia
	νοίκιασμα	ni·kiaz·ma

How much is it per …?	Πόσο κοστίζει για κάθε …;	po·so ko·sti·zi yia ka·the …
caravan	τροχόσπιτο	tro·kho·spi·to
person	άτομο	a·to·mo
tent	τέντα	te·da
vehicle	αυτοκίνητο	af·to·ki·ni·to

Can I camp here?
Μπορώ να κατασκηνώσω εδώ;
bo·ro na ka·ta·ski·no·so e·tho

Can I park next to my tent?
Μπορώ να παρκάρω δίπλα στην τέντα μου;
bo·ro na par·ka·ro thi·pla stin te·da mu

Who do I ask to stay here?
Ποιον ρωτάω για να μείνω εδώ;
pion ro·ta·o yia na mi·no e·tho

Could I borrow …?
Μπορώ να δανειστώ …;
bo·ro na tha·ni·sto …

Is it coin-operated?
Λειτουργεί με κέρματα;
li·tur·yi me ker·ma·ta

Is the water drinkable?
Είναι το νερό πόσιμο;
i·ne to ne·ro po·si·mo

When you're making a request, make it sound more polite by starting your question with μήπως *mi·*pos, the equivalent of the English 'Do you, by any chance, ...?'.

Do you, by any chance, have a room with a view?

Μήπως έχετε ένα	*mi·*pos *e·*hete *e·*na
δωμάτιο με θέα;	tho·*ma·*tio me *the·*a

See the **phrasebuilder** for more on requests.

renting

νοικιάζοντας

I'm here about the ... for rent.	Είμαι εδώ για το ... που νοικιάζεται.	*i·*me e·*tho* yia to ... pu ni·*kia·*ze·te
Do you have a/an ... for rent?	Έχεις ένα ... για νοίκιασμα;	*e·*his *e·*na ... yia ni·*kiaz·*ma
apartment	διαμέρισμα	thi·a·*me·*riz·ma
house	σπίτι	*spi·*ti
room	δωμάτιο	tho·*ma·*ti·o

I'm here about the ... for rent.	Είμαι εδώ για την ... που νοικιάζεται.	*i·*me e·*tho* yia tin ... pu ni·*kia·*ze·te
Do you have a ... for rent?	Έχεις μια ... για νοίκιασμα;	*e·*his mia ... yia ni·*kiaz·*ma
cabin	καμπίνα	ka·*bi·*na
villa	έπαυλη	*e·*pav·li

furnished	με έπιπλα	me *e·*pi·pla
partly furnished	με λίγα έπιπλα	me *li·*gha *e·*pi·pla
unfurnished	χωρίς έπιπλα	kho·*ris* e·pi·pla

accommodation

73

staying with locals

Can I stay at your place?
Μπορώ να μείνω στο   bo·ro na mi·no sto
σπίτι σου;   spi·ti su

Is there anything I can do to help?
Μπορώ να κάνω κάτι για   bo·ro na ka·no ka·ti yia
να βοηθήσω;   na vo·i·thi·so

I have my own ...	Έχω το δικό μου ...	e·kho to thi·ko mu ...
mattress	στρώμα	stro·ma
sleeping bag	σλίπινγκ μπαγκ	sli·ping bag

Can I ...?	Μπορώ να ...;	bo·ro na ...
bring anything	φέρω κάτι	fe·ro ka·ti
for the meal	για το φαγητό	yia to fa·yi·to
do the dishes	πλύνω τα πιάτα	pli·no ta pia·ta
set/clear the	στρώσω/μαζέψω	stro·so/ma·zep·so
table	το τραπέζι	to tra·pe·zi
take out the	βγάλω έξω τα	vgha·lo ek·so ta
rubbish	σκουπίδια	sku·pi·thia

Thanks for your hospitality.
Ευχαριστώ για τη   ef·kha·ri·sto yia ti
φιλοξενία σας.   fi·lok·se·ni·a sas

If you're dining with your hosts, see **eating out**, page 157, for additional phrases.

foreign visitors

Punctuality for social engagements is not taken as seriously as you might be used to. An invitation for 9pm means that most people won't show up before 9.30pm. An evening coffee can sometimes extend to dinner, and not end until after midnight. Such a long visit is known in Greek as an αρμένικη βίζιτα ar·me·ni·ki vi·si·ta (Armenian visit).

looking for ...

ψάχνοντας για ...

Where's ...?	Πού είναι ...;	pu *i*·ne ...
a department store	ένα κατάστημα	*e*·na ka·*ta*·sti·ma
the flea market	το παζάρι	to pa·*za*·ri
the food market	η αγορά τροφίμων	i a·gho·*ra* tro·*fi*·mon
a kiosk	ένα περίπτερο	*e*·na pe·*rip*·te·ro
the street market	η λαϊκή αγορά	i la·i·*ki* a·gho·*ra*
a supermarket	ένα σούπερ-μάρκετ	*e*·na *su*·per *mar*·ket
a souvenir shop	ένα κατάστημα με σουβενίρ	*e*·na ka·*ta*·sti·ma me su·ve·*nir*

On which day is the street market held?

Ποια μέρα έχει λαϊκή;	pia *me*·ra *e*·hi la·i·*ki*

Where can I buy (a padlock)?

Πού μπορώ να αγοράσω (μια κλειδαριά);	pu bo·*ro* na a·gho·*ra*·so (mia kli·ṭha·*ria*)

For phrases on directions, see **directions**, page 63.

listen for ...

Μπορώ να σας βοηθήσω; bo·*ro* na sas vo·i·*thi*·so	Can I help you?
Τίποτε άλλο; *ti*·po·te *a*·lo	Anything else?
Όχι, δεν έχουμε. *o*·hi ṭhen *e*·khu·me	No, we don't have any.
Να το τυλίξω; na to ti·*lik*·so	Shall I wrap it?

making a purchase

I'm just looking.
Απλά κοιτάζω.   a·*pla* ki·*ta*·zo

I'd like to buy (an adaptor plug).
Θα ήθελα να αγοράσω   tha *i*·the·la na a·gho·*ra*·so
(ένα μετασχηματιστή).   (*e*·na me·ta·shi·ma·ti·*sti*)

Can I look at it?
Μπορώ να το κοιτάξω;   bo·*ro* na to ki·*tak*·so

Do you have any others?
Έχετε άλλα;   *e*·he·te *a*·la

How much is it?
Πόσο κάνει;   *po*·so *ka*·ni

Can you write down the price?
Μπορείς να γράψεις την τιμή;   bo·*ris* na *ghrap*·sis tin ti·*mi*

Does it have a guarantee?
Έχει εγγύηση;   *e*·hi e·*gi*·i·si

Could I have it wrapped?
Μπορείς να μου το τυλίξεις;   bo·*ris* na mu to ti·*lik*·sis

Could I have a bag/receipt, please?
Μπορώ να έχω μια τσάντα/   bo·*ro* na *e*·kho mia *tsa*·da/
απόδειξη, παρακαλώ;   a·*po*·thik·si pa·ra·ka·*lo*

Can I have it sent overseas?
Μπορείς να το στείλεις   bo·*ris* na to *sti*·lis
στο εξωτερικό;   sto ek·so·te·ri·*ko*

Can you order it for me?
Μπορείς να το παραγγείλεις   bo·*ris* na to pa·ra·*gi*·lis
για μένα;   yia *me*·na

Can I pick it up later?
Μπορώ να το πραλάβω   bo·*ro* na to pa·ra·*la*·vo
αργότερα;   ar·*gho*·te·ra

It's faulty.
Είναι ελαττωματικό.   *i*·ne e·la·to·ma·ti·*ko*

bargain	ευκαιρία f	ef·ke·*ri*·a
rip-off	γδάρσιμο n	*ghthar*·si·mo
sale	έκπτωση f	*ek*·pto·si
specials	προσφορές f pl	pros·fo·*res*

Do you accept ...?	Δέχεστε ...;	*the*·he·ste ...
credit cards	πιστωτικές κάρτες	pi·sto·ti·*kes kar*·tes
debit cards	χρεωτικές κάρτες	khre·o·ti·*kes kar*·tes
travellers cheques	ταξιδιωτικές επιταγές	tak·si·thio·ti·*kes* e·pi·ta·*yes*
I'd like ..., please.	Θα ήθελα ..., παρακαλώ.	tha *i*·the·la ... pa·ra·ka·*lo*
a refund	επιστροφή χρημάτων	e·pi·stro·*fi* khri·*ma*·ton
my change	τα ρέστα μου	ta *re*·sta mu
to return this	να επιστρέψω αυτό	na e·pi·*strep*·so af·to

bargaining

παζάρεμα

That's too expensive.

Είναι πάρα πολύ ακριβό.   *i*·ne *pa*·ra po·*li* a·kri·*vo*

I don't have that much money.

Δεν έχω τόσα πολλά χρήματα.   then *e*·kho *to*·sa po·*la khri*·ma·ta

Do you have something cheaper?

Έχεις κάτι πιο φτηνό;   *e*·his *ka*·ti pio fti·*no*

Can you lower the price?

Μπορείς να κατεβάσεις   bo·*ris* na ka·te·va·*sis*
την τιμή;   tin ti·*mi*

How much for (two)?

Πόσο κάνει για (δύο);   *po*·so *ka*·ni yia (*thi*·o)

I'll give you (five euros).

Θα σου δώσω (πέντε ευρώ).   tha su *tho*·so (*pe*·de ev·*ro*)

I'll give you (five Cyprus pounds).

Θα σου δώσω (πέντε   tha su *tho*·so (*pe*·de
λίρες Κύπρου).   *li*·res *ki*·pru)

books & reading

βιβλία και διάβασμα

Is there an English-language bookshop/section?

Υπάρχει ένα βιβλιοπωλείο/   i·*par*·hi *e*·na viv·li·o·po·*li*·o/
τμήμα Αγγλικής γλώσσας;   *tmi*·ma ang·gli·*kis* ghlo·sas

Can you recommend a book for me?

Μπορείς να μου συστήσεις   bo·*ris* na mu si·*sti*·sis
ένα βιβλίο;   *e*·na viv·*li*·o

Do you have Lonely Planet guidebooks?

Έχετε βιβλία-οδηγούς του   *e*·he·te viv·*li*·a·o·thi·*ghus* tu
Λόνλι Πλάνετ;   *lon*·li *pla*·net

Do you have ...?	Έχεις ένα ...;	*e*·his *e*·na ...
a book by (Nikos	βιβλίο (του Νίκου	viv·*li*·o (tu *ni*·ku
Kazantzakis)	Καζαντζάκη)	ka·za·*dza*·ki)
an entertainment	οδηγό	o·thi·*gho*
guide	διασκεδάσεων	thias·ke·*tha*·se·on

I'd like a ...	Θα ήθελα ...	tha *i*·the·la ...
dictionary	ένα λεξικό	*e*·na lek·si·*ko*
newspaper	μια εφημερίδα	mia e·fi·me·*ri*·tha
(in English)	(στα Αγγλικά)	(sta ang·gli·*ka*)
notepad	ένα μπλοκ για	*e*·na blok yia
	σημειώσεις	si·mi·*o*·sis

clothes

My size is …	Το νούμερό	to nu·me·ro
	μου είναι …	mu i·ne …
(40)	(σαράντα)	(sa·ra·da)
small	μικρό	mi·kro
medium	μεσαίο	me·se·o
large	μεγάλο	me·gha·lo

Can I try it on?

Μπορώ να το προβάρω;   bo·ro na to pro·va·ro

It doesn't fit.

Δε μου κάνει.   the mu ka·ni

electronic goods

Where can I buy duty-free electronic goods?

Πού μπορώ να αγοράσω   pu bo·ro na a·gho·ra·so
αφορολόγητα ηλεκτρονικά   a·fo·ro·lo·yi·ta i·lek·tro·ni·ka
είδη;   i·thi

Is this the latest model?

Είναι αυτό το τελευταίο   i·ne af·to to te·lef·te·o
μοντέλο;   mo·de·lo

Is this (240) volts?

Είναι αυτό   i·ne af·to
(240) βολτ;   (thia·ko·sia sa·ra·da) volt

I need an adaptor plug.

Χρειάζομαι ένα   khri·a·zo·me e·na
μετασχηματιστή.   me·ta·shi·ma·ti·sti

---

boy-words & girl-words

Some phrases in this book are marked with m/f – they refer as a rule to the speaker. Follow the m (masculine) form if you're a 'he' and the f (feminine) form if you're a 'she'.

hairdressing

I'd like (a) ...	Θα ήθελα ένα ...	tha *i·the·la *e·na ...
blow wave	στέγνωμα	*stegh·no·ma
	με πιστολάκι	me pis·to·*la·ki
colour	βάψιμο	*vap·si·mo
haircut	κούρεμα	*ku·re·ma
my beard	ψαλίδισμα	psa·*li·thiz·ma
trimmed	στο μούσι μου	sto *mu·si mu
shave	ξύρισμα	*ksi·riz·ma

Don't cut it too short.

Μην τα κόψεις πολύ κοντά. min ta *kop·sis po·*li ko·*da

Please use a new blade.

Παρακαλώ χρησιμοποίησε pa·ra·ka·*lo khri·si·mo·*pi·i·se
καινούργιο ξυράφι. ke·*nur·yio ksi·*ra·fi

Shave it all off!

Ξύρισέ τα όλα. *ksi·ri·*se ta *o·la

I should never have let you near me!

Δεν θα έπρεπε ποτέ να σε then tha *e·pre·pe po·*te na se
αφήσω κοντά μου! a·*fi·so ko·*da mu

barber	κουρέας m	ku·*re·as
beauty salon	ινστιτούτο	in·sti·*tu·to
	αισθητικής n	es·thi·ti·*kis
for both sexes	και για τα δύο φύλα	ke yia ta *thi·o *fi·la
men's	κομμωτής	ko·mo·*tis
hairdresser	για άντρες m	yia *a·dres
women's	κομμωτής	ko·mo·*tis
hairdresser	για γυναίκες m	yia yi·*ne·kes

music & DVD

I'd like a CD/DVD.
Θα ήθελα ένα CD/DVD. tha i·the·la e·na si·di/di·vi·di

I'm looking for something by (Anna Vissi).
Ψάχνω για κάτι psakh·no yia ka·ti
(της Άννας Βίσση). (tis a·na vi·si)

What's his/her best recording?
Ποια είναι η καλύτερη pia i·ne i ka·li·te·ri
ηχογράφησή του/της; i·kho·ghra·fi·si tu/tis

Does this work on all DVD players?
Παίζει σε όλα τα DVD; pe·zi se o·la ta di·vi·di

Is this for a (PAL/NTSC) system?
Είναι κατάλληλο για i·ne ka·ta·li·lo yia
σύστημα (PAL/NTSC); si·sti·ma (pal/en·ti·es·si)

video & photography

Can you …?	Μπορείς να …;	bo·ris na …
develop	εμφανίσεις	em·fa·ni·sis
digital	ψηφιακές	psi·fi·a·kes
photos	φωτογραφίες	fo·to·ghra·fi·es
develop this	εμφανίσεις	em·fa·ni·sis
film	αυτό το φιλμ	af·to to film
load my film	βάλεις το φιλμ	va·lis to film
	στη μηχανή μου	sti mi·kha·ni mu
recharge the	φορτίσεις την	for·ti·sis tin
battery for	μπαταρία για την	ba·ta·ri·a yia tin
my digital	ψηφιακή μου	psi·fi·a·ki mu
camera	μηχανή	mi·kha·ni
transfer	μεταφέρεις	me·ta·fe·ris
photos from	φωτογραφίες από	fo·to·ghra·fi·es a·po
my camera	την φωτογραφική	ti fo·to·ghra·fi·ki
to CD	μου μηχανή στο CD	mu mi·kha·ni sto si·di

I need ... film for this camera.	Χρειάζομαι φιλμ ... για αυτή τη μηχανή.	khri·*a*·zo·me film ... yia af·*ti* ti mi·kha·*ni*
APS	APS	e·i·pi·es
B&W	μαυρόασπρο	mav·*ro*·a·spro
colour	έγχρωμο	*eng*·khro·mo
slide	σλάιντ	*sla*·id
(200) speed	ταχύτητα (200)	ta·*hi*·ti·ta (thia·ko·*si*·on)

Do you have ... for this camera?	Έχεις ... για αυτή τη φωτογραφική μηχανή;	*e*·his ... yia af·*ti* ti fo·to·ghra·fi·*ki* mi·kha·*ni*
batteries	μπαταρίες	ba·ta·*ri*·es
memory cards	κάρτες μνήμης	*kar*·tes mni·mis

I need a cable to connect my camera to a computer.
Χρειάζομαι ένα καλώδιο για να συνδέσω τη μηχανή μου στο κομπιούτερ.

khri·*a*·zo·me *e*·na ka·*lo*·thi·o yia na sin·*the*·so ti mi·kha·*ni* mu sto kom·*piu*·ter

I need a cable to recharge this battery.
Χρειάζομαι ένα καλώδιο για να φορτίσω αυτή τη μπαταρία.

khri·*a*·zo·me *e*·na ka·*lo*·thi·o yia na for·*ti*·so af·*ti* ti ba·ta·*ri*·a

I need a video cassette for this camera.
Χρειάζομαι μια βιντεοκασέτα για αυτή τη μηχανή.

khri·*a*·zo·me mia vi·de·o·ka·*se*·ta yia af·*ti* ti mi·kha·*ni*

Do you have disposable (underwater) cameras?
Έχεις (υποβρύχιες) φωτογραφικές μηχανές μιας χρήσης;

e·his (i·pov·*ri*·hi·es) fo·to·ghra·fi·*kes* mi·kha·*nes* mias *khri*·sis

When will it be ready?
Πότε θα είναι έτοιμο;

po·te tha *i*·ne *e*·ti·mo

How much is it?
Πόσο κάνει;

po·so *ka*·ni

I need a passport photo taken.
Θέλω να βγάλω φωτογραφία για διαβατήριο.

the·lo na *vga*·lo fo·to·ghra·*fi*·a yia thia·va·*ti*·ri·o

I'm not happy with these photos.

Δεν είμαι ικανοποιημένος/
ικανοποιημένη με αυτές
τις φωτογραφίες. **m/f**

then *i*·me i·ka·no·pi·i·*me*·nos/
i·ka·no·pi·i·*me*·ni me af·*tes*
tis fo·to·ghra·*fi*·es

I don't want to pay the full price.

Δεν θέλω να πληρώσω
ολόκληρη την τιμή.

then *the*·lo na pli·*ro*·so
o·*lo*·kli·ri tin ti·*mi*

repairs

Can I have my ... repaired here?	Μπορώ να επισκευάσω εδώ ...;	bo·*ro* na e·pi·ske·*va*·so e·*tho* ...
backpack	το σάκο μου	to *sa*·ko mu
camera	τη φωτογραφική μηχανή μου	ti fo·to·ghra·fi·*ki* mi·kha·*ni* mu
shoes	τα παπούτσια μου	ta pa·*pu*·tsia mu
sunglasses	τα γιαλιά μου του ήλιου	ta yia·*lia* mu tu *i*·liu

When will my ... be ready?	Πότε θα είναι έτοιμα τα ...;	*po*·te tha *i*·ne e·*ti*·ma ta ...
glasses	γιαλιά μου	yia·*lia* mu
shoes	παπούτσια μου	pa·*put*·sia mu
sunglasses	γιαλιά μου του ήλιου	yia·*lia* mu tu *i*·liu

When will my camera be ready?

Πότε θα είναι έτοιμη η
φωτογραφική μηχανή μου;

po·te tha *i*·ne e·*ti*·mi i
fo·to·ghra·fi·*ki* mi·kha·*ni* mu

When will my backpack be ready?

Πότε θα είναι έτοιμος
ο σάκος μου;

po·te tha *i*·ne e·*ti*·mos
o *sa*·kos mu

backgammon board	τάβλι n	*tav·li*
baskets	καλάθια n pl	ka·*la*·thia
bouzouki	μπουζούκι n	bu·*zu*·ki
bronzeware	μπρούτζινα n pl	*bru*·dzi·na
carpets	χαλιά n pl	kha·*lia*
ceramics	κεραμικά n pl	ke·ra·mi·*ka*
copperware	χάλκινα n pl	*khal*·ki·na
cushion covers	μαξιλαροθήκες f pl	mak·si·la·ro·*thi*·kes
evil eye (blue eye warding off evil spirits)	φυλαχτό n	fi·lakh·*to*
icons	εικόνες f pl	i·*ko*·nes
lace	δαντέλλα f	than·*te*·la
leather work	δερμάτινα n pl	ther·*ma*·ti·na
pottery	είδη αγγειοπλαστικής n pl	*i*·thi a·gi·o·pla·sti·*kis*
rugs	τάπητες m pl	*ta*·pi·tes
sculptures	γλυπτά n pl	ghlip·*ta*
worry beads	κομπολόγια n pl	ko·bo·*lo*·yia
woven shoulder bag	υφαντή τσάντα ώμου f	i·fa·*di* tsa·da *o*·mu
... jewellery	... κοσμήματα n pl	... koz·*mi*·ma·ta
filigree	φιλιγκράν	fi·li·*gran*
gold	χρυσά	khri·*sa*
silver	ασημένια	a·si·*me*·nia

post office

ταχυδρομείο

I want to send a …	Θέλω να στείλω …	*the*·lo na *sti*·lo …
fax	ένα φαξ	*e*·na faks
letter	ένα γράμμα	*e*·na *ghra*·ma
parcel	ένα δέμα	*e*·na *the*·ma
postcard	μια κάρτα	mia *kar*·ta
telegram	ένα τηλεγράφημα	*e*·na ti·le·*ghra*·fi·ma
I want to buy a/an …	Θέλω να αγοράσω ένα …	*the*·lo na a·gho·*ra*·so *e*·na …
aerogram	αερόγραμμα	a·e·ro·*ghra*·ma
envelope	φάκελο	*fa*·ke·lo
stamp	γραμματόσημο	ghra·ma·*to*·si·mo
customs declaration	δήλωση τελωνείου f	*thi*·lo·si te·lo·*ni*·u
domestic a	εσωτερικό	e·so·te·ri·*ko*
fragile a	εύθραυστο	*ef*·thraf·sto
international a	διεθνές	thi·eth·*nes*
mail	αλληλογραφία f	a·li·lo·ghra·*fi*·a
mailbox	ταχυδρομικό κουτί n	ta·hi·*thro*·mi·*ko* ku·*ti*
postcode	ταχυδρομικός τομέας m	ta·hi·*thro*·mi·*kos* to·*me*·as

snail mail

airmail	αεροπορικώς	a·e·ro·po·ri·*kos*
express mail	εξπρές	eks·*pres*
registered mail	συστημένο	si·sti·*me*·no
sea mail	ατμοπλοϊκώς	at·mo·plo·i·*kos*
surface mail	δια ξηράς	thi·*a* ksi·*ras*

Please send it by airmail to (Australia).

Παρακαλώ στείλτε το
αεροπορικώς στην
(Αυστραλία).

pa·ra·ka·*lo* stil·te to
a·e·ro·po·ri·*kos* stin
(af·stra·*li*·a)

Please send it by surface mail to (New Zealand).

Παρακαλώ στείλτε το δια
ξηράς στην (Νέα Ζηλανδία).

pa·ra·ka·*lo* stil·te to thi·*a*
ksi·*ras* stin (*ne*·a zi·nan·*thi*·a)

It contains (souvenirs).

Περιέχει (σουβενίρ).

pe·ri·e·hi (su·ve·*nir*)

Where's the poste restante section?

Πού είναι το ποστ ρεστάντ;

pu *i*·ne to post re·*stant*

Is there any mail for me?

Υπάρχουν γράμματα
για μένα;

i·*par*·khun *ghra*·ma·ta
yia *me*·na

I'd like to collect a parcel.

Θα ήθελα να παραλάβω
ένα δέμα.

tha *i*·the·la na pa·ra·*la*·vo
e·na *the*·ma

Where can I find a fax and telegram service?

Πού μπορώ να βρω
υπηρεσία για φαξ και
για τηλεγράφημα;

pu bo·*ro* na vro
i·pi·re·*si*·a yia faks ke
yia ti·le·*ghra*·fi·ma

How much is a fax per page?

Πόσο κοστίζει το φαξ
η σελίδα;

po·so ko·*sti*·zi to faks
i se·*li*·tha

Do you have Internet services?

Έχετε υπηρεσία
Διαδικτύου;

e·he·te i·pi·re·*si*·a
thi·a·thik·*ti*·u

---

medusa

Medusa, famous for turning mortals to stone, had hair much like the tentacles of a jellyfish. In fact the jellyfish is named after her in Greek (μέδουσα *me*·thu·sa), French (*méduse* me·*dooz*) and Spanish (*medusa* me·*doo*·sa), to name just a few languages.

phone

τηλέφωνο

What's your phone number?
Τι αριθμό τηλεφώνου έχεις;   ti a·rith·*mo* ti·le·fo·nu *e*·his

Where's the nearest public phone?
Πού είναι το πιο κοντινό   pu *i*·ne to pio ko·di·*no*
δημόσιο τηλέφωνο;   ṭhi·*mo*·si·o ti·*le*·fo·no

Where's the nearest telephone office?
Πού είναι το πιο κοντινό   pu *i*·ne to pio ko·di·*no*
τηλεφωνικό κέντρο;   ti·le·fo·ni·*ko* ke·dro

Do you have a metered phone?
Έχεις τηλέφωνο με μετρητή;   *e*·his ti·*le*·fo·no me me·tri·*ti*

Can I look at a phone book?
Μπορώ να κοιτάξω τον   bo·*ro* na ki·*tak*·so ton
τηλεφωνικό κατάλογο;   ti·le·fo·ni·*ko* ka·*ta*·lo·gho

I want to ...	Θέλω να ...	*the*·lo na ...
buy a (2000 unit) phonecard	αγοράσω μια τηλεφωνική κάρτα (2000 μονάδων)	a·gho·*ra*·so mia ti·le·fo·ni·*ki kar*·ta (ṭhi·o hi·*lia*·ṭhon mo·*na*·ṭhon)
buy a discount card	αγοράσω μια κάρτα με έκπτωση	a·gho·*ra*·so mia *kar*·ta me *ek*·pto·si
call (Singapore)	τηλεφωνήσω (στη Σιγγαπούρη)	ti·le·fo·*ni*·so (sti sing·ga·*pu*·ri)
make a (local) call	κάμω ένα (τοπικό) τηλέφωνο	*ka*·mo e·na (to·pi·*ko*) ti·*le*·fo·no
reverse the charges	αντιστρέψω τα έξοδα	a·di·*strep*·so ta *ek*·so·ṭha
speak for (three) minutes	μιλήσω για (τρία) λεπτά	mi·*li*·so yia (*tri*·a) lep·*ta*

Ποιος μιλάει;
pios mi·*la*·i | **Who's calling?**

Σε ποιον θέλετε να μιλήσετε;
se pion *the*·le·te
na mi·*li*·se·te | **Who do you want to speak to?**

Μια στιγμή.
mia stigh·*mi* | **One moment.**

Δεν είναι εδώ.
then *i*·ne e·*tho* | **He's/She's not here.**

Λάθος αριθμός.
la·thos a·rith·*mos* | **Wrong number.**

How much does ... cost?	Πόσο κοστίζει ...;	*po*·so ko·*sti*·zi ...
a (three)-minute call	ένα τηλεφώνημα (τριών) λεπτών	*e*·na ti·le·*fo*·ni·ma (tri·*on*) lep·*ton*
each extra minute	κάθε έξτρα λεπτό	*ka*·the *eks*·tra lep·*to*

The number is ...
Ο αριθμός είναι ... | o a·rith·*mos i*·ne ...

What's the code for (New Zealand)?
Ποιος είναι ο κωδικός αριθμός για (τη Νέα Ζηλανδία); | pios *i*·ne o ko·thi·*kos* a·rith·*mos* yia (ti *ne*·a zi·lan·*thi*·a)

It's engaged.
Είναι κατειλημμένη. | *i*·ne ka·ti·li·*me*·ni

I've been cut off.
Με διέκοψαν. | me thi·*e*·kop·san

The connection's bad.
Η σύνδεση είναι κακή. | i *sin*·the·si *i*·ne ka·*ki*

Hello.
Εμπρός. | e·*bros*

It's ...
Είμαι ... | *i*·me ...

Is … there?
Είναι … εκεί;   *i*·ne … e·*ki*

Can I speak to …?
Μπορώ να μιλήσω με …;   bo·*ro* na mi·*li*·so me …

Can I leave a message?
Μπορώ να αφήσω ένα μήνυμα;   bo·*ro* na a·*fi*·so e·na *mi*·ni·ma

Please tell him/her I called.
Παρακαλώ πες του/της   pa·ra·ka·*lo* pes tu/tis
ότι τηλεφώνησα.   *o*·ti ti·le·*fo*·ni·sa

My number is …
Ο αριθμός μου είναι …   o a·rith·*mos* mu *i*·ne …

I don't have a contact number.
Δεν έχω αριθμό για   then e·kho a·rith·*mo* yia
επικοινωνία.   e·pi·ki·no·*ni*·a

I'll call back later.
Θα τηλεφωνήσω αργότερα.   tha ti·le·fo·*ni*·so ar·*gho*·te·ra

mobile/cell phone

κινητό τηλέφωνο

I'd like a …	Θα ήθελα …	tha *i*·the·la …
charger for	ένα φορτιστή για	e·na for·ti·*sti* yia
my phone	το τηλέφωνό μου	to ti·*le*·fo·no mu
mobile/cell	να νοικιάσω ένα	na ni·*kia*·so e·na
phone for hire	κινητό τηλέφωνο	ki·ni·*to* ti·*le*·fo·no
prepaid mobile/	ένα	e·na
cell phone	προπληρωμένο	pro·pli·ro·*me*·no
	κινητό τηλέφωνο	ki·ni·*to* ti·*le*·fo·no
SIM card for	μια κάρτα SIM	mia *kar*·ta sim
your network	για το δίκτυό σας	yia to *thik*·tio sas

What are the rates?
Ποιες είναι οι τιμές;   pies *i*·ne i ti·*mes*

(40c) per (30) seconds.
(40λ) για (30)   (sa·*ra*·da lep·*ta*) yia (tri·*a*·da)
δευτερόλεπτα.   thef·te·*ro*·lep·ta

communications

the internet

Where's the local Internet cafe?

Πού είναι το τοπικό		pu *i*·ne to to·pi·*ko*
καφενείο με διαδίκτυο;		ka·fe·*ni*·o me thi·a·*thik*·ti·o

I'd like to ...	Θα ήθελα να ...	tha *i*·the·la na ...
check my	ελέγξω την	e·*leng*·so tin
email	ηλεκτρονική	i·lek·tro·ni·*ki*
	αλληλογραφία μου	a·li·lo·ghra·*fi*·a mu
get Internet	έχω πρόσβαση	e·kho *pros*·va·si
access	στο Διαδίκτυο	sto thi·a·*thik*·ti·o
use a printer	χρησιμοποιήσω	khri·si·mo·pi·*i*·so
	έναν εκτυπωτή	e·nan ek·ti·po·*ti*
use a scanner	χρησιμοποιήσω	khri·si·mo·pi·*i*·so
	ένα σκάνερ	e·na *ska*·ner

Do you have ...?	Έχετε ...;	*e*·he·te ...
Macs	Κομπιούτερ Mac	kom·*piu*·ter mak
PCs	Κομπιούτερ PC	kom·*piu*·ter pi si
a Zip drive	Zip drive	zip *dra*·iv

How much	Πόσο κοστίζει	*po*·so ko·*sti*·zi
per ...?	κάθε ...;	*ka*·the ...
hour	ώρα	o·ra
page	σελίδα	se·*li*·tha

How do I log on?

Πώς μπαίνω μέσα;   pos *be*·no *me*·sa

Please change it to the (English)-language setting.

Παρακαλώ άλλαξέ το στην   pa·ra·ka·*lo* a·lak·*se* to stin
(αγγλική) γλώσσα.   (ang·gli·*ki*) *glo*·sa

Do you have (English) keyboards?

έχεις (Αγγλικό) πληκτρολόγιο;   *e*·his (ang·gli·*ko*) plik·tro·*lo*·yi·o

It's crashed.

κατέρρευσε.   ka·*te*·ref·se

I've finished.

Τελείωσα.   te·*li*·o·sa

What time does the bank open?

Τι ώρα ανοίγει η τράπεζα;   ti o·ra a·ni·yi i tra·pe·za

Where's a/an ...?	Πού είναι ...;	pu i·ne ...
automated teller machine	μια αυτόματη μηχανή χρημάτων	mia af·to·ma·ti mi·kha·ni khri·ma·ton
foreign exchange office	ένα γραφείο αλλαγής χρημάτων	e·na ghra·fi·o a·la·yis khri·ma·ton

Where can I ...?	Πού μπορώ να ...;	pu bo·ro na ...
I'd like to ...	Θα ήθελα να ...	tha i·the·la na ...
cash a cheque	εξαργυρώσω μια επιταγή	ek·sar·yi·ro·so mia e·pi·ta·yi
change money	αλλάξω χρήματα	a·lak·so khri·ma·ta
change a travellers cheque	αλλάξω μια ταξιδιωτική επιταγή	a·lak·so mia tak·si·thio·ti·ki e·pi·ta·yi
get a cash advance	κάμω μια ανάληψη σε μετρητά	ka·mo mia a·na·lip·si se me·tri·ta
withdraw money	αποσύρω χρήματα	a·po·si·ro khri·ma·ta
What's the ...?	Ποια είναι ... ;	pia i·ne ...
exchange rate	η τιμή συναλλάγματος	i ti·mi si·na·lagh·ma·tos
charge for that	η χρέωση για αυτό	i khre·o·si yia af·to

Has my money arrived yet?

Έχουν φτάσει τα
χρήματά μου;

e·khun *fta*·si ta
khri·ma·*ta* mu

How long will it take to arrive?

Σε πόσο καιρό θα φτάσουν;

se *po*·so ke·ro tha *fta*·sun

The automated teller machine took my card.

Η αυτόματη μηχανή
χρημάτων κράτησε
την κάρτα μου.

i af·*to*·ma·ti mi·kha·*ni*
khri·*ma*·ton *kra*·ti·se
tin *kar*·ta mu

I've forgotten my PIN.

Ξέχασα τον κωδικό
αριθμό μου.

kse·ha·sa ton ko·thi·*ko*
a·rith·*mo* mu

Can I use my credit card to withdraw money?

Μπορώ να χρησιμοποιήσω
την πιστωτική μου κάρτα
για να αποσύρω χρήματα;

bo·*ro* na khri·si·mo·pi·*i*·so
tin pi·sto·ti·*ki* mu *kar*·ta
yia na a·po·*si*·ro *khri*·ma·ta

---

listen for ...

διαβατήριο n	thia·va·*ti*·ri·o	**passport**
ταυτότητα f	taf·*to*·ti·ta	**identification**

Δεν μπορούμε να το κάνουμε αυτό.
  then bo·*ru*·me na
  to *ka*·nu·me af·*to*
We can't do that.

Τελείωσαν τα χρήματά σας.
  te·*li*·o·san ta *khri*·ma·*ta* sas
You have no funds left.

Υπάρχει ένα πρόβλημα.
  i·*par*·hi *e*·na *prov*·li·ma
There's a problem.

Υπογράψτε εδώ.
  i·po·*ghrap*·ste e·*tho*
Sign here.

I'd like a/an ...	Θα ήθελα ...	tha i·the·la ...
audio set	ακουστικά	a·ku·sti·ka
catalogue	ένα κατάλογο	e·na ka·ta·lo·gho
guide	έναν οδηγό	e·nan o·thi·gho
guidebook in	έναν οδηγό στα	e·nan o·thi·gho sta
(English)	(Αγγλικά)	(ang·gli·ka)
(local) map	ένα (τοπικό)	e·na (to·pi·ko)
	χάρτη	khar·ti
Do you have	Έχετε	e·he·te
information	πληροφορίες για	pli·ro·fo·ri·es yia
on ... sights?	... χώρους;	... kho·rus
ancient	αρχαίους	ar·he·us
archaic	αρχαϊκούς	ar·kha·i·kus
archeological	αρχαιολογικούς	ar·he·o·lo·yi·kus
architectural	αρχιτεκτονικούς	ar·hi·tek·to·ni·kus
Byzantine	Βυζαντινούς	vi·za·di·nus
classical	κλασσικούς	kla·si·kus
cultural	πολιτιστικούς	po·li·ti·sti·kus
Hellenistic	Ελληνιστικούς	e·li·ni·sti·kus
historical	ιστορικούς	i·sto·ri·kus
neoclassical	νεοκλασσικούς	ne·o·kla·si·kus
Orthodox	Ορθόδοξους	or·tho·dok·sus
Ottoman	Οθωμανικούς	o·tho·ma·ni·kus
religious	θρησκευτικούς	thris·kef·ti·kus
Roman	Ρωμαϊκούς	ro·ma·i·kus

signs

Ανδρών	an·thron	Men
Είσοδος	i·so·thos	Entrance
Έξοδος	ek·so·thos	Exit
Τουαλέτες	tu·a·le·tes	Toilets
Γυναικών	yi·ne·kon	Women

I'd like to see (the) ...	Θα ήθελα να δω ...	tha *i*·the·la na tho ...
Acropolis	την Ακρόπολη	tin ak·*ro*·po·li
amphitheatre	το αμφιθέατρο	to am·fi·*the*·a·tro
Archeological Museum	το Αρχαιολογικό Μουσείο	to ar·he·o·lo·yi·*ko* mu·*si*·o
Byzantine frescoes	Βυζαντινά φρέσκο	vi·za·di·*na* *fres*·ko
labyrinth	τον λαβύρινθο	ton la·*vi*·rin·tho
mosaics	τα μωσαϊκά	ta mo·sa·i·*ka*
Mt Athos monasteries	τα μοναστήρια του Αγίου Όρους	ta mo·na·*sti*·ria tu a·*yi*·u *o*·rus
Mycaenian tombs	Μυκηναϊκούς τάφους	mi·ki·na·i·*kus* *ta*·fus
oracle of Delphi	το μαντείο των Δελφών	to ma·*di*·o ton thel·*fon*
palace	το παλάτι	to pa·*la*·ti
ruins	τα ερείπια	ta e·*ri*·pi·a
sculptures	τα γλυπτά	ta ghlip·*ta*
statues	τα αγάλματα	ta a·*ghal*·ma·ta
temple	το ναό	to na·*o*

What's that?
Τι είναι εκείνο;   ti *i*·ne e·*ki*·no

Who made it?
Ποιος το έκαμε;   pios to *e*·ka·me

How old is it?
Πόσο χρονώ είναι;   *po*·so khro·*no i*·ne

When was this discovered?
Πότε ανακαλύφτηκε αυτό;   *po*·te a·na·ka·*lif*·ti·ke af·*to*

When were the excavations done?
Πότε έγιναν οι ανασκαφές;   *po*·te e·yi·nan i a·nas·ka·*fes*

Could you take a photograph of me?
Μπορείς να μου πάρεις   bo·*ris* na mu *pa*·ris
μια φωτογραφία;   mia fo·to·ghra·*fi*·a

Can I take a photo (of you)?
Μπορώ να (σου) πάρω   bo·*ro* na (su) *pa*·ro
μια φωτογραφία;   mia fo·to·ghra·*fi*·a

getting in

είσοδος

What time does it open?
Τι ώρα ανοίγει;   ti *o*·ra a·*ni*·yi

What time does it close?
Τι ώρα κλείνει;   ti *o*·ra *kli*·ni

Is it open every day?
Είναι ανοιχτό κάθε μέρα;   *i*·ne a·nikh·*to ka*·the *me*·ra

What's the admission charge?
Πόσο κοστίζει η είσοδος;   *po*·so ko·*sti*·zi i *i*·so·thos

Can I go in wearing these clothes?
Μπορώ να μπω με αυτά   bo·*ro* na bo me af·*ta*
τα ρούχα;   ta *ru*·kha

Is there a discount for …?	Υπάρχει έκπτωση για …;	i·*par*·hi *ek*·pto·si yia …
children	παιδιά	pe·*thia*
families	οικογένειες	i·ko·*ye*·ni·es
groups	γκρουπ	grup
older people	υπερήλικους	i·pe·*ri*·li·kus
pensioners	συνταξιούχους	si·dak·si·u·khus
students	σπουδαστές	spu·tha·*stes*

tours

Can you recommend a tour?
Μπορείς να συστήσεις κάποια περιήγηση;
bo·*ris* na si·*sti*·sis *ka*·pia pe·ri·*i*·yi·si

When's the next tour?
Πότε είναι η επόμενη περιήγηση;
po·te *i*·ne i e·*po*·me·ni pe·ri·*i*·yi·si

How long is the tour?
Πόσην ώρα διαρκεί η περιήγηση;
po·sin o·ra thi·ar·*ki* i pe·ri·*i*·yi·si

The guide will pay.
Ο/Η οδηγός θα πληρώσει. m/f
o/i o·thi·*ghos* tha pli·*ro*·si

The guide has paid.
Ο/Η οδηγός έχει πληρώσει. m/f
o/i o·thi·*ghos* e·hi pli·*ro*·si

What time should we be back?
Τι ώρα πρέπει να επιστρέψουμε;
ti o·ra *pre*·pi na e·pi·*strep*·su·me

I'm with them.
Είμαι με αυτούς.
i·me me af·*tus*

I've lost my group.
Έχασα την ομάδα μου.
e·kha·sa tin o·*ma*·tha mu

doing business

επιχειρησήσεις

I'm attending a ...	Παρακολουθώ ...	pa·ra·ko·lu·tho ...
conference	ένα συνέδριο	e·na sin·e·thri·o
course	μια σειρά μαθημάτων	mia si·ra ma·thi·ma·ton
meeting	μια συνεδρίαση	mia sin·e·thri·a·si
trade fair	μια εμπορική έκθεση	mia e·bo·ri·ki ek·the·si
I'm with ...	Είμαι με ...	i·me me ...
(Olympiaki)	(την Ολυμπιακή)	(tin o·li·bi·a·ki)
my colleague	τον συνάδελφό μου m	ton sin·a·thel·fo mu
	την συναδέλφισσά μου f	tin sin·a·thel·fi·sa mu
my colleagues	τους συναδέλφους μου	tus sin·a·thel·fus mu

I'm alone.
Είμαι μόνος/μόνη. m/f   i·me mo·nos/mo·ni

I have an appointment with ...
Έχω ένα ραντεβού με ...   e·kho e·na ra·de·vu me ...

I'm staying at (the Xenia), room (10).
Μένω στο (Ξενία),   me·no sto (kse·ni·a)
δωμάτιο (10).   tho·ma·ti·o (the·ka)

I'm here for (two) days/weeks.
Είμαι εδώ για (δύο)   i·me e·tho yia (thi·o)
μέρες/εβδομάδες.   me·res/ev·tho·ma·thes

Here's my business card.
Ορίστε η κάρτα μου.   o·ri·ste i kar·ta mu

Can I have your business card?
Μπορώ να έχω την κάρτα σου;   bo·ro na e·kho tin kar·ta su

Here's my ...	Ορίστε ... μου.	o·ri·ste ... mu
What's your ...?	Ποια είναι η δική	pia i·ne i thi·ki
	σου η ...;	su i ...
address	διεύθυνση	thi·ef·thin·si
email address	ηλεκτρονική	i·lek·tro·ni·ki
	διεύθυνση	thi·ef·thin·si

Here's my ...	Εδώ είναι	e·tho i·ne
number.	ο αριθμός ... μου.	o a·rith·mos ... mu
What's your	Ποιος είναι ο	pios i·ne o
... number?	δικός σου ο	thi·kos su o
	αριθμός ...;	a·rith·mos ...
fax	του φαξ	tu faks
mobile	του κινητού	tu ki·ni·tu
pager	του	tu
	τηλεειδοποιητή	ti·le·i·tho·pi·i·ti
work	της δουλειάς	tis thu·lias

Where's the ...?	Πού είναι ...;	pu i·ne ...
business	ο χώρος	o kho·ros
centre	εργασίας	er·gha·si·as
conference	το συνέδριο	to sin·e·thri·o
meeting	η συνεδρίαση	i sin·e·thri·a·si

I need (a/an) ...	Χρειάζομαι ...	khri·a·zo·me ...
computer	ένα κομπιούτερ	e·na kom·piu·ter
Internet	σύνδεση στο	sin·the·si sto
connection	διαδύκτιο	thi·a·thik·ti·o
interpreter	διερμηνέα	thi·er·mi·ne·a
more business	περισσότερες	pe·ri·so·te·res
cards	κάρτες	kar·tes
some space to	χώρο να τοποθε-	kho·ro na to·po·the·
set up	τήσω τα πράγματα	ti·so ta ragh·ma·ta
to send a fax	να στείλω ένα φαξ	na sti·lo e·na faks

Thank you for your time.

Ευχαριστώ για το χρόνο σου.   ef·kha·ri·sto yia to khro·no su

That went very well.

Πήγε πολύ καλά.   pi·ye po·li ka·la

Shall we go for a drink/meal?

Πάμε για ποτό/φαγητό;   pa·me yia po·to/fa·yi·to

looking for a job

Where are jobs advertised?
Πού διαφημίζονται
οι δουλειές;
pu thi·a·fi·*mi*·zo·de
i thu·*lies*

I'm enquiring about the position advertised.
ζητώ πληροφορίες για τη
θέση που διαφημίστηκε.
zi·to pli·ro·fo·*ri*·es yia ti
the·si pu thi·a·fi·*mi*·sti·ke

I've had experience.
Έχω πείρα.
e·kho *pi*·ra

What's the wage?
Τι μισθό έχει;
ti mi·*stho* e·hi

I'm looking for … work.	Ψάχνω για δουλειά …	*psakh*·no yia thu·*lia* …
bar	σε μπαρ	se bar
casual	προσωρινή	pro·so·ri·*ni*
English-teaching	να διδάσκω αγγλικά	na thi·*tha*·sko ang·gli·*ka*
fruit-picking	να μαζεύω φρούτα	na ma·*ze*·vo *fru*·ta
full-time	με πλήρη απασχόληση	me *pli*·ri a·pa·*skho*·li·si
labouring	χειρωνακτική	hi·ro·nak·ti·*ki*
office	γραφείου	ghra·*fi*·u
part-time	μερικής απασχόλησης	me·ri·*kis* a·pa·*skho*·li·sis
waitering	γκαρσόν	gar·*son*

Do I need (a/an)…?	Χειάζομαι …;	khri·*a*·zo·me …
contract	συμβόλαιο	sim·*vo*·le·o
experience	πείρα	*pi*·ra
insurance	ασφάλεια	as·*fa*·li·a
my own transport	δικό μου μεταφορικό μέσο	thi·*ko* mu me·ta·fo·ri·*ko me*·so
paperwork	ντοκουμέντα	do·ku·*men*·ta
uniform	στολή	sto·*li*
work permit	άδεια εργασίας	*a*·thi·a er·gha·*si*·as

Here is/are my ...	Ορίστε ...	o·ri·ste ...
bank account details	ο τραπεζικός μου λογαριασμός	o tra·pe·zi·kos mu lo·gha·riaz·mos
CV/résumé	το βιογραφικό μου σημείωμα	to vi·o·ghra·fi·ko mu si·mi·o·ma
residency permit	η άδεια παραμονής μου	i a·thi·a pa·ra·mo·nis mu
visa	η βίζα μου	i vi·za mu
work permit	η άδεια εργασίας μου	i a·thi·a er·gha·si·as mu

What time do I ...?	Τι ώρα ...;	ti o·ra ...
finish	τελειώνω	te·li·o·no
have a break	έχω διάλειμμα	e·kho thia·li·ma
start	αρχίζω	ar·hi·zo

I can start ...	Μπορώ να αρχίσω ...	bo·ro na ar·hi·so ...
Can you start ...?	Μπορείς να αρχίσεις ...;	bo·ris na ar·hi·sis ...
at (eight) o'clock	στις (οχτώ)	stis (okh·to)
next week	την επόμενη εβδομάδα	tin e·po·me·ni ev·tho·ma·tha
today	σήμερα	si·me·ra
tomorrow	αύριο	av·ri·o

advertisement	διαφήμιση f	thi·a·fi·mi·si
contract	συμβόλαιο n	sim·vo·le·o
employee	υπάλληλος m&f	i·pa·li·los
employer	εργοδότης m	er·gho·tho·tis
	εργοδότρια f	er·gho·tho·tri·a
job	δουλειά f	thu·lia
work experience	πείρα στη δουλειά f	pi·ra sti thu·lia

I have a disability.
Έχω μια αναπηρία. *e*·kho mia a·na·pi·*ri*·a

I need assistance.
Χρειάζομαι βοήθεια. khri·*a*·zo·me vo·*i*·thi·a

What services do you have for people with a disability?
Τι υπηρεσίες έχετε για ti i·pi·re·*si*·es *e*·he·te yia
άτομα με ειδικές ανάγκες; *a*·to·ma me i·thi·*kes* a·*na*·ges

Are there disabled toilets?
Υπάρχουν τουαλέτες για i·*par*·khun tu·a·*le*·tes yia
άτομα με ειδικές ανάγκες; *a*·to·ma me i·thi·*kes* a·*na*·ges

Are there disabled parking spaces?
Υπάρχει πάρκνινγκ για i·*par*·hi *par*·king yia
άτομα με ειδικές ανάγκες; *a*·to·ma me i·thi·*kes* a·*na*·ges

Is there wheelchair access?
Υπάρχει δρόμος για i·*par*·hi *thro*·mos yia
αναπηρικές καρέκλες; a·na·pi·ri·*kes* ka·*re*·kles

How wide is the entrance?
Πόσο πλατιά είναι η είσοδος; *po*·so pla·*tia i*·ne i *i*·so·thos

Is there somewhere I can sit down?
Υπάρχει κάπου να καθίσω; i·*par*·hi *ka*·pu na ka·*thi*·so

I'm deaf.
Είμαι κουφός. *i*·me ku·*fos*

I have a hearing aid.
Έχω ακουστικά. *e*·kho a·ku·sti·*ka*

Are guide dogs permitted?
Επιτρέπεται στα σκυλιά e·pi·*tre*·pe·te sta ski·*lia*
για τυφλούς; yia ti·*flus*

How many steps are there?
Πόσα σκαλοπάτια υπάρχουν; *po*·sa ska·lo·*pa*·tia i·*par*·khun

Is there a lift?
Υπάρχει ασανσέρ; i·*par*·khi a·san·*ser*

Are there rails in the bathroom?

Υπάρχουν στηρίγματα
στο μπάνιο;

i·*par*·khun sti·*righ*·ma·ta
sto *ba*·nio

Could you call me a disabled taxi?

Μπορείς να καλέσεις
ένα ταξί για άτομα με
ειδικές ανάγκες;

bo·*ris* na ka·*le*·sis
e·na tak·*si* yia *a*·to·ma me
i·thi·kes a·*na*·ges

Could you help me cross the street safely?

Μπορείς να με βοηθήσεις
να περάσω το δρόμο
με ασφάλεια;

bo·*ris* na me vo·i·*thi*·sis
na pe·*ra*·so to *thro*·mo
me as·*fa*·li·a

guide dog	σκυλί για τυφλούς n	ski·*li* yia ti·*flus*
older person	υπερήλικος m	i·pe·*ri*·li·kos
	υπερήλικη f	i·pe·*ri*·li·ki
person with a	άτομο με ειδικές	*a*·to·mo me i·thi·*kes*
disability	ανάγκες n	a·*na*·ges
ramp	ράμπα f	*ram*·pa
walking frame	περπατούσα f	per·pa·*tu*·sa
walking stick	μπαστούνι n	ba·*stu*·ni
wheelchair	αναπηρική	a·na·pi·ri·*ki*
	καρέκλα f	ka·*re*·kla

gobbledy gook

So you're having one of those days when you can't make
heads or tails of the Greek signs around you, and you're
dying to say 'It's all Greek to me!'. In your shoes, a Greek
speaker would say:

This is Chinese to me.

Αυτά για μένα είναι Κινέζικα.   af·*ta* yia *me*·na *i*·ne ki·*ne*·zi·ka

travelling with children

ταξιδεύοντας με παιδιά

Is there a ...?	Υπάρχει ...;	i·par·hi ...
baby change room	δωμάτιο για άλλαγμα μωρών	tho·*ma*·ti·o yia *a*·lagh·ma mo·*ron*
child-minding service	υπηρεσία διαφύλαξης παιδιών	i·pi·re·*si*·a thi·a·*fi*·lak·sis pe·*thion*
children's menu	παιδικό μενού	pe·thi·ko me·*nu*
child's portion	παιδική μερίδα	pe·thi·*ki* me·*ri*·tha
crèche	βρεφοκομείο	vre·fo·ko·*mi*·o
discount for children	έκπτωση για παιδιά	*ek*·pto·si yia pe·*thia*
family ticket	οικογενειακό εισιτήριο	i·ko·ye·ni·a·*ko* i·si·*ti*·ri·o

I need a/an ...	Χρειάζομαι ...	khri·*a*·zo·me ...
baby seat	κάθισμα μωρού	*ka*·thiz·ma mo·*ru*
(English-speaking) babysitter	(αγγλομαθή) μπέημπι σίτερ	(ang·glo·ma·*thi*) be·i·bi *si*·ter
booster seat	ανυψωμένο κάθισμα	a·nip·so·*me*·no *ka*·thiz·ma
cot	παιδικό κρεβάτι	pe·thi·ko kre·*va*·ti
highchair	παιδική καρέκλα	pe·thi·*ki* ka·*re*·kla
plastic sheet	πλαστικό σεντόνι	pla·sti·ko se·*do*·ni
plastic bag	πλαστική σακούλα	pla·sti·*ki* sa·*ku*·la
potty	γιογιό	yio·*yio*
pram	παιδικό καροτσάκι	pe·thi·ko ka·rot·*sa*·ki
sick bag	σακούλα εμετού	sa·*ku*·la e·me·*tu*
stroller	καροτσάκι	ka·rot·*sa*·ki

Where's the	Πού είναι το πιο	pu i·ne to pio
nearest …?	κοντινό …;	ko·di·no …
park	πάρκο	par·ko
playground	γήπεδο	yi·pe·do
toy shop	κατάστημα	ka·ta·sti·ma
	παιγνιδιών	pegh·ni·thion

Where's the	Πού είναι η πιο	pu i·ne i pio
nearest …?	κοντινή …;	ko·di·ni …
drinking	βρύση με	vri·si me
fountain	πόσιμο νερό	po·si·mo ne·ro
swimming pool	πισίνα	pi·si·na
tap	βρύση	vri·si
theme park	παιδική χαρά	pe·thi·ki kha·ra

Do you sell …?	Πουλάτε …;	pu·la·te …
baby wipes	πετσέτες για	pet·se·tes yia
	σκούπισμα	sku·piz·ma
	μωρών	mo·ron
painkillers	παυσίπονα	paf·si·po·na
for infants	για μωρά	yia mo·ra
disposable	πάνες μιας	pa·nes mias
nappies/diapers	χρήσης	khri·sis
tissues	χαρτομάντηλα	khar·to·ma·di·la

Do you hire out …?	Νοικιάζετε …;	ni·kia·ze·te …
prams	παιδικά	pe·thi·ka
	καροτσάκια	ka·rot·sa·kia
strollers	καροτσάκια	ka·rot·sa·kia

Are there any good places to take children around here?

Υπάρχουν καλά μέρη εδώ	i·par·khun ka·la me·ri e·tho
κοντά για τα παιδιά;	ko·da yia ta pe·thia

Is there space for a pram?

Υπάρχει χώρος για το	i·par·hi kho·ros yia to
παιδικό καροτσάκι;	pe·thi·ko ka·rot·sa·ki

Are children allowed?

Επιτρέπεται στα παιδιά;	e·pi·tre·pe·te sta pe·thia

Where can I change a nappy?

Πού μπορώ να αλλάξω	pu bo·ro na a·lak·so
την πάνα;	tin pa·na

Do you mind if I breast-feed here?
Σε πειράζει αν θηλάσω   se pi·ra·zi an thi·la·so
εδώ το μωρό;   e·tho to mo·ro

Could I have some paper and pencils, please?
Μπορώ να έχω λίγο χαρτί   bo·ro na e·kho li·gho khar·ti
και μολύβια, παρακαλώ.   ke mo·li·via pa·ra·ka·lo

Is this suitable for (five)-year-old children?
Είναι αυτό κατάλληλο για   i·ne af·to ka·ta·li·lo yia
παιδιά (πέντε) χρονών;   pe·thia (pe·de) khro·no

Do you know a dentist/doctor who is good with children?
Ξέρεις ένα οδοντίατρο/   kse·ris e·na o·tho·di·a·tro/
γιατρό που είναι καλός   yia·tro pu i·ne ka·los
με τα παιδιά;   me ta pe·thia

If your child is sick, see **health**, page 195.

talking with children

μιλώντας με τα παιδιά

What's your name?
Πώς σε λένε;   pos se le·ne

How old are you?
Πόσο χρονό είσαι;   po·so khro·no i·se

When's your birthday?
Πότε είναι τα   po·te i·ne ta
γενέθλιά σου;   ye·neth·li·a su

Do you go to school/kindergarten?
Πηγαίνεις στο σχολείο/   pi·ye·nis sto skho·li·o/
νηπιαγωγείο;   ni·pi·a·gho·yi·o

What grade are you in?
Σε ποια τάξη είσαι;   se pia tak·si i·se

Do you like …?	Σου αρέσει …;	su a·re·si …
music	η μουσική	i mu·si·ki
school	το σχολείο	to skho·li·o
your teacher	ο δάσκαλός σου **m**	o tha·ska·los su
	η δασκάλα σου **f**	i tha·ska·la su

children

105

Do you like sport?
Σου αρέσουν τα σπορ;   su a·*re*·sun ta spor

What do you do after school?
Τι κάνεις μετά το σχολείο;   ti *ka*·nis me·*ta* to skho·*li*·o

Do you learn English?
Μαθαίνεις αγγλικά;   ma·*the*·nis ang·gli·*ka*

talking about children

When's the baby due?
Πότε είναι να γεννηθεί   *po*·te *i*·ne na ye·ni·*thi*
το μωρό;   to mo·*ro*

What are you going to call the baby?
Πώς θα το ονομάσεις   pos tha to·o·no·*ma*·sis
το μωρό;   to mo·*ro*

Is this your first child?
Είναι το πρώτο σου παιδί;   *i*·ne to *pro*·to su pe·*thi*

How many children do you have?
Πόσα παιδιά έχεις;   *po*·sa pe·*thia* e·his

What a beautiful child!
Τι όμορφο παιδί!   ti *o*·mor·fo pe·*thi*

Is it a boy or a girl?
Είναι αγόρι ή κορίτσι;   *i*·ne a·*gho*·ri i ko·*rit*·si

How old is he/she?
Πόσο χρονώ είναι;   *po*·so khro·*no i*·ne

Does he/she go to school?
Πηγαίνει στο σχολείο;   pi·*ye*·ni sto skho·*li*·o

What's his/her name?
Πώς τον/την λένε;   pos ton/tin *le*·ne

Is he/she well-behaved?
Είναι καλό παιδί;   *i*·ne ka·*lo* pe·*thi*

He/She has your eyes.
Έχει τα μάτια σου.   *e*·hi ta *ma*·tia su

He/She looks like you.
Σου μοιάζει.   su *mia*·zi

basics

βασικά

Yes.	Ναι.	ne
No.	Όχι.	*o*·hi
Please.	Παρακαλώ.	pa·ra·ka·*lo*
Thank you (very much).	Ευχαριστώ (πολύ).	ef·kha·ri·*sto* (po·*li*)
You're welcome.	Παρακαλώ.	pa·ra·ka·*lo*
Sorry.	Συγνώμη.	si·*ghno*·mi
Excuse me.	Με συγχωρείτε.	me sing·kho·*ri*·te
I beg your pardon?	Ορίστε;/Συγνώμη;	o·*ri*·ste/si·*ghno*·mi
Here you are.	Ορίστε.	o·*ri*·ste

greetings & goodbyes

χαιρετισμοί και αποχαιρετισμοί

Greeks shakes hands when greeting each other and saying goodbye. When greeting friends, male or female, they kiss each other on both cheeks.

Hello/Hi.	Γεια σου.	yia su
Good afternoon.	Χαίρετε.	*he*·re·te
Good morning.	Καλή μέρα.	ka·*li me*·ra
Good evening.	Καλή σπέρα.	ka·*li spe*·ra

when in greece ...

Be sure not to turn up empty-handed when you visit a Greek friend's house. It's customary to bring ένα κουτί γλυκά *e*·na ku·*ti* ghli·*ka* (a box of sweets) or μια ανθοδέσμη mia an·tho·*thes*·mi (a bunch of flowers).

meeting people

107

How are you?
Τι κάνεις;   ti *ka*·nis;

So-so.
Έτσι και έτσι.   *et*·si ke *et*·si

Fine. And you?
Καλά. Εσύ;   ka·*la* e·*si*

What's your name?
Πώς σε λένε;   pos se *le*·ne

My name is …
Με λένε …   me *le*·ne …

I'm pleased to meet you.
Χαίρω πολύ.   *he*·ro po·*li*

I'd like to introduce you to … (a man).
Θα ήθελα να σε   tha *i*·the·la na se
συστήσω στο …   si·*sti*·so sto …

I'd like to introduce you to … (a woman).
Θα ήθελα να σε   tha *i*·the·la na se
συστήσω στη …   si·*sti*·so sti …

This is my …	Από εδώ …	a·po e·*thi* …
child	το παιδί μου	to pe·*thi* mu
colleague	ο συνάδελφός μου m	o sin·*a*·thel·*fos* mu
	η συναδέλφισσά μου f	i sin·a·*thel*·fi·*sa* mu
friend	ο φίλος μου m	o *fi*·los mu
	η φίλη μου f	i *fi*·li mu
husband	ο σύζυγός μου	o *si*·zi·ghos mu
partner	ο σύντροφός μου m	o *si*·dro·fos mu
(intimate)	η σύντροφός μου f	i *si*·dro·fos mu
wife	η σύζυγός μου	i *si*·zi·*ghos* mu

For other family members, see **family**, page 114.

See you later/Goodbye/Bye.
Αντίο.   a·*di*·o

Good night.
Καλή νύχτα.   ka·*li* *nikh*·ta

Bon voyage!
Καλό ταξίδι!   ka·*lo* tak·*si*·ṭhi

addressing people

The Greek language has two forms of the word 'you'. Use the polite form εσείς *e·sis* with adult strangers, elders, or those in a position of authority. In all other cases, you can use the informal form εσύ *e·si*. The polite form is simply the plural form of 'you', and you use it even when addressing one person. In this book we've chosen the appropriate form for the situation that the phrase is used in – it's normally the polite form unless we've marked it otherwise. For phrases where either form might be suitable, we've given both.

Also note that when speaking to older people you know well, their first name comes after Κύριε *ki·ri·e* (Sir), or Κυρία *ki·ri·a* (Madam).

Mr/Sir	Κύριε	*ki·ri·e*
Ms/Mrs	Κα	*ki·ri·a*
Miss	Δις	*thes·pi·nis*
Madam	Κυρία	*ki·ri·a*

on friendly terms

People will indicate when you can use the informal form of the word 'you' (εσύ *e·si*). If you want to initiate a more informal conversation with a Greek acquaintance, say:

Please speak to me in the singular.
Μίλα μου στον ενικό.   *mi·la mu ston e·ni·ko*

And here are a few casual terms to address your Greek pals:

friend	φίλε/φίλη m/f	*fi·le/fi·li*
dude	ρε μάγκα	re *ma·ga*
mate (Cyprus only)	κουμπάρε	ku·*ba·re*

making conversation

How are you going?
Πώς πάμε;   pos *pa*·me

What's happening?
Τι γίνεται;   ti *yi*·ne·te

What's new?
Τι νέα;   ti *ne*·a

What a beautiful day!
Τι όμορφη μέρα!   ti o·mor·fi *me*·ra

Nice/Awful weather, isn't it?
Καλός/απαίσιος καιρός,   ka·*los*/a·pe·si·os ke·*ros*
έτσι δεν είναι;   *et*·si then i·ne

Where are you going?
Πού πηγαίνεις;   pu pi·*ye*·nis

What are you doing?
Τι κάνεις;   ti *ka*·nis

What's this called?
Πώς το λένε αυτό;   pos to *le*·ne af·*to*

That's (beautiful), isn't it!
Είναι (όμορφο),   *i*·ne (o·mor·fo)
έτσι δεν είναι!   *et*·si then *i*·ne

---

don't mention the war

Sometimes, discretion is the better part of conversation –
these topics are best avoided:

• anything linked to Το Μακεδονικό to ma·ke·tho·ni·*ko*
(the Macedonian issue). A northern region of Greece is
called Macedonia, and many Greek patriots object to the
Former Yugoslav Republic of Macedonia usurping 'their'
name.

• any mention of Το Κυπριακό to kip·ri·a·*ko* (the Cyprus
problem). Displaced Greek Cypriots object to the Turkish
occupation of Northern Cyprus.

Can I take a photo (of you)?
 Μπορώ να (σου) πάρω   bo·*ro* na (su) *pa*·ro
 μια φωτογραφία;   mia fo·to·ghra·*fi*·a

Do you live here?
 Μένεις εδώ;   *me*·nis e·*tho*

Are you here on holiday?
 Είσαι εδώ για διακοπές;   *i*·se e·*tho* yia thia·ko·*pes*

I'm here …   Είμαι εδώ για …   *i*·me e·*tho* yia …
 for a holiday   διακοπές   thia·ko·*pes*
 on business   δουλειά   thu·*lia*
 to study   σπουδές   spu·*thes*

How long are you here for?
 Πόσον καιρό θα είσαι εδώ;   *po*·son ke·*ro* tha *i*·se e·*tho*

I'm here for (four) weeks/days.
 Θα είμαι εδώ για (τέσσερις)   tha *i*·me e·*tho* yia (*te*·se·ris)
 εβδομάδες/μέρες.   ev·tho·*ma*·thes/*me*·res

Do you like it here?
 Σου αρέσει εδώ;   su a·*re*·si e·*tho*

I love it here.
 Μου αρέσει εδώ.   mu a·*re*·si e·*tho*

nationalities

Where are you from?
 Από πού είσαι;   a·*po* pu *i*·se

I'm from …   Είμαι από …   *i*·me a·*po* …
 Australia   την Αυστραλία   tin af·stra·*li*·a
 Canada   τον Καναδά   ton ka·na·*tha*
 Singapore   τη Σιγγαπούρη   ti si·ga·*pu*·ri

age

How old ...?	Πόσο χρονώ ...;	po·so khro·no ...
are you	είσαι	i·se
is your son	είναι ο γιος σου	i·ne o yios su
is your daughter	είναι η κόρη σου	i·ne i ko·ri su

I'm ... years old.
Είμαι ... χρονώ.   i·me ... khro·no

He/She is ... years old.
Αυτός/αυτή είναι ... χρονών.   af·tos/af·ti i·ne ... khro·no

I'm younger than I look.
Είμαι νεότερος/νεότερη   i·me ne·o·te·ros/ne·o·te·ri
από ό,τι φαίνομαι. **m/f**   a·po o·ti fe·no·me

For your age, see **numbers & amounts**, page 35.

---

local talk

Absolutely!	Απολύτως!	a·po·li·tos
Don't stress!	Μην κάνεις έτσι!	min ka·nis et·si
Enough!	Αρκετά!	ar·ke·ta
Exactly!	Ακριβώς!	a·kri·vos
Great!	Απίθανο!	a·pi·tha·no
Hey!	Εε!	e·e
I don't care.	Δεν με νιάζει.	then me nia·zi
I don't give a stuff.	Δεν δίνω δεκάρα.	then thi·no the·ka·ra
It's OK.	Είναι εντάξει.	i·ne e·dak·si
Just a minute.	Μισό λεπτό.	mi·so lep·to
Just joking.	Αστειεύομαι.	a·sti·e·vo·me
Maybe.	Ίσως.	i·sos
No problem.	Δεν υπάρχει	then i·par·hi
	πρόβλημα.	prov·li·ma
No way!	Αποκλείεται!	a·po·kli·e·te
Rubbish!	Σαχλαμάρες!	sakh·la·ma·res
Sure.	Σίγουρα.	si·ghu·ra
Well now ...	Λοιπόν ...	li·pon ...
You're wrong.	Κάνεις λάθος.	ka·nis la·thos

the call of the wild ... and the domesticated

Dogs in Greece don't 'woof' – instead, they say ghav. Greek cows, on the other hand, seem to speak English. Here are some animal noises as they sound to Greek ears:

bird	τσίου-τσίου	*tsi*·u *tsi*·u
cat	νιάου	*nia*·ou
chick	κο-κο-κο	ko·ko·*ko*
cow	μου	mu
crow	κρα	kra
dog	γαβ	ghav
hen	κα-κα-κα	ka·ka·*ka*
rooster	κι-κιρίκου	ki·ki·*ri*·ku

occupations & studies

What's your occupation?

Τι δουλειά κάνεις;	ti thu·*lia ka*·nis

I'm a ...	Είμαι ...	*i*·me ...
businessperson	επιχειρηματίας m&f	e·pi·hi·ri·ma·*ti*·as
journalist	δημοσιογράφος m&f	thi·mo·si·o·*ghra*·fos
salesperson	πωλητής m	po·li·*tis*
	πωλήτρια f	po·*li*·tri·a
student	σπουδαστής m	spu·tha·*stis*
	σπουδάστρια f	spu·*tha*·stri·a
teacher	δάσκαλος m	*tha*·ska·los
	δασκάλα f	tha·*ska*·la
waiter	γκαρσόν	gar·*son*
waitress	γκαρσόνα	gar·*so*·na

I work in ...	Δουλεύω ...	thu·*le*·vo ...
administration	στη διοίκηση	sti thi·*i*·ki·si
health	στην υγεία	stin i·*yi*·a
sales &	στις πωλήσεις	stis po·*li*·sis
marketing	και μάρκετινγκ	ke *mar*·ke·ting

I'm ...	Είμαι ...	*i*·me ...
retired	συνταξιούχος m/f	si·dak·si·*u*·khos
self-	ιδιωτικός/ιδιωτική	i·thi·o·ti·*kos*/i·thi·o·ti·*ki*
employed	υπάλληλος m/f	i·*pa*·li·los
unemployed	άνεργος/άνεργη m/f	*an*·er·ghos/*an*·er·yi

What are you studying?	Τι σπουδάζεις;	ti spu·*tha*·zis

I'm studying ...	Σπουδάζω ...	spu·*tha*·zo ...
Greek	Ελληνικά	e·li·ni·*ka*
languages	γλώσσες	*ghlo*·ses
science	θετικές επιστήμες	the·ti·*kes* e·pi·*sti*·mes

family

οικογένεια

Are you married? (to a man)
Είσαι παντρεμένος;   *i*·se pa·dre·*me*·nos

Are you married? (to a woman)
Είσαι παντρεμένη;   *i*·se pa·dre·*me*·ni

I live with someone. (with a woman)
Ζω με κάποια.   zo me *ka*·pia

I live with someone. (with a man)
Ζω με κάποιον.   zo me *ka*·pion

I'm ...	Είμαι ...	*i*·me ...
married	παντρεμένος m	pa·dre·*me*·nos
	παντρεμένη f	pa·dre·*me*·ni
separated	χωρισμένος m	kho·riz·*me*·nos
	χωρισμένη f	kho·riz·*me*·ni
single	ανύπαντρος m	a·*ni*·pa·dros
	ανύπαντρη f	a·*ni*·pa·dri

Do you have a/an ...?
Έχεις ...;   *e*·his ...

I (don't) have a/an ...
(Δεν) έχω ...   (then) *e*·kho ...

aunt	θεία f	*thi*·a
brother	αδερφό m	a·*ther*·fo
brother-in-law	γαμπρό m	gha·*bro*
cousin	ξάδερφο m	ksa·*ther*·fo
	ξαδέρφη f	ksa·*ther*·fi
daughter	κόρη f	*ko*·ri
daughter-in-law	νύφη f	*ni*·fi
family	οικογένεια f	i·ko·*ye*·ni·a
father	πατέρα m	pa·*te*·ra
father-in-law	πεθερό m	pe·the·*ro*
granddaughter	εγγονή f	e·go·*ni*
grandfather	παπού m	pa·*pu*
grandmother	γιαγιά f	yia·*yia*
grandson	εγγονό m	e·go·*no*
husband	σύζυγο m	*si*·zi·gho
mother	μητέρα f	mi·*te*·ra
mother-in-law	πεθερά f	pe·the·*ra*
nephew	ανιψιό m	a·nip·*sio*
niece	ανιψιά f	a·nip·*sia*
partner (intimate)	σύντροφο m&f	*si*·dro·fo
sister	αδερφή f	a·ther·*fi*
sister-in-law	νύφη f	*ni*·fi
son	γιο m	yio
son-in-law	γαμπρό m	gha·*bro*
uncle	θείο m	*thi*·o
wife	σύζυγο f	*si*·zi·gho

farewells

Tomorrow is my last day here.
Αύριο είναι η τελευταία   *av*·ri·o *i*·ne i te·lef·*te*·a
μέρα μου εδώ.   *me*·ra mu e·*tho*

It's been great meeting you.
Είναι υπέροχο που σε   *i*·ne i·*pe*·ro·kho pu se
συνάντησα.   si·*na*·di·sa

If you come to (Scotland) you can stay with me.
Αν έρθεις (στη Σκωτία) an *er*·this (sti sko·*ti*·a)
μπορείς να μείνεις μαζί μου. bo·*ris* na *mi*·nis ma·*zi* mu

Here's my address.
Εδώ είναι η διεύθυνσή μου. e·*tho i*·ne i thi·*ef*·thin·*si* mu

What's your address?
Ποια είναι η δική σου pia *i*·ne i thi·*ki* su
διεύθυνση; thi·*ef*·thin·si

What's your …? Ποιο είναι το … σου; pio *i*·ne to … su
Here's my … Εδώ είναι το … μου. e·*tho i*·ne to … mu
  phone number τηλέφωνό ti·*le*·fo·*no*
  email address ημέιλ i·*me*·il

Keep in touch!
Μη χαθούμε! mi kha·*thu*·me

We'll talk again soon.
Θα τα πούμε. tha ta *pu*·me

Farewell.
Γεια χαρά. yia ha·*ra*

Adieu.
Αντίο. a·*di*·o

well-wishing		
Bless you!	Ο Θεός να σε φυλάει!	o the·*os* na se fi·*la*·i
Bon voyage!	Καλό ταξίδι!	ka·*lo* tak·*si*·thi
Congratulations!	Συγχαρητήρια!	sing·kha·ri·*ti*·ri·a
Good luck!	Καλή τύχη!	ka·*li ti*·hi
Happy Birthday!	Χαρούμενα γενέθλια!	kha·*ru*·me·na ye·*ne*·thli·a
Have a nice/ good time!	Καλά/Ωραία να περάσεις!	ka·*la*/or·*e*·a na pe·*ra*·sis
Merry Christmas!	Καλά Χριστούγεννα!	ka·*la* khri·*stu*·ye·na

If you're lost for words on a special occasion, just wish people Χρόνια πολλά! *khro*·nia po·*la* (Many years!) – this works for just about any festive occasion.

common interests

κοινά ενδιαφέροντα

What do you do in your spare time?

Τι κάνεις τον ελεύθερο	ti *ka*·nis ton e·*lef*·the·ro	
χρόνο σου;	*khro*·no su	

Do you like ...?	Σου αρέσει ...;	su a·*re*·si ...
I (don't) like ...	(Δεν) μου αρέσει ...	(then) mu a·*re*·si ...
billiards	το μπιλιάρδο	to bi·*liar*·tho
chess	το σκάκι	to *ska*·ki
cooking	η μαγειρική	i ma·yi·ri·*ki*
dancing	ο χορός	o kho·*ros*
dominoes	το ντόμινο	to *do*·mi·no
drawing	το σχέδιο	to *she*·thi·o
gardening	η κηπουρική	i ki·pu·ri·*ki*
music	η μουσική	i mu·si·*ki*
painting	η ζωγραφική	i zo·ghra·fi·*ki*
reading	το διάβασμα	to *thia*·vaz·ma

Do you like ...?	Σου αρέσουν ...;	su a·*re*·sun ...
I (don't) like ...	(Δεν) μου αρέσουν	(then) mu a·*re*·sun
	τα ...	ta ...
films	φιλμ	film
sport	σπορ	spor

Do you like ...?	Σου αρέσει να ...;	su a·*re*·si na ...
shopping	ψωνίζεις	pso·*ni*·zis
travelling	ταξιδεύεις	tak·si·*the*·vis

I (don't) like ...	(Δεν) μου αρέσει	(then) mu a·*re*·si
	να ...	na ...
shopping	ψωνίζω	pso·*ni*·zo
travelling	ταξιδεύω	tak·si·*the*·vo

For sporting activities, see **sport**, page 141.

astrology	αστρολογία f	a·stro·lo·*yi*·a
backgammon	τάβλι n	*tav*·li
bouzouki	μπουζούκι n	bu·*zu*·ki
(instrument)		
current affairs	επίκαιρα θέματα n pl	e·*pi*·ke·ra *the*·ma·ta
playing cards	χαρτιά n pl	khar·*tia*
politics	πολιτική f	po·li·ti·*ki*
sirtaki	συρτάκι n	sir·*ta*·ki
(Greek dancing)		

music

μουσική

What music do you like?

Τι μουσική σου αρέσει; ti mu·si·*ki* su a·*re*·si

Which bands/singers do you like?

Τι μπάντες/τραγουδιστές ti *ba*·des/tra·ghu·*thi*·stes
σου αρέσουν; su a·*re*·sun

traditional greek dances

Many traditional dances are specific to certain regions of Greece, while others are popular throughout the country. The most common ones are the Ζεμπέκικο ze·*be*·ki·ko (Zembekiko), the Τσάμικο *tsa*·mi·ko (Tsamiko), Καλαματιανό ka·la·ma·tia·*no* (Kalamatiano) – also called the Συρτό sir·*to* (Sirto) – and the Χασαποσέρβικο ha·sa·po·*ser*·vi·ko (Zorba Dance).

In most of these dances, the participants hold hands to form a semicircle and, moving in repetitive steps, they follow the lead dancer in an anticlockwise direction. The one exception is the Zembekiko, which is danced by individuals – although sometimes called the 'drunken sailor's dance' for its seeming clumsiness, it actually takes great skill to perform.

Other popular dances are the Κότσαρι *kot*·sa·ri (Kotsari), the Κρητικός kri·ti·*kos* (Kritikos) and the Ποντιακός po·di·a·*kos* (Pontiakos).

Do you ...?		
dance	Χορεύεις;	kho·*re*·vis
go to concerts	Πηγαίνεις σε κονσέρτα;	pi·*ye*·nis se kon·*ser*·ta
listen to music	Ακούς μουσική;	a·*kus* mu·si·*ki*
play an instrument	Παίζεις κανένα όργανο;	*pe*·zis ka·*ne*·na *or*·gha·no
sing	Τραγουδάς;	tra·ghu·*thas*
blues	μπλουζ n	bluz
classical music	κλασσική μουσική f	kla·si·*ki* mu·si·*ki*
electronic music	ηλεκτρονική μουσική f	i·lek·tro·ni·*ki* mu·si·*ki*
Greek folk music	Ελληνική παραδοσιακή μουσική f	e·li·ni·*ki* pa·ra·tho·si·a·*ki* mu·si·*ki*
jazz	τζαζ f	tzaz
pop music	ποπ f	pop
rembetika	ρεμπέτικα n pl	re·*be*·ti·ka
rock music	μουσική ροκ f	mu·si·*ki* rok
traditional music	παραδοσιακή μουσική f	pa·ra·tho·si·a·*ki* mu·si·*ki*

Planning to go to a concert? See **tickets**, page 46, and **going out**, page 127.

cinema & theatre

Σινεμά και θέατρο

I feel like going to a ...	Θέλω να πάω σε ...	*the*·lo na *pa*·o se ...
ballet	μπαλέτο	ba·*le*·to
film	φιλμ	film
play	έργο	*er*·gho

interests

119

What's showing at the cinema/theatre tonight?
Τι παίζει στο σινεμά/   ti *pe*·zi sto si·ne·*ma*/
θέατρο απόψε;   the·a·tro a·*pop*·se

Is it in English/Greek?
Είναι στα Αγγλικά/Ελληνικά;   *i*·ne sta ang·gli·*ka*/e·li·ni·*ka*

Does it have (English) subtitles?
Έχει (Αγγλικούς) υπότιτλους;   *e*·hi (ang·gli·*kus*) i·*po*·tit·lus

Is this seat taken?
Είναι αυτή η θέση πιασμένη;   *i*·ne af·*ti* i *the*·si piaz·*me*·ni

Have you seen …?
Έχεις δει …;   *e*·his thi …

Who's in it?
Ποιος παίζει σ' αυτό;   pios *pe*·zi saf·*to*

Did you like the (film)?
Σου άρεσε το (φιλμ);   su *a*·re·se to (film)

I thought it was …	Νομίζω πως ήταν …	no·*ni*·zo pos *i*·tan …
excellent	εξαιρετικό	ek·se·re·ti·*ko*
long	μεγάλο	me·*gha*·lo
OK	εντάξει	e·*dak*·si

I (don't) like …	(Δεν) μου αρέσουν …	(then) mu a·*re*·sun …
action movies	οι ταινίες δράσης	i te·*ni*·es *thra*·sis
animated films	τα φιλμ κινου-μένων σχεδίων	ta film ki·nu·*me*·non she·*thi*·on
comedies	οι κωμωδίες	i ko·mo·*thi*·es
documentaries	τα ντοκυμαντέρ	ta do·ki·man·*ter*
drama	τα δραματικά έργα	ta thra·ma·ti·*ka* er·gha
Greek cinema	τα ελληνικά έργα	ta e·li·ni·*ka* er·gha
horror movies	τα έργα τρόμου	ta *er*·gha *tro*·mu
sci-fi	τα έργα επιστημονικής φαντασίας	ta *er*·gha e·pi·sti·mo·ni·*kis* fa·da·*si*·as
short films	τα φιλμ μικρής διάρκειας	ta film mi·*kris* thi·*ar*·ki·as
thrillers	τα θρίλερ	ta *thri*·ler
war movies	τα πολεμικά έργα	ta po·le·mi·*ka* er·gha

feelings & opinions
αισθήματα και γνώμες

feelings

αισθήματα

Are you …?	Είσαι …;	*i*·se …
I'm (not) …	(Δεν) Είμαι …	(ţhen) *i*·me …
annoyed	ενοχλημένος m	e·no·khli·*me*·nos
	ενοχλημένη f	e·no·khli·*me*·ni
disappointed	απογοητευμένος m	a·po·gho·i·tev·*me*·nos
	απογοητευμένη f	a·po·gho·i·tev·*me*·ni
embarrassed	αμήχανος m	a·*mi*·kha·nos
	αμήχανη f	a·*mi*·kha·ni
happy	ευτυχισμένος m	ef·ti·hiz·*me*·nos
	ευτυχισμένη f	ef·ti·hiz·*me*·ni
hot	ζεστός m	ze·*stos*
	ζεστή f	ze·*sti*
hungry	πεινασμένος m	pi·naz·*me*·nos
	πεινασμένη f	pi·naz·*me*·ni
in a hurry	βιαστικός m	via·sti·*kos*
	βιαστική f	via·sti·*ki*
sad	στενοχωρημένος m	ste·no·kho·ri·*me*·nos
	στενοχωρημένη f	ste·no·kho·ri·*me*·ni
surprised	έκπληκτος m	*ek*·plik·tos
	έκπληκτη f	*ek*·plik·ti
thirsty	διψασμένος m	ţhip·saz·*me*·nos
	διψασμένη f	ţhip·saz·*me*·ni
tired	κουρασμένος m	ku·raz·*me*·nos
	κουρασμένη f	ku·raz·*me*·ni
worried	ανύσυχος m	a·*ni*·si·khos
	ανύσυχη f	a·*ni*·si·hi
I'm (not) cold.	(Δεν) Κρυώνω.	(ţhen) kri·*o*·no

If you're not feeling well, see **health**, page 195.

feelings & opinions

mixed feelings

a little	λίγο	*li*·gho
I'm a little sad.	Είμαι λίγο στενοχωρημένος/ στενοχωρημένη. m/f	*i*·me *li*·gho ste·no·kho·ri·*me*·nos ste·no·kho·ri·*me*·ni
very	πολύ	po·*li*
I feel very lucky.	Αισθάνομαι πολύ τυχερός/τυχερή. m/f	es·*tha*·no·me po·*li* ti·he·*ros*/ti·he·*ri*
extremely	πάρα πολύ	*pa*·ra po·*li*
I'm extremely sorry.	Λυπάμαι πάρα πολύ.	li·*pa*·me *pa*·ra po·*li*

opinions

γνώμες

Did you like it?
Σου άρεσε;   su *a*·re·se

What do you think of it?
Τι νομίζεις για αυτό;   ti no·*mi*·zis yia af·*to*

I thought it was ...	Νομίζω ήταν ...	no·*mi*·zo *i*·tan ...
It's ...	Είναι ...	*i*·ne ...
awful	απαίσιο	a·*pe*·si·o
beautiful	όμορφο	*o*·mor·fo
boring	πληκτικό	plik·ti·*ko*
great	καταπληκτικό	ka·ta·plik·ti·*ko*
interesting	ενδιαφέρον	en·thia·*fe*·ron
OK	εντάξει	e·*dak*·si
strange	παράξενο	pa·*rak*·se·no
too expensive	πάρα πολύ ακριβό	*pa*·ra po·*li* a·kri·*vo*

politics & social issues

Who do you vote for?
Ποιον ψηφίζεις; pion psi·*fi*·zis

I support the ... party.	Εγώ υποστηρίζω το κόμμα ...	e·*gho* i·po·sti·*ri*·zo to *ko*·ma ...
I'm a member of the ... party.	Είμαι μέλος του κόμματος ...	*i*·me *me*·los tu *ko*·ma·tos ...
coalition	συνασπισμός	si·nas·piz·*mos*
communist	κομμουνιστικό	ko·mu·ni·sti·*ko*
conservative	συντηρητικό	si·di·ri·ti·*ko*
democratic	δημοκρατικό	thi·mo·kra·ti·*ko*
green	οικολογικό	i·ko·lo·yi·*ko*
liberal	φιλελεύθεροι	fil·e·*lef*·the·ri
republican	ρεπουμπλικανικό	re·pu·bli·ka·ni·*ko*
social	κοινωνικό	ki·no·ni·*ko*
democratic	δημοκρατικό	thi·mo·kra·ti·*ko*
socialist	σοσιαλιστικό	so·si·a·li·sti·*ko*

Did you hear about ...?
Άκουσες για ...; *a*·ku·ses yia ...

Do you agree with it?
Συμφωνείς με αυτό ...; sim·fo·*nis* me af·*to* ...

I (don't) agree with ...
(Δεν) Συμφωνώ με ... (then) sim·fo·*no* me ...

How do people feel about ...?
Πώς αισθάνονται οι pos es·*tha*·no·de i
άνθρωποι για ...; *an*·thro·pi yia ...

How can we support ...?
Πώς μπορούμε να pos bo·*ru*·me na
υποστηρίξουμε ...; i·po·sti·*rik*·su·me ...

How can we protest against ...?
Πώς μπορούμε να pos bo·*ru*·me na
διαμαρτυρηθούμε για ...; thi·a·mar·ti·ri·*thu*·me yia ...

'no' means 'yes'

Although it may sound like 'no', remember that ναι ne really means 'yes'.

abortion	εκτρώσεις f	ek·tro·sis
animal rights	δικαιώματα	thi·ke·o·ma·ta
	των ζώων n	ton zo·on
civil servants	δημοσίους	tus thi·mo·si·us
	υπαλλήλους m	i·pa·li·lus
crime	έγκλημα n	eng·li·ma
democracy	δημοκρατία f	thi·mo·kra·ti·a
diaspora	διασπορά f	thi·a·spo·ra
discrimination	διακρίσεις f	thi·a·kri·sis
drugs	ναρκωτικά n	nar·ko·ti·ka
the economy	οικονομία f	i·ko·no·mi·a
education	εκπαίδευση f	ek·pe·thef·si
the environment	περιβάλλον n	pe·ri·va·lon
equal opportunity	ίσες ευκαιρίες f	i·ses ef·ke·ri·es
euthanasia	ευθανασία f	ef·tha·na·si·a
the European	Ευρωπαϊκή	ev·ro·pa·i·ki
Union	Ένωση f	e·no·si
gay rights	δικαιώματα	thi·ke·o·ma·ta
	των γκέι n	ton ge·i
globalisation	παγκοσμιοποίηση f	pa·goz·mi·o·pi·i·si
human rights	ανθρώπινα	an·thro·pi·na
	δικαιώματα n	thi·ke·o·ma·ta
immigration	μετανάστευση f	me·ta·na·stef·si
inequality	ανισότητα f	a·ni·so·ti·ta
inflation	πληθωρισμό m	pli·tho·riz·mo
the military junta	στρατιωτική	stra·ti·o·ti·ki
	χούντα f	khu·da
the Macedonian	Μακεδονικό	ma·ke·tho·ni·ko
question	ζήτημα n	zi·ti·ma
the monarchy	μοναρχία f	mo·nar·hi·a
NATO	ΝΑΤΟ n	na·to
parliament	κοινοβούλιο n	ki·no·vu·li·o

SOCIAL

124

the partition of Cyprus	διχοτόμηση της Κύπρου f	thi·kho·*to*·mi·si tis *ki*·pru
party politics	πολιτική του κόμματος f	po·li·ti·*ki* tu *ko*·ma·tos
privatisation	ιδιωτικοποίηση f	i·*thi*·o·ti·ko·*pi*·i·si
poverty	φτώχεια f	*fto*·hia
racism	ρατσισμό n	rat·siz·*mo*
refugees	πρόσφυγες m	*pros·fi*·yes
relations with Turkey	σχέσεις με την Τουρκία f	*she*·sis me tin tur·*ki*·a
sexism	σεξισμό m	sek·siz·*mo*
social welfare	κοινωνική πρόνοια f	ki·no·ni·*ki pro*·ni·a
strikes	απεργίες f	ap·er·*yi*·es
terrorism	τρομοκρατία f	tro·mo·kra·*ti*·a
traffic restrictions	περιορισμό της κυκλοφορίας m	pe·ri·o·riz·*mo* tis ki·klo·fo·*ri*·as
unemployment	ανεργία f	an·er·*yi*·a
US military bases	στρατιωτικές βάσεις των ΗΠΑ f	stra·ti·o·ti·*kes va*·sis ton *i*·pa
the war in (the Balkans)	πολέμους (στα Βαλκάνια) m	po·*le*·mus (sta val·*ka*·ni·a)

the environment

το περιβάλλον

Is there a ... problem here?
Υπάρχει κλάποιο πρόβλημα εδώ με ...;
   i·*par*·hi *ka*·pio *pro*·vli·ma e·*tho* me ...

What should be done about ...?
Τι θα πρέπει να γίνει με ...;
   ti tha *pre*·pi na *yi*·ni me ...

beach cleaning	καθαρισμό	ka·tha·riz·mo
	των ακτών m	ton ak·ton
conservation	προστασία	pro·sta·si·a
	του περιβάλλοντος f	tu pe·ri·va·lo·dos
deforestation	αποδάσωση f	a·po·tha·so·si
drought	ανομβρία f	a·nom·vri·a
earthquakes	σεισμούς m	siz·mus
ecosystem	οικοσύστημα n	i·ko·si·sti·ma
endangered	είδη υπό	i·thi i·po
species	εξαφάνιση n	ek·sa·fa·ni·si
erosion	διάβρωση f	thi·av·ro·si
forest fires	φωτιές στα δάση f	fo·tyes sta tha·si
genetically	γενετικά	ye·ne·ti·ka
modified food	μεταλλαγμένο	me·ta·lagh·me·no
	φαγητό n	fa·yi·to
hunting	κυνήγι n	ki·ni·yi
hydroelectricity	υδροηλεκτρισμό m	i·thro·i·lek·triz·mo
irrigation	άρδευση f	ar·thef·si
marine	θαλάσσια	tha·la·si·a
reserves	διαφύλαξη f	thi·a·fi·lak·si
national parks	εθνικά πάρκα n	eth·ni·ka par·ka
nuclear energy	πυρηνική ενέργεια f	pi·ri·ni·ki e·ner·yi·a
nuclear testing	πυρηνικές δοκιμές f	pi·ri·ni·kes tho·ki·mes
ozone layer	στρώμα του όζοντος n	stro·ma tu o·zo·dos
pesticides	φυτοφάρμακα n	fi·to·far·ma·ka
pollution	μόλυνση f	mo·lin·si
recycling	πρόγραμμα	pro·ghra·ma
program	ανκύκλωσης n	a·na·ki·klo·sis
smog	νέφος n	ne·fos
toxic waste	τοξικά απόβλητα n	tok·si·ka a·pov·li·ta
urban	αστική	a·sti·ki
encroachment	εξάπλωση f	ek·sa·plo·si
water supply	παροχή ύδατος f	pa·ro·hi i·tha·tos
Is this a	Είναι αυτό	i·ne af·to
protected …?	προστατευόμενο …;	pro·sta·te·vo·me·no
forest	δάσος	tha·sos
park	πάρκο	par·ko
species	είδος	i·thos

going out
βγαίνουμε έξω

where to go

πού να πάμε

What's there to do in the evenings?

Τι μπορούμε να κάνουμε το βράδι;		ti bo·*ru*·me na *ka*·nu·me to *vra*·thi

What's on …?	Τι γίνεται …;	ti *yi*·ne·te …
locally	εδώ γύρω	e·*tho yi*·ro
this weekend	αυτό το Σαββατοκύριακο	af·*to* to sa·va·to·*ki*·ria·ko
today	σήμερα	*si*·me·ra
tonight	απόψε	a·*pop*·se
Where can I find …?	Πού μπορώ να βρω …;	pu bo·*ro* na vro …
a *bouzouki* place (venue with live Greek music)	ταβέρνα με μπουζούκια	ta·*ver*·na me bu·*zu*·kia
clubs	κλαμπ	klab
gay venues	Χώρους συνάντησης για γκέη	*kho*·rus si·*na*·di·sis yia *ge*·i
an open-air cinema	θερινό κινηματογράφο	the·ri·*no* ki·ni·ma·to·*ghra*·fo
places to eat	εστιατόρια	e·sti·a·*to*·ri·a
pubs	μπυραρίες	bi·ra·*ri*·es
Is there a local … guide?	Υπάρχει τοπικός οδηγός για …;	i·*par*·hi to·pi·*kos* o·*thi*·*ghos* yia …
entertainment	διασκεδάσεις	thias·ke·*tha*·sis
film	φιλμ	film
gay	γκέη	*ge*·i
music	μουσική	mu·si·*ki*

127

I feel like going	Έχω όρεξη να	e·kho o·rek·si na
to a ...	πάω σε ...	pa·o se ...
ballet	μπαλέτο	ba·le·to
bar	μπαρ	bar
café	καφενείο	ka·fe·ni·o
concert	κονσέρτο	kon·ser·to
film	φιλμ	film
karaoke bar	καράόκι μπαρ	ka·ra·o·ki bar
nightclub	νυχτερινό κέντρο	nikh·te·ri·no ke·dro
party	πάρτυ	par·ti
performance	θέαμα	the·a·ma
play	έργο	er·gho
pub	μπυραρία	bi·ra·ri·a
rebetika club	κέντρο με	ke·dro me
	ρεμπέτικα	re·be·ti·ka
restaurant	εστιατόριο	e·sti·a·to·ri·o
sports match	αθλητικό	ath·li·ti·ko
	παιγνίδι	pegh·ni·thi

For more on bars and drinks, see **romance**, page 131, and **eating out**, pages 166–170.

invitations

προσκλήσεις

What are you	Τι κάνεις ...;	ti ka·nis ...
doing ...?		
now	τώρα	to·ra
this weekend	το Σαββατοκύριακο	to sa·va·to·ki·ria·ko
tonight	απόψε	a·pop·se

Do you know a good restaurant?
Ξέρεις κανένα καλό   kse·ris ka·ne·na ka·lo
εστιατόριο;   e·sti·a·to·ri·o

My round.
Η σειρά μου.   i si·ra mu

We're having a party.
Έχουμε πάρτι.   e·khu·me par·ti

Would you like to go (for a) ...?	Θα ήθελες να πας ...;	tha *i*·the·les na pas ...
coffee	για καφέ	yia ka·*fe*
dancing	για χορό	yia kho·*ro*
drink	για ποτό	yia po·*to*
meal	για φαγητό	yia fa·yi·*to*
out somewhere	κάπου έξω	*ka*·pu *ek*·so
walk	βόλτα	*vol*·ta

responding to invitations

απαντώντας σε προσκλήσεις

Sure!
Μάλιστα!   *ma*·li·sta

Yes, I'd love to.
Ναι, θα ήθελα πολύ.   ne tha *i*·the·la po·*li*

That's very kind of you.
Πολύ ευγενικό εκ   po·*li* ev·ye·ni·*ko* ek
μέρους σου.   *me*·rus su

No, I'm afraid I can't.
Όχι, φοβάμαι πως δεν .   o·hi fo·*va*·me pos then
μπορώ   bo·*ro*

What about tomorrow?
Τι θα έλεγες για αύριο;   ti tha *e*·le·yes yia *av*·ri·o

Where shall we go?
Πού θα πάμε;   pu tha *pa*·me

arranging to meet

κανονίζοντας για συνάντηση

What time will we meet?
Τι ώρα θα συναντηθούμε;   ti *o*·ra tha si·na·di·*thu*·me

Where will we meet?
Πού θα συναντηθούμε;   pu tha si·na·di·*thu*·me

Let's meet at …	Ας	as
	συναντηθούμε …	si·na·di·thu·me …
(eight) o'clock	στις (οχτώ)	stis (okh·to)
the entrance	στην είσοδο	stin i·so·tho

I'll pick you up.
Θα σε πάρω εγώ.   tha se pa·ro e·gho

Are you ready?
Είσαι έτοιμος/έτοιμη; m/f   i·se e·ti·mos/e·ti·mi

I'm ready.
Είμαι έτοιμος/έτοιμη. m/f   i·me e·ti·mos/e·ti·mi

Where will you be?
Πού θα είσαι;   pu tha i·se

If I'm not there by (nine), don't wait for me.
Αν δεν είμαι εκεί μέχρι   an then i·me e·ki me·khri
(τις εννέα), μή με περιμένεις.   (tis e·ne·a) mi me pe·ri·me·nis

I'm looking forward to it.
Το περιμένω πώς και πώς.   to pe·ri·me·no pos ke pos

OK!	Εντάξει!	e·dak·si
I'll see you then.	Θα σε δω τότε.	tha se tho to·te
Sorry I'm late.	Συγνώμη που	sigh·no·mi pu
	άργησα.	ar·yi·sa

drugs

ναρκωτικά

Do you have a light?
Έχεις φωτιά;   e·his fo·tia

Do you want to have a smoke?
Θέλεις να καπνίσεις;   the·lis na kap·ni·sis

I don't take drugs.
Δεν παίρνω ναρκωτικά.   then per·no nar·ko·ti·ka

I take … occasionally.
Παίρνω … καμιά φορά.   per·no … ka·mia fo·ra

I'm high.
Είμαι μαστουρωμένος.   i·me ma·stu·ro·me·nos

asking someone out

Where would you like to go (tonight)?
Πού θα ήθελες να πάμε   pu tha *the*·lis na *pa*·me
(απόψε);   (a·*pop*·se)

Would you like to do something (tomorrow)?
Θα ήθελες να κάνουμε   tha *i*·the·les na *ka*·nu·me
κάτι (αύριο);   *ka*·ti (av·ri·o)

Yes, I'd love to.
Ναι, θα το ήθελα πολύ.   ne tha to *i*·the·la po·*li*

Sorry, I can't.
Συγνώμη, δεν μπορώ.   sigh·*no*·mi then bo·*ro*

pick-up lines

Would you like a drink?
Θα ήθελες ένα ποτό;   tha *i*·the·les *e*·na po·*to*

You look like someone I know. (to a man)
Μοιάζεις με κάποιον που ξέρω.   *mia*·zis me *ka*·pion pu *kse*·ro

You look like someone I know. (to a woman)
Μοιάζεις με κάποια που ξέρω.   *mia*·zis me *ka*·pia pu *kse*·ro

You're a fantastic dancer. (to a man)
Είσαι απίθανος χορευτής.   *i*·se a·*pi*·tha·nos kho·ref·*tis*

You're a fantastic dancer. (to a woman)
Είσαι απίθανη χορεύτρια.   *i*·se a·*pi*·tha·ni kho·*ref*·tria

Can I …?	Μπορώ να …;	bo·ro na …
dance with you	χορέψω μαζί σου	kho·rep·so ma·zi su
sit here	καθίσω εδώ	ka·thi·so e·tho
take you home	σε πάρω στο σπίτι	se pa·ro sto spi·ti

rejections

No, thank you.
Όχι, ευχαριστώ.
o·hi ef·kha·ri·sto

I'd rather not.
Νομίζω όχι.
no·mi·zo o·hi

I'm here with my boyfriend.
Είμαι εδώ με τον φίλο μου.
i·me e·tho me ton fi·lo mu

I'm here with my girlfriend.
Είμαι εδώ με την φίλη μου.
i·me e·tho me tin fi·li mu

Excuse me, I have to go now.
Συγνώμη, πρέπει να πηγαίνω τώρα.
sigh·no·mi pre·pi na pi·ye·no to·ra

Leave me alone! (a man)
Άσε με ήσυχο!
a·se me i·si·kho

Leave me alone! (a woman)
Άσε με ήσυχη!
a·se me i·si·khi

Piss off!
Άντε από δω, ρε!
a·de a·po tho re

local talk

He's a babe.
Είναι κούκλος.   *i*·ne *ku*·klos

She's a babe.
Είναι κούκλα.   *i*·ne *ku*·kla

He's hot.
Είναι θερμός.   *i*·ne ther·*mos*

She's hot.
Είναι θερμή.   *i*·ne ther·*mi*

He's a bastard.
Είναι μπάσταρδος.   *i*·ne *ba*·star·thos

She's a bitch.
Είναι καριόλα.   *i*·ne ka·*rio*·la

He/She gets around.
Σεργιανάει.   ser·yia·*na*·i

getting closer

I like you very much.
Μου αρέσεις πολύ.   mu a·*re*·sis po·*li*

You're great.
Είσαι θαύμα.   *i*·se *thav*·ma

Can I kiss you?
Μπορώ να σε φιλήσω;   bo·*ro* na se fi·*li*·so

Do you want to come inside for a while?
Θέλεις να έρθεις μέσα,   *the*·lis na *er*·this *me*·sa
για λίγο;   yia *li*·gho

Do you want a massage?
Θέλεις ένα μασάζ;   *the*·lis *e*·na ma·*saz*

Can I stay over?
Μπορώ να μείνω τη νύχτα; bo·*ro* na *mi*·no ti *nikh*·ta

sex

Kiss me.	Φίλα με.	*fi*·la me
I want you.	Σε θέλω.	se *the*·lo
Touch me here.	Πιάσε με εδώ.	*pia*·se me e·*tho*
Let's go to bed.	Πάμε στο κρεβάτι.	*pa*·me sto kre·*va*·ti

Do you like this?
Σου αρέσει αυτό; su a·*re*·si af·*to*

I (don't) like that.
(Δεν) Μου αρέσει αυτό. (ţhen) mu a·*re*·si af·*to*

I think we should stop now.
Νομίζω πως πρέπει να no·*mi*·zo pos *pre*·pi na
σταματήσουμε τώρα. sta·ma·*ti*·su·me *to*·ra

Do you have a condom?
Έχεις προφυλακτικό; *e*·his pro·fi·lak·ti·*ko*

Let's use a condom.
Ας χρησιμοποιήσουμε as khri·si·mo·pi·*i*·su·me
προφυλακτικό. pro·fi·lak·ti·*ko*

I won't do it without protection.
Δεν το κάνω χωρίς ţhen to *ka*·no kho·*ris*
προφύλαξη. pro·*fi*·lak·si

It's my first time.
Είναι η πρώτη μου φορά. *i*·ne i *pro*·ti mu fo·*ra*

Don't worry, I'll do it myself.
Μην ανησυχείς, θα το min a·ni·si·*his* tha to
κάνω μόνος/μόνη μου. **m/f** *ka*·no *mo*·nos/*mo*·ni mu

It helps to have a sense of humour.
Βοηθάει να έχεις την vo·i·*tha*·i na *e*·his tin
αίσθηση του χιούμορ. *es*·thi·si tu *hiu*·mor

Oh my god!
Ω, θεέ μου! o the·*e* mu

That's great.
Είναι απίθανο. *i*·ne a·*pi*·tha·no

Easy tiger! (to a man)
σιγά ρε γόη!   si·*gha* re *gho*·i

Easy tiger! (to a woman)
σιγά ρε γόισσα!   si·*gha* re *gho*·i·sa

faster	πιο γρήγορα	pio *ghri*·gho·ra
harder	πιο γερά	pio ye·*ra*
slower	πιο αργά	pio ar·*gha*
softer	πιο μαλακά	pio ma·la·*ka*

That was …	Ήταν …	*i*·tan …
amazing	καταπληκτικό	ka·ta·plik·ti·*ko*
romantic	ρομαντικό	ro·ma·di·*ko*
wild	άγριο	*a*·ghri·o

love

αγάπη

I think we're good together.
Νομίζω ταιριάζουμε.   no·*mi*·zo te·*ria*·zu·me

I love you.
Σ'αγαπώ.   sa·gha·*po*

Will you …?	Θα …;	tha …
go out with me	έρθεις έξω	er·*this* ek·so
	μαζί μου	ma·*zi* mu
marry me	με παντρευτείς	me pa·dref·*tis*
meet my	συναντήσεις τους	si·na·*di*·sis tus
parents	γονείς μου	gho·*nis* mu

sweet talk

my baby	μωρό μου	mo·*ro* mu
my darling	μάνα μου	*ma*·na mu
my doll	κουκλί μου	ku·*kli* mu
my hunk	τζουτζούκο μου	tzu·*tzu*·ko mu
my soul	ψυχούλα μου	psi·*hu*·la mu
my treasure	χρυσό μου	khri·*so* mu
sweetheart	καρδούλα μου	kar·*thu*·la mu

problems

Are you seeing someone else? (to a woman)
βλέπεις κάποιον άλλο;   *e*·his ka·pion *a*·lon

Are you seeing someone else? (to a man)
βλέπεις κάποια άλλη;   *e*·his ka·pia *a*·li

He/She is just a friend.
Είναι απλά φίλος/φίλη.   *i*·ne a·*pla fi*·los/*fi*·li

You're just using me for sex.
Με θέλεις μόνο για το σεξ.   me *the*·lis *mo*·no yia to seks

I never want to see you again.
Δεν θέλω να σε ξαναδώ.   then *the*·lo na se ksa·na·*tho*

I don't think it's working out.
Δεν νομίζω ότι δουλεύει.   then no·*mi*·zo o·ti thu·*le*·vi

We'll work it out.
Θα τα βρούμε.   tha ta *vru*·me

leaving

I have to leave (tomorrow).
Πρέπει να φύγω (αύριο).   *pre*·pi na *fi*·gho (*av*·ri·o)

I'll …	Θα …	tha …
keep in touch	βρίσκομαι σε επαφή	*vris*·ko·me se e·pa·*fi*
miss you	μου λείψεις	mu *lip*·sis
visit you	σε επισκεφτώ	se e·pis·kef·*to*

it's a tragedy

The poet Thespis (Θέσπις *thes*·pis) was one of the founders of the theatrical tragedy genre during the 6th century BC. His name survives in the English word 'Thespian', meaning 'dramatic' or 'relating to drama or theatre'.

πίστη και πολιτιστικές διαφορές

religion

θρησκεία

What's your religion?
Ποια είναι η θρησκεία σου;   pia i·ne i thris·ki·a su

I'm not religious.
Δεν είμαι θρήσκος.   then i·me thris·kos

I'm ...	Είμαι ...	i·me ...
agnostic	αγνωστικιστής m	agh·no·sti·ki·stis
	αγνωστικίστρια f	agh·no·sti·ki·stri·a
Buddhist	Βουδιστής m	vu·thi·stis
	Βουδίστρια f	vu·thi·stri·a
Catholic	Καθολικός m	ka·tho·li·kos
	Καθολική f	ka·tho·li·ki
Christian	Χριστιανός m	khri·stia·nos
	Χριστιανή f	khri·stia·ni
Hindu	Ινδουιστής m	in·thu·i·stis
	Ινδουίστρια f	in·thu·i·stri·a
Jewish	Ιουδαίος m	i·u·the·os
	Ιουδαία f	i·u·the·a
Muslim	Μουσουλμάνος m	mu·sul·ma·nos
	Μουσουλμάνα f	mu·sul·ma·na
Orthodox	Ορθόδοξος m	or·tho·thok·sos
	Ορθόδοξη f	or·tho·thok·si
I (don't) believe in ...	(Δεν) Πιστευω ...	(then) pi·ste·vo ...
astrology	στην αστρολογία	stin a·stro·lo·yi·a
fate	στη μοίρα	sti mi·ra
God	στο Θεό	sto the·o

Can I ... here?	Μπορώ να ... εδώ;	bo·ro na ... e·tho
Where can I ...?	Πού μπορώ να ...;	pu bo·ro na ...
attend mass	παρακολουθήσω	pa·ra·ko·lu·thi·so
	τη λειτουργία	ti li·tur·yi·a
attend a	παρακολουθήσω	pa·ra·ko·lu·thi·so
service	την ακολουθία	tin a·ko·lu·thi·a
pray	προσευχηθώ	pro·sef·hi·tho
worship	προσκυνήσω	pros·ki·ni·so

cultural differences

πολιτιστικές διαφορές

Is this a local or national custom?
Είναι αυτό τοπικό ή
εθνικό έθιμο;
*i·*ne af·*to* to·pi·*ko* i
eth·ni·*ko* e·thi·mo

I'm not used to this.
Δεν είμαι συνηθισμένος
σ'αυτό.
then *i·*me si·ni·thiz·*me·*nos
saf·*to*

I'd rather not join in.
Θα προτιμούσα να μη
λάβω μέρος.
tha pro·ti·*mu·*sa na mi
*la·*vo *me·*ros

I'll try it.
Θα το δοκιμάσω.
tha to tho·ki·*ma·*so

I didn't mean to do anything wrong.
Δεν ήθελα να κάμω κάτι
που δεν έπρεπε.
then *i·*the·la na *ka·*mo ka·ti
pu then *e·*pre·pe

I didn't mean to say anything wrong.
Δεν ήθελα πω κάτι
που δεν έπρεπε.
then *i·*the·la po *ka·*ti
pu then *e·*pre·pe

I don't want to offend you.
Δεν θέλω να σε προσβάλω.
then *the·*lo na se proz·*va·*lo

I'm sorry, it's	Συγνώμη, είναι	sigh·*no·*mi *i·*ne
against my ...	αντίθετο με ... μου.	a·*di·*the·to me ... mu
beliefs	την πίστη	tin *pi·*sti
religion	τη θρησκεία	ti thris·*ki·*a

When's the museum open?
Πότε είναι ανοιχτό το μουσείο; *po·te i·*ne a·nikh·*to* to mu·*si·*o

When's the gallery open?
Πότε είναι ανοιχτή
η πινακοθήκη; *po·*te *i·*ne a·nikh·*ti*
i·pi·na·ko·*thi·*ki

What kind of art are you interested in?
Τι είδους τέχνη σε ενδιαφέρει; ti *i·*thus *tekh·*ni se en·thia·*fe·*ri

I'm interested in …
Με ενδιαφέρει … me en·thia·*fe·*ri …

What's in the collection?
Τι υπάρχει στη συλλογή; ti i·*par·*hi sti si·lo·*yi*

It's an exhibition of …
Είναι μια έκθεση … *i·*ne mia *ek·*the·si …

Where are the exhibits from (Knossos)?
Πού είναι τα εκθέματα
από την (Κνωσσό); pu *i·*ne ta ek·*the·*ma·ta
a·*po* tin (kno·*so*)

What style is this?
Τι στυλ είναι αυτό; ti stil *i·*ne af·*to*

Is it an original or a copy?
Είναι αυθεντικό ή αντίγραφο; *i·*ne af·the·di·*ko* i a·*di·*ghra·fo

What do you think of …?
Πώς σου φαίνεται …; pos su *fe·*ne·te …

I like the works of …
Μου αρέσουν τα έργα … mu a·*re·*sun ta *er·*gha

It reminds me of …
Μου θυμίζει … mu thi·*mi·*zi …

Byzantine	Βυζαντινός	vi·za·di·*nos*
classical	κλασσικός	kla·si·*kos*
Hellenistic	Ελληνιστικός	e·li·ni·sti·*kos*
modern	μοντέρνος	mo·*der·*nos
Roman	Ρωμαϊκός	ro·ma·i·*kos*

... civilisation	... πολιτισμός m	... po·li·tiz·mos
Cycladic	Κυκλαδικός	ki·kla·thi·kos
Minoan	Μινωικός	mi·no·i·kos
Mycenean	Μυκηναϊκός	mi·ki·ma·i·kos
... style	... ρυθμός m	... rith·mos
Corinthian	Κορινθιακός	ko·rin·thi·a·kos
Doric	Δωρικός	tho·ri·kos
Ioanian	Ιωνικός	i·o·ni·kos
architecture	αρχιτεκτονική f	ar·hi·tek·to·ni·ki
artwork	καλλιτέχνημα n	ka·li·tekh·ni·ma
column	κολόνα f	ko·lo·na
curator	έφορος μουσείου m	e·fo·ros mu·si·u
decorative arts	διακοσμητικές τέχνες f pl	thi·a·koz·mi·ti·kes tekh·nes
etching	χαλκογραφία f	khal·ko·ghra·fi·a
exhibit	έκθεση f	ek·the·si
exhibition hall	αίθουσα έκθεσης f	e·thu·sa ek·the·sis
fresco	φρέσκο n	fres·ko
metalwork	μεταλλικά αντικείμενα n pl	me·ta·li·ka a·di·ki·me·na
mosaic	μωσαϊκό n	mo·sa·i·ko
painter	ζωγράφος m	zo·ghra·fos
painting (artwork)	πίνακας m	pi·na·kas
painting (the art)	ζωγραφική f	zo·ghra·fi·ki
period	περίοδος f	pe·ri·o·thos
permanent collection	μόνιμη συλλογή f	mo·ni·mi si·lo·yi
print	αντίγραφο n	a·di·ghra·fo
sculptor	γλύπτης m	ghlip·tis
sculpture	γλυπτική f	ghlip·ti·ki
shield	ασπίδα f	a·spi·tha
spear	δόρυ n	tho·ri
sword	σπαθί n	spa·thi
statue	άγαλμα n	a·ghal·ma
terracotta pot	αγγείο τερακότα n	a·gi·o te·ra·ko·ta
tunic	χιτώνας m	hi·to·nas
vessel	αγγείο n	a·gi·o

sporting interests

αθλητικά ενδιφέροντα

What sport do you follow/play?
Τι σπορ ακολουθείς/παίζεις;   ti spor a·ko·lu·*this/pe*·zis

I follow (basketball).
Παρακολουθώ (μπάσκετ).   pa·ra·ko·lu·*tho (ba*·sket)

I play (football).
Παίζω (ποδόσφαιρο).   *pe*·zo (po·*thos*·fe·ro)

I do ...	Κάνω ...	*ka*·no ...
athletics	αθλήματα	ath·*li*·ma·ta
hiking	πεζοπορία	pe·zo·po·*ri*·a
sailing	ιστιοπλοΐα	i·sti·o·plo·*i*·a
scuba diving	υπόγειες	i·*po*·yi·es
	καταδύσεις	ka·ta·*thi*·sis
sailboarding	γουιντσέρφινγκ	ghu·id·*ser*·fing
water-skiing	θαλάσσιο σκι	tha·*la*·si·o ski

For more sports, see the **dictionary**.

top sport		
soccer	ποδόσφαιρο n	po·*thos*·fe·ro
	ευρωπαϊκό	ev·ro·pa·i·*ko*
basketball	μπάσκετ n	*bas*·ket
volleyball	βόλεϋ n	*vo*·le·i
gymnastics	κλασικός	kla·si·*kos*
	αθλητισμός m	ath·li·tiz·*mos*
swimming	κολύμπι n	ko·*lim*·bi

To exercise you brain, try Greece's favourite nonphysical pastime:

backgammon	τάβλι n	*tav*·li

I …	Εγώ …	e·gho …
cycle	κάνω ποδήλατο	ka·no po·thi·la·to
run	τρέχω	tre·kho
walk	βαδίζω	va·thi·zo

Do you like (football)?
Σου αρέσει (το ποδόσφαιρο);   su a·re·si (to po·thos·fe·ro)

Yes, very much.
Ναι, πάρα πολύ.   ne pa·ra po·li

Not really.
Όχι.   o·hi

I like watching it.
Μου αρέσει να το κοιτάζω.   mu a·re·si na to ki·ta·zo

What's your favourite team?
Ποια ομάδα υποστηρίζεις;   pia o·ma·tha i·po·sti·ri·zis

Who's your favourite sportsperson?
Ποιος αθλητής σου αρέσει;   pios ath·li·tis su a·re·si

going to a game

πηγαίνοντας σε ένα παιγνίδι

Would you like to go to a game?
Θα ήθελες να πας σε   tha i·the·les na pas se
ένα παιγνίδι;   e·na pegh·ni·thi

Who are you supporting?
Ποιον υποστηρίζεις;   pion i·po·sti·ri·zis

Who's playing/winning?
Ποιος παίζει/κερδίζει;   pios pe·zi/ker·thi·zi

scoring

What's the score?	Ποιο είναι το σκορ;	pio i·ne to skor
draw/even	ισοπαλία	i·so·pa·li·a
love/zero/nil	μηδέν	mi·then
match-point	πόντος για	po·dos yia
	παιγνίδι	pegh·ni·thi

What a …!	Τι …!	ti …
goal	γκολ	gol
hit	χτύπημα	*khti*·pi·ma
kick	κλωτσιά	klot·*sia*
pass	πάσα	*pa*·sa
performance	απόδοση	a·*po*·ţho·si

That was a … game!	Ήταν … παιγνίδι!	*i*·tan … pegh·*ni*·ţhi
bad	άσχημο	*a*·shi·mo
boring	πληκτικό	plik·ti·*ko*
great	υπέροχο	i·*pe*·ro·kho

playing sport

παίζοντας σπορ

Do you want to play?
Θέλεις να παίξεις; *the*·lis na *pek*·sis

Can I join in?
Να παίξω και εγώ; na *pek*·so ke e·*gho*

That would be great.
Αυτό θα ήταν υπέροχο. af·*to* tha *i*·tan i·*pe*·ro·kho

I can't.
Δεν μπορώ. ţhen bo·*ro*

I have an injury.
Έχω ένα τραύμα. *e*·kho e·na *trav*·ma

Your/My point.
Δικός σου/μου πόντος. ţhi·*kos* su/mu *po*·dos

Kick it to me!
κλώτσα την σε μένα!   *klot*·sa tin se *me*·na

Pass it to me!
ρίξ'την σε μένα!   *riks*·tin se *me*·na

You're a good player.
Είσαι καλός παίχτης.   *i*·se ka·*los pekh*·tis

Thanks for the game.
Ευχαριστώ για το παιγνίδι.   ef·kha·ri·*sto* yia to pegh·*ni*·ţhi

Where's a good place to …?	Πού είναι ένα καλό μέρος για να … κανείς;	pu *i*·ne *e*·na ka·*lo me*·ros yia na … ka·*nis*
fish	ψαρέψει	psa·*rep*·si
go horse riding	κάμει ιππασία	*ka*·mi i·pa·*si*·a
run	τρέξει	*trek*·si
snorkel	κάμει κατάδυση	*ka*·mi ka·*ta*·ţhi·si
surf	σερφάρει	ser·*fa*·ri

Where's the nearest ...?	Πού είναι το πιο κοντινό ...;	pu *i*·ne to pio ko·*di*·no ...
golf course	γήπεδο του γκολφ	*yi*·pe·ţho tu golf
gym	γυμναστήριο	yim·na·*sti*·ri·o
tennis court	γήπεδο του τένις	*yi*·pe·ţho tu *te*·nis

Where's the nearest swimming pool?

Πού είναι η πιο κοντινή πισίνα; pu *i*·ne i pio ko·di·*ni* pi·*si*·na

Do I have to be a member to attend?

Πρέπει να είμαι μέλος
για να πάω;

pre·pi na *i*·me *me*·los
yia na *pa*·o

Is there a women-only session?

Υπάρχει ορισμένη ώρα
μόνο για γυναίκες;

i·*par*·hi o·riz·*me*·ni *o*·ra
mo·no yia yi·*ne*·kes

Can I book a lesson?

Μπορώ να κλείσω ένα
μάθημα;

bo·*ro* na *kli*·so *e*·na
ma·thi·ma

Where are the changing rooms?

Πού είναι τα αποδυτήρια; pu *i*·ne ta a·po·ţhi·*ti*·ri·a

What's the charge per ...?	Πόσο κοστίζει ...;	*po*·so ko·*sti*·zi ...
day	την ημέρα	tin i·*me*·ra
game	το παιγνίδι	to pegh·*ni*·ţhi
hour	την ώρα	tin *o*·ra
visit	την επίσκεψη	tin e·*pis*·kep·si

Can I hire a ...?	Μπορώ να νοικιάσω ...;	bo·*ro* na ni·*kia*·so ...
ball	μια μπάλα	mia *ba*·la
bicycle	ένα ποδήλατο	*e*·na po·*ţhi*·la·to
court	το γήπεδο	to *yi*·pe·ţho
racquet	μια ρακέτα	mia ra·*ke*·ta

fishing

Where are the good spots?
Πού είναι τα καλά μέρη;　　　　pu *i*·ne ta ka·*la* me·ri

Do I need a fishing permit?
Χρειάζομαι άδεια για　　　　khri·*a*·zo·me *a*·thi·a yia
ψάρεμα;　　　　*psa*·re·ma

Do you do fishing tours?
Κάνετε εκδρομές για　　　　*ka*·ne·te ek·thro·*mes* yia
ψάρεμε;　　　　*psa*·re·ma

What's the best bait?
Ποιο είναι το καλύτερο　　　　pio *i*·ne to ka·*li*·te·ro
δόλωμα;　　　　*tho*·lo·ma

Are they biting?
Τσιμπάει;　　　　tsi·*ba*·i

What kind of fish are you landing?
Τι ψάρι βγάζεις;　　　　ti *psa*·ri *vgha*·zis

How much does it weigh?
Πόσο ζυγίζει;　　　　*po*·so zi·*yi*·zi

bait	δόλωμα n	*tho*·lo·ma
fishing line	πετονιά f	pe·to·*nia*
flare	φανάρι n	fa·*na*·ri
float	φελλός f	fe·*los*
hooks	αγκίστρια n pl	a·*gi*·stri·a
lifejacket	σωσίβιο n	so·*si*·vi·o
lure	δόλωμα n	*tho*·lo·ma
rod	καλάμι n	ka·*la*·mi
sinkers	βαρύδια n pl	va·*ri*·thia

not biting?

Fishing with dynamite used to be a popular pastime in Greece, but this 'sport' has been outlawed because of its environmental impact. Look out for signs warning Απαγορεύεται η χρήση δυναμίτη (No Dynamite).

horse riding

How much is a (one-)hour ride?
Πόσο κοστίζει η ιππασία | *po·*so kos·*ti·*zi i i·pa·*si·*a
(την) ώρα; | (tin) *o·*ra

How long is the ride?
πόση ώρα διαρκεί η | *po·*si *o·*ra ṭhi·ar·*ki* i
διαδρομή με το άλογο; | ṭhi·a·ṭhro·*mi* me to *a·*lo·gho

I'm (not) an experienced rider.
(Δεν) Είμαι πεπειραμένος | (ṭhen) *i·*me pe·pi·ra·me·*nos*
αναβάτης. | a·na·*va·*tis

Can I rent a hat and boots?
Μπορώ να νοικάσω ένα | bo·*ro* na ni·*kia·*so *e·*na
καπέλο και μπότες; | ka·*pe·*lo ke *bo·*tes

bit	στομίδα f	sto·*mi·*ṭha
bridle	χαλινάρι n	kha·li·*na·*ri
canter	τριποδισμός m	tri·po·*ṭhiz·mos*
crop	μαστίγιο ιππασίας n	mas·*ti·*yi·o i·pa·*si·*as
gallop	καλπασμός m	kal·paz·*mos*
groom	ιπποκόμος m	i·po·*ko·*mos
horse	άλογο n	*a·*lo·gho
pony	πουλάρι n	pu·*la·*ri
race	κούρσα f	*kur·*sa
reins	γκέμια n pl	*ge·*mia
saddle	σέλλα f	*se·*la
stable	στάβλος m	*stav·*los
stirrup	σκάλα f	*ska·*la
trot	τροχασμός m	tro·khaz·*mos*
walk	βάδισμα n	*va·*ṭhiz·ma

soccer/football

Who plays for (Iraklis)?
Ποιος παίζει στον (Ηρακλή);   pios *pe*·zi ston (i·ra·*kli*)

He's a great (player).
Είναι μεγάλος (παίχτης).   *i*·ne me·*gha*·los (*pekh*·tis)

He played brilliantly in the match against (Italy).
Έπαιξε υπέροχα στο ματς   *e*·pek·se i·*pe*·ro·kha sto mats
εναντίον (της Ιταλίας).   e·na·*di*·on (tis i·ta·*li*·as)

Which team is at the top of the league?
Ποια ομάδα είναι στην   pia o·*ma*·ṭha *i*·ne stin
κορυφή της πρώτης εθνικής;   ko·ri·*fi* tis *pro*·tis eth·ni·*kis*

What a great/terrible team!
Τι μεγάλη/κουρέλα ομάδα!   ti me·*gha*·li/ku·*re*·la o·*ma*·ṭha

ball	μπάλα f	*ba*·la
coach	προπονητής m	pro·po·ni·*tis*
corner (kick)	κόρνερ n	*kor*·ner
expulsion	αποβολή n	a·po·vo·*li*
fan	οπαδός m	o·pa·*ṭhos*
foul	φάουλ n	*fa*·ul
free kick	φρίκικ n	*fri*·kik
goal (structure)	γκολπόστ n	gol·*post*
goalkeeper	γκολκήπερ m	gol·*ki*·per
manager	μάνατζερ m	*ma*·na·dzer
offside	οφσάιτ n	of·*sa*·it
penalty	πέναλτι n	*pe*·nal·ti
player	παίχτης m	*pekh*·tis
red card	κόκκινη κάρτα f	*ko*·ki·ni *kar*·ta
referee	διαιτητής m	ṭhi·e·ti·*tis*
throw in	αναπληρωματικός m	a·na·pli·ro·ma·ti·*kos*
yellow card	κίτρινη κάρτα n	*ki*·tri·ni *kar*·ta

tennis & table tennis

I'd like to …	Θα ήθελα να …	tha i·the·la na …
book a time to play	κλείσω ώρα να παίξω	kli·so o·ra na pek·so
play table tennis	παίξω πινγκ πονγκ	pek·so ping pong
play tennis	παίξω τένις	pek·so te·nis

Can we play at night?
Μπορούμε να παίξουμε τη νύχτα;
bo·ru·me na pek·su·me ti nikh·ta

I need my racquet restrung.
Η ρακέτα μου χρειάζεται επισκευή.
i ra·ke·ta mu khri·a·ze·te e·pis·ke·vi

ace	άσος m	a·sos
advantage	πλεονέκτημα n	ple·o·nek·ti·ma
bat	ρακέτα f	ra·ke·ta
clay	πήλινη σφαίρα f	pi·li·ni sfe·ra
fault	φάουλ n	fa·ul
game, set, match	παιγνίδι, σετ, ματς n	pegh·ni·thi set mats
grass	γρασίδι n	ghra·si·thi
hard court	σκληρό γήπεδο n	skli·ro yi·pe·tho
net	δίχτυ n	thikh·ti
ping-pong ball	μπαλάκι του πινγκ πονγκ n	ba·la·ki tu ping pong
play doubles v	παίζουμε ζευγάρια	pe·zu·me zev·gha·ria
racket	ρακέτα f	ra·ke·ta
serve v	σερβ	serv
tennis ball	μπαλάκι του τένις n	ba·la·ki tu te·nis
table-tennis table	τραπέζι του πινγκ πονγκ n	tra·pe·zi tu ping pong

water sports

Can I hire (a) …?	Μπορώ να νοικιάσω …;	bo·ro na ni·kia·so …
boat	μια βάρκα	mia var·ka
canoe	ένα κανό	e·na ka·no
kayak	ένα καγιάκ	e·na ka·yiak
life jacket	ένα σωσίβιο	e·na so·si·vi·o
snorkelling gear	μια στολή κατάδυσης	mia sto·li ka·ta·thi·sis
water-skis	θαλάσσια σκι	tha·la·si·a ski
wetsuit	αδιάβροχη στολή	a·thiav·ro·hi sto·li

Are there any …?	Υπάρχουν …;	i·par·khun …
reefs	ξέρες	kse·res
rips	δύνες	thi·nes
water hazards	θαλάσσιοι κίνδυνοι	tha·la·si·i kin·thi·ni

guide	οδηγός m&f	o·thi·ghos
motorboat	βάρκα με μηχανή f	var·ka me mi·kha·ni
oars	κουπιά n pl	ku·pia
sailboarding	γουιντσέρφινγκ n	ghu·id·ser·fing
sailing boat	βάρκα με ιστία f	var·ka me i·sti·a
surfboard	σέρφμπορντ n	serf·bord
surfing	σέρφινγκ n	ser·fing
wave	κύμα n	ki·ma

diving in

During the summer months, ask around for diving classes:

Is there a diving school here?

Υπάρχει σχολή καταδύσεων εδώ;	i·par·hi skho·li ka·ta·thi·se·on e·tho

Do you offer diving lessons (in English)?

Προσφέρετε μαθήματα καταδύσεων (στα αγγλικά);	pros·fe·re·te ma·thi·ma·ta ka·ta·thi·se·on (sta ang·gli·ka)

hiking

πεζοπορία

Where can I ...?	Πού μπορώ να ...;	pu bo·ro na ...
buy supplies	αγοράσω προμήθειες	a·gho·ra·so pro·mi·thi·es
find someone who knows this area	βρω κάποιον που ξέρει αυτή την περιοχή	vro ka·pion pu kse·ri af·ti tin pe·ri·o·hi
get a map	πάρω ένα χάρτη	pa·ro e·na khar·ti
hire hiking gear	νοικιάσω εξοπλισμό για πεζοπορία	ni·kia·so ek·so·pliz·mo yia pe·zo·po·ri·a

How ...?	Πόσο ...;	po·so ...
high is the climb	ψηλό είναι το ανέβασμα	psi·lo i·ne to a·ne·vaz·ma
long is the trail	μακρύ είναι το μονοπάτι	ma·kri i·ne to mo·no·pa·ti

Do we need to take ...?	Χρειάζεται να πάρουμε ...;	khri·a·ze·te na pa·ru·me ...
bedding	σκεπάσματα	ske·paz·ma·ta
food	φαγητό	fa·yi·to
water	νερό	ne·ro

Do we need a guide?
Χρειαζόμαστε οδηγό;   khri·a·zo·ma·ste o·thi·gho

Are there guided treks?
Υπάρχουν μονοπάτια   i·par·khun mo·no·pa·tia
με σήματα;   me si·ma·ta

Is there a path to (Profitis Ilias)?
Υπάρχει μονοπάτι για   i·par·hi mo·no·pa·ti yia
(τον Προφήτη Ηλία);   (ton pro·fi·ti i·li·a)

Is it safe?
Είναι ασφαλές; *i*·ne as·fa·*les*

Is it steep?
Είναι απόκρημνο; *i*·ne a·*po*·krim·no

Are there any rockfalls?
Πέφτουν πουθενά πέτρες; *pef*·tun pu·the·*na* pet·res

Is there a hut?
Υπάρχει κανένα καλύβι; i·*par*·hi ka·*ne*·na ka·*li*·vi

When does it get dark?
Πότε σκοτεινιάζει; *po*·te sko·ti·*nia*·zi

Is the track …?	Είναι ο δρόμος …;	*i*·ne o ţhro·mos …
(well-)	σημαδεμένος	si·ma·ţhe·*me*·nos
marked	(καλά)	(ka·*la*)
open	ανοιχτός	a·nikh·*tos*
scenic	γραφικός	ghra·fi·*kos*

Which is the …	Ποια είναι η πιο	pia *i*·ne i pio
route?	… διαδρομή;	… ţhi·a·ţhro·*mi*
easiest	εύκολη	*ef*·ko·li
most interesting	ενδιαφέρουσα	en·ţhia·*fe*·ru·sa
shortest	κοντινή	ko·di·*ni*

Where can I	Πού μπορώ	pu bo·*ro*
find the …?	να βρω το …	na vro to …
camping	χώρο του	*kho*·ro tu
ground	κάμπινγκ	*kam*·ping
nearest village	πιο κοντινό	pio ko·di·*no*
	χωριό	kho·*rio*
showers	ντουζ	duz
toilets	την τουαλέτα	tin tu·a·*le*·ta

Where have you come from?
Από πού ήρθες; a·*po* pu *ir*·thes

How long did it take?
Πόση ώρα σου πήρε; *po*·si *o*·ra su *pi*·re

Does this path go to …?
Πηγαίνει αυτό το pi·*ye*·ni af·*to* to
μονοπάτι στο …; mo·no·*pa*·ti sto …

Can I go through here?

Μπορώ να πάω μέσα
από εδώ;

bo·*ro* na *pa*·o *me*·sa
a·*po* e·*tho*

Is the water OK to drink?

Είναι εντάξει το νερό
για να πιω;

i·ne e·*dak*·si to ne·*ro*
yia na pio

I'm lost.

Χάθηκα.

kha·thi·ka

beach

παραλία

Where's the ...	Πού είναι η ...	pu *i*·ne i ...
beach?	παραλία;	pa·ra·*li*·a
best	καλύτερη	ka·*li*·te·ri
nearest	κοντινότερη	ko·di·*no*·te·ri
public	δημόσια	thi·*mo*·si·a

Where's the nudist beach?

Πού είναι η πλαζ γυμνιστών;

pu *i*·ne i plaz yim·ni·*ston*

Do we have to pay?

Πρέπει να πληρώσουμε;

pre·pi na pli·*ro*·su·me

What time is high/low tide?

Τι ώρα είναι η παλίρροια/
άμπωτις;

ti *o*·ra *i*·ne i pa·*li*·ri·a/
a·bo·tis

Is it safe to dive/swim here?

Είναι ασφαλές να κάμω
βουτιές/κολυμπήσω εδώ;

i·ne as·fa·*les* na *ka*·mo
vu·*ties*/ko·li·*bi*·so e·*tho*

listen for ...

Είναι επικίνδυνο!
i·ne e·pi·*kin*·thi·no **It's dangerous!**

Πρόσεχε το υπόγειο ρεύμα!
pro·*se*·he to i·*po*·yi·o *rev*·ma **Be careful of the undertow!**

outdoors

153

| Απαγορεύεται το κολύμπι | a·pa·gho·*re*·ve·te to ko·*li*·bi | **No Swimming** |
| Απαγορεύονται οι βουτιές | a·pa·gho·*re*·vo·de i vu·*ties* | **No Diving** |

Are there any ...?	Υπάρχουν ...;	i·*par*·khun ...
currents	ρεύματα	*rev*·ma·ta
jelly fish	μέδουσες	*me*·ţhu·ses
rocks	βράχια	*vra*·hia
sea urchins	αχινοί	a·hi·*ni*

How much for a/an ...?	Πόσο για μια ...;	*po*·so yia mia ...
chair	καρέκλα	ka·*re*·kla
hut	καλύβα	ka·*li*·va
umbrella	ομπρέλα	o·*bre*·la

weather

καιρός

What's the weather like?

Πώς είναι ο καιρός; pos *i*·ne o ke·*ros*

What will the weather be like tomorrow?

Πώς θα είναι ο καιρός αύριο; pos tha *i*·ne o ke·*ros* av·ri·o

It's ...	Είναι ...	*i*·ne ...
cloudy	συννεφιά	si·ne·*fia*
dry	ξηρασία	ksi·ra·*si*·a
fine	καλός καιρός	ka·*los* ke·*ros*
freezing	παγωνιά	pa·gho·*nia*
humid	υγρασία	i·ghra·*si*·a
mild	μαλακός καιρός	ma·la·*kos* ke·*ros*
sunny	λιακάδα	lia·*ka*·ţha

It's ...		
raining	Βρέχει.	*vre*·hi
snowing	Χιονίζει.	hio·*ni*·zi
windy	Φυσάει.	fi·*sa*·i
drizzling	Ψιχαλίζει.	psi·kha·*li*·zi

It's ...	Κάνει ...	*ka*·ni ...
cold	κρύο	*kri*·o
hot	πολλή ζέστη	po·*li* ze·sti
warm	ζέστη	*ze*·sti

Where can I buy a/an ...?	Πού μπορώ να αγοράσω ...;	pu bo·*ro* na a·gho·*ra*·so ...
rain jacket	ένα αδιάβροχο	*e*·na a·*thiav*·ro·kho
umbrella	μια ομπρέλα	mia o·*bre*·la

weathering the local storms

heatwave	καύσωνας m	*kaf*·so·nas
strong northerly wind	μελτέμι n	mel·*te*·mi
strong cold wind	βαρδάρης m	var·*tha*·ris
thunderstorm	καταιγίδα f	ka·te·*yi*·tha

flora & fauna

χλωρίδα και πανίδα

What ... is that?	Τι ... είναι εκείνο;	ti ... *i*·ne e·*ki*·no
animal	ζώο	*zo*·o
flower	λουλούδι	lu·*lu*·thi
plant	φυτό	fi·*to*
tree	δέντρο	*the*·dro

What's it used for?

Σε τι χρησιμοποιείται;   se ti khri·si·mo·pi·*i*·te

Can you eat the fruit?

Μπορείς να φας τον καρπό;   bo·*ris* na fas ton kar·*po*

Is it ...?	Είναι ...;	*i*·ne ...
common	κοινό	ki·*no*
dangerous	επικίνδυνο	e·pi·*kin*·thi·no
endangered	υπό εξαφάνιση	i·*po* ek·sa·*fa*·ni·si
poisonous	δηλητηριώδες	thi·li·ti·ri·*o*·thes
protected	προστατευόμενο	pro·sta·te·*vo*·me·no

local plants & animals

basil	βασιλικός m	va·si·li·*kos*
carnation	γαρύφαλο n	gha·*ri*·fa·lo
carob	χαρούπι n	kha·*ru*·pi
Dalmatian pelican	Δαλματικός πελεκάνος m	thal·ma·ti·*kos* pe·le·*ka*·nos
dolphin	δελφίνι n	thel·*fi*·ni
falcon	γεράκι n	ye·*ra*·ki
fig	σύκο n	*si*·ko
iris	κρίνος m	*kri*·nos
lizard	σαύρα f	*sav*·ra
monk seal	φώκια f	*fo*·kia
olive	ελιά f	e·*lia*
orchid	ορχιδέα f	or·hi·*the*·a
pine	πεύκο n	*pef*·ko
rose	τριαντάφυλλο n	tri·a·*da*·fi·lo
sea gull	γλάρος m	*gla*·ros
sea turtle	θαλάσσια χελώνα f	tha·*la*·si·a khe·*lo*·na
snake	φίδι n	*fi*·thi
swallow	χελιδόνι n	he·li·*tho*·ni
wildflowers	αγριολούλουδα n pl	a·ghri·o·*lu*·lu·tha

basics

βασικά

breakfast	πρόγευμα n	*pro*·yev·ma
lunch	γεύμα n	*yev*·ma
dinner	δείπνο n	*thip*·no
snack	μεζεδάκι n	me·ze·*tha*·ki
eat v	τρώγω	*tro*·gho
drink v	πίνω	*pi*·no

I'd like …	Θα ήθελα …	tha *i*·the·la …
Please.	Παρακαλώ.	pa·ra·ka·*lo*
Thank you.	Ευχαριστώ.	ef·kha·ri·*sto*
I'm starving!	Πεινώ τρομερά!	pi·*no* tro·me·*ra*
Enjoy your meal.	Καλή όρεξη.	ka·*li* o·rek·si

food glorious food

For breakfast, Greeks usually have a hot cup of milk, tea or coffee with φρυγανιά fri·gha·*nia* (dry sweet toast). If eating out, a typical order is a τυρόπιτα ti·*ro*·pi·ta (cheese pie) or σπανακόπιτα spa·na·*ko*·pi·ta (spinach pie).

Lunch, the day's main meal, is an early afternoon affair, usually followed by a απογευματινός ύπνος a·po·yev·ma·ti·*nos* ip·nos (siesta). A typical lunch will be a meat dish with rice, pasta or potatoes, or fish with a side salad. Legume dishes such as φακές fa·*kes* (lentil broth) and φασολάδα fa·so·*la*·tha (bean broth) are especially popular in winter.

Dinner is a light meal eaten between eight and nine o'clock.

Dessert is rarely served. Instead, seasonal fresh fruit finishes off a meal.

finding a place to eat

Can you recommend a ...?	Μπορείς να συστήσεις ένα ...;	bo·ris na si·sti·sis e·na ...
bar	μπαρ	bar
café	καφεστιατόριο	ka·fe·sti·a·to·ri·o
restaurant	ρεστωράν	re·sto·ran
Where would you go for (a) ...?	Πού θα πήγαινες για ...;	pu tha pi·ye·nes yia ...
celebration	μια γιορτή	mia yior·ti
cheap meal	ένα φτηνό γεύμα	e·na fti·no yev·ma
local specialities	τοπικές λιχουδιές	to·pi·kes li·khu·thies
I'd like to reserve a table for ...	Θα ήθελα να κρατήσω ένα τραπέζι για ...	tha i·the·la na kra·ti·so e·na tra·pe·zi yia ...
(two) people	(δύο) άτομα	(thi·o) a·to·ma
(eight) o'clock	τις (οχτώ)	stis (okh·to)

listen for ...

Δεν υπάρχει άδειο τραπέζι. then i·par·hi a·thio tra·pe·zi	We're full.
Κλείσαμε. kli·sa·me	We're closed.
Μια στιγμή. mia stigh·mi	One moment.
Πού θα θέλατε να καθίσετε; pu tha the·la·te na ka·thi·se·te	Where would you like to sit?
Τι μπορώ να σας φέρω; ti bo·ro na sas fe·ro	What can I get for you?
Ορίστε! o·ri·ste	Here you go!

I'd like (a/the) ..., please.	Θα ήθελα ..., παρακαλώ.	tha *i*·the·la ... pa·ra·ka·*lo*
children's menu	ένα μενού για παιδιά	*e*·na me·*nu* yia pe·*thia*
drink list	τον κατάλογο με τα ποτά	ton ka·*ta*·lo·gho me ta po·*ta*
half portion	μισή μερίδα	mi·*si* me·*ri*·tha
menu (in English)	ένα μενού (στα αγγλικά)	*e*·na me·*nu* (sta ang·gli·*ka*)
mixed plate	μια ποικιλία	mia pi·ki·*li*·a
nonsmoking	στους μη καπνίζοντες	stus mi kap·*ni*·zo·des
smoking	στους καπνίζοντες	stus kap·*ni*·zo·des
table for (five)	ένα τραπέζι για (πέντε)	*e*·na tra·*pe*·zi yia (*pe*·de)
table outside	ένα τραπέζι έξω	*e*·na tra·*pe*·zi *ek*·so

Are you still serving food?
Σερβίρετε ακόμη φαγητό;   ser·*vi*·re·te a·*ko*·mi fa·ghi·*to*

How long is the wait?
Πόση ώρα θα περιμένουμε;   *po*·si o·ra tha pe·ri·*me*·nu·me

eateries

Act like a local and order some μερικά παξιμάδια me·ri·*ka* pak·si·*ma*·thia (dried bread) for dunking in your coffee or other hot drinks the next time you're at one of these eateries:

καφετηρία f	ka·fe·ti·*ri*·a	cafeteria
καφενείο n	ka·fe·*ni*·o	coffee shop
γλακτοπωλείο n	gha·lak·to·po·*li*·o	dairy shop
φαστφουντάδικο n	fast·fun·*da*·thi·ko	fast-food eatery
ουζερί n	u·ze·*ri*	ouzeria
οινοπωλείο n	i·no·po·*li*·o	liquor shop
ταβέρνα f	ta·*ver*·na	taverna

at the restaurant

What would you recommend?
Τι θα συνιστούσες;   ti tha si·ni·*stu*·ses

What are you serving today?
Τι έχετε σήμερα;   ti *e*·he·te si·me·ra

What's that called?
Πώς το λένε αυτό;   pos to *le*·ne af·*to*

What's in that dish?
Τι περιέχει αυτό το φαγητό;   ti pe·ri·*e*·hi af·*to* to fa·ghi·*to*

I'll have that.
Θα πάρω αυτό.   tha *pa*·ro af·*to*

listen for ...

Πώς θα το θέλατε ψημένο;
pos tha to *the*·la·te
psi·*me*·no

How would you like that cooked?

Σας αρέσει ...;
sas a·*re*·si ...

Do you like ...?

Συνιστώ ...
si·ni·*sto* ...

I suggest the ...

Is it savoury or sweet?
Είναι πικάντικο ή γλυκό;
        i·ne pi·*ka*·di·ko i ghli·*ko*

I'd like it hot, please.
Θα το ήθελα ζεστό,
παρακαλώ.
        tha to *i*·the·la ze·*sto*
        pa·ra·ka·*lo*

Does it take long to prepare?
Θα αργήσει να ετοιμαστεί;
        tha ar·*ghi*·si na e·ti·ma·*sti*

Is it self-serve?
Είναι σελφ σέρβις;
        i·ne self *ser*·vis

Is there a cover charge?
Υπάρχει προσαύξηση τιμής;
        i·*par*·hi pro·*saf*·ksi·si ti·*mis*

Is service included in the bill?
Συμπεριλαμβάνεται
και η εξυπηρέτηση στο
λογαριασμό;
        si·be·ri·lam·*va*·ne·te
        ke i ek·si·pi·*re*·ti·si sto
        lo·gha·riaz·*mo*

Are these complimentary?
Είναι αυτά δωρεάν;
        i·ne af·*ta* tho·re·*an*

How much is that?
Πόσο κάνει αυτό;
        po·so *ka*·ni af·*to*

I'd like (a/the) ...	Θα ήθελα ...	tha *i*·the·la ...
chicken	το κοτόπουλο	to ko·*to*·pu·lo
local speciality	μια τοπική	mia to·pi·*ki*
	λιχουδιά	li·khu·*thia*
meal fit for	ένα λουκούλλειο	e·na lu·*ku*·li·o
a king	γεύμα	*yev*·ma
menu	το μενού	to me·*nu*
sandwich	ένα σάντουιτς	e·na sa·du·its
that dish	εκείνο το φαγητό	e·*ki*·no to fa·yi·*to*

look for ...

Ορεκτικά	o·rek·ti·*ka*	Appetisers
Σούπες	*su*·pes	Soups
Προδόρπια	pro·*thor*·pi·a	Entrees
Σαλάτες	sa·*la*·tes	Salads
Κύρια φαγητά	*ki*·ri·a fa·yi·*ta*	Main Courses
Ψητά της ώρας	psi·*ta* tis o·ras	Freshly Grilled
		Dishes
Μαγειρεμένα	ma·yi·re·*me*·na	Precooked
φαγητά	fa·yi·*ta*	Dishes
Σαλάτες	sa·*la*·tes	Side Dishes
Μακαρόνια	ma·ka·*ro*·nia	Pasta
Ψάρια	*psa*·ria	Fish
Θαλασσινά	tha·la·si·*na*	Seafood
Επιδόρπια	e·pi·*thor*·pi·a	Desserts
Ποτά	po·*ta*	Drinks
Απεριτίφ	a·pe·ri·*tif*	Apéritifs
Αναψυκτικά	a·nap·sik·ti·*ka*	Soft Drinks
Οινοπνευματώδη	i·nop·nev·ma·to·*thi*	Spirits
ποτά	po·*ta*	
Μπύρες	*bi*·res	Beers
Σαμπάνια	sam·*pa*·nia	Sparkling Wines
Άσπρο κρασί	*as*·pro kra·*si*	White Wines
Κόκκινο κρασί	*ko*·ki·no kra·*si*	Red Wines
Επιδόρπια κρασιά	e·pi·*thor*·pi·a kra·*sia*	Dessert Wines
Ρετσίνα	ret·*si*·na	Retsina
Χωνευτικά	kho·nef·ti·*ka*	Digestifs

street food

If you've got the munchies, try one of these snacks:

κουλούρι n	ku·*lu*·ri	crisp sesame-coated bread rings
γύρος m	*yi*·ros	spit-roast lamb
πασατέμπο n	pa·sa·*tem*·po	pumpkin seeds
σουβλάκι n	suv·*la*·ki	skewered marinated meat
σπανακόπιτα f	spa·na·*ko*·pi·ta	spinach & cheese pie
τυρόπιτα f	ti·*ro*·pi·ta	cheese pie
ψημένα κάστανα n pl	psi·*me*·na *ka*·sta·ma	roasted chestnuts
ψημένο καλαμπόκι n	psi·*me*·no ka·la·*bo*·ki	roasted corn

I'd like it with/ without …	Θα το ήθελα με/ χωρίς …	tha to *i*·the·la me/ kho·*ris* …
cheese	τυρί	ti·*ri*
chilli	πιπεριά	pi·pe·*ria*
chilli sauce	σάλτσα πιπεριάς	*salt*·sa pi·pe·*rias*
garlic	σκόρδο	*skor*·tho
ketchup	σάλτσα	*salt*·sa
nuts	καρύδια	ka·*ri*·thia
oil	λάδι	*la*·thi
pepper	πιπέρι	pi·*pe*·ri
salt	αλάτι	a·*la*·ti
tomato sauce	σάλτσα ντομάτας	*salt*·sa do·*ma*·tas
vinegar	ξύδι	*ksi*·thi

For additional items, see the **culinary reader**, page 175.
For other specific meal requests, see **vegetarian & special meals**, page 173.

eating out

163

at the table

Please bring (a/the) …	Παρακαλώ φέρε …	pa·ra·ka·*lo* fe·re …
bill	το λογαριασμό	to lo·gha·riaz·*mo*
cloth	ένα τραπεζομάντηλο	*e*·na tra·pe·zo·*ma*·di·lo
glass	ένα ποτήρι	*e*·na po·*ti*·ri
serviette	μια πετσέτα	mia pet·*se*·ta
wineglass	ένα ποτήρι κρασιού	*e*·na po·*ti*·ri kra·*siu*

This is …	Αυτό είναι …	af·*to* i·ne …
(too) cold	(πολύ) κρύο	(po·*li*) kri·o
spicy	πιπεράτο	pi·pe·*ra*·to
superb	καταπληκτικό	ka·ta·plik·ti·*ko*

There's a mistake in the bill.
Υπάρχει κάποιο λάθος
στο λογαριασμό.
i·*par*·hi ka·pio la·thos
sto lo·gha·riaz·*mo*

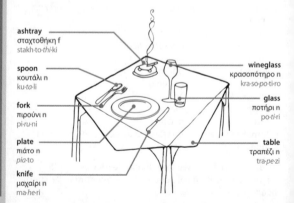

ashtray
σταχτοθήκη f
stakh·to·*thi*·ki

spoon
κουτάλι n
ku·*ta*·li

fork
πιρούνι n
pi·*ru*·ni

plate
πιάτο n
pia·to

knife
μαχαίρι n
ma·*he*·ri

wineglass
κρασοπότηρο n
kra·so·po·*ti*·ro

glass
ποτήρι n
po·*ti*·ri

table
τραπέζι n
tra·*pe*·zi

talking food

I love this dish.
Μου αρέσει πολύ αυτό   mu a·re·si po·li af·to
το φαγητό.   to fa·yi·to

I love the local cuisine.
Μου αρέσει η τοπική κουζίνα.   mu a·re·si i to·pi·ki ku·zi·na

That was delicious!
Ήταν νοστιμότατο!   i·tan no·sti·mo·ta·to

My compliments to the chef.
Τα συγχαρητήριά μου στο σεφ.   ta sing·kha·ri·ti·ri·a mu sto sef

methods of preparation

μέθοδος παρασκευής

I'd like it …	Θα το ήθελα …	tha to i·the·la …
I don't want it …	Δεν το θέλω …	then to the·lo …
boiled	βρασμένο	vraz·me·no
broiled	ψημένο στη σχάρα	psi·me·no sti skha·ra
deep-fried	τηγανισμένο σε καυτό λίπος	ti·gha·niz·me·no se kaf·to li·pos
fried	τηγανητό	ti·gha·ni·to
grilled	στα κάρβουνα	sta kar·vu·na
mashed	πουρέ	pu·re
reheated	ξαναζεσταμένο	ksa·na·ze·sta·me·no
steamed	βρασμένο στον ατμό	vraz·me·no ston at·mo

how would you like that?

medium	ψημένο	psi·me·no
	κανονικά	ka·no·ni·ka
rare	μισοψημένο	mi·sop·si·me·no
well-done	καλοψημένο	ka·lop·si·me·no

nonalcoholic drinks

… mineral water	… μεταλλικό νερό n	… me·ta·li·ko ne·ro
sparkling	γαζόζα	gha·zo·za
still	χωρίς ανθρακικό	kho·ris an·thra·ki·ko
(hot) water	(ζεστό) νερό n	(ze·sto) ne·ro
bottled water	εμφιαλωμένο νερό n	em·fi·a·lo·me·no ne·ro
tap water	νερό βρύσης n	ne·ro vri·sis
apple juice	χυμός μήλου m	hi·mos mi·lu
hot chocolate	ζεστό κακάο n	ze·sto ka·ka·o
herbal tea	τσάι από βότανα n	tsa·i a·po vo·ta·na
morello cherry juice	βισινάδα f	vi·si·na·tha
orange juice	χυμός πορτοκάλι m	hi·mos por·to·ka·li
soft drink	αναψυκτικό n	a·nap·sik·ti·ko
(cup of) tea	(ένα φλυτζάνι) τσάι n	(e·na fli·dza·ni) tsa·i
(cup of) coffee	(ένα φλυτζάνι) καφέ m	(e·na fli·dza·ni) ka·fe
with milk	με γάλα	me gha·la
with lemon	με λεμόνι	me le·mo·ni
sweetened	με ζάχαρη	me za·kha·ri
unsweetened	χωρίς ζάχαρη	kho·ris za·kha·ri

coffee time

black	χωρίς γάλα	kho·ris gha·la
decaffeinated	χωρίς καφεΐνη	kho·ris ka·fe·i·ni
Greek	ελληνικός	e·li·ni·kos
iced	φραπέ	fra·pe
instant	στιγμιαίος	stigh·mi·e·os
medium	μέτριος	me·tri·os
plain (no sugar)	σκέτος	ske·tos
strong	δυνατός	thi·na·tos
sweet	γλυκός	ghli·kos
weak	ελαφρύς	e·la·fris
white	με γάλα	me gha·la

κουμανταρία f	ku·ma·da·*ri*·a	traditional Cypriot wine
ζιβανία f	zi·va·*ni*·a	a clear Cypriot apéritif made from grapes
ούζο n	*u*·zo	spirit distilled from grapes with a strong aniseed flavour
ρετσίνα f	ret·*si*·na	pine-resinated wine, served chilled
τσίπουρο n	*tsi*·pu·ro	spirit made from grapes, high in alcohol
τσικουδιά f	tsi·ku·*thia*	Crete's version of τσίπουρο

alcoholic drinks

οινοπνευματώδη ποτά

To get drinks at a bar in Greece, you don't have to memorise numerous standard measurements – standard serves are ordered using 'one'. For example: μία μπύρα *mi*·a *bi*·ra (one beer) or ένα ούζο *e*·na *u*·zo (one ouzo). See also **numbers & amounts**, page 35.

beer	μπύρα f	*bi*·ra
brandy	μπράντι n	*bran*·di
champagne	σαμπάνια f	sam·*pa*·nia
cocktail	κοκτέηλ n	kok·*te*·il
a shot of ...	ένα ... m	*e*·na ...
gin	τζιν	dzin
rum	ρούμι	*ru*·mi
whisky	ουίσκι	u·*i*·ski

a shot of ...	μία ... f	mia ...
tequila	τεκίλα	te·ki·la
vodka	βότκα	vot·ka

a bottle/glass	ένα μπουκάλι/	e·na bu·ka·li/
of ... wine	ποτήρι ... κρασί n	po·ti·ri ... kra·si
dessert	επιδόρπιο	e·pi·thor·pi·o
dry	ξηρό	ksi·ro
red	κόκκινο	ko·ki·no
rosé	ροζέ	ro·ze
sparkling	σαμπάνια	sam·pa·nia
sweet	γλυκό	ghli·ko
white	άσπρο	a·spro

a ... of beer	ένα ... μπύρα n	e·na ... bi·ra
glass	ποτήρι	po·ti·ri
pint	μεγάλο ποτήρι	me·gha·lo po·ti·ri
small bottle	μικρό μπουκάλι	mi·kro bu·ka·li
large bottle	μεγάλο μπουκάλι	me·gha·lo bu·ka·li

a ... of beer	μια ... μπύρα f	mia ... bi·ra
carafe	καράφα	ka·ra·fa
jug	κανάτα	ka·na·ta

give it a go

Try more traditional Greek delicacies from these eateries:

αρτοποιείο n	ar·to·pi·i·o	bakery
ζαχαροπλαστείο n	za·kha·ro·pla·sti·o	patisserie or sweet shop
φαστφουντάδικο n	fast·fu·da·thi·ko	fast-food eatery
καντίνα f	kan·ti·na	canteen or food van
πιτσαρία f	pit·sa·ri·a	barbecue-style eatery
σουβλατζίδικο n	suv·lat·zi·thi·ko	kebab and souvlaki shop
τυροπωλείο n	ti·ro·po·li·o	cheese shop
ψαροταβέρνα f	psa·ro·ta·ver·na	taverna serving fish
ψησταριά f	psi·sta·ria	eatery serving spit-roasted meats

FOOD

168

in the bar

Excuse me!
Συγνώμη!   sigh·*no*·mi

I'm next.
Είναι η δική μου σειρά.   *i*·ne i ţhi·*ki* mu si·*ra*

I'll have …
Θα πάρω …   tha *pa*·ro …

Same again, please.
Από τα ίδια, παρακαλώ.   a·*po* ta *i*·thia pa·ra·ka·*lo*

No ice, thanks.
Όχι πάγο, ευχαριστώ.   *o*·hi *pa*·gho ef·kha·ri·*sto*

I'll buy you a drink.
Θα σε κεράσω εγώ.   tha se ke·*ra*·so e·*gho*

What would you like?
Τι θα ήθελες;   ti tha *i*·the·les

I don't drink alcohol.
Δεν πίνω αλκοόλ.   ţhen *pi*·no al·ko·*ol*

It's my round.
Είναι η σειρά μου.   *i*·ne i si·*ra* mu

How much is that?
Πόσο κάνει αυτό;   *po*·so *ka*·ni af·*to*

Do you serve meals here?
Σερβίρετε φαγητό εδώ;   ser·*vi*·re·te fa·yi·*to* e·ţho

listen for …

Τι θα πάρεις; ti tha *pa*·ris	**What are you having?**
Νομίζω ήπιες αρκετά. no·*mi*·zo *i*·pies ar·ke·*ta*	**I think you've had enough.**
Τελευταίες παραγγελίες. te·lef·*te*·es pa·ra·ghe·*li*·es	**Last orders.**
Τα ποτά τα κερνάει το κατάστημα. ta po·*ta* ta ker·*na*·i to ka·*ta*·sti·ma	**Drinks are on the house.**

eating out

169

drinking up

Cheers!
Εις υγείαν! — is i·*yi*·an

I feel fantastic!
Είμαι στα κέφια μου! — *i*·me sta *ke*·fia mu

I think I've had one too many.
Νομίζω ήπια παραπάνω. — no·*mi*·zo *i*·pia pa·ra·*pa*·no

I'm feeling drunk.
Μέθυσα. — *me*·thi·sa

I'm pissed.
Είμαι σκνίπα στο μεθύσι. — *i*·me *skni*·pa sto me·*thi*·si

I feel ill.
Δεν αισθάνομαι καλά. — then es·*tha*·no·me ka·*la*

Where's the toilet?
Πού είναι η τουαλέτα; — pu *i*·ne i tu·a·*le*·ta

I'm tired, I'd better go home.
Είμαι κουρασμένος/
κουρασμένη, καλύτερα
να πάω σπίτι. m/f
— *i*·me ku·raz·*me*·nos/
ku·raz·*me*·ni ka·*li*·te·ra
na *pa*·o *spi*·ti

Can you call a taxi for me?
Μπορείς να μου καλέσεις
ένα ταξί; — bo·*ris* na mu ka·*le*·sis
e·na tak·*si*

I don't think you should drive.
Νομίζω ότι δεν πρέπει να
οδηγήσεις. — no·*mi*·zo *o*·ti then *pre*·pi na
o·thi·*yi*·sis

---

pot plant

When you're in Greece, make sure that you don't eat the
decoration – βασιλικός va·si·li·*kos* (basil) is favoured as an
ornamental plant and is rarely used in cooking.

φροντίζοντας για τον εαυτό σου

What's the local speciality?
Ποιες είναι οι τοπικές
λιχουδιές;
pies *i*·ne i to·pi·*kes*
li·khu·*thies*

What's that?
Τι είναι εκείνο;
ti *i*·ne e·*ki*·no

Can I taste it?
Μπορώ να το δοκιμάσω;
bo·*ro* na to tho·ki·*ma*·so

Can I have a bag, please?
Μπορώ να έχω μια
σακούλα, παρακαλώ;
bo·*ro* na *e*·kho mia
sa·*ku*·la pa·ra·ka·*lo*

How much is (a kilo of cheese)?
Πόσο κάνει (ένα κιλό τυρί);
po·so *ka*·ni (*e*·na ki·*lo* ti·*ri*)

I'd like …	Θα ήθελα …	tha *i*·the·la …
(three) pieces	(τρία) κομμάτια	(*tri*·a) ko·*ma*·tia
(six) slices	(έξι) φέτες	(*ek*·si) *fe*·tes
that one	εκείνο	e·*ki*·no
this one	αυτό	af·*to*

Less.	Πιο λίγο.	pio *li*·gho
A bit more.	Λιγάκι πιο πολύ.	li·*gha*·ki pio po·*li*
Enough.	Αρκετά.	ar·ke·*ta*

For more on quantities, see **numbers & amounts**, page 35.

---

listen for …

Δεν υπάρχει άλλο.	
then i·*par*·hi *a*·lo	**There isn't any.**
Μπορώ να σας βοηθήσω;	
bo·*ro* na sas vo·i·*thi*·so	**Can I help you?**
Τι θα θέλατε;	
ti tha *the*·la·te	**What would you like?**
Τίποτε άλλο;	
ti·po·te *a*·lo	**Anything else?**

cooked	μαγειρεμένο	ma·yi·re·*me*·no
cured	παστό	pa·*sto*
dried	ξηρό	ksi·*ro*
fresh	φρέσκο	*fre*·sko
frozen	κατεψυγμένο	ka·tep·sigh·*me*·no
grilled	στα κάρβουνα	sta *kar*·vu·na
raw	ωμό	o·*mo*
roasted	ψητό	psi·*to*
savoury	πικάντικο	pi·*ka*·di·ko
smoked	καπνιστό	kap·ni·*sto*
sweet	γλυκό	ghli·*ko*

Do you have ...?	Έχετε κάτι ...;	e·he·te *ka*·ti ...
anything cheaper	πιο φτηνό	pio fti·*no*
other kinds	διαφορετικό	ţhia·fo·re·ti·*ko*

Where can I find the ... section?	Πού μπορώ να βρω το μέρος με ...;	pu bo·*ro* na vro to *me*·ros me ...
bread	το ψωμί	to pso·*mi*
dairy	τα γαλακτικά	ta gha·lak·ti·*ka*
fish	τα ψάρια	ta *psa*·ria
frozen goods	τα κατεψυγμένα	ta ka·tep·sigh·*me*·na
fruit and vegetable	τα φρούτα και τα λαχανικά	ta *fru*·ta ke ta la·kha·ni·*ka*
meat	το κρέας	to *kre*·as
poultry	τα πουλερικά	ta pu·le·ri·*ka*
seafood	τα θαλασσινά	ta tha·la·si·*na*

Could I please borrow a ...?	Μπορώ παρακαλώ να δανειστώ ...;	bo·*ro* pa·ra·ka·*lo* na ţha·ni·*sto* ...
I need a ...	Χρειάζομαι ...	khri·*a*·zo·me ...
chopping board	μια σανίδα κοπής	mia sa·*ni*·ţha ko·*pis*
frying pan	ένα τηγάνι	*e*·na ti·*gha*·ni
knife	ένα μαχαίρι	*e*·na ma·*he*·ri
saucepan	μια κατσαρόλα	mia kat·sa·*ro*·la

For more cooking implements, see the **dictionary**.

vegetarian & special meals
φαγητά για χορτοφάγους και ειδικά φαγητά

ordering food

Do you have ... food? Έχετε φαγητό ...; *e·he·te fa·yi·to ...*

halal	χαλάλ	kha·*lal*
kosher	κόσια	*ko*·si·a
Lent	Σαρακοστιανό	sa·ra·ko·stia·*no*
pulse-based	με όσπρια	me *os*·pri·a
vegetarian	για χορτοφάγους	yia khor·to·*fa*·ghus

Is there a ... restaurant near here?
Υπάρχει ένα εστιατόριο ... *i·par·hi e·na e·sti·a·to·ri·o ...*
εδώ κοντά; *e·tho ko·da*

Is it cooked in/with ...?
Είναι μαγειρεμένο *i·ne ma·yi·re·me·no*
σε/με ...; *se/me ...*

Could you prepare a meal without ...?
Μπορείτε να κάνετε *bo·ri·te na ka·ne·te*
φαγητό χωρίς ...; *fa·yi·to kho·ris ...*

I don't eat ...	Δεν τρώω ...	*then tro·gho ...*
butter	βούτυρο	*vu*·ti·ro
eggs	αβγά	av·*gha*
fish	ψάρι	*psa*·ri
fish stock	ζουμί από ψάρι	zu·*mi* a·po *psa*·ri
lamb	αρνί	ar·*ni*
(red) meat	(κόκκινο) κρέας	(*ko*·ki·no) *kre*·as
meat stock	ζουμί από κρέας	zu·*mi* a·po *kre*·as
oil	λάδι	*la*·thi
olives	ελιές	e·*lies*
pork	χοιρινό	hi·ri·*no*
poultry	πουλερικά	pu·le·ri·*ka*

Is this …?	Είναι αυτό …;	i·ne af·to …
decaffeinated	χωρίς καφεΐνη	kho·ris ka·fe·i·ni
gluten-free	χωρίς γλουτένη	kho·ris ghlu·te·ni
low in fat	χαμηλό σε λίπος	kha·mi·lo se li·pos
low in sugar	χαμηλό σε ζάχαρη	kha·mi·lo se za·kha·ri
organic	οργανικό	or·gha·ni·ko
salt-free	χωρίς αλάτι	kho·ris a·la·ti

special diets & allergies

I'm on a special diet.

Κάνω ειδική δίαιτα.	ka·no i·thi·ki thi·e·ta

I'm allergic to …	Είμαι αλλεργικός/ αλλεργική … m/f	i·me a·ler·yi·kos a·ler·yi·ki …
dairy produce	στα γαλακτικά	sta gha·lak·ti·ka
eggs	στα αβγά	sta av·gha
gluten	στη γλουτένη	sti ghlu·te·ni
honey	στο μέλι	sto me·li
MSG	στο MSG	sto em si dzi
nuts	στους ξηρούς καρπούς	stus ksi·rus kar·pus
seafood	στα θαλασσινά	sta tha·la·si·na
shellfish	στα οστρακοειδή	sta os·tra·ko·i·thi

I'm (a) …	Είμαι …	i·me …
Buddhist	Βουδιστής m	vu·thi·stis
	Βουδίστρια f	vu·thi·stri·a
Hindu	Ινδουιστής m	in·thu·i·stis
	Ινδουίστρια f	in·thu·i·stri·a
Jewish	Ιουδαίος m	i·u·the·os
	Ιουδαία f	i·u·the·a
Muslim	Μουσουλμάνος m	mu·sul·ma·nos
	Μουσουλμάνα f	mu·sul·ma·na
vegan	βέγκαν m&f	ve·gan
vegetarian	χορτοφάγος m&f	khor·to·fa·ghos

This miniguide lists dishes and ingredients used in Greek cuisine. It's designed to help you get the most out of your gastronomic experience by providing you with food terms that you may see on menus. For certain dishes we've marked the region or city where they're most popular.

The **culinary reader** has been ordered according to the Greek alphabet:

Αα Ββ Γγ Δδ Εε Ζζ Ηη Θθ Ιι Κκ Λλ Μμ
Νν Ξξ Οο Ππ Ρρ Σσ/ς Ττ Υυ Φφ Χχ Ψψ Ωω

Α α

αβγολέμονο ⓝ av·gho·*le*·mo·no *egg and lemon sauce added to meat, chicken or fish soup and other dishes*

αβγοτάραχο ⓝ av·gho·*ta*·ra·kho *dried & salted grey mullet roe, coated in beeswax*

αγγινάρες ⓕ pl au·gi·*na*·res *globe artichokes*
— **αλαπολίτα** a·la·po·*li*·ta *'Constantinople-style artichokes' – artichokes, carrots & potatoes in dill-spiked chicken stock*
— **καλογρές** ka·lo·*ghres* *'nuns' – artichoke hearts braised in creamy onion broth (Crete)*

αγγουροντομάτα σαλάτα ⓕ ang·gu·ro·do·*ma*·ta sa·*la*·ta *cucumber slices, tomato wedges & parsley with oil, lemon juice, salt & pepper*

αγγουροσαλάτα ⓕ ang·gu·ro·sa·*la*·ta *sliced cucumbers sprinkled with salt & served with oil & vinegar*

άγρια χόρτα ⓝ pl *a*·ghri·a *khor*·ta *seasonal wild greens*

άγρια σπαράγγια ⓝ pl *a*·ghri·a spa·*rang*·gi·a *wild asparagus*

άγριες αγγινάρες ⓕ pl *a*·ghri·es ang·gi·*na*·res *small prickly artichokes, eaten few with salt & lemon juice*

αμπελοπούλια ⓝ pl am·be·lo·*pu*·lia *tiny birds preserved in vinegar & wine, eaten whole (Cyprus)*

αμελέτητα ⓝ pl a·me·*le*·ti·ta *lamb testicles*

αμπελοφάσουλα ⓝ pl am·be·lo·*fa*·su·la *green beans*

αμπερόριζα ⓕ am·be·ro·*ri*·za *rose geranium (leaves are used as a flavouring for cakes, pastries & preserved fruits)*

αμύγδαλα ⓝ pl *migh*·tha·la *almonds*

αμυγδαλωτά ⓝ pl a·migh·tha·lo·*ta* *almond shortbread sprinkled with icing sugar & chopped almonds*

αμυγδαλωτό γλύκισμα ⓝ a·migh·tha·lo·to *ghli*·kiz·ma *nougat*

αναρή ⓕ a·na·*ri* *soft ricotta-like cheese from goat's or sheep's milk (Cyprus)*

αρακάς ⓜ a·ra·*kas* *fresh peas*
— **λαδερός** la·the·ros *peas stewed with carrots, garlic bulbs & herbs in oil & paprika (Corfu)*

αρνάκι ⓝ ar·*na*·ki *milk-lamb (very young lamb)*
— **γεμιστό** ye·mi·sto *Easter dish of stuffed roast lamb (Dodecanese Islands)*

αρνί ⓝ ar·*ni* *lamb*
— **βραστό** vra·sto *slow-boiled mutton served with mutton-stock soup (Crete)*
— **γιαχνί** yiakh·*ni* *lamb stewed with tomatoes, onions, carrots & celery*
— **γιουβέτσι με κριθαράκι** yiu·ve·tsi me kri·tha·*ra*·ki *lamb baked with tomatoes & barley-shaped pasta in an earthenware pot*
— **εξοχικό** ek·so·*hi*·ko *'country-style lamb' – baked filo parcels of lamb, potato, feta & κεφαλοτύρι*

— φρικασέ με μαρούλι
fri·ka·*se* me ma·*ru*·li poached lamb with
shredded lettuce, egg & lemon sauce
— κεφαλάκι ριγανάτο
ke·fa·*la*·ki ri·gha·*na*·to lamb's head (gen-
erally roasted) complete with tongue,
cheek, brains & eyes
— κοκκινιστό ko·ki·ni·*sto* lamb braised
in white wine with onions & bay leaves
— οψτό of·*to* roast lamb on the spit
— στη σούβλα sti *suv*·la spit-roast
lamb basted with olive oil, lemon juice &
garlic – a traditional Easter dish
— στο φούρνο sto *fur*·no
roasted leg or shoulder of lamb
αρνίσια παϊδάκια ⓝ pl ar·*ni*·sia
pa·i·*tha*·kia marinated & chargrilled
lamb cutlets
αστακός a·sta·*kos* ⓜ
lobster, usually boiled or chargrilled
αφέλια ⓝ pl a·*fe*·lia meat braised with
potato & mushrooms in red wine
αχηβάδα ⓕ a·hi·*va*·tha clam
αχινοί ⓜ pl a·hi·*ni* sea urchins
— σαλάτα sa·*la*·ta sea urchin salad
— γεμιστοί ye·mi·*sti* sea urchin stuffed
with rice, onions & tomatoes

Β β

βασιλόπιτα ⓕ va·si·*lo*·pi·ta New Year loaf
decorated with almonds – whoever finds
the coin in the bread gets good luck
βατόμουρο ⓝ va·*to*·mu·ro
blackberry · raspberry
βατραχοπόδαρα τηγανητά ⓝ pl
va·tra·kho·po·*tha*·ra ti·gha·ni·*ta*
fried frog's legs (Western Greece)
βυσσινάδα ⓕ vi·si·*na*·tha
syrup of morello cherries – mixed with
cold water for summer-time cordials
βύσσινο ⓝ *vi*·si·no
morello cherry · sour black cherry
— γλυκό ghli·*ko* morello cherry preserve
βλίτο ⓝ *vli*·to amaranth – its sweet nutty
flavour & soft texture make it popular for
warm salads
βοδινό ⓝ vo·*thi*·no beef
— καπαμά ka·pa·*ma* beef stewed with
tomatoes, red wine, cinnamon & cloves

— με λαχανικά me la·kha·ni·*ka* beef
braised with carrots, potatoes & celery
βολβοί ⓜ pl vol·*vi* grape hyacinth bulbs
— βραστοί vra·*sti* bulbs boiled, dressed
with dill vinaigrette & accompanied by
σκορδαλιά
βρούβα ⓕ *vru*·va charlock · field green
with sharp peppery taste

Γ γ

γαϊδουρελιά ⓕ gha·i·thu·re·*lia* 'donkey
olive' – named so because of its large size
γαλακτομπούρεκο ⓝ gha·lak·to·*bu*·re·ko
baked custard-cream filo pie sprinkled
with a lemony syrup
γαλοπούλα ⓕ gha·lo·*pu*·la turkey
— γεμιστή ye·mi·*sti* stuffed roast turkey
γαλύπες ⓕ pl gha·*li*·pes a sea anemone
— τηγανητές ti·gha·ni·*tes*
lightly battered & fried sea anemone
γαλυπε κεφτέδες ⓝ pl
gha·li·po·kef·*te*·thes sea anemone rissoles
γαρδούμια ⓝ pl ghar·*thu*·mia small offal
rolls made from strips of lamb's stomach,
bound with intestines then roasted
γαρίδες ⓕ pl gha·*ri*·thes prawns · shrimps
— σαγανάκι sa·gha·*na*·ki
prawns fried with tomatoes & red wine,
topped with feta & baked
— τηγανητές ti·gha·ni·*tes* fried prawns
— βραστές vra·*stes* boiled prawns
accompanied by λαδολέμονο
— γιουβετσάκι yiu·vet·*sa*·ki prawns
with tomatoes, parsley, oregano & feta
chunks baked in earthenware pots
γαριδοσαλάτα ⓕ gha·ri·tho·sa·*la*·ta
prawn salad
γαύρος ⓜ *ghav*·ros fresh anchovy
γεμιστά ⓝ pl ye·mi·*sta* stuffed vegetables
γεμιστός ye·mi·*stos* method of stuffing
meat, fish or vegetables prior to cooking
γιαούρτι ⓝ yia·*ur*·ti thick, heavy yogurt
with a tangy bite, made from sheep's,
goat's or cow's milk
— αγελάδος a·ye·*la*·thos
cow's milk yogurt
— φρούτων *fru*·ton fruit yogurt
— με μέλι me *me*·li yogurt with honey
— πρόβειο *pro*·vio sheep's milk yoghurt

γιαουρτογλού ⓕ yia·ur·to·*ghlu*
pie cooked with finely sliced grilled meat,
topped with a yogurt sauce

γιαουρτόπιτα ⓕ yia·ur·to·pi·ta
light moist cake made with yogurt,
sugar, lemon rind & lots of eggs

γίδα βραστή ⓕ *yi*·tha vra·*sti*
aromatic dish of boiled goat

γύρος *yi*·ros 'to spin' – seasoned lamb
packed onto a spit & rotisseried upright,
carved for meat platters or served in
πίτα with tomatoes, onions & **τζατζίκι**

γιορτή ⓕ yior·*ti* small pieces of pork & goat
boiled with corn, topped with melted
butter, cinnamon & pepper (Samos)

γιουβαρλάκια ⓝ pl yiu·var·*la*·kia egg-
shaped rissoles of minced beef or lamb
simmered in a light stock

γιουβέτσι ⓝ yiu·*vet*·si casserole of meat &
seafood with tomatoes & barley pasta
— **με θαλασσινά** me tha·la·si·*na*
casserole of seafood, barley pasta, tomatoes & chicken stock (Ionian Islands)

γιουσλεμέδες ⓜ pl yiuz·le·*me*·thes golden
pies filled with eggs & **κεφαλοτύρι**,
deep-fried then served with grated cheese
(Lesvos)

γλιστρίδα ⓕ ghli·*stri*·tha purslane –
small-leafed plant with lemony flavour &
crisp texture used mainly in salads
— **με κάππαρόφυλλα σαλάτα**
me ka·pa·ro·fi·la sa·*la*·ta purslane leaves,
sliced tomatoes, black olives & caper
leaves with oil & lemon dressing
— **με γιαούρτι** me yia·ur·ti
chopped purslane beaten with strained
yogurt, garlic, lemon, salt & oil (Crete)

γλυκά κουταλιού ⓝ pl ghli·ka ku·ta·*liu*
'spoon sweets' – preserved fruits

γλυκάνισο ⓝ ghli·*ka*·ni·so aniseed

γλυκά ταψιού ⓝ pl ghli·*ka* tap·siu
sweets made with filo pastry

γλύκισμα ⓝ pl *ghli*·kiz·ma
sweet pastry • cake

γλυκοκολοκύθα ⓕ ghli·ko·ko·lo·*ki*·tha
marrow • pumpkin • squash

γλώσσα ⓕ *ghlo*·sa tongue (fish) • generic
name for any flat fish

— **μοσχαρίσια κρασάτη**
mo·sha·ri·sia kra·*sa*·ti tongue (fish) fried
in butter, then poached in white wine

γουρουνάκι (του γάλακτος) ⓝ
ghu·ru·*na*·ki (tu *gha*·lak·tos)
piglet • suckling pig
— **στη σούβλα** sti suv·la whole suckling
pig spit-roasted until tender
— **γεμιστό με φέτα** ye·mi·*sto* me fe·ta
suckling pig stuffed with feta & roasted

γυαλιστερές ⓕ pl yia·li·ste·*res*
shellfish eaten alive with a squeeze of
lemon juice (Dodecanese Islands)

Δ δ

δάχτυλα ⓝ pl *thakh*·ti·la 'fingers' – deep-
fried, nut-filled pastries (Cyprus)

δίπλες ⓕ pl *thi*·ples sweet pastry, deep-
fried & drizzled with honey & sesame seeds
— **Δράμας** *thra*·mas
yogurt pie with vine leaves

δρύλιοι αλευρολέμονο ⓜ pl *thri*·li
a·lev·ro·le·mo·no wild greens in lemon

Ε ε

ελαιόλαδο ⓝ e·le·o·la·*tho* olive oil

ελαιόπιτες ⓕ pl e·le·o·pi·tes
small olive & leek pies (Cyprus)

ελαιότη ⓕ e·le·o·ti bread with a layer of
chopped black olives & onions (Cyprus)

ελαιόψωμο ⓝ e·le·op·so·mo olive bread

ελιές ⓕ pl e·*lies* olives
— **Αμφίσσης** am·*fi*·sis large blue-black
olives with nutty flavour
— **Αταλάντης** a·ta·*lan*·dis big fruity
greenish-purple or purple olives
— **χαμούρες** ha·*mu*·res
dried newly fallen olives
— **Ιονίων πράσινες** i·o·ni·on pra·si·nes
mild green olives (Ionian Islands)
— **Καλαμάτας** ka·la·*ma*·tas large black
olives with pungent flavour
— **μαύρες** mav·res black olives
— **Ναυπλίου** naf·*pli*·u
nutty flavoured green olives (Nafplio)
— **παστές** pa·*stes* dried salted olives
— **πελτέ** pel·te olive paste
— **πράσινες** pra·si·nes green olives

— **τσακιστές** tsa·ki·stes cracked green
olives marinated in oil, lemon & herbs
— **τουρσί** tur·si pickled olives
ελίτσες ① pl e·lit·ses tiny sweet black olives
εντόσθια ① pl en·do·sthi·a offal • innards
(usually lamb)
— **κοκκινιστά** ko·ki·ni·sta
chicken giblets in a rich gravy
— **πουλιών** pu·lion giblets

Ζ ζ

ζαχαροπούλια ① za·kha·ro·pu·lia
marzipan sweets (Lesvos)
ζαχαρωτό με αμύγδαλο ①
za·kha·ro·to me a·migh·tha·lo marzipan
ζαμπόν ① zam·bon ham
ζαργάνα ① zar·gha·na garfish
ζύμη ① zi·mi pastry
— **με γιαούρτι** me yia·ur·ti baked pasta
dish consisting of homemade macaroni,
strained yogurt & onions (Kos)

Θ θ

θαλασσινά ① pl tha·la·si·na seafood
— **του Αιγαίου** tu e·ye·u paella-style
rice dish cooked with seafood (Hydra)
θρούμπες ① pl thru·mbes ripe black
olives
θυμάρι ① thi·ma·ri thyme

Ι ι

ιμάμ-μπαϊλντί ① i·mam·ba·il·di
Turkish-inspired dish of eggplant stuffed
with eggplant pulp, tomato, garlic,
onion, parsley, then baked

Κ κ

καβούρι ① ka·vu·ri crab
— **βραστό** vra·sto
crab boiled & dressed with **λαδολέμονο**
καϊμάκι ① to ka·i·ma·ki froth that forms
on top of Greek coffee while it brews
— **πηγμένο** pigh·me·no clotted cream
κακαβιά ① ka·ka·via saltwater fish soup
καλαμαράκια ① pl ka·la·ma·ra·kia baby
squid

καλαμάρι ① ka·la·ma·ri squid
— **γεμιστό** ye·mi·sto squid stuffed with
rice & baked in a lemony broth
— **Λεβριανά** lev·ria·na
squid stewed in dry red wine with green
olives, tomatoes, onions & parsley
— **με ρύζι** me ri·zi
fried squid with onions simmered with
water, crushed tomatoes, rice & cinnamon
— **τηγανητό** ti·gha·ni·to squid cut in
rings or strips, lightly battered & fried
καλιτσούνια ① pl ka·lit·su·nia
small cheese pies
καπαμάς ① ka·pa·mas method of stewing
meat with tomatoes, wine, cinnamon &
sometimes red capsicum & cloves
κάππαρη ① ka·pa·ri capers, usually
pickled & eaten as an appetiser
κάπρος ① ka·pros wild boar
καραμέλα ① ka·ra·me·la candy • caramel
καραβίδα ① ka·ra·vi·tha crayfish
καρύδια ① pl ka·ri·thia walnuts
— **γεμιστά** ye·mi·sta walnuts & roasted
almonds preserved in syrup (Cyprus)
καρυδόπιτα ① ka·ri·tho·pi·ta
rich moist walnut cake
κάσιου ① ka·siu cashews
καταΐφι ① ka·ta·i·fi 'angel hair' pastry –
syrupy nest-like nut-filled rolls
κατσικάκι ① kat·si·ka·ki goat • kid
— **πατούδο** pa·tu·tho
roast kid stuffed with liver, rice, bread-
crumbs, feta & raisins or **κεφαλοτύρι**,
bacon, rice & dill (Cyclades)
— **ψητό** psi·to roast kid, sometimes
served with a spicy red wine sauce
καφές ① ka·fes coffee
— **ελληνικός** e·li·ni·kos
freshly brewed Greek coffee
— **γλυκός** ghli·kos sweet coffee
— **μέτριος** me·tri·os medium-strength
coffee with a little sugar
— **πολλά βαρύς** po·la va·ris
strong coffee
— **σκέτος** ske·tos sugarless coffee
— **βαρύγλυκος** va·ri·ghli·kos
strong & sweet coffee
κεφαλάκι ① ke·fa·la·ki head – usually
refers specifically to lamb's head

κεφτεδάκια ⓝ pl kef·te·*tha*·kia
miniature meat rissoles served at parties

κεφαλοτύρι ⓝ ke·fa·lo·*ti*·ri *'head cheese'*
– known as 'kefalotiri', a hard, pale
yellow cheese made from sheep and
goat's milk

κεφτέδες ⓝ pl kef·te·*thes*
small tasty rissoles, often made with
minced lamb, pork or veal
   — **στη σχάρα** sti *skha*·ra
   chargrilled meat rissoles

κιχώρι ⓝ ki·*kho*·ri chicory • *green leaves*

κιμαδόπιτα ⓕ ki·ma·*tho*·pi·ta
mincemeat pie

κιμάς ki·*mas* ⓜ
sauce made from mincemeat, onions &
tomatoes served with pasta or rice

κλιματόφυλλο ⓝ kli·ma·to·fi·lo *vine leaf*

κοψίσι ⓝ ko·*fi*·si *pie made from boiled &*
shredded dried fish mixed with onion,
garlic, rice & tomatoes (Kefallonia)

κόκκοι καφέ ⓜ pl *ko*·ki ka·fe *coffee beans*

κοκκινέλι ⓝ ko·ki·*ne*·li *red resinated wine*

κόκκινη πιπεριά ⓕ *ko*·ki·ni pi·pe·*ria*
red capsicum (pepper)

κοκκινιστό ⓝ ko·ki·ni·*sto*
'reddened' – method of simmering meat,
chicken or rice with tomatoes

κόκκινο φασόλι ⓝ *ko*·ki·no fa·*so*·li
red kidney bean
   — **λάχανο** *la*·kha·no *red cabbage*

κοκκινοπίπερο ⓝ ko·ki·no·*pi*·pe·ro
cayenne (spice)

κόκορας ⓜ *ko*·ko·ras *rooster*
   — **κρασάτος** kra·*sa*·tos
   lightly floured rooster fried with onions &
   spices, then cooked in red wine sauce

κοκορέτσι ⓝ ko·ko·*ret*·si
chopped lamb offal wrapped in lamb's
intestines & grilled

κοκορόζουμο ⓝ ko·ko·ro·*zu*·mo
lemony rooster broth used as a post-
party pick-me-up (Cyclades)

κολιός ⓜ ko·li·os *mackerel*
   — **λαδορίγανη** la·*tho*·ri·gha·ni
   mackerel baked with oil, lemon, oregano,
   garlic & parsley
   — **σε κλημματόφυλλα** kli·ma·*to*·fi·la
   mackerel in vine leaves

κολιτσάνοι ⓜ pl ko·lit·*sa*·ni *a sea anemone*

κολοκέτα ⓝ pl ko·lo·*ke*·ta
pastries stuffed with red pumpkin,
raisins & cracked wheat (Cyprus)

κολοκύθα ⓕ ko·lo·*ki*·tha
marrow • pumpkin • squash

κολοκυθάκια ⓝ pl ko·lo·ki·*tha*·kia *zucchini*
   — **με αβγά** me av·*gha*
   zucchini & egg omelette
   — **τηγανητά** ti·gha·ni·*ta*
   zucchini battered & deep-fried, served
   with lemon & **σκορδαλιά**
   — **βραστά** vra·*sta* *boiled baby zucchini*
   with oil & lemon dressing

κολοκύθι ⓝ ko·lo·*ki*·thi
marrow • pumpkin • squash

κολοκυθόανθοι ⓜ pl ko·lo·ki·*tho*·an·thi
zucchini flowers
   — **τηγανητοί** ti·gha·ni·*ti*
   zucchini flowers & cheese fritters (Andros)
   — **γεμιστοί** ye·mi·*sti* *zucchini flower*
   ντολμάδες *stuffed with rice, tomato &*
   parsley & simmered until tender

κολοκυθοκεφτέδες
ko·lo·ki·tho·kef·te·thes *rissoles of puréed*
zucchini, parsley, onion, mint & garlic

κολοκυθόπιτα ⓕ ko·lo·ki·*tho*·pi·ta
zucchini pie

κόλυβα ⓝ pl *ko*·li·va *wheat mixed with*
fruit, pomegranate seeds, sugar & nuts –
eaten after the death of a family member
& on the anniversary of their death

κομπόστα ⓕ ko·*bo*·sta
compote • stewed fruit

κονσερβολιά ⓕ kon·ser·vo·*lia* *common*
type of olive from the central mainland

κοντοσούβλι ⓝ kon·do·*suv*·li
spit-roast pieces of lamb or pork seasoned
with onions, oregano, salt & pepper

κορωναίικη ⓕ ko·ro·ne·*i*·ki *a smaller, oil-*
bearing variety of the kalamata olive

κοτόπιτα ⓕ ko·*to*·pi·ta *chicken filo pastry*

κοτόπουλο ⓝ ko·*to*·pu·lo *chicken*
   — **χυλοπίτες** hi·lo·*pi*·tes *whole chicken &*
   noodles simmered in tomato, onion &
   cinnamon broth until liquid is absorbed
   — **λεμονάτο** le·mo·*na*·to *roast chicken*
   basted with butter & lemon juice
   — **με μπάμιες** me *ba*·mies *chicken &*
   okra braised in tomato & onion gravy

κοτόσουπα ① ko·to·su·pa
soup made from boiled whole chicken

κρασί ⑩ kra·si wine
— **άσπρο** a·spro white wine
— **κόκκινο** ko·ki·no red wine
— **λευκό** lef·ko white wine
— **ροζέ** ro·ze rosé wine

κρέας ⑩ kre·as meat
— **ελαφιού** e·la·fiu venison
— **στη στάμνα** sti stam·na
meat cooked in a pot
— **στο φούρνο με πατάτες** sto fur·no
me pa·ta·tes roast meat with potatoes

κρεατικά ⑩ pl kre·a·ti·ka
meat dishes, mostly stewed or roasted

κρεατόπιτα ① kre·a·to·pi·ta
lamb or veal pie, usually with cinnamon
— **Κεφαλλονίτικη** ke·fa·lo·ni·ti·ki
meat pie cooked with onions, eggs, rice,
potatoes, tomatoes & spices (Kefallonia)
— **της Κρήτης** tis kri·tis
pie of alternating layers of cubed lamb
(or goat) & **μυζήθρα** covered in butter &
baked in shortcrust pastry (Crete)

κρεατόσουπα ① kre·a·to·su·pa nourish-
ing broth made from boiled meat –
sometimes thickened with rice &
αβγολέμονο

κρεμμυδόπιτα ① kre·mi·tho·pi·ta
pie with a filling of **μυζήθρα**, grated
onion, eggs & dill (Mykonos)

Κρητική κρεατόπιτα ①
kri·ti·ki kre·a·to·pi·ta
see **κρεατόπιτα της Κρήτης**

κριθαράκι ⑩ kri·tha·ra·ki
tiny spindle-shaped barley pasta used
for pasta dishes, soups & casseroles
— **με βούτυρο και τυρί** me vu·ti·ro
ke ti·ri pasta baked with brown butter,
cheese, lemon juice & herbs

κουκουβάγια ① ku·ku·va·yia
see **παξιμάδια σαλάτα**

κουκιά ⑩ pl ku·kia broad beans
— **ξερά βραστά** kse·ra vra·sta broad
beans boiled in water & lemon juice &
served with oil, dill & onion rings
— **με αγριαγκινάρες**
me a·ghri·ang·gi·na·res
broad beans with artichokes

κουλουκόψωμο ⑩ ku·lu·kop·so·mo
see **παξιμάδια με ντομάτες και φέτα**

κουλουράκια ⑩ pl ku·lu·ra·kia
cookies • biscuits • buns
— **με πετιμέζι** me pe·ti·me·zi
sweet buns made with syrup, cinnamon
& spices

κουλούρι ⑩ ku·lu·ri crisp sesame-coated
bread rings sold on streets & outside
church after Sunday mass • generic
name for circular rolls, buns & biscuits

κουλούρια αστυπαλίτικα ① pl ku·lu·ri·a
a·sti·pa·li·ti·ka saffron biscuits (Astypalea)

κουμκουάτ ⑩ kum·ku·at cumquat
— **λικέρ** li·ker cumquat liqueur (Corfu)

Κουμανταρία ① ku·man·da·ri·a
heavy dessert wine originally made
during the Crusades by the Knights of
the Order of St John (Cyprus)

κουνέλι ⑩ ku·ne·li rabbit
— **κρασάτο** kra·sa·to rabbit casserole
with red wine, garlic & bay leaves
— **με καρύδι** me ka·ri·thi marinated
rabbit, fried & simmered in white wine
infused with coarsely ground walnuts
— **με γιαούρτι** me yia·ur·ti
rabbit marinated in lemon juice & black
pepper, then baked with a creamy egg &
yogurt sauce
— **στιφάδο** sti·fa·tho rabbit ragout
spiced with cloves, cinnamon & cumin

κουπέπια ⑩ pl ku·pe·pia ντολμάδες
made with minced lamb & veal, served
hot with **αβγολέμονο** sauce (Cyprus)

κούπες ① pl ku·pes deep-fried pastries of
mincemeat, onion & spices (Cyprus)

κουραμπιέδες ⑩ pl ku·ra·bie·thes
buttery almond shortbread

κυδώνι ⑩ ki·tho·ni quince
— **μπελτές** bel·tes quince jelly
— **γλυκό** ghli·ko quince preserve
flavoured with rose geranium
— **στο φούρνο** sto fur·no buttered
quince baked in a water & sugar solution
until liquid has caramelised
— **γεμιστό** ye·mi·sto
large quince stuffed with minced beef,
rice, onions, raisins, cloves & nutmeg

κυδωνόπαστο ⓝ ki·tho·no·pa·sto
*dark-red quince paste dried until firm, cut
in small diamonds & dusted with sugar*

Λ λ

λαβράκι ⓝ lav·ra·ki *sea bass*
— **στο αλάτι** sto a·la·ti *whole sea bass
buried in salt & baked – the salt-encrusted
skin is slit & the flesh is eaten from the
bone with an oil & lemon dressing*

λαγάνα ⓕ la·gha·na *bread sprinkled with
sesame seeds baked on the first day of Lent*

λαγός ⓜ la·ghos *hare*
— **στιφάδο** sti·fa·tho *hare ragout
spiced with cumin & cloves, usually
marinated in vinegar prior to cooking*

λαγωτό ⓝ la·gho·to *hare ragout (Kefallonia)*

λαδόξιδο ⓝ la·thok·si·tho *vinaigrette of
oil, vinegar, parsley, salt & pepper*

λαδολέμονο ⓝ la·tho·le·mo·no
*thick dressing of oil beaten with lemon
juice, salt & pepper*

λάχανα ⓝ pl la·kha·na *seasonal wild greens*
— **με λαρδί** mel lar·thi *casserole of seasonal greens & fatty bacon (Mykonos)*

λαχανικά ⓝ pl la·kha·ni·ka *vegetables*
— **της θάλασσας** tis tha·la·sas
sea vegetables

λάχανο ⓝ la·kha·no *cabbage*
— **κοκκινιστό** ko·ki·ni·sto
*cabbage stewed with tomatoes, onions,
parsley, dill & paprika (Corfu)*
— **με κιμά** me ki·ma *cabbage braised
with onions, mincemeat & tomatoes,
finished with fresh butter (Chios)*

λαχανοσαλάτα ⓕ la·kha·no·sa·la·ta
*shredded white cabbage sprinkled with
oil, lemon juice & salt*

λεμονάτος ⓜ le·mo·na·tos
method of cooking with oil & lemon juice

λιθρίνι ⓝ li·thri·ni *sea bream*

λουκάνικα ⓝ pl lu·ka·ni·ka *pork sausages
seasoned with coriander & orange peel •
generic word for sausages & frankfurters*

λουκανόπιτες ⓕ pl lu·ka·no·pi·tes
filo-wrapped sausages

λουκουμάδες ⓜ pl lu·ku·ma·thes
*rosette-shaped, light-as-air doughnuts
served hot with honey & cinnamon*

λουκούμι ⓝ lu·ku·mi *Turkish delight*

λουκούμια ⓝ pl lu·ku·mia
wedding shortbread (Cyprus)

λούντζα ⓕ lun·dza *spicy ham made from
cured smoked pork fillet (Cyprus, Cyclades)*
— **με χαλούμι** me kha·lu·mi *grilled ham
topped with melted* **χαλούμι** *(Cyprus)*

λουβιά ⓝ pl lu·via *black-eyed peas*
— **με λάχανα** me la·kha·na *warm salad
of black-eyed peas & seasonal greens
with oil & lemon dressing (Cyprus)*

λουζές ⓜ lu·zes *salted fillet of pork stuffed
into thick pig's intestine & sun-dried
(Mykonos)*

λιαστός ⓜ lia·stos *sun-dried*

Μ μ

μαγειρίτσα ⓕ ma·yi·rit·sa *lamb's offal
soup thickened with rice &* **αβγολέμονο**,
eaten to celebrate the end of Lent

μακαρόνια ⓝ pl ma·ka·ro·nia
macaroni • spaghetti
— **με κιμά** me ki·ma *pasta with a sauce of
mincemeat, tomatoes, onions & red wine*
— **με σάλτσα** me sal·tsa *pasta with
tomato, onion & oregano sauce*
— **με βούτυρο και τυρί** me vu·ti·ro ke
ti·ri *pasta with butter sauce & cheese*
— **στο φούρνο** sto fur·no *pasta baked
in cheese & butter sauce*

μαντί ⓝ man·di *small pasta pockets filled
with mincemeat, cooked in meat broth
seasoned with capsicum & served with a
yogurt & garlic sauce (Northern Greece)*

μάραθο ⓝ ma·ra·tho *fennel*
— **με ούζο σούπα** me u·zo su·pa
ouzo & fennel soup

μαχαλεπί ⓝ ma·kha·le·pi *creamy custard
pudding in rose-water syrup (Cyprus)*

μαχλέπι ⓝ ma·khle·pi
*pungent bitter-sweet black cherry pips
used for spicing breads & stuffings*

μαρίδα πικάντικη ⓕ ma·ri·tha
pi·kan·di·ki *whitebait, tomato & mint
fritters (Rhodes)*

μαρίδες ⓕ pl ma·ri·thes *whitebait*
— **λιαστές** lia·stes *whitebait seasoned
with oregano & strung out to dry then
chargrilled & served with oil & lemon juice*

— τηγανητές ti·gha·ni·tes whitebait rolled in flour & deep fried until crisp, served with lemon wedges

μαστίχα ① ma·sti·kha mastic • crystallised resin from the mastic bush, eaten as chewing gum & used as a flavouring (Chios)

μαυρομάτικα φασόλια ⑩ pl mav·ro·ma·ti·ka fa·so·lia black-eyed peas
— με χόρτα me khor·ta black-eyed peas stewed with greens, onions, tomatoes, parsley, mint & garlic (Crete)

μεγαρίτικη ① me·gha·ri·ti·ki olives grown in Attica, near Athens, named after the city of Megara

μελανούρι ⑩ me·la·nu·ri sea bream

μεζές ⑩ me·zes snack

μεζεδάκια ⑩ me·ze·tha·ki tasty morsels served with ouzo – favourites include olives, salted cucumber slices, feta, salted anchovies, mackerel & mini-meat rissoles

μέλι ⑩ me·li honey
— με ξηρούς καρπούς me ksi·rus kar·pus honey poured over walnuts or almonds

μελιτζάνες ① pl me·li·dza·nes eggplant
— στο φούρνο sto fur·no sliced eggplant fried with potatoes, & baked with tomatoes, cumin, parsley & feta
— τηγανητές ti·gha·ni·tes see κολοκυθάκια τηγανητά

μελιτζανοσαλάτα ① me·li·dza·no·sa·la·ta smoky purée of grilled mashed eggplant, onion, garlic, oil & lemon

μελιτίνι ⑩ me·li·ti·ni golden pastry tarts filled with fresh cheese, eggs & sugar, traditionally eaten at Easter

μελόπιτα ① me·lo·pi·ta cheesecake made with μυζήθρα & clear honey

μηλοπιτάκια ⑩ pl mi·lo·pi·ta·kia crescent-shaped apple & walnut pies

μοσχάρι ⑩ mo·sha·ri veal
— κατσαρόλας με αρακά kat·sa·ro·las me a·ra·ka veal stewed with fresh peas in white wine & thyme
— κοκκινιστό με μακαρόνια ko·ki·ni·sto me ma·ka·ro·nia veal stewed with tomatoes, served with spaghetti
— ψητό psi·to rolled veal rubbed with lemon juice, pepper & salt, pot-roasted with onion & tomatoes & wine

— στιφάδο sti·fa·tho veal ragout with garlic, peppercorns & bay leaves

μουσακάς ⑩ mu·sa·kas thick-sliced eggplant & mincemeat arranged in layers, topped with béchamel & baked
— με αγγινάρες me ang·gi·na·res alternating layers of minced veal & artichoke hearts

μουσταλευριά ① mu·sta·lev·ri·a dark gelatinous pudding made from boiled grape must, thickened with flour & sprinkled with cinnamon, seeds & nuts

μούστος ⑩ mu·stos grape must collected from crushed wine grapes
— κουλούρα ku·lu·ra hard, turban-shaped grape must buns

μπακαλιάρος ⑩ ba·ka·lia·ros dried salt cod soaked for several hours prior to cooking

μπουρδέτο ⑩ bur·the·to salt cod stew
— κροκετάκια kro·ke·ta·kia deep-fried salt cod mashed with potato & nutmeg
— πλακί pla·ki salt cod simmered with onions, potatoes, celery, carrots & garlic in a tomato-based sauce
— τηγανητός ti·gha·ni·tos salt cod fried in crisp, golden batter, traditionally accompanied with σκορδαλιά

μπακλαβάς ⑩ pl ba·kla·vas nut-filled layers of filo bathed in honey syrup

μπάμιες ① pl ba·mies okra
— λαδερές la·the·res okra stewed in oil
— γιαχνί yia·khni okra braised with pulped tomatoes & onions

μπαρμπούνια ⑩ pl bar·bu·nia small, sweet-fleshed red mullet
— ψητά στον άνιθο psi·ta ston a·ni·tho red mullet on a bed of dill
— στη σκάρα sti ska·ra red mullet basted with oil & lemon & chargrilled
— τηγανητά ti·gha·ni·ta red mullet rolled in seasoned flour & fried

μπεκάτσα ① be·kat·sa woodcock
— κρασάτη kra·sa·ti woodcock casserole with dry red wine, tomatoes & spices, served on fried bread

μπεκρή μεζέ ① be·kri me·ze 'drunken μεζέ' – meat cooked in tomato & wine sauce

μπομπότα ⓕ bo-*bo*-ta
  sweet corn bread studded with raisins, walnuts, cloves & flavoured with cinnamon & orange juice (Zakynthos)

μπισκότα ⓝ pl bi-*sko*-ta biscuits • cookies

μπιζελόσουπα ⓕ bi-ze-*lo*-su-pa
  fragrant pea soup loaded with dill

μπόλια bo-li-a ⓕ
  lacy caul of fat encasing lamb's stomach

μπριάμι ⓝ bri-a-mi casserole of sliced potatoes, zucchini, capsicums, tomatoes & herbs • roast vegetables

μπριζόλες ⓕ pl bri-*zo*-les chops • steak

μπουγάτσα ⓕ bu-*ghat*-sa creamy semolina pudding wrapped in pastry & baked

μπουρδέτο ⓝ bur-*the*-to
  hot fish casserole spiked with paprika

μπουρεκάκια ⓝ pl bu-re-*ka*-kia little filo pies in cigar, cigarette & envelope shapes

μπουρέκια ⓝ pl bu-*re*-kia filo pies shaped into thin long rolls, batons & pinwheels
  — **με ανεβί** me a-ne-*ri* deep-fried pastry pouches stuffed with cheese (Cyprus)

μυαλά ⓝ pl mia-*la* brains
  — **αρνίσια λαδολέμονο** ar-*ni*-si-a la-*tho-le*-mo-no poached lamb's brains
  — **τηγανητά** ti-gha-ni-*ta* fried brains

μύδια ⓝ pl *mi*-thia mussels
  — **κρασάτα** kra-*sa*-ta
  poached mussels in a white wine sauce
  — **τηγανητά** ti-gha-ni-*ta* mussels shucked, lightly battered, fried in hot oil & served with a garlic yogurt sauce
  — **γεμιστά** ye-mi-*sta* mussels stuffed with rice, onions & parsley, slow-simmered in fish stock, tomato purée & white wine

μυζήθρα ⓕ mi-*zi*-thra
  soft mild ricotta-like cheese made from sheep's or goat's milk (sweet or savoury)

μυζηθρόπιτες ⓕ pl mi-zi-*thro*-pi-tes delicate deep-fried pies with **μυζήθρα** (Crete)

N ν

νεγκόσκα ⓕ ne-*go*-ska variety of red grape

νεραντζάκι γλυκό ⓝ ne-ran-*dza*-ki ghli-*ko* preserved small bitter green oranges

νεράπη ⓕ ne-*ra*-ti
  variety of cheese pie (Crete)

νουμπουλό ⓝ num-bu-*lo*
  bacon-flavoured sausage (Corfu)

ντολμάδες dol-*ma*-thes ⓜ pl
  dolmades – parcels of rice-wrapped leaves (usually vine leaves) & cooked in water, oil & lemon juice
  — **φυλλιανές** fi-li-a-*nes* Christmas & New Year dish of onion sleeves stuffed with minced veal, pork & rice (Lesvos)
  — **με αυγολέμονο** me av-gho-*le*-mo-no dolmades with rice, minced lamb, tomatoes, mint & cumin, served hot with αλευρολέμονο
  — **με κουκιά** me ku-*kia*
  dolmades with boiled & sliced broad beans & dried ox meat, cooked on a bed of beef bones (Northern Greece)
  — **με λαχανόφυλλα** me la-kha-*no*-fi-la stuffed cabbage leaves, served hot with αβγολέμονο
  — **γιαλαντζί** yia-lan-*dzi*
  'fraud' – stuffed meatless dolmades
  — **Σμυρναίικα** zmir-*ne*-i-ka
  dolmades stuffed with sautéed onions, rice, eggplant, oregano, dill, garlic & cooked in tomato broth

ντομάτες ⓕ pl do-*ma*-tes tomatoes
  — **λιαστές** lia-*stes* sun-dried tomatoes
  — **γεμιστές** ye-mi-*stes*
  large tomatoes stuffed with rice, tomato pulp, onion, garlic & herbs

ντοματοκεφτέδες ⓜ pl
  do-ma-to-kef-*te*-thes
  deep-fried tomato rissoles

ντοματομπελτές ⓜ do-ma-to-pel-*tes*
  tomato paste

ντοματόσουπα ⓕ do-ma-to-su-pa soup made with tomatoes & sometimes pasta

νυχάκι ⓝ ni-*kha*-ki kalamata table olive (Messenia & Laconia)

Ξ ξ

ξεροτήγανα ⓝ pl kse-ro-*ti*-gha-na see **δίπλες**

ξινόχοντρος ⓜ ksi-*no*-khon-dros ground wheat cooked in sour milk & dried

ξινομυζήθρα ⓕ ksi-no-mi-*zi*-thra
  savoury **μυζήθρα**

O o

οινοπνευματώδη ⑩ pl i·nop·nev·ma·to·thi *alcoholic spirits*

οστρακοειδή ⑩ pl o·stra·ko·i·thi *shellfish*

ούζο ⑩ u·zo *clear spirit distilled from grape seeds, stems & skins with a strong aniseed flavour*

ορτή σαλάτα ① of·ti sa·la·ta *grilled salad of potatoes, onions & σταφιδολιές, foil-wrapped & chargrilled (Crete)*

ορτό ⑩ of·to *sausage made from pig's intestines, rice, walnuts, pistachios, raisins, cinnamon & orange peel (Crete)*

ουρά βοδιού ① u·ra vo·thiu *oxtail*

Π π

παϊδάκια ⑩ pl pai·i·tha·kia *chops · cutlets*

παξιμάδια ⑩ pl pak·si·ma·thia *hard wheat or barley rusks eaten slightly moistened with water at meal times (both wheat & barley varieties are common)*
— **με ντομάτες και φέτα** me do·ma·tes ke fe·ta **παξιμάδια** *moistened with water or tomato juice & topped with sliced tomatoes, feta, oregano, oil, salt & pepper – very popular snack or light lunch*
— **σαλάτα** sa·la·ta **παξιμάδια** *broken into pieces, moistened with water & sprinkled with diced tomatoes, crumbled feta or oregano, oil, salt & pepper*

παλαμίδα ① pa·la·mi·tha *bonito · tunny fish (a variety of tuna)*
— **ψητή με χόρτα** psi·ti me khor·ta *marinated bonito steaks*

παλικάρια ⑩ pl pa·li·ka·ri·a *mix of legumes & grains boiled & tossed with oil, onions & dill*

πανέ pa·ne *crumbed & fried*

παντρεμένοι ⑩ pl pan·dre·me·ni *beans with other foods (rice, meat, tomatoes)*

παντζάρι ⑩ pan·dza·ri *beetroot*
— **σαλάτα** sa·la·ta *boiled thickly sliced beetroot dressed with vinaigrette & served with σκορδαλιά*

παντσέττα ① pan·tse·ta *pancetta*

— **γεμιστή στο φούρνο** ye·mi·sti sto fur·no *pig's stomach stuffed with parmesan, garlic, onions & oregano, basted with oil, wine & lemon juice & baked with potatoes (Zakynthos)*

πάπια ① pa·pia *duck*
— **με σάλτσα ροδιού** me sal·tsa ro·thiu *fried duck breast served with sauce made from pomegranate seeds, lemon juice, duck stock & walnuts (Northern Greece)*
— **σαλμί** sal·mi *whole duck seared in oil, then jointed & cooked in its own juices, wine, orange juice & onions*

πάπρικα ① pa·pri·ka *paprika*

παπουτσάκι ⑩ pa·put·sa·ki *'little shoe' – stuffed baby eggplant topped with béchamel sauce & baked*

παρμεζάνα ① par·me·za·na *parmesan*

πασατέμπος ⑩ pa·sa·te·bos *'pass the time' – roasted pumpkin seeds sold as a snack*

πάστα ① pa·sta *gateau*

παστέλι ⑩ pa·ste·li *sweet honey & sesame seed wafers*

παστιτσάδα ① pa·stit·sa·tha *pot-roasted veal with tomato, red wine, cloves, cinnamon & paprika (Corfu)*

παστίτσιο ⑩ pa·stit·si·o *baked layers of buttery macaroni & minced lamb topped with white sauce & grated κεφαλοτύρι*

παστός pa·stos *salted & dried*

παστουρμάς ⑩ pa·stur·mas *spicy dried ox meat*

πατάτες ① pl pa·ta·tes *potatoes*
— **γιαχνί** yia·khni *potatoes stewed with tomatoes, onions & oregano*
— **κεφτέδες** kef·te·thes *fried potato, feta & parsley rissoles*
— **λεμονάτες** le·mo·na·tes *potatoes roasted with oil, lemon juice, oregano, salt & pepper*
— **πουρέ** pu·re *mashed potatoes*
— **στο φούρνο** sto fur·no *potatoes baked or roasted with oil, salt & oregano*
— **τηγανητές** ti·gha·ni·tes *fried potato slices*

πατατοσαλάτα ① pa·ta·to·sa·la·ta *potato salad*

πατατού ① pa·ta·tu *baked mashed potato pie (Cyclades)*

πατσάς pat-*sas* ⓜ tripe • rich-textured & surprisingly delicate-flavoured soup made with the stomach of a young lamb & finished with **αβγολέμονο**

πατούδα ⓕ pa-*tu*-ṭha pastries filled with walnuts, almonds & cinnamon, baked, sprinkled with orange flower water & dredged in icing sugar (Crete)

πεϊνιρλί ⓝ pe-i-nir-*li* savoury pastries with a variety of fillings such as mincemeat, feta, ham & egg, & dried ox meat

πέρδικες ⓕ pl *per*-ṭhi-kes partridges
— **με ελιές και σέλινο** me e-*lies* ke *se*-li-no partridges browned in butter & simmered in their own juices with green olives, sliced celery & tomatoes

πέρκα ⓕ *per*-ka sea perch

πέστροφα ⓕ *pe*-stro-fa trout

πεταλίδες ⓕ pl pe-ta-*li*-ṭhes limpets
— **με θαλασσινούς χοχλιούς** me tha-la-si-*nus* kho-khli-*us* limpets & sea snails stewed with ripe tomatoes, onions & black pepper (Lesvos)

πετιμέζι ⓝ pe-ti-*me*-zi syrup made from unfermented grape juice, used to flavour rolls, cakes & sweets – when mixed with cold water makes a refreshing drink

πιλάφι ⓝ pi-*la*-fi pilau – rice & stock cooked to a creamy consistency – served to complement boiled meat or chicken
— **με ντομάτες** me do-*ma*-tes pilau with the addition of tomatoes, meat stock, garlic, parsley, salt & pepper
— **με γαρίδες** me gha-*ri*-ṭhes pilau with prawns, onions & oregano
— **με μύδια** me *mi*-ṭhia pilau with fresh mussels, onions & white wine
— **με περδίκια** me per-*ṭhi*-ki-a pilau with partridge, tomato & cloves (Kefallonia)

πιπέρι ⓝ pi-*pe*-ri black pepper

πιροσκί ⓝ pi-ro-*ski* deep-fried, dough-wrapped sausage roll

πίτα ⓕ *pi*-ta pie – filo is the most common pastry used • flat doughy circular bread seared on grill until golden, mainly used for wrapping **σουβλάκι** & **γύρος**

πιτσούνια ⓝ pl pit-*su*-nia squab • love-bird • any tiny bird used for cooking

— **κρασάτα** kra-*sa*-ta baby squabs doused in red wine, tomato pulp, cinnamon & cloves then braised
— **με κουκουνάρια** me ku-ku-*na*-ria squab ignited with brandy, splashed with retsina & dressed with a garlic cream sauce (Northern Greece)
— **με κουκιά** me ku-*kia* stewed squab & fresh broad beans cooked in chicken stock, white wine, dill, garlic & lots of black pepper

πλακί pla-*ki* method of baking or braising with tomatoes, onion, garlic & parsley

ποδαράκια ⓝ pl po-ṭha-*ra*-kia trotters
— **αρνίσια** ar-*ni*-si-a boiled lamb's trotters browned in butter & garlic, roasted, then finished with egg & lemon sauce

πόρτο ⓝ *por*-to port

πορτοκάλι ⓝ por-to-*ka*-li orange
— **γλυκό** ghli-*ko* preserved orange

ποτό ⓝ po-*to* drinks • spirits (on menus)

πράσα ⓝ pl *pra*-sa leeks
— **αλευρολέμονο** a-lev-ro-*le*-mo-no braised leeks in lemony sauce
— **με δαμάσκηνα** me ṭha-*ma*-ski-na leeks & prunes sprinkled with cinnamon & nutmeg
— **με ρύζι** me *ri*-zi leeks & celery simmered with rice & crushed tomatoes

πρασάκια με πατάτες ⓝ pl pra-*sa*-ki-a me pa-*ta*-tes leeks & sliced potatoes cooked in butter, chicken stock, onions, oregano & parsley

πρασόπιτα ⓕ pra-*so*-pi-ta pie made with braised leeks, feta, **μυζήθρα** & skim milk (Western Greece)

Ρ ρ

ραβιόλες ⓕ pl ra-vi-*o*-les pasta envelopes stuffed with a mixture of cheese & mint, served with melted butter & grated cheese (Cyprus)

ραδίκι ⓝ ra-*ṭhi*-ki chicory • term used for common varieties of **χόρτα**
— **σαλάτα** sa-*la*-ta spring salad of young dandelion leaves splashed with oil & lemon

ρακί ⓝ ra-ki fiery village spirit made from grapes, like ouzo but without the aniseed taste, high in alcohol

ραφιόλια ⓝ pl ra-fi-o-li-a sweet half-moon filo pastries stuffed with cheese, eggs, cinnamon, orange rind & ouzo (Cyclades)

ρεβανί ⓝ re-va-ni very sweet semolina sponge, flavoured with vanilla & orange juice & smothered with honey syrup

ρεβίθια ⓝ pl re-vi-thia chickpeas
— **αλευρολέμονο** a-lev-ro-le-mo-no chickpeas simmered in a rich lemony broth
— **στο φούρνο** sto fur-no casserole of chickpeas, onions, garlic & bay leaves – favourite fasting food during Lent
— **σούπα** su-pa chickpea soup

ρεβιθοκεφτέδες ⓜ pl re-vi-tho-kef-te-thes rissoles of mashed chickpeas, potatoes, onion, parsley & black pepper

ρέγγα ⓕ reng-ga smoked herrings, eaten plain or grilled with oil & lemon

ρέσσι ⓝ re-si pilau made with burghul & lamb (including the tail) & served at weddings (Cyprus)

ρετσίνα ⓕ ret-si-na retsina – pine-resinated wine, often served chilled

ριγανάτος ⓜ ri-gha-na-tos seasoned with oregano, salt & pepper

ρίγανη ⓕ ri-gha-ni pungent Greek oregano

ριζάδα ⓕ ri-za-tha thick soup made with rice & shellfish or tiny game birds (Corfu)

ριζόγαλο ⓝ ri-zo-gha-lo vanilla-flavoured rice pudding sprinkled with cinnamon

ρόδι ⓝ ro-thi pomegranate – used to flavour sweets, syrups, cakes & salads

ροδόνερο ⓝ ro-tho-ne-ro fragrant rose-water used to flavour cakes, pies & sweets

ροφός ⓜ ro-fos grouper • blackfish

ρολό από κιμά ⓝ ro-lo a-po ki-ma baked mincemeat roll with hard-boiled eggs cuddled in the middle

ρύζι ⓝ ri-zi rice

Σ σ

σαλάχι ⓝ sa-la-hi ray fish • skate
— **σαλάτα** sa-la-ta boiled ray fish salad dressed with λαδολέμονο

σαλιγκάρια ⓝ pl sa-ling-ga-ri-a snails – cooked in the shell & eaten with a fork

— **φρικασέ** fri-ka-se large snails sautéed in oil & stewed with zucchini, onions, fresh dill & finished with αβγολέμονο
— **με σάλτσα** me sal-tsa snails cooked with crushed tomatoes, tomato paste, onions & oregano
— **συμπεθεριό** sim-be-the-rio 'in-laws' – snails cooked with sliced eggplant, tomato pulp & ξινόχοντρος
— **στα κάρβουνα** sta kar-vu-na live snails chargrilled & doused with λαδολέμονο & bay leaves (Cyclades)
— **στιφάδο** sti-fa-tho snail ragout with bay leaves (Crete)

σαλμί ⓝ sal-mi method of casseroling game with red wine, vegetables & herbs

σάλτσα ⓕ sal-tsa sauce • generic term for tomato sauce
— **από ζωμό κρέατος** a-po zo-mo kre-a-tos gravy
— **άσπρη** a-spri béchamel sauce with egg
— **άσπρη ξινή** a-spri ksi-ni 'sharp white sauce' – made with butter, flour, meat stock, eggs & lemon
— **αυγολέμονο** av-gho-le-mo-no see αβγολέμονο
— **ντομάτα** do-ma-ta tomato sauce with bay leaves
— **ντομάτα με κιμά** do-ma-ta me ki-ma tomato & mincemeat sauce
— **μαρινάτα** ma-ri-na-ta marinade
— **μουστάρδα** mu-star-tha mustard & garlic beaten with lemon juice
— **ταρτάρ** tar-tar tartare sauce

Σάμος sa-mos rich golden dessert wine (Samos)

σαρακοστιανά ⓝ pl sa-ra-ko-sti-a-na see νηστήσιμα

σαρδέλες ⓕ pl sar-the-les sardines
— **παστές** pa-stes salted sardines
— **στο φούρνο** sto fur-no sardines baked with oil, lemon, garlic & oregano

σαρμάς ⓜ sar-mas pie-like offal dish (Northern Greece)

σβίγγοι ⓜ pl zving-gi deep-fried fritters served with honey, cinnamon & cognac syrup

σελινόριζα ① se·li·*no*·ri·za celeriac
— **με αυγολέμονο** me av·gho·*le*·mo·no creamy dish of celeriac in chicken stock & finished with egg & lemon sauce
— **με πράσα** me *pra*·sa braised celeriac wedges & leek strips thickened with **αβγολέμονο**

σέσκουλο ⓝ se·sku·lo swiss chard, type of **χόρτα**
— **με κιμά** me ki·*ma* silverbeet sautéed with chopped onion in butter & cooked with minced lamb, rice, dill, lemon juice & salt

σεσκουλόρυζο ⓝ se·sku·*lo*·ri·zo
see **σπανακόρυζο**

σεφταλιά ① sef·ta·*lia* pork rissoles wrapped in sheep's caul & chargrilled (Cyprus)

σκαλτσοτσέτα ① pl skal·tsot·se·ta paper-thin slices of fillet steak skewered & simmered in oil, water & tomatoes

σκορδαλιά ① skor·*tha*·lia thick paste of walnuts, bread, potatoes, olive oil, lemon & garlic

σκόρδο ⓝ *skor*·tho garlic
— **στούμπι** *stu*·bi vinegar bottled with a garlic bulb, used for dressing vegetable dishes & salads (Ionian Islands)
— **τσιγαριστά** tsi·gha·ri·*sta* fried whole garlic bulbs • peeled & sliced garlic cloves fried & simmered in white wine, tomato paste, salt & pepper (Ithaca)

σκουμπρί ⓝ sku·*bri* mackerel

σνακς ⓝ pl snaks snacks

σοφρίτο ⓝ so·*fri*·to fried veal slices braised in a sauce of crushed garlic, wine vinegar, parsley, mint & brandy (Corfu)

σοκολάτα ① so·ko·*la*·ta chocolate
— **γάλα** *gha*·la hot chocolate

σουσάμι ⓝ su·*sa*·mi sesame seed

σούβλα ① *suv*·la spit-roasted • skewers • method of chargrilling meat or fish

σουβλάκι ⓝ suv·*la*·ki souvlaki – tender chunks of seasoned or marinated meat (or fish) skewered & chargrilled
— **με πίτα** me *pi*·ta souvlaki with **πίτα**

σούγλι ⓝ *sugh*·li sun-dried baby bogue fish coated in batter & fried (Cyclades)

σούπα ① *su*·pa soup
— **ειδάτη** ksi·*tha*·ti sour soup of lentils, parsley & vinegar

— **με τσουκνίδες** me tsuk·*ni*·thes electric-green soup of stinging nettles & diced potatoes cooked in chicken stock & thickened with milk

σουπιές ① pl su·*pies* cuttlefish
— **κρασάτες** kra·*sa*·tes cuttlefish cooked in wine
— **με σάλτσα μελάνης** me *sal*·tsa me·*la*·nis cuttlefish cooked in a rich sauce made from its own black ink & wine (Crete)
— **με σπανάκι** me spa·*na*·ki cuttlefish cooked with spinach, onions, dill & mint

σουτζουκάκια ⓝ pl su·dzu·*ka*·kia rissoles of minced lamb, veal or pork braised in a very spicy tomato gravy

σουτζούκι ① su·*dzu*·ki strings of almonds dipped in syrup & sun-dried

σπάλα ① *spa*·la shoulder of meat
— **μοσχαρίσια** mos·kha·*ri*·si·a silverside

σπανακόπιτα ① spa·na·*ko*·pi·ta spinach filo pie, often includes feta or **κεφαλοτύρι**, eggs & herbs

σπανακόρυζο ⓝ spa·na·*ko*·ri·zo sautéed spinach, rice, spring onions & dill simmered in water until liquid is absorbed

σπετζοφάι ⓝ spe·dzo·*fa*·i sliced pork sausages stewed with sweet green peppers, eggplant, tomatoes & oregano

σπλήνα ① *spli*·na spleen
— **γεμιστή** ye·mi·*sti* calf's spleen stuffed with chopped sautéed liver, onion, garlic & herbs, then roasted

σπληνάντερο ⓝ spli·*nan*·de·ro spit-roast sausage made from intestine stuffed with sliced spleen & garlic

σταφίδες ① pl sta·*fi*·thes raisins • currants

σταφιδολιές ① pl sta·fi·*tho*·lies type of olive sun-dried until wrinkled, lightly salted & packed, or immersed in oil

σταφιδωτά ⓝ pl sta·fi·*tho*·ta oval short-bread biscuits with chewy raisin centres

σταφύλια ⓝ pl sta·*fi*·li·a grapes

στάκα ① *sta*·ka creamy butter made from fresh goat's or sheep's milk, used to flavour pies, stuffed vegetables & pilau
— **με αβγά** me av·*gha* omelette with **στάκα** (Crete)

στάμνα ⊙ *stam*·na method of cooking meat & potatoes in a pot sealed with wet clay & baked in charcoal embers

στιφάδο ⊙ sti·*fa*·tho meat, game or seafood ragout

στραγάλια ⊙ pl stra·*gha*·lia roasted chickpeas for snacking

σύκο ⊙ *si*·ko fig
— **αποστολιάτικο** a·po·sto·*lia*·ti·ko young green fig
— **γλυκό** ghli·ko green fig preserve
— **στο φούρνο** sto *fur*·no figs baked in a syrup of honey, vanilla, orange juice & orange flower water

συκόπιτα ⊙ si·*ko*·pi·ta fig cake (Corfu)

συκόψωμο ⊙ si·*kop*·so·mo heavy aromatic fig cake • dried green figs minced & mixed with ouzo shaped into balls, flattened, dried & wrapped in vine leaves

συκωταριά ⊙ si·ko·ta·*ria* innards • offal

συκώτι ⊙ si·*ko*·ti liver
— **κρασάτα** kra·*sa*·ta chopped liver marinated in red wine
— **λαδορίγανη** la·tho·*ri*·gha·ni grilled liver with oil, lemon & oregano
— **μαρινάτα** ma·ri·*na*·ta thinly sliced livers fried & finished with vinegar, white wine & rosemary
— **με κρεμμυδάκια** me kre·mi·*tha*·kia livers fried with spring onions & cloves in a sauce of white wine & tomato juice

σφακιανόπιτες ⊙ pl sfa·ki·a·*no*·pi·tes cheese pies consisting of balls of cheese wrapped in dough, then fried & served with a dollop of honey

σφουγγάτο ⊙ sfung·*ga*·to Spanish-style omelette made with more vegetables than eggs, fried or baked (Rhodes)

Τ τ

ταβάς ⊙ ta·*vas* casserole of seasoned beef or lamb, fried onions, diced tomatoes, oil, vinegar & cinnamon

ταλατούρι ⊙ ta·la·*tu*·ri τζατζίκι flavoured with mint (Cyprus)

ταραμάς ⊙ ta·ra·*mas* salted pressed roe of the grey mullet or cod

ταράξακο ⊙ ta·*rak*·sa·ko dandelion

ταχίνι ⊙ ta·*hi*·ni sesame seed paste

ταχινόσουπα ⊙ ta·hi·*no*·su·pa creamy lemony soup made from sesame paste (popular during Lent)

τελεμές ⊙ te·le·*mes* heavily salted feta-style cheese

τηγανόψωμο ⊙ ti·gha·*nop*·so·mo fried tomato & spring onion bread (Santorini)

τίλιο ⊙ *ti*·li·o infusion of lime leaves

τζατζίκι ⊙ dza·*dzi*·ki refreshing purée of grated cucumber, yogurt & garlic

τσόχος ⊙ *tso*·khos milk thistle • mild sweet-tasting green used in warm salads, pies & stews • type of χόρτα

της ώρας tis *o*·ras dishes cooked to order, such as steaks or chops

τσουρέκι ⊙ tot·su·*re*·ki braided Easter bread spiced with lemon rind & cherry pips, sprinkled with almonds & crushed μαστίχα

τραχανόσουπα ⊙ tra·kha·*no*·su·pa thick gruel of granulated pasta cooked in chicken broth with butter, lemon juice

τριαντάφυλλο γλυκό ⊙ tri·an·*da*·fi·lo ghli·*ko* delicate soft jam made from dark red rose petals

τσικουδιά ⊙ tsi·ku·*thia* see ρακί

τσιπούρα ⊙ tsi·*pu*·ra gilt head bream • snapper

τσίπουρο ⊙ *tsi*·pu·ro see ρακί

τσίρος ⊙ *tsi*·ros small dried mackerel

τσουκνίδες ⊙ pl tsu·*kni*·thes stinging nettles used in salads & soups

τουρσί ⊙ tur·*si* pickles • pickled

τούρτα ⊙ *tur*·ta cake • gateau • tart

τυρί ⊙ ti·*ri* cheese
— **μπλε** ble blue cheese
— **ημίσκληρο** i·mi·*skli*·ro semi-firm cheese
— **κατσικίσιο** kat·si·*ki*·si·o goat's cheese
— **κρεμώδες** kre·*mo*·thes cream cheese
— **μαλακή μυζήθρα** ma·la·*ki* mi·zi·thra cottage cheese
— **μαλακό** ma·la·*ko* soft cheese
— **σαγανάκι** sa·gha·na·ki sharp, hard cheese fried until crispy on the outside & soft in the centre, served with a squeeze of lemon juice
— **σκληρό** skli·*ro* hard cheese

τυρόπηγμα ⊙ ti·ro·*pigh*·ma curd

τυρόπιτα ① ti·ro·pi·ta *cheese pies, the classic mixture is feta & **κεφαλοτύρι** wrapped in flaky filo pastry & baked*

τυροβολιά ① ti·ro·vo·lia *cheese variety*

Φ φ

φάβα ① fa·va *yellow split pea purée served with raw onion rings*
— **παντρεμένη** pan·dre·me·ni *'married' – leftover* **φάβα** *served as a hot dish with the addition of tomatoes & cumin*

φαγρί ⑩ fa·ghri *sea bream*

φακές ① pl fa·kes *lentils*
— **με μακαρόνια** me ma·ka·ro·nia *lentils simmered in water & vinegar with mint, garlic & pearl pasta (Astypalea)*
— **σούπα** su·pa *lentil soup*

Φανουρόπιτα ① fa·nu·ro·pi·ta *cake spiced with dried fruit, brandy & cinnamon – served on Saint Fanourios Day*

φασκόμηλο ⑩ fa·sko·mi·lo *sage*

φασολάδα ① fa·so·la·tha *thick fragrant soup of beans, tomatoes, tomato paste, carrots, celery, garlic & parsley*

φασολάκια ⑩ pl fa·so·la·kia *green beans*
— **λαδερά** la·the·ra *green beans cooked in oil with tomatoes & onions*
— **σαλάτα** sa·la·ta *boiled fresh green beans with* **λαδολέμονο** *or* **λαδόξιδο**

φασόλια ⑩ pl fa·so·li·a *dried beans – usually refers to white haricot/lima beans*
— **μάραθο** ma·ra·tho *dried beans browned in oil & onions, simmered with tomato pulp & fennel leaves*
— **σαλάτα** sa·la·ta *bean salad*

φέτα ① fe·ta
feta – white, crumbly, salty cheese
— **σχάρας** skha·ras *grilled feta*

φέτες ψαριού με ντομάτα και σταφίδες ① pl fe·tes psa·riu me do·ma·ta ke sta·fi·thes *fish with tomato & currants*

φιλέτο ⑩ fi·le·to *fillet • steak*

φιρίκια ① pl fi·ri·ki·a
small crisp apples (Northern Greece)
— **με αμύγδαλα** me a·migh·tha·la *baked* **φιρίκια** *stuffed with almonds*
— **γεμιστά** ye·mi·sta *φιρίκια stuffed with minced veal, coriander & cumin*

φιστίκια ⑩ pl fi·sti·ki·a *peanuts*
— **Αιγίνης** e·yi·nis *pistachios*

φλαούνες ① pl fla·u·nes *baked savoury tarts (Cyprus)*

φοινίκια ⑩ pl fi·ni·ki·a *honey-dipped shortbread sprinkled with cinnamon & marked with a criss-cross design*

φρικασέ ⑩ fri·ka·se *meat or vegetable stew thickened & flavoured with* **αβγολέμονο**

φρουταλιά ① fru·ta·lia *omelette-type dish consisting of eggs, potatoes, parsley & sliced smoked pork sausages (Andros)*

φρυγαδέλια ⑩ pl fri·gha·the·lia *liver parcels in lamb's caul, fried or skewered & chargrilled (Northern Greece, Thessaly)*

φύλλο ⑩ fi·lo *flaky tissue-thin pastry used for pies & sweet pastries*

Χ χ

χαβιάρι ⑩ kha·via·ri *caviar*

χαλβάς ⑩ khal·vas
rich creamy sweet made from sesame seeds & honey, flavoured with pistachio, chocolate or almonds
— **σιμιγδαλένιος** si·migh·tha·le·nios *moist cake of semolina & honey, decorated with almonds & cinnamon*
— **της Ρίνας** tis ri·nas *baked semolina & almond cake served hot with sugar syrup*

χαλορίνι ⑩ kha·lo·ri·ni
pouch-shaped cheese filled with crushed coriander (Cyprus)

χαλούμι ⑩ kha·lu·mi
firm, white, sheep's milk cheese with elastic texture & salty taste (Cyprus)

χαλουμόπιτες ① pl kha·lu·mo·pi·tes *savoury cake made with* **χαλούμι,** *eggs, mint, sultanas &* **μαστίχα** *(Cyprus)*

χαλουμόφωμο ⑩ kha·lu·mop·so·mo *bread baked with chunks of* **χαλούμι** *(Cyprus)*

χαμομήλι ⑩ kha·mo·mi·li *chamomile*

χαμψιά ① kham·psia *fresh anchovy*

χαμψοπίλαφο ⑩ kham·pso·pi·la·fo *onion & anchovy pilau seasoned with oregano*

χείλη της χανούμισσας ① pl hi·li tis kha·nu·mi·sas *'the Turkish lady's lips' – crunchy honey cakes (Rhodes)*

χέλι ⑩ he·li *eel*
— **πλακί** pla·ki *eel baked with tomatoes, onions, potatoes & herbs (Corfu)*

χοιρινές ① pl hi·ri·*nes* pork chops

— **κρασάτες** kra·*sa*·tes pork chops simmered in red wine

— **στη σχάρα** sti skha·ra pork chops chargrilled with salt, pepper & lemon juice

— **τηγανητές** ti·gha·ni·tes fried pork chops

χοιρινό ⓝ hi·ri·no pork

— **με κυδώνια** me ki·*tho*·nia pork & quinces simmered in red wine spiced with orange peel & cinnamon

— **με πράσα** me pra·sa pork & leek casserole

— **με σέλινο αυγολέμονο** me se·li·no av·gho·le·mo·no pork & celery in egg & lemon sauce

— **μπούτι ψητό** *bu*·ti psi·to crispy, roast leg of pork

— **παστό** pa·*sto* salted pork

χοιρομέρι ⓝ hi·ro·*me*·ri cured leg of ham (Cyprus, Zakynthos)

χόντρος ⓜ khon·dros hand-milled wheat used in soups, dolmades, snail dishes & stews (see also **ξινόχοντρος**)

χόρτα ① pl khor·ta wild or cultivated greens used in salads, pie fillings, casseroles or boiled & served hot with an oil & lemon dressing

— **τσιγάρι** tsi·*gha*·ri lightly fried wild greens

χορτόπιτα ① khor·to·pi·ta pies made from seasonal greens

χορτοσαλάτα ① khor·to·sa·*la*·ta warm salad of greens dressed with salt, oil & lemon

χορτόσουπα ① khor·*to*·su·pa vegetable soup

χουρμάδες ⓜ pl khur·*ma*·thes dates

χοχλιοί ⓜ pl kho·khli·i snails

— **μπουμπουριστοί** bu·bu·ri·sti 'upside-down' – live snails deep-fried & doused with vinegar & rosemary

χριστόψωμο ⓝ khri·stop·so·mo sweet Christmas bread baked in the shape of a cross

χταπόδι ⓝ khta·po·thi octopus

— **βραστό** vra·sto boiled octopus coated with oil & lemon sauce

— **κεφτέδες** kef·*te*·thes rissoles of minced octopus, onion, mint & cheese

— **κρασάτο** kra·*sa*·to octopus cooked in red wine sauce

— **λιαστό** lia·sto sun-dried, chargrilled octopus sprinkled with oil & lemon juice

— **με μακαρόνι κοφτό** me ma·ka·ro·ni kof·to casserole of octopus, tomatoes, macaroni & red wine

— **στα κάρβουνα** sta kar·vu·na grilled octopus

— **στιφάδο** sti·*fa*·tho octopus ragout

— **τουρσί** tur·si pickled octopus

χυλόφτα ⓝ pl hi·lof·ta macaroni served with hot butter & grated cheese (Crete)

χωριάτικη σαλάτα ① kho·ri·a·ti·ki sa·*la*·ta 'village salad' – salad of tomatoes, cucumber, olives & feta (known outside Greece as 'Greek salad')

Ψ ψ

ψάρι ⓝ *psa*·ri fish

— **μαρινάτο** ma·ri·*na*·to fish fried until golden, served with a piquant sauce of garlic, rosemary & vinegar (also called **ψάρι σαβόρι**)

— **πλακί** pla·*ki* whole fish basted with oil, lemon & parsley, baked on a bed of chopped tomatoes & onions

— **σαβόρι** sa·vo·ri see **ψάρι μαρινάτο**

— **Σπετσιώτο** spet·si·o·to fish baked with bread crumbs & white wine (Spetses)

— **στη σχάρα** sti skha·ra chargrilled fish

— **στο φούρνο λαδορίγανη** sto fur·no la·tho·ri·gha·ni sliced fish & potato wedges baked in a broth of oil, water & lemon juice

— **τηγανητό** ti·gha·ni·to battered fish

— **βραστό με λαχανικά** vra·sto me la·kha·ni·ka poached fish with vegetables – the broth is often strained, thickened with **αβγολέμονο**

ψαροκεφτέδες ⓜ pl psa·ro·kef·*te*·thes fried fish rissoles

ψαρονέφρι ⓝ psa·ro·ne·fri pork fillet steak

ψαρόσουπα ① psa·ro·su·pa fish soup thickened with rice & **αβγολέμονο**

ψητός psi·tos an all-purpose term for grilling, baking & barbecueing

ψωμιά με ανάγλυφες διακοσμήσεις ⓝ pl pso·mia me a·na·ghli·fes thi·a·koz·mi·sis decorated bread (usually made with doughs of different colours) eaten at festivals, baptisms & weddings

ουσιώδη

emergencies

έκτακτη ανάγκη

Help!	Βοήθεια!	vo·i·thia
Stop!	Σταμάτα!	sta·ma·ta
Go away!	Φύγε!	fi·ye
Thief!	Κλέφτης!	klef·tis
Fire!	Φωτιά!	fo·tia
Watch out!	Πρόσεχε!	pro·se·he

Call an ambulance!
Κάλεσε το ασθενοφόρο.   ka·le·se to as·the·no·fo·ro

Call the doctor!
Κάλεσε ένα γιατρό.   ka·le·se e·na yia·tro

Call the police!
Κάλεσε την αστυνομία.   ka·le·se tin a·sti·no·mi·a

It's an emergency.
Είναι μια έκτακτη ανάγκη.   i·ne mia ek·tak·ti a·na·gi

There's been an accident.
Έγινε ατύχημα.   e·yi·ne a·ti·hi·ma

Could you please help?
Μπορείς να βοηθήσεις,   bo·ris na vo·i·thi·sis
παρακαλώ;   pa·ra·ka·lo

---

signs

Αστυνομία	a·sti·no·mi·a	Police
Αστυνομικός	a·sti·no·mi·kos	Police Station
Σταθμός	stath·mos	
Νοσοκομείο	no·so·ko·mi·o	Hospital
Σταθμός Πρώτων	stath·mos pro·ton	Emergency
Βοηθειών	vo·i·thi·on	Department

Is it safe …?	**Είναι ασφαλές …;**	*i*·ne as·fa·*les* …
at night	τη νύχτα	ti *nikh*·ta
for gay people	για γκέι	yia *ge*·i
for travellers	για ταξιδιώτες	yia tak·si·*thio*·tes
for women	για γυναίκες	yia yi·*ne*·kes
on your own	χωρίς παρέα	kho·*ris* pa·*re*·a

I'm lost.
Έχω χαθεί. *e*·kho kha·*thi*

Where are the toilets?
Πού είναι η τουαλέτα; pu *i*·ne i tu·a·*le*·ta

Is that a UN zone?
Είναι αυτή η ζώνη του ΟΗΕ; *i*·ne af·*ti* i *zo*·ni tu o·*i*·e

Where's the demarcation line?
Πού είναι η διαχωριστική pu *i*·ne i thi·a·kho·ri·sti·*ki*
γραμμή; ghra·*mi*

Are there military bases in this region?
Υπάρχουν στρατιωτικές i·*par*·khun stra·ti·o·ti·*kes*
βάσεις σ' αυτή την περιοχή; *va*·sis saf·*ti* tin pe·ri·o·*hi*

police

Where's the police station?
Πού είναι ο αστυνομικός pu *i*·ne o a·sti·no·mi·*kos*
σταθμός; stath·*mos*

Please telephone the Tourist Police.
Παρακαλώ τηλεφώνα την pa·ra·ka·*lo* ti·le·*fo*·na tin
τουριστική αστυνομία. tu·ri·sti·*ki* a·sti·no·*mi*·a

I want to report an offence.
Θέλω να αναφέρω *the*·lo na a·na·*fe*·ro
μια παρανομία. mia pa·ra·no·*mi*·a

It was him/her.
Ήταν αυτός/αυτή. *i*·tan af·*tos*/af·*ti*

I have insurance.
Έχω ασφάλεια. *e*·kho as·*fa*·li·a

I've been ...	Με έχουν ...	me e·khun ...
He/She has been ...	Τον/Την έχουν ...	ton/tin e·khun ...
assaulted	κακοποιήσει	ka·ko·pi·i·si
raped	βιάσει	vi·a·si
robbed	ληστέψει	li·step·si

the police may say ...

Κατηγορείσαι για ...	
ka·ti·gho·ri·se yia ...	You're charged with ...
Αυτός κατηγορείται για ...	
af·ti ka·ti·gho·ri·te yia ...	He's charged with ...
Αυτή κατηγορείται για ...	
af·ti ka·ti·gho·ri·te yia ...	She's charged with ...

διατάραξη	thi·a·ta·rak·si	disturbing the
ησυχίας	i·si·hi·as	peace
εξαγωγή	ek·sa·gho·yi	exporting
αρχαιοτήτων χωρίς	ar·he·o·ti·ton kho·ris	antiquities with-
άδεια	a·thi·a	out a permit
κακοποίηση	ka·ko·pi·i·si	assault
κλοπή από	klo·pi a·po	shoplifting
κατάστημα	ka·ta·sti·ma	
κλοπή	klo·pi	theft
μετακίνηση	me·ta·ki·ni·si	removing
αρχαιοτήτων	ar·he·o·ti·ton	antiquities
μη κατοχή	mi ka·to·hi	not having
βίζας	vi·zas	a visa
κατοχή	ka·to·hi	possession
(παράνομων	(pa·ra·no·mon	(of illegal
ουσιών)	u·si·on)	substances)
υπέρβαση της	i·per·va·si tis	overstaying
βίζας	vi·zas	a visa

Είναι πρόστιμο για ...	i·ne pro·sti·mo yia ...	It's a ... fine.
πάρκινγκ	par·king	parking
ταχύτητα	ta·hi·ti·ta	speeding

I've lost my ...	Έχασα ... μου.	e·kha·sa ... mu
My ... was/were stolen.	Έκλεψαν ... μου.	e·klep·san ... mu
bags	τις βαλίτσες	tis va·lit·se
money	τα χρήματά	ta khri·ma·ta
passport	το διαβατήριό	to thia·va·ti·rio

What am I accused of?

Για τι πράγμα
κατηγορούμαι;

yia ti *pra*·ghma
ka·ti·gho·*ru*·me

I didn't realise I was doing anything wrong.

Δεν κατάλαβα ότι έκαμα
κάτι λάθος.

then ka·*ta*·la·va o·ti e·ka·ma
ka·ti *la*·thos

I didn't do it.

Δεν το έκαμα.

then to e·ka·ma

I'm sorry.

Συγνώμη.

sigh·*no*·mi

Can I pay an on-the-spot fine?

Μπορώ να πληρώσω ένα
πρόστιμο επί τόπου;

bo·*ro* na pli·*ro*·so e·na
pro·sti·mo e·*pi* to·pu

I want to contact my embassy.

Θέλω να έρθω σε επαφή
με την πρεσβεία μου.

the·lo na *er*·tho se e·pa·*fi*
me tin prez·*vi*·a mu

Can I make a phone call?

Μπορώ να κάμω ένα
τηλεφώνημα;

bo·*ro* na *ka*·mo e·na
ti·le·*fo*·ni·ma

Can I have a lawyer (who speaks English)?

Μπορώ να έχω ένα
δικηγόρο (που να
μιλάει αγγλικά);

bo·*ro* na e·kho e·na
thi·ki·*gho*·ro (pu na
mi·*la*·i ang·gli·*ka*)

This drug is for personal use.

Αυτό το φάρμακο είναι
για προσωπική χρήση.

af·*to* to *far*·ma·ko *i*·ne
yia pro·so·pi·*ki* hri·si

I have a prescription for this drug.

Έχω συνταγή για αυτό
το φάρμακο.

e·kho si·da·*yi* yia af·*to*
to *far*·ma·ko

I (don't) understand.

(Δεν) καταλαβαίνω.

(then) ka·ta·la·*ve*·no

doctor

γιατρός

Where's the nearest …?	Πού είναι το πιο κοντινό…;	pu *i*·ne to pio ko·di·*no* …
emergency department	πρώτων βοηθειών	*pro*·ton vo·i·thi·*on*
hospital	νοσοκομείο	no·so·ko·*mi*·o
medical centre	ιατρικό κέντρο	i·a·tri·*ko ke*·dro
(night) pharmacy	(νυχτερινό) φαρμακείο	(nikh·te·ri·*no*) far·ma·*ki*·o

Where's the nearest …?	Πού είναι ο πιο κοντινός …;	pu *i*·ne o pio ko·di·*nos* …
dentist	οδοντίατρος	o·tho·di·*a*·tros
doctor	γιατρός	yia·*tros*
optometrist	οφθαλμίατρος	of·thal·*mi*·a·tros

I need a doctor (who speaks English).
Χρειάζομαι ένα γιατρό (που να μιλάει αγγλικά). — khri·*a*·zo·me *e*·na yia·*tro* (pu na mi·*la*·i ang·gli·*ka*)

Could I see a female doctor?
Μπορώ να δω μια γυναίκα γιατρό; — bo·*ro* na tho mia yi·*ne*·ka yia·*tro*

Could the doctor come here?
Μπορεί ο γιατρός να έρθει εδώ; — bo·*ri* o yia·*tros* na *er*·thi e·*tho*

Is there an after-hours emergency number?
Υπάρχει τηλεφωνικός αριθμός για επείγουσες ανάγκες τη νύχτα; — i·*par*·hi ti·le·fo·ni·*kos* a·rith·*mos* yia e·*pi*·ghu·ses a·*na*·ges ti *nikh*·ta

I've run out of my medication.
Μου έχουν τελειώσει τα φάρμακά μου. — mu *e*·khun te·li·o·si ta *far*·ma·*ka* mu

This is my usual medicine.
Αυτά είναι τα συνηθισμένα
μου φάρμακα.
af·*ta i*·ne ta si·ni·thiz·*me*·na
mu *far*·ma·ka

What's the correct dosage?
Ποια είναι η σωστή δόση;
pia *i*·ne i so·*sti tho*·si

I don't want a blood transfusion.
Δεν θέλω μετάγγιση
αίματος.
then *the*·lo me·*ta*·gi·si
e·ma·tos

Please use a new syringe.
Παρακαλώ χρησιμοποίησε
καινούργια σύριγγα.
pa·ra·ka·*lo* khri·si·mo·*pi*·i·se
ke·*nur*·yia *si*·ri·ga

I have my own syringe.
Έχω δική μου σύριγγα.
e·kho thi·*ki* mu *si*·ri·ga

I've been vaccinated against ...
Έχω κάμει εμβόλιο για ...
e·kho *ka*·mi em·*vo*·li·o yia

He/She has been **vaccinated** **against ...**	Αυτός/Αυτή έχει κάμει εμβόλιο για ...	af·*tos*/af·*ti* e·khi *ka*·mi em·*vo*·li·o yia ...
hepatitis	ηπατίτιδα	i·pa·*ti*·ti·tha
A/B/C	A/B/C	*e*·i/bi/si
tetanus	τέτανο	*te*·ta·no
typhoid	τύφο	*ti*·fo

I need new ...	Χρειάζομα ...	khri·*a*·zo·me ...
contact	καινούργιους	ke·*nur*·yius
lenses	φακούς επαφής	fa·*kus* e·pa·*fis*
glasses	καινούργια γιαλιά	ke·*nur*·yia yia·*lia*

My prescription is ...
Η συνταγή μου είναι ...
i si·da·*yi* mu *i*·ne ...

How much will it cost?
Πόσο θα κοστίσει;
po·so tha ko·*sti*·si

Can I have a receipt for my insurance?
Μπορώ να έχω μια
απόδειξη για την
ασφάλειά μου;
bo·*ro* na *e*·kho mia
a·*po*·thik·si yia tin
as·*fa*·li·a mu

the doctor may say ...

Ποιο είναι το πρόβλημα;
pio *i*·ne to *prov*·li·ma — **What's the problem?**

Πού πονάει;
pu po·*na*·i — **Where does it hurt?**

Έχετε πυρετό;
e·he·te pi·re·*to* — **Do you have a temperature?**

Πόσον καιρό είστε έτσι;
po·son ke·ro *i*·ste et·si — **How long have you been like this?**

Το είχατε αυτό πριν;
to *i*·kha·te af·*po* prin — **Have you had this before?**

Έχετε σεξουαλικές σχέσεις;
e·he·te sek·su·a·li·*kes she*·sis — **Are you sexually active?**

Μήπως είχατε σεξ χωρίς προφύλαξη;
mi·pos *i*·kha·te seks kho·*ris* pro·*fi*·lak·si — **Have you had unprotected sex?**

Πίνετε;/Καπνίζετε;
pi·ne·te/ka·*pni*·ze·te — **Do you drink/smoke?**

Παίρνετε ναρκωτικά;
per·ne·te nar·ko·ti·*ka* — **Do you take drugs?**

Είστε αλλεργικός σε κάτι;
i·ste a·ler·yi·*kos* se *ka*·ti — **Are you allergic to anything?**

Παίρνετε φάρμακα;
per·ne·te *far*·ma·ka — **Are you on medication?**

Πόσον καιρό ταξιδεύετε;
po·son ke·ro tak·si·*the*·ve·te — **How long are you travelling for?**

Πρέπει να μπείτε στο νοσοκομείο.
pre·pi na *bi*·te sto no·so·ko·*mi*·o — **You need to be admitted to hospital.**

Πρέπει να το ελέγξετε όταν επιστρέψετε στη χώρα σας.
pre·pi na to e·*leng*·kse·te o·tan e·pi·*strep*·se·te sti *kho*·ra sas — **You should have it checked when you go home.**

health

197

Πρέπει να επιστρέψετε στη
χώρα σας για θεραπεία.
*pre·pi na e·pi·strep·se·te sti
kho·ra sas yia the·ra·pi·a* | You should return home for treatment.

Είστε υποχονδριακός/υποχονδριακή. **m/f**
*i·ste i·po·khon·thri·a·kos/
po·khon·thri·a·ki* | You're a hypochondriac.

symptoms & conditions

συμπτώματα και καταστάσεις

I'm sick.
Είμαι άρρωστος.   *i·me a·ro·stos*

My friend is (very) sick. (about a man)
Ο φίλος μου είναι   *o fi·los mu i·ne*
(πολύ) άρρωστος.   *(po·li) a·ro·stos*

My friend is (very) sick. (about a woman)
Η φίλη μου είναι   *i fi·li mu i·ne*
(πολύ) άρρωστη.   *(po·li) a·ro·sti*

My child is (very) sick.
Το παιδί μου   *to pe·thi mu*
είναι (πολύ) άρρωστο.   *i·ne (po·li) a·ro·sto*

He/She is having a/an ...	Αυτός/Αυτή έχει ...	af·tos/af·ti e·hi ...
allergic reaction	αλλεργική αντίδραση	a·ler·yi·ki a·di·thra·si
asthma attack	προσβολή από άσθμα	proz·vo·li a·po as·thma
epileptic fit	επιληπτική κρίση	e·pi·lip·ti·ki kri·si
heart attack	καρδιακή προσβολή	kar·thi·a·ki pros·vo·li

He/She has been ...	Αυτός/Αυτή ...	af·tos/af·ti ...
injured	έχει τραυματιστεί	e·hi trav·ma·ti·sti
vomiting	κάνει εμετό	ka·ni e·me·to

I've been …

injured	Έχω τραυματιστεί.	e·kho trav·ma·ti·*sti*
vomiting	Κάνω εμετό.	ka·no e·me·*to*

I've been bitten/ stung by a … Με έχει δαγκώσει/ τσιμπήσει … me *e*·hi tha·*go*·si/ tsi·*bi*·si …

bee	μέλισσα	*me*·li·sa
jellyfish	μέδουσα	*me*·thu·sa
sea urchin	αχινός	a·hi·*nos*
snake	φίδι	*fi*·thi
wasp	σφήκα	*sfi*·ka
weever fish	δράκαινα	*thra*·ke·na

I feel … Αισθάνομαι … es·*tha*·no·me …

anxious	ανυπόμονος/η m/f	a·ni·*po*·mo·nos/i
better	καλύτερα m&f	ka·*li*·te·ra
depressed	θλιμμένος/η m/f	thli·*me*·nos/i
dizzy	ζαλάδα m&f	za·*la*·tha
hot and cold	ζέστη και κρύο m&f	ze·sti ke *kri*·o
nauseous	ναυτία m&f	naf·*ti*·a
shivery	ρίγος m&f	*ri*·ghos
strange	παράξενα m&f	pa·*rak*·se·na
weak	αδύνατος/η m/f	a·*thi*·na·tos/i
worse	χειρότερα m&f	hi·*ro*·te·ra

It hurts here.
Πονάει εδώ. po·*na*·i e·*tho*

I can't sleep.
Δεν μπορώ να κοιμηθώ. then bo·*ro* na ki·mi·*tho*

I think it's the medication I'm on.
Νομίζω είναι τα φάρμακα no·*mi*·zo *i*·ne ta *far*·ma·ka
που παίρνω. pu *per*·no

I'm on medication for …
Παίρνω φάρμακα για … *per*·no *far*·ma·ka yia …

He/She is on medication for …
Αυτός/αυτή παίρνει af·*tos*/af·*ti per*·ni
φάρμακα για … *far*·ma·ka yia …

I have (a/an) …
Έχω …   e·kho …

He/She has (a/an) …
Αυτός/αυτή έχει …   af·tos/af·ti e·hi …

I've recently had (a/an) …
Είχα πρόσφατα …   i·kha pros·fa·ta …

He/She has recently had (a/an) …
Αυτός/αυτή είχε πρόσφατα …   af·tos/af·ti i·he pros·fa·ta …

AIDS	Έηντς n	e·idz
asthma	άσθμα n	as·thma
burn	έγκαυμα n	e·gav·ma
cold	κρύωμα n	kri·o·ma
constipation	δυσκοιλιότητα f	this·ki·li·o·ti·ta
cough	βήχα m	vi·kha
dehydration	αφυδάτωση f	a·fi·tha·to·si
diabetes	διαβήτη m	thia·vi·ti
diarrhoea	διάρροια f	thi·a·ri·a
encephalitis	εγκεφαλίτιδα f	e·ge·fa·li·ti·tha
fever	πυρετό m	pi·re·to
headache	πονοκέφαλο m	po·no·ke·fa·lo
heatstroke	ηλιακή	i·lia·ki
	συμφόρηση f	sim·fo·ri·si
indigestion	δυσπεψία f	this·pep·si·a
(fungal)	(μυκητώδη)	(mi·ki·to·thi)
infection	μόλυνση f	mo·lin·si
insect bite	τσίμπημα από	tsi·bi·ma a·po
	έντομο n	e·do·mo
Lyme disease	νόσο του lyme f	no·so tu la·im
nausea	ναυτία f	naf·ti·a
pain	πόνο m	po·no
rabies	λύσσα f	li·sa
rash	εξάνθημα n	ek·san·thi·ma
sea sickness	ναυτία f	naf·ti·a
sore throat	πονόλαιμο m	po·no·le·mo
sprain	στραμπούλισμα n	stra·bu·liz·ma
stomachache	στομαχόπονο m	sto·ma·kho·po·no
sunburn	ηλιακό έγκαυμα n	i·li·a·ko e·gav·ma
tick typhus	τσιμπούρι τύφου n	tsi·bu·ri ti·fu

women's health

(I think) I'm pregnant.
(Νομίζω) Είμαι έγγυος.   (no·mi·zo) i·me e·gi·os

I'm on the pill.
Παίρνω το Χάπι.   per·no to kha·pi

I haven't had my period for (six) weeks.
Δεν έχω περίοδο για (έξι)   then e·kho pe·ri·o·tho yia (ek·si)
εβδομάδες.   ev·tho·ma·thes

I've noticed a lump here.
Παρατήρησα ένα   pa·ra·ti·ri·sa e·na
εξόγκωμα εδώ.   ek·so·go·ma e·tho

Do you have something for (period pain)?
Έχετε κάτι για (πόνο για   e·he·te ka·ti yia (po·no yia
την περίοδο);   tin pe·ri·o·tho)

I have a …	Έχω …	e·kho …
urinary tract infection	μόλυνση στον ουρικό σωλήνα	mo·lin·si ston u·ri·ko so·li·na
yeast infection	μυκωτική μόλυνση	mi·ko·ti·ki mo·lin·si

---

the doctor may say …

Χρησιμοποιείτε αντισυλληπτικά; khri·si·mo·pi·i·te a·di·si·lip·ti·ka	**Are you using contraception?**
Έχετε περίοδο; e·he·te pe·ri·o·tho	**Are you menstruating?**
Είστε έγγυος; i·ste e·gi·os	**Are you pregnant?**
Πότε είχατε περίοδο τελευταία; po·te i·kha·te pe·ri·o·tho te·lef·te·a	**When did you last have your period?**
Είστε έγγυος. i·ste e·gi·os	**You're pregnant.**

I need (a/the) ...	Χρειάζομαι ...	khri·*a*·zo·me ...
contraception	αντισυλληπτικό	a·di·si·lip·ti·*ko*
morning-after pill	το χάπι του επόμενου πρωινού	to *kha*·pi tu e·*po*·me·nu pro·i·*nu*
pregnancy test	τεστ εγγυμοσύνης	test e·gi·mo·*si*·nis

allergies

αλλεργίες

I have a skin allergy.
Έχω αλλεργία στο δέρμα.   e·kho a·ler·*yi*·a sto *ther*·ma

I'm allergic to ...	Είμαι αλλεργικός/ αλλεργική ... m/f	*i*·me a·ler·yi·*kos* a·ler·yi·*ki*
He's allergic to ...	Αυτός είναι αλλεργικός ...	af·*tos i*·ne a·ler·yi·*kos* ...
She's allergic to ...	Αυτή είναι αλλεργική ...	af·*ti i*·ne a·ler·yi·*ki* ...
antibiotics	στα αντιβιωτικά	sta a·di·vi·o·ti·*ka*
anti- inflammatories	στα αντιφλεγμονώδη	sta a·di·flegh·mo·*no*·thi
aspirin	στην ασπιρίνη	stin as·pi·*ri*·ni
bees	στις μέλισσες	stis *me*·li·ses
codeine	στην κωδεΐνη	stin ko·the·*i*·ni
penicillin	στην πενικιλλίνη	stin pe·ni·ki·*li*·ni
pollen	στη γύρη	sti *yi*·ri
sulphur-based drugs	στα φάρμακα με θείο	sta *far*·ma·ka me *thi*·o
wasps	στις σφήκες	stis *sfi*·kes

inhaler	αναπνευστήρας m	a·nap·nef·*sti*·ras
injection	ένεση f	*e*·ne·si
antihistamines	αντιισταμίνες f	a·di·i·sta·*mi*·nes

For food-related allergies, see **vegetarian & special meals**, page 173.

parts of the body

μέρη του σώματος

My ... hurts.
Πονάει ...   po·na·i ...

I can't move my ...
Δεν μπορώ να κουνήσω ...   ţhen bo·ro na ku·ni·so ...

I have a cramp in my ...
Έχω κράμπα ...   e·kho kra·ba ...

My ... is swollen.
Είναι πρησμένο ...   i·ne priz·me·no ...

It hurts when you touch it.
Πονάει όταν το αγγίζεις.   po·ne o·tan to a·gi·zis

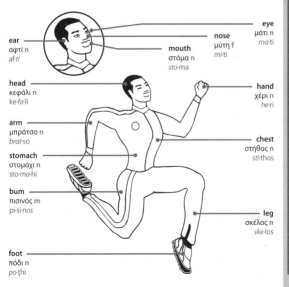

eye
μάτι n
ma·ti

nose
μύτη f
mi·ti

ear
αφτί n
af·ti

mouth
στόμα n
sto·ma

head
κεφάλι n
ke·fa·li

hand
χέρι n
he·ri

arm
μπράτσο n
brat·so

chest
στήθος n
sti·thos

stomach
στομάχι n
sto·ma·hi

bum
πισινός m
pi·si·nos

leg
σκέλος n
ske·los

foot
πόδι n
po·ţhi

alternative treatments

I don't use (Western medicine).
Δεν χρησιμοποιώ
(συμβατική ιατρική).

then khri·si·mo·pi·o
(sim·va·ti·ki i·a·tri·ki)

I prefer …	Προτιμώ …	pro·ti·mo …
Can I see someone	Μπορώ να δω	bo·ro na tho
who practises …?	κάποιον που	ka·pion pu
	ασκεί …;	a·ski …
acupuncture	βελονισμό	ve·lo·niz·mo
naturopathy	φυσική θεραπεία	fi·si·ki the·ra·pi·a
reflexology	αντανακλαστική	a·da·na·kla·sti·ki

pharmacist

I need something for (a headache).
Χρειάζομαι
κάτι για (πονοκέφαλο).

khri·a·zo·me
ka·ti yia (po·no·ke·fa·lo)

Do I need a prescription for (antihistamines)?
Χρειάζομαι συνταγή για
(αντιισταμίνες);

khri·a·zo·me si·da·yi yia
(a·di·i·sta·mi·nes)

I have a prescription.
Έχω συνταγή.

e·kho si·da·yi

---

come again?

If you need something repeated in a consultation or conversation, say Ορίστε; o·ris·te (Sorry?). Use Συγνώμη sigh·no·mi (Sorry) when you need to apologise.

How many times a day?
Πόσες φορές την ημέρα;　　po·ses fo·res tin i·me·ra

Will it make me drowsy?
Θα με κάμει να νυστάζω;　　tha me ka·mi na ni·sta·zo

antiseptic	αντισηπτικό n	a·di·sip·ti·ko
condoms	προφυλακτικά n pl	pro·fi·lakh·ti·ka
contraceptives	αντισυλληπτικά n pl	a·di·si·lip·ti·ka
insect repellent	εντομοαπωθητικό n	e·do·mo·a·po·thi·ti·ko
laxative	καθαρτικό n	ka·thar·ti·ko
painkillers	παυσίπονα	paf·si·po·na
(for infants)	(για μωρά) n pl	(yia mo·ra)
rehydration	ενυδρωτικά	en·i·thro·ti·ka
salts	άλατα n pl	a·la·ta
spray for insect	σπρέι για	spre·i yia
bites	τσιμπήματα	tsi·bi·ma·ta
	κουνουπιών n	ku·nu·pion
sunburn lotion	λοσιόν για ηλιακό	lo·sion yia i·li·a·ko
	έγκαυμα n	e·gav·ma
sunscreen	αντηλιακό n	a·di·i·li·a·ko
talcum powder	ταλκ n	talk
thermometer	θερμόμετρο n	ther·mo·me·tro
zinc cream	ψευδαργυρούχος	psev·thar·yi·ru·khos
	αλοιφή f	a·li·fi

dentist

I have a …	Έχω …	e·ho …
broken tooth	ένα σπασμένο δόντι	e·na spaz·me·no tho·di
cavity	ένα κούφιο δόντι	e·na ku·fio tho·di
toothache	πονόδοντο	po·no·tho·do

I've lost a filling.
Έχασα ένα σφράγισμα.   e·kha·sa e·na sfra·yiz·ma

My dentures are broken.
Οι μασέλες μου έσπασαν.   i ma·se·les mu e·spa·san

My gums hurt.
Πονούν τα ούλα μου.   po·nun ta u·la mu

I need an anaesthetic/a filling.
Χρειάζομαι αναισθητικό/   khri·a·zo·me a·nes·thi·ti·ko/
σφράγισμα.   sfra·yiz·ma

I don't want it extracted.
Δεν θέλω να το βγάλω.   then the·lo na to vgha·lo

Ouch!
Όου!   o·u

the dentist may say …

Ανοίξτε το στόμα πολύ a·nik·ste to sto·ma po·li.	Open wide.
Δεν θα πονέσει καθόλου. then tha po·ne·si ka·tho·lu	This won't hurt a bit.
Δαγκώστε αυτό. tha·go·ste af·to	Bite down on this.
Μην κινείστε. min ki·ni·ste	Don't move.
Ξεβγάλτε! ksev·ghal·te	Rinse!
Γυρίστε πίσω, δεν τελείωσα. yi·ri·ste pi·so then te·li·o·sa	Come back, I haven't finished.

A

Greek nouns in the **dictionary** have their gender indicated by ⑩ masculine, ① feminine or ⑪ neuter. If it's a plural noun you'll also see pl. When a word that could be either a noun or a verb has no gender indicated, it's a verb. Adjectives are given in the masculine form only – see **adjectives & adverbs** in the **phrasebuilder** for more on how to form feminine and neuter adjectives. Both nouns and adjectives are provided in the nominative case only – refer to the **phrasebuilder** for more information on **case**. Note that we've also added the abbreviations a adjective and v verb for added clarity where required.

A

aboard (επάνω στο) κατάστρωμα
(e·*pa*·no sto) ka·*tas*·tro·ma
abortion έκτρωση ① *ek*·tro·si
about περίπου pe·*ri*·pu
above από πάνω a·*po pa*·no
abroad στο εξωτερικό sto ek·so·te·ri·*ko*
accident ατύχημα ⑪ a·*ti*·hi·ma
accommodation κατάλυμα ⑪ ka·*ta*·li·ma
account λογαριασμός ⑩ lo·gha·riaz·*mos*
across απέναντι a·*pe*·na·di
activist ακτιβιστής/ακτιβίστρια ⑩/①
a·kti·vi·*stis*/a·kti·*vi*·stri·a
actor ηθοποιός ⑩&① i·tho·pi·*os*
acupuncture βελονισμός ⑩ ve·lo·niz·*mos*
adaptor μετασχηματιστής ⑩
me·ta·shi·ma·ti·*stis*
addiction εθισμός ⑩ e·thiz·*mos*
address διεύθυνση ① thi·*ef*·thin·si
administration διοίκηση ① thi·*i*·ki·si
admission (price) τιμή εισόδου ⑩
ti·*mi* i·so·*thu*
admit δέχομαι *the*·kho·me
adult ενήλικος/ενήλικη ⑩/①
e·*ni*·li·kos/e·*ni*·li·ki
advertisement διαφήμιση ① thi·a·*fi*·mi·si
advice συμβουλή ① sim·vu·*li*
Aegean Αιγαίο ⑪ e·*ye*·o
aerobics αερόμπικς ⑪ pl a·e·ro·biks
aeroplane αεροπλάνο ⑪ a·e·ro·*pla*·no
Africa Αφρική ① a·fri·*ki*
after μετά me·*ta*
(this) afternoon (αυτό το) απόγευμα ⑪
(af·*to* to) a·*po*·yev·ma

aftershave κολόνια ξυρίσματος ①
ko·*lo*·ni·a ksi·*riz*·ma·tos
again πάλι *pa*·li
age ηλικία ① i·li·*ki*·a
(three days) ago (τρεις μέρες) πριν
(tris *me*·res) prin
agree συμφωνώ sim·fo·*no*
agriculture γεωργία ① ye·or·*yi*·a
ahead εμπρός e·*bros*
AIDS Έηντς ⑪ e·idz
air αέρας ⑩ a·*e*·ras
air-conditioned με ερκοντίσιον
me er·kon·*di*·si·on
air conditioning έρκοντίσιον ⑪
er kon·*di*·si·on
airline αερογραμμή ① a·e·ro·ghra·*mi*
airmail αεροπορικό ταχυδρομείο ⑪
a·e·ro·po·ri·*ko* ta·hi·*thro*·mi·o
airplane αεροπλάνο ⑪ a·e·ro·*pla*·no
airport αεροδρόμιο ⑪ a·e·ro·*thro*·mi·o
airport tax δασμός αεροδρομίου ⑩
thaz·*mos* a·e·ro·*thro*·mi·u
aisle (on plane) διάδρομος (αεροπλάνου)
⑩ thi·*a*·thro·mos (a·e·ro·*pla*·nu)
alarm clock ξυπνητήρι ⑪ ksi·pni·*ti*·ri
Albania Αλβανία ① al·va·*ni*·a
alcohol αλκοόλ ⑪ al·ko·*ol*
all όλοι ⑩ *o*·li
allergy αλλεργία ① a·ler·*yi*·a
almond αμύγδαλο ⑪ a·*migh*·tha·lo
almost σχεδόν she·*thon*
alone μόνος *mo*·nos
already ήδη *i*·thi
also επίσης e·*pi*·sis

altar βωμός ⓜ vo·*mos*
altitude ύψος ⓝ *ip*·sos
always πάντα *pa*·da
ambassador πρέσβης/πρέσβειρα ⓜ/ⓕ
  prez·vis/*prez*·vi·ra
ambulance νοσοκομειακό ⓝ
  no·so·ko·mi·a·*ko*
America Αμερική ⓕ a·me·ri·*ki*
American football
  Αμερικανικό ποδόσφαιρο ⓝ
  a·me·ri·ka·ni·*ko* po·*thos*·fe·ro
amphitheatre αμφιθέατρο ⓝ
  am·fi·*the*·a·tro
anaemia αναιμία ⓕ a·ne·*mi*·a
anarchist αναρχικός/αναρχική ⓜ/ⓕ
  a·nar·hi·*kos*/a·nar·hi·*ki*
ancient a αρχαίος ar·*he*·os
and και ke
angry θυμωμένος thi·mo·*me*·nos
animal ζώο ⓝ *zo*·o
ankle αστράγαλος ⓜ a·*stra*·gha·los
another ένας άλλος *e*·nas *a*·los
answer απάντηση ⓕ a·*pa*·di·si
ant μυρμήγκι ⓝ mir·*mi*·gi
antibiotics αντιβιοτικά ⓝ pl a·di·vi·o·ti·*ka*
antinuclear αντιπυρηνικό ⓝ
  a·di·pi·ri·ni·*ko*
antique αντίκα ⓕ an·*ti*·ka
antiseptic αντισηπτικό ⓝ a·di·si·lip·ti·*ko*
any καθόλου ka·*tho*·lu
anxious ανυπόμονος/ανυπόμονη ⓜ/ⓕ
  a·ni·*po*·mo·nos/a·ni·*po*·mo·ni
apartment διαμέρισμα ⓝ thi·a·*me*·riz·ma
appendix (body) σκωληκοειδίτης ⓜ
  sko·li·ko·i·*thi*·tis
apple μήλο ⓝ *mi*·lo
appointment ραντεβού ⓝ ra·de·*vu*
apricot βερύκοκο ⓝ ve·*ri*·ko·ko
April Απρίλιος ⓜ a·*pri*·li·os
archaic αρχαϊκός ar·kha·i·*kos*
archaeological αρχαιολογικός
  ar·he·o·lo·yi·*kos*
architect αρχιτέκτονας ⓜ&ⓕ
  ar·hi·*tek*·to·nas
architecture αρχιτεκτονική ⓕ
  ar·hi·tek·to·ni·*ki*
argue συζητώ si·zi·*to*
arm χέρι ⓝ *he*·ri
aromatherapy αρωμοθεραπεία ⓕ
  a·ro·mo·the·ra·*pi*·a

arrest v συλλαμβάνω si·lam·*va*·no
arrivals αφίξεις ⓕ pl a·*fik*·sis
arrive φτάνω *fta*·no
art τέχνη ⓕ *tekh*·ni
art gallery πινακοθήκη ⓕ pi·na·ko·*thi*·ki
artist καλλιτέχνης/καλλιτέχνιδα ⓜ/ⓕ
  ka·li·*tekh*·nis/ka·li·*tekh*·ni·ʈha
ashtray σταχτοθήκη ⓕ stakh·to·*thi*·ki
Asia Ασία ⓕ a·*si*·a
ask (a question) ρωτάω ro·*ta*·o
ask (for something) ζητάω zi·*ta*·o
asparagus σπαράγγι ⓝ spa·*ra*·gi
aspirin ασπιρίνη ⓕ a·spi·*ri*·ni
asthma άσθμα ⓝ *asth*·ma
astrology αστρολογία ⓕ a·stro·lo·*yi*·a
at σε se
athletics αθλητικά ⓝ pl a·thli·ti·*ka*
atmosphere ατμόσφαιρα ⓕ at·*mos*·fe·ra
aubergine μελιτζάνα ⓕ me·li·*dza*·na
August Αύγουστος ⓜ *av*·ghu·stos
aunt θεία ⓕ *thi*·a
Australia Αυστραλία ⓕ af·stra·*li*·a
Australian Rules Football
  Αυστραλέζικο ποδόσφαιρο ⓝ
  af·stra·*le*·zi·ko po·*thos*·fe·ro
automated teller machine (ATM)
  αυτόματη μηχανή χρημάτων ⓕ
  af·to·ma·ti mi·kha·*ni* khri·*ma*·ton
autumn φθινόπωρο ⓝ fthi·*no*·po·ro
avenue λεωφόρος ⓕ le·o·*fo*·ros
avocado αβοκάντο ⓝ a·vo·*ka*·do
awful απαίσιος a·*pe*·si·os

B

B&W (film) μαυρόασπρο (φιλμ) ⓝ
  mav·ro·a·spro (film)
baby μωρό ⓝ mo·*ro*
baby food φαγητό για μωρά ⓝ
  fa·yi·to yia mo·*ra*
baby powder ταλκ ⓝ talk
babysitter μπέμπι σίτερ ⓕ be·i·bi *si*·ter
back (body) πλάτη ⓕ *pla*·ti
back (position) πίσω *pi*·so
backgammon τάβλι ⓝ *tav*·li
backpack σακίδιο ⓝ sa·*ki*·thi·o
bacon μπέικον ⓝ *be*·i·kon
bad κακός ka·*kos*
bag σάκος ⓝ *sa*·kos

baggage αποσκευές ① pl a·po·ske·*ves*

baggage allowance
επιτρεπόμενες αποσκευές ① pl
e·pi·tre·*po*·me·nes a·po·ske·*ves*

baggage claim παραλαβή αποσκευών
① pa·ra·la·*vi* a·po·ske·*von*

bakery φούρνος ⑩ *fur*·nos

balance (account) υπόλοιπο
(λογαριασμού) ⑩
i·*po*·li·po (lo·gha·riaz·*mu*)

Balcans Βαλκάνια ⑩ pl val·*ka*·ni·a

balcony μπαλκόνι ⑩ bal·*ko*·ni

ball (sport) μπάλα ① *ba*·la

ballet μπαλέτο ⑩ ba·*le*·to

banana μπανάνα ① ba·*na*·na

band (music) μπάντα ① *ba*·da

bandage επίδεσμος ⑩ e·*pi*·thez·mos

Band-Aid τσιρότο ⑩ tsi·*ro*·to

bank τράπεζα ① *tra*·pe·za

bank account τραπεζικός λογαριασμός
⑩ tra·pe·zi·kos lo·gha·riaz·*mos*

banknote χαρτονόμισμα ⑩
khar·to·*no*·miz·ma

baptism βάπτιση ① *vap*·ti·si

bar μπαρ ⑩ bar

barber κουρέας ⑩ ku·*re*·as

bar work δουλειά σε μπαρ ① thu·*lia* se bar

baseball μπέιζμπολ ⑩ *be*·iz·bol

basket καλάθι ① ka·*la*·thi

basketball μπάσκετ ⑩ *ba*·sket

bath μπάνιο ⑩ *ba*·nio

bathing suit μαγιό ⑩ ma·*yio*

bathroom μπάνιο ⑩ *ba*·nio

battery μπαταρία ① ba·ta·*ri*·a

be είμαι *i*·me

beach παραλία ① pa·ra·*li*·a

beach volleyball βόλεϊ παραλίας ⑩
vo·le·i pa·ra·*li*·as

bean φασόλι ⑩ fa·so·li

beansprouts φύτρα φασολιών ①
fit·ra fa·so·*lion*

beautiful όμορφος o·*mor*·fos

beauty salon ινστιτούτο αισθητικής ⑩
in·sti·*tu*·to es·thi·ti·*kis*

because διότι thi·o·ti

bed κρεβάτι ⑩ kre·*va*·ti

bedding σκεπάσματα ⑩ pl ske·*paz*·ma·ta

bed linen σεντόνια ⑩ pl se·*do*·nia

bedroom υπνοδωμάτιο ⑩
ip·no·tho·*ma*·ti·o

bee μέλισσα ① *me*·li·sa

beef βοδινό ⑩ vo·thi·*no*

beer μπύρα ① *bi*·ra

beetroot παντζάρι ① pat·*za*·ri

before πριν prin

beggar ζητιάκος/ζητιάνα ⑩/①
zi·*tia*·nos/zi·*tia*·na

behind πίσω *pi*·so

Belgium Βέλγιο ⑩ *vel*·yi·o

below κάτω *ka*·to

beside δίπλα *thi*·pla

best a ο καλύτερος o ka·*li*·te·ros

bet στοίχημα ⑩ *sti*·hi·ma

better καλύτερος/καλύτερη ⑩/①
ka·*li*·te·ros/ka·*li*·te·ri

between ανάμεσα a·*na*·me·sa

bible Βίβλος ① *viv*·los

bicycle ποδήλατο ⑩ po·*thi*·la·to

big μεγάλος me·*gha*·los

bigger μεγαλύτερος me·gha·*li*·te·ros

biggest ο μεγαλύτερος o me·gha·*li*·te·ros

bike ποδήλατο ⑩ po·*thi*·la·to

bike chain αλυσίδα ποδηλάτου ①
a·li·*si*·tha po·thi·*la*·tu

bike lock κλειδαριά ποδηλάτου ①
kli·tha·*ria* po·thi·*la*·tu

bike path δρόμος ποδηλάτου ⑩
thro·mos po·thi·*la*·tu

bike shop κατάστημα ποδηλάτου ⑩
ka·*ta*·sti·ma po·thi·*la*·tu

bill (restaurant etc) λογαριασμός ⑩
lo·gha·riaz·*mos*

billiards μπιλιάρδο ① bi·*liar*·tho

binoculars κιάλια ⑩ pl *kia*·lia

bird πουλί ⑩ pu·*li*

birthday γενέθλια ⑩ pl ye·*ne*·thli·a

birth certificate πιστοποιητικό
γεννήσεως ⑩ pi·sto·pi·i·ti·*ko* ye·ni·se·os

biscuit μπισκότο ⑩ bi·*sko*·to

bite (dog) δαγκωματιά ① tha·go·ma·*tia*

bite (insect) τσίμπημα ⑩ *tsi*·bi·ma

bitter πικρός pi·*kros*

black a μαύρος *mav*·ros

bladder κύστη ① *ki*·sti

blanket κουβέρτα ① ku·*ver*·ta

blind a τυφλός ti·*flos*

blister φουσκάλα ① fu·*ska*·la

blocked μπλοκαρισμένος blo·ka·riz·*me*·nos

blood αίμα ⑩ *e*·ma

blood group ομάδα αίματος ①
o·*ma*·tha *e*·ma·tos

blood pressure πίεση αίματος ①
pi·e·si e·ma·tos

blood test εξέταση αίματος ①
ek·se·ta·si e·ma·tos

blue a μπλε ble

board (transport) v ανεβαίνω a·ne·ve·no

boarding house πανσιόν ① pan·sion

boarding pass κάρτα επιβίβασης ①
kar·ta e·pi·vi·va·sis

boat βάρκα ① var·ka

body σώμα ⑩ so·ma

boiled βρασμένος vraz·me·nos

bone κόκαλο ⑩ ko·ka·lo

book βιβλίο ⑩ viv·li·o

book (reserve) v κλείνω θέση kli·no the·si

booked out πλήρες pli·res

bookshop βιβλιοπωλείο ⑩ viv·li·o·po·li·o

boot (footwear) μπότα ① bo·ta

boots (footwear) μπότες ① pl bo·tes

border σύνορο ⑩ si·no·ro

bored βαριεστημένος va·ri·e·sti·me·nos

boring ανιαρός a·ni·a·ros

borrow δανείζομαι tha·ni·zo·me

botanical garden βοτανικός κήπος ⑩
vo·ta·ni·kos ki·pos

both και οι δύο ke i thi·o

bottle μπουκάλι ⑩ bu·ka·li

bottle opener ανοιχτήρι ⑩ a·nikh·ti·ri

bottle shop κάβα ① ka·va

bottom (body) πισινός ⑩ pi·si·nos

bottom (position) κάτω κα·to

bouzouki (traditional music)
μπουζούκι ⑩ bu·zu·ki

bouzouki place μπουζουκτσίδικο ⑩
bu·zuk·tsi·thi·ko

bowl μπωλ ⑩ bol

box κουτί ⑩ ku·ti

boxer shorts σλιπάκι ⑩ sli·pa·ki

boxing μποξ ⑩ boks

boy αγόρι ⑩ a·gho·ri

boyfriend φίλος ⑩ fi·los

bra σουτιέν ⑩ su·ti·en

brakes φρένα ⑩ pl fre·na

brandy κονιάκ ⑩ ko·niak

brave γενναίος ye·ne·os

bread ψωμί ⑩ pso·mi

bread rolls ψωμάκια ⑩ pl pso·ma·kia

break v σπάω spa·o

break down χαλάω ha·la·o

breakfast πρόγευμα ⑩ pro·yev·ma

breast (body) στήθος ⑩ sti·thos

breathe αναπνέω a·nap·ne·o

bribe v δωροδοκώ tho·ro·tho·ko

bridge γεφύρι ⑩ ye·fi·ri

briefcase ⑩ χαρτοφύλακας khar·to·fi·la·kas

brilliant λαμπρός la·bros

bring φέρνω fer·no

broccoli μπρόκολο ⑩ bro·ko·lo

brochure μπροσούρα ① bro·su·ra

broken σπασμένος spaz·me·nos

broken down χαλασμένος
kha·laz·me·nos

bronchitis βρογχίτιδα ① vro·hi·ti·tha

bronze μπρούτζος ⑩ bru·dzos

brother αδερφός ⑩ a·ther·fos

brown καφέ ka·fe

bruise σημάδι από χτύπημα ⑩
si·ma·thi a·po khti·pi·ma

brush βούρτσα ① vur·tsa

bucket κουβάς ⑩ ku·vas

Buddhist Βουδιστής/Βουδίστρια
vu·thi·stis/vu·thi·stri·a ⑩/①

budget προϋπολογισμός ⑩
pro·i·po·lo·yiz·mos

buffet μπουφές ⑩ bu·fes

bug κοριός ⑩ ko·rios

build v χτίζω khti·zo

builder χτίστης ⑩ khti·stis

building κτήριο ⑩ kti·ri·o

Bulgaria Βουλγαρία ① vul·gha·ri·a

bumbag πορτοφόλι μέσης ⑩
por·to·fo·li me·sis

burn έγκαυμα ⑩ e·gav·ma

burnt καμένος ka·me·nos

bus (city) αστικό λεωφορείο ⑩
a·sti·ko le·o·fo·ri·o

bus (intercity) υπεραστικό λεωφορείο ⑩
i·per·a·sti·ko le·o·fo·ri·o

bus station σταθμός λεωφορείου ⑩
stath·mos le·o·fo·ri·u

bus stop στάση λεωφορείου ①
sta·si le·o·fo·ri·u

business επιχείρηση ① e·pi·hi·ri·si

business class μπίζνες κλας biz·nes klas

businessperson επιχειρηματίας ⑩&①
e·pi·hi·ri·ma·ti·as

business trip ταξίδι εργασίας ⑩
tak·si·thi er·gha·si·as

busker περιοδεύων τραγουδιστής ⑩
pe·ri·o·the·von tra·ghu·thi·stis
περιοδεύουσα τραγουδίστρια ①
pe·ri·o·the·vu·sa tra·ghu·thi·stri·a

busy απασχολημένος a·pa·skho·li·*me*·nos

but αλλά a·*la*

butcher χασάπης *kha·sa·pis*

butcher's shop κρεοπωλείο ⓝ kre·o·po·*li·o*

butter βούτυρο ⓝ *vu·*ti·ro

butterfly πεταλούδα ⓕ pe·ta·*lu·*tha

button κουμπί ⓝ ku·*bi*

buy v αγοράζω a·gho·*ra·*zo

Byzantine Βυζαντινός vi·za·di·*nos*

C

cabin καμπίνα ⓕ ka·*bi·*na

cabbage μάπα ⓕ *ma·*pa

cable car τελεφερίκ ⓝ te·le·fe·*rik*

café καφεστιατόριο ⓝ ka·fe·sti·a·to·*ri·o*

cafeteria καφετηρία ⓕ ka·fe·ti·*ri·a*

cake γλυκό ⓝ ghli·*ko*

cake shop ζαχαροπλαστείο ⓝ za·kha·ro·pla·*sti·o*

calculator αριθμομηχανή ⓕ a·rith·mo·mi·kha·*ni*

calendar ημερολόγιο ⓝ i·me·ro·*lo·*yi·o

call v καλώ ka·*lo*

camera φωτογραφική μηχανή ⓕ fo·to·ghra·fi·*ki* mi·kha·*ni*

camera shop κατάστημα φωτογραφικών ειδών ⓝ ka·ta·sti·ma fo·to·ghra·fi·*kon* i·*thon*

camp v κατασκηνώνω ka·ta·ski·*no·*no

camping ground χώρος για κάμπινγκ ⓜ *kho·*ros yia *kam·*ping

camping store κατάστημα ειδών κατασκήνωσης ⓝ ka·ta·sti·ma i·*thon* ka·ta·ski·no·sis

campsite χώρος για κάμπινγκ ⓜ *kho·*ros yia *kam·*ping

can (be able) v μπορώ bo·*ro*

can (tin) κουτί ⓝ ku·*ti*

can opener ανοιχτήρι ⓝ a·nikh·*ti·*ri

Canada Καναδάς ⓜ ka·na·*thas*

cancel ακυρώνω a·ki·*ro·*no

cancer καρκίνος ⓜ kar·*ki·*nos

candle κερί ⓝ ke·*ri*

candy καραμέλα ⓕ ka·ra·*me·*la

cantaloupe πεπόνι ⓝ pe·*po·*ni

capsicum πιπεριά ⓕ pi·pe·*ria*

car αυτοκίνητο ⓝ af·to·*ki·*ni·to

caravan τροχόσπιτο ⓝ tro·*kho·*spi·to

cardiac arrest καρδιακή προσβολή ⓕ kar·*thi·*a·*ki* proz·vo·*li*

cards (playing) χαρτιά ⓝ pl khar·*tia*

care (for someone) φροντίζω fro·*di·*zo

car hire ενοικίαση αυτοκινήτου ⓕ e·ni·*ki·*a·si af·to·ki·*ni·*tu

carob χαρούπι ⓝ kha·*ru·*pi

car owner's title τίτλος κατόχου αυτοκινήτου ⓜ *tit·*los ka·to·khu af·to·ki·*ni·*tu

car park χώρος στάθμευσης αυτικινήτων ⓜ *kho·*ros *stath·*mef·sis af·to·ki·*ni·*tu

car registration άδεια κυκλοφορίας αυτοκινήτου ⓕ *a·*thia ki·klo·fo·*ri·*as af·to·ki·*ni·*tu

carrot καρότο ⓝ ka·*ro·*to

carry μεταφέρω me·ta·*fe·*ro

carton χαρτοκιβώτιο ⓝ khar·to·ki·*vo·*ti·o

cash μετρητά ⓝ pl me·tri·*ta*

cash (a cheque) v εξαργυρώνω ek·sar·yi·*ro·*no

cash register ταμείο ⓝ ta·*mi·*o

cashew κάσιου ⓝ *ka·*si·u

cashier ταμίας ⓜ&ⓕ ta·*mi·*as

casino καζίνο ⓝ ka·*zi·*no

cassette κασέτα ⓕ ka·*se·*ta

castle κάστρο ⓝ *ka·*stro

casual work ημερομίσθια εργασία ⓕ i·me·ro·*mi·*sthi·a er·gha·*si·*a

cat γάτα ⓕ *gha·*ta

catamaran καταμαράν ⓝ ka·ta·ma·*ran*

cathedral μητρόπολη ⓕ mi·*tro·*po·li

Catholic Καθολικός/Καθολική ⓜ/ⓕ ka·tho·li·*kos*/ka·tho·li·*ki*

cauliflower κουνουπίδι ⓝ ku·nu·*pi·*thi

cave σπηλιά ⓕ spi·*lia*

CD σι ντι ⓝ si di

celebration γιορτή ⓕ yior·*ti*

cellphone κινητό ⓝ ki·ni·*to*

cemetery κοιμητήριο ⓝ ki·mi·*ti·*ri·o

cent σεντ ⓝ sent

centimetre εκατοστόμετρο ⓝ e·ka·to·*sto·*me·tro

centre κέντρο ⓝ *ke·*dro

ceramics κεραμικά ⓝ pl ke·ra·mi·*ka*

cereal δημητριακά ⓝ pl thi·mi·tri·a·*ka*

certificate πιστοποιητικό ⓝ pi·sto·pi·i·ti·*ko*

chain αλυσίδα ⓕ a·li·*si·*tha

chair καρέκλα ⓕ ka·*re·*kla

chairlift (skiing) τελεφερίκ ⓝ te·le·fe·*rik*

champagne σαμπάνια ⓕ sam·*pa·*nia

championships αγώνες πρωταθλήματος ⑩ pl a·gho·nes pro·ta·thli·ma·tos

chance πιθανότητα ① pi·tha·no·ti·ta

change αλλαγή ① a·la·yi

change (coins) ψιλά ⑩ pl psi·la

change (from sale) ρέστα ⑩ pl re·sta

change (money) v αλλάζω a·la·zo

changing room (in shop) δοκιμαστήριο ρούχων ⑩ tho·ki·ma·sti·ri·o ru·khon

charming χαριτωμένος kha·ri·to·me·nos

charter flight πτήση τσάρτερ ① pti·si tsar·ter

chat up (somebody) v ψήνω psi·no

cheap φτηνός fti·nos

cheat απατεώνας/απατεώνισσα ⑩/① a·pa·te·o·nas/a·pa·te·o·ni·sa

check v ελέγχω e·leng·kho

check (banking) προσωπική επιταγή ① pro·so·pi·ki e·pi·ta·yi

check (bill) λογαριασμός ⑩ lo·gha·riaz·mos

check-in (desk) ρεσεψιόν ① re·sep·sion

checkpoint σημείο ελέγχου ⑩ si·mi·o e·leng·khu

cheese τυρί ⑩ ti·ri

cheese shop τυροπωλείο ⑩ ti·ro·po·li·o

chef ⑩ σεφ sef

chemist (shop) φαρμακείο ⑩ far·ma·ki·o

chemist (pharmacist) φαρμακοποιός ⑩&① far·ma·ko·pi·os

cheque προσωπική επιταγή ① pro·so·pi·ki e·pi·ta·yi

cherry κεράσι ⑩ ke·ra·si

chess σκάκι ⑩ ska·ki

chessboard σκακιέρα ① ska·kie·ra

chest (body) στήθος ⑩ sti·thos

chestnut κάστανο ⑩ ka·sta·no

chewing gum μαστίχα ① ma·sti·kha

chicken κοτόπουλο ⑩ ko·to·pu·lo

chicken pox ανεμοβλογιά ① a·ne·mov·lo·yia

chickpea στραγάλι ⑩ stra·gha·li

child παιδί ⑩ pe·thi

childminding επιτήρηση παιδιών ① e·pi·ti·ri·si pe·thion

children παιδιά ⑩ pl pe·thia

child seat παιδικό κάθισμα ⑩ pe·thi·ko ka·thiz·ma

chilli πιπεριά ① pi·pe·ria

chilli sauce σάλτσα πιπεριάς ① sal·tsa pi·pe·rias

chipura τσίπουρο ⑩ tsi·pu·ro

chiropractor χειροπράκτωρ ⑩&① hi·ro·prak·stor

chocolate σοκολάτα ① so·ko·la·ta

choose διαλέγω thia·le·gho

chopping board σανίδα κοπής ① sa·ni·tha ko·pis

chopsticks τσοπ στικς ⑩ pl tsop stiks

Christian Χριστιανός/Χριστιανή ⑩/① khri·stia·nos/khri·stia·ni

Christian name μικρό όνομα ⑩ mi·kro o·no·ma

Christmas Χριστούγεννα ⑩ pl khri·stu·ye·na

Christmas Day ημέρα Χριστουγέννων ① i·me·ra khri·stu·ye·non

Christmas Eve παραμονή Χριστουγέννων ① pa·ra·mo·ni khri·stu·ye·non

church εκκλησία ① e·kli·si·a

cider κρασί από μήλο ⑩ kra·si a·po mi·lo

cigar πούρο ⑩ pu·ro

cigarette τσιγάρο ⑩ tsi·gha·ro

cigarette lighter αναπτήρας ⑩ a·nap·ti·ras

cinema σινεμά ⑩ si·ne·ma

circus τσίρκο ⑩ tsir·ko

citizenship ιθαγένεια ① i·tha·ye·ni·a

city πόλη ① po·li

city centre κέντρο της πόλης ⑩ ke·dro tis po·lis

civil rights πολιτικά δικαιώματα ⑩ pl po·li·ti·ka thi·ke·o·ma·ta

civil servant δημόσιος υπάλληλος ⑩&① thi·mo·si·os i·pa·li·los

class (category) τάξη ① tak·si

classical κλασικός kla·si·kos

class system ταξικό σύστημα ⑩ tak·si·ko si·sti·ma

clean a καθαρός ka·tha·ros

clean v καθαρίζω ka·tha·ri·zo

cleaning καθάρισμα ⑩ ka·tha·riz·ma

client πελάτης/πελάτισσα ⑩/① pe·la·tis/pe·la·ti·sa

cliff γκρεμός ⑩ gre·mos

climb v αναρριχούμαι a·na·ri·khu·me

cloakroom ιματιοφυλάκιο ① i·ma·ti·o·fi·la·ki·o

clock ρολόι ⑩ ro·lo·i

close v κοντινός ko·di·nos

close v κλείνω kli·no

closed κλεισμένος kliz·me·nos

clothesline μύλος (για ρούχα) ⑩ *mí*·los (yia ru·kha)

clothing ρούχα ⑩ pl *ru*·kha

clothing store κατάστημα ρούχων ⑩ ka·*ta*·sti·ma *ru*·khon

cloud σύννεφο ⑩ *sí*·ne·fo

cloudy συννεφιασμένος si·ne·fiaz·*me*·nos

clutch (car) συμπλέκτης ⑩ si·*ble*·ktis

coach (sport) προπονητής/προπονήτρια ⑩/① pro·po·ni·*tís*/pro·po·ni·tri·a

coalition συνασπισμός ⑩ sin·as·piz·*mos*

coast ακτή ① ak·*tí*

coat παλτό ⑩ pal·*to*

cocaine κοκαΐνη ① ko·ka·*í*·ni

cockroach κοριός ⑩ ko·*rios*

cocktail κοκτέηλ ⑩ kok·*te*·il

cocoa κακάο ⑩ ka·*ka*·o

coconut ινδική καρύδα ① in·thi·*ki* ka·*ri*·tha

coffee καφές ⑩ ka·*fes*

coffee shop καφενείο ⑩ ka·fe·*ni*·o

coins κέρματα ⑩ pl *ker*·ma·ta

cold κρύο ⑩ *kri*·o

cold a κρυωμένος kri·o·*me*·nos

colleague συνάδελφος/συναδέλφισσα ⑩/① si·*na*·thel·fos/si·na·*thel*·fi·sa

collect call κλήση με αντιστροφή της επιβάρυνσης ① *kli*·si me a·dis·tro·*fí* tis e·pi·*va*·rin·sis

college κολλέγιο ⑩ ko·*le*·yi·o

colour χρώμα ⑩ *khro*·ma

column κολώνα ① ko·*lo*·na

comb χτένα ① *khte*·na

come έρχομαι *er*·kho·me

comedy κωμωδία ① ko·mo·*thi*·a

comfortable άνετος *a*·ne·tos

commission προμήθεια ① pro·*mi*·thi·a

communications (profession) επικοινωνίες ① pl e·pi·ki·no·*ni*·es

communion κοινωνία ① ki·no·*ni*·a

communist κομμουνιστής/κομμουνίστρια ⑩/① ko·mu·ni·*stís*/ko·mu·ni·stri·a

companion σύντροφος/συντρόφισσα ⑩/① si·dro·fos/si·*dro*·fi·sa

company (firm) εταιρεία ① e·te·*ri*·a

company (friends) συντροφιά ① si·dro·*fia*

compass πυξίδα ① pik·*sí*·tha

complain παραπονούμαι pa·ra·po·*nu*·me

complaint παράπονο ⑩ pa·*ra*·po·no

complimentary (free) δωρεάν tho·re·*an*

computer κομπιούτερ ⑩ kom·*piu*·ter

computer game παιγνίδι στο κομπιούτερ ⑩ pegh·*ni*·thi sto kom·*piu*·ter

concert κονσέρτο ⑩ kon·*ser*·to

concussion κλονισμός ⑩ klo·niz·*mos*

conditioner (hair) κοντίσιονερ ⑩ kon·di·si·o·ner

condom προφυλακτικό ⑩ pro·fi·lak·ti·*ko*

conference (big) συνέδριο ⑩ si·*ne*·thri·o

conference (small) σεμινάριο ⑩ se·mi·*na*·ri·o

confession εξομολόγηση ① ek·so·mo·*lo*·ghi·si

confirm (a booking) επικυρώνω e·pi·ki·*ro*·no

conjunctivitis επιπεφυκίτις ⑩ e·pi·pe·fi·*kí*·tis

connection σύνδεσμος ⑩ *sin*·thez·mos

conservative a συντηρητικός si·di·ri·ti·*kos*

constipation δυσκοιλία ① this·ki·*li*·a

consulate προξενείο ① prok·se·*ni*·o

contact lenses φακοί επαφής ⑩ pl fa·*ki* e·pa·*fis*

contact lens solution υγρό φακών επαφής ⑩ i·*ghro* fa·kon e·pa·*fis*

contraceptives αντισυλληπτικά ⑩ pl a·di·si·lip·ti·*ka*

contract συμβόλαιο ⑩ sim·*vo*·le·o

convenience store σούπερ μάρκετ ⑩ *su*·per *mar*·ket

convent μοναστήρι γυναικών ⑩ mo·na·*stí*·ri yi·ne·*kon*

cook μάγειρας/μαγείρισσα ⑩/① *ma*·yi·ras/ma·*yí*·ri·sa

cook v μαγειρεύω ma·yi·*re*·vo

cookie μπισκότο ⑩ bis·*ko*·to

cooking μαγείρεμα ⑩ ma·*yi*·re·ma

cool (temperature) δροσερό thro·se·*ro*

copper χαλκός ⑩ khal·*kos*

copy αντίγραφο ⑩ a·*dí*·ghra·fo

Corinthian Κορινθιακός ko·rin·thi·a·*kos*

corkscrew ανοιχτήρι ⑩ a·nikh·*tí*·ri

corn καλαμπόκι ⑩ ka·la·*bo*·ki

corner γωνία ① gho·*ni*·a

cornflakes κορν φλέικς ⑩ pl korn *fle*·iks

corrupt διεφθαρμένος thi·ef·thar·*me*·nos

cost v κοστίζω ko·*sti*·zo

cotton βαμπάκι ⑩ va·*ba*·ki

cotton balls μπαλάκια από βαμπάκι ⑩ pl ba·*la*·kia a·po va·*ba*·ki

cotton buds ξιλάκι με βαμπάκι ⑩ ksi·*la*·ki me va·*ba*·ki

cough v βήχω *vi*·kho
cough medicine φάρμακο για το βήχα
ⓝ *far*·ma·ko yia to *vi*·kha
count v μετράω me·*tra*·o
counter (at bar) πάγκος ⓜ *pa*·gos
country χώρα ⓕ *kho*·ra
countryside εξοχή ⓕ ek·so·*hi*
coupon κουπόνι ⓝ ku·*po*·ni
courgette κολοκυθάκι ⓝ ko·lo·ki·*tha*·ki
court (legal) δικαστήριο ⓝ thi·ka·*sti*·ri·o
court (tennis) γήπεδο ⓝ *yi*·pe·tho
couscous κουσκούς ⓝ kus·*kus*
cover charge προσαύξηση τιμής ⓕ
pro·*saf*·ksi·si ti·*mis*
cow γελάδα ⓕ ye·*la*·tha
cracker (biscuit) γαλέτα ⓕ gha·*le*·ta
craft τέχνη ⓕ *tekh*·ni
crash ⓜ κρότος *kro*·tos
crazy τρελλός tre·*los*
cream κρέμα ⓕ *kre*·ma
crèche παιδικός σταθμός ⓜ
pe·thi·*kos* stath·*mos*
credit πίστωση ⓕ *pi*·sto·si
credit card πιστωτική κάρτα ⓕ
pi·sto·ti·*ki* *kar*·ta
cricket (sport) κρίκετ ⓝ *kri*·ket
crop σοδειά ⓕ so·*thia*
cross (religious) σταυρός ⓜ stav·*ros*
crowded γεμάτο (κόσμο)
ye·*ma*·to (koz·mo)
cruise κρουαζέρα ⓕ kru·a·*ze*·ra
cucumber αγγούρι ⓝ a·*gu*·ri
cup φλυτζάνι ⓝ fli·*dza*·ni
cupboard ντουλάπι ⓝ du·*la*·pi
currency exchange τιμή συναλλάγματος
ⓕ ti·*mi* si·na·*lagh*·ma·tos
current (electricity) ρεύμα ⓝ *rev*·ma
current affairs επίκαιρα θέματα ⓝ pl
e·*pi*·ke·ra *the*·ma·ta
curry κάρι ⓝ *ka*·ri
cushion cover μαξιλαροθήκη ⓕ
mak·si·la·ro·*thi*·ki
custom έθιμο ⓝ e·*thi*·mo
customs τελωνείο ⓝ te·lo·*ni*·o
cut v κόβω *ko*·vo
cutlery μαχαιροπήρουνα ⓝ pl
ma·he·ro·*pi*·ru·na
CV βιογραφικό σημείωμα ⓝ
vi·o·ghra·fi·*ko* si·*mi*·o·ma
Cycladic Κυκλαδικός ki·kla·thi·*kos*

cycle v κάνω ποδήλατο
ka·no po·*thi*·la·to
cycling ποδηλασία ⓕ po·thi·la·*si*·a
cyclist ποδηλάτης/ποδηλάτισσα ⓜ/ⓕ
po·thi·*la*·tis/po·thi·*la*·ti·sa
Cypriot (person) Κύπριος/Κύπρια ⓜ/ⓕ
ki·pri·os/*ki*·pri·a
Cypriot (wine etc) κυπριακός/κυπριακή
ⓜ/ⓕ ki·pri·a·*kos*/ki·pri·a·*ki*
Cyprus Κύπρος ⓕ *ki*·pros
cystitis κύστη ⓕ *ki*·sti

D

dad μπαμπάς ⓜ ba·*bas*
daily καθημερινός ka·thi·me·ri·*nos*
dairy shop γαλακτοπωλείο ⓝ
gha·lak·to·po·*li*·o
dance v χορεύω kho·*re*·vo
dancing χορός kho·*ros*
dangerous επικίνδυνος e·pi·*kin*·thi·nos
dark (night) a σκοτεινός sko·ti·*nos*
dark (colour) a σκούρος *sku*·ros
date (a person) v βγαίνω (με κάποιον)
vye·no (me *ka*·pion)
date (appointment) ραντεβού ⓝ ra·de·*vu*
date (day) ημερομηνία ⓕ i·me·ro·mi·*ni*·a
date (fruit) χουρμάς ⓜ khur·*mas*
date of birth ημερομηνία γεννήσεως ⓕ
i·me·ro·mi·*ni*·a ye·*ni*·se·os
daughter κόρη ⓕ *ko*·ri
dawn αυγή ⓕ av·*yi*
day ημέρα ⓕ i·*me*·ra
day after tomorrow
μεθαύριο me·*thav*·ri·o
day before yesterday
προχθές prokh·*tes*
dead α νεκρός ne·*kros*
deaf α κουφός ku·*fos*
deal (cards) μοιράζω (χαρτιά)
mi·ra·zo (khar·*tia*)
December Δεκέμβριος ⓜ de·*kem*·vri·os
decide αποφασίζω a·po·fa·*si*·zo
deck κατάστρωμα ⓝ ka·*ta*·stro·ma
deep βαθύς va·*this*
deforestation αποδάσωση ⓕ
a·po·*tha*·so·si
degrees (temperature) βαθμοί ⓜ pl
vath·*mi*

dehydration αφυδάτωση ① a·fi·*tha*·to·si
delay καθυστέρηση ① ka·thi·*ste*·ri·si
delicatessen ντελικατέσεν ① de·li·ka·*te*·sen
delineation line διαχωριστική γραμμή ①
  thi·a·kho·ri·sti·*ki* ghra·*mi*
deliver παραδίνω pa·ra·*thi*·no
democracy δημοκρατία ① *thi*·mo·kra·*ti*·a
demonstration διαδήλωση ① thi·a·*thi*·lo·si
Denmark Δανία ① tha·*ni*·a
dental floss οδοντιατρική κλωστή ①
  o·tho·di·a·tri·*ki* klo·*sti*
dentist οδοντίατρος ⑩&① o·tho·*di*·a·tros
deodorant αποσμητικό ⑩ a·poz·mi·ti·*ko*
depart (leave) αναχωρώ a·na·kho·*ro*
department store κατάστημα ⑩
  ka·*ta*·sti·ma
departure αναχώρηση ① a·na·*kho*·ri·si
departure gate θύρα αναχώρησης ①
  thi·ra a·na·*kho*·ri·sis
deposit (bank) κατάθεση ① ka·*ta*·the·si
deposit (on house etc) προκαταβολή ①
  pro·ka·ta·vo·*li*
depressed θλιμμένος/θλιμμένη ⑩/①
  thli·*me*·nos/thli·*me*·ni
derailleur εκτροχιασμός ⑩
  ek·tro·hi·az·*mos*
descendent απόγονος ⑩ a·*po*·gho·nos
desert έρημος ① *e*·ri·mos
design σχέδιο ⑩ *skhe*·thi·o
dessert επιδόρπιο ⑩ e·pi·*thor*·pi·o
destination προορισμός ⑩ pro·o·riz·*mos*
details λεπτομέρειες ① pl lep·to·*me*·ri·es
diabetes διαβήτης ⑩ thi·a·*vi*·tis
dial tone ήχος κλήσης ⑩ *i*·khos *kli*·sis
diaper πάνα ① *pa*·na
diaphragm διάφραγμα ⑩ thi·*a*·ghra·ma
diarrhoea διάρροια ① thi·*a*·ri·a
diary ημερολόγιο ⑩ i·me·ro·*lo*·yi·o
diaspora διασπορά ① thi·a·spo·*ra*
dice ζάρια ⑩ pl *za*·ria
dictionary λεξικό ⑩ lek·si·*ko*
die v πεθαίνω pe·*the*·no
diet δίαιτα ① *thi*·e·ta
different διαφορετικός thia·fo·re·ti·*kos*
difficult δύσκολος *thi*·sko·los
digital a ψηφιακός psi·fi·a·*kos*
dining car βαγόνι φαγητού ⑩
  va·*gho*·ni fa·yi·*tu*
dinner δείπνο ⑩ *thip*·no
direct a άμεσος *a*·me·sos

direct-dial κατ' ευθείαν γραμμή ①
  ka·tef·*thi*·an gra·*mi*
direction κατεύθυνση ① ka·*tef*·thin·si
director διευθυντής/διευθύντρια ⑩/①
  thi·ef·thi·*dis*/thi·ef·*thi*·dri·a
dirty a βρώμικος *vro*·mi·kos
disabled a ανάπηρος a·*na*·pi·ros
disco ντισκοτέκ ① di·sko·*tek*
discount έκπτωση ① *ek*·pto·si
discrimination διάκριση ① thi·*a*·kri·si
disease ασθένεια ① a·*sthe*·ni·a
dish πιάτο ⑩ *pia*·to
disk (CD-ROM) σι ντι ρομ ⑩ si di rom
disk (floppy) δισκέτα ① thi·*ske*·ta
diving βουτιά ① vu·*tia*
diving equipment εξαρτήματα
  βουτηχτή ⑩ pl ek·sar·*ti*·ma·ta vu·tikh·*ti*
divorced a
  διαζευγμένος/διαζευγμένη ⑩/①
  thi·a·zev·*ghme*·nos/thi·a·zev·*ghme*·ni
dizzy ζαλισμένος/ζαλισμένη ⑩/①
  za·liz·*me*·nos/za·liz·*me*·ni
do v κάνω *ka*·no
doctor γιατρός ⑩&① yia·*tros*
documentary ντοκυμαντέρ ⑩
  do·ki·man·*ter*
dog σκυλί ⑩ ski·*li*
dole επίδομα ανεργίας ⑩
  e·*pi*·tho·ma an·er·*yi*·as
doll κούκλα ① *ku*·kla
dollar δολλάριο ⑩ tho·*la*·ri·o
dolphin δελφίνι ⑩ thel·*fi*·ni
dhomatia (room for rent)
  δωμάτια (για νοίκιασμα) ⑩ pl
  tho·*ma*·ti·a (yia *ni*·kiaz·ma)
dominoes ντόμινο ⑩ *do*·mi·no
door πόρτα ① *por*·ta
dope (drugs) ναρκωτικά ⑩ pl nar·ko·ti·*ka*
Doric Δωρικός *tho*·ri·kos
double a διπλός thi·*plos*
double bed διπλό κρεβάτι ⑩
  thi·*plo* kre·va·*ti*
double room διπλό δωμάτιο ⑩
  thi·*plo* tho·*ma*·ti·o
down κάτω *ka*·to
downhill κατηφορικά ka·ti·fo·ri·*ka*
dozen ντουζίνα ① du·*zi*·na
drama δράμα ⑩ *thra*·ma
dream όνειρο ⑩ o·*ni*·ro
dress ⑩ φόρεμα ① *fo*·re·ma

dried ξηρός ksi·*ros*
dried fruit ξηρά φρούτα ⓝ pl ksi·*ra* fru·ta
drink ποτό ⓝ po·*to*
drink v πίνω *pi*·no
drink (alcoholic) ποτό (αλκοολικό) ⓝ po·*to* (al·ko·o·li·ko)
drive v οδηγώ o·thi·*gho*
drivers licence άδεια οδήγησης ⓕ *a*·thi·a o·*thi*·yi·sis
drizzle ψιχάλα ⓕ psi·*kha*·la
drug (illegal) ναρκωτικό ⓝ nar·ko·ti·*ko*
drug addiction εθισμός στα ναρκωτικά ⓜ e·thiz·*mos* sta nar·ko·ti·*ka*
drug dealer έμπορος ναρκωτικών ⓜ&ⓕ *e*·bo·ros nar·ko·ti·*kon*
drug trafficking κυκλοφορία ναρκωτικών ⓕ ki·klo·fo·*ri*·a nar·ko·ti·*kon*
drug user ναρκομανής ⓜ&ⓕ nar·ko·ma·*nis*
drugs (illicit) ναρκωτικά ⓝ pl nar·ko·ti·*ka*
drum τύμπανο ⓝ *ti*·ba·no
drunk μεθυσμένος me·thiz·*me*·nos
dry a στεγνός stegh·*nos*
dry v στεγνώνω stegh·*no*·no
duck πάπια ⓕ *pa*·pia
dummy (pacifier) πιπίλα ⓕ pi·*pi*·la
DVD Ντι-Βι-Ντί ⓝ di·vi·*di*

E

each καθένας ka·*the*·nas
ear αφτί ⓝ af·*ti*
early νωρίς no·*ris*
earn κερδίζω ker·*thi*·zo
earplugs ωτοασπίδες ⓕ pl o·to·a·*spi*·thes
earrings σκουλαρίκια ⓝ pl sku·la·*ri*·kia
Earth Γη ⓕ yi
earthquake σεισμός ⓜ siz·*mos*
east ανατολή ⓕ a·na·to·*li*
Easter Πάσχα ⓝ *pas*·kha
easy εύκολο *ef*·ko·lo
eat τρώω *tro*·gho
economy class τουριστική θέση ⓕ tu·ri·sti·*ki the*·si
ecstasy (drug) έκσταση ⓕ *ek*·sta·si
eczema έκζεμα ⓝ *ek*·ze·ma
education εκπαίδευση ⓕ ek·*pe*·thef·si
egg αβγό ⓝ av·*gho*
eggplant μελιτζάνα ⓕ me·li·*dza*·na

election εκλογή ⓕ ek·lo·*yi*
electrical store κατάστημα ηλεκτρικών ειδών ⓝ ka·*ta*·sti·ma i·lek·tri·*kon* i·*thon*
electricity ηλεκτρισμός ⓜ i·lek·triz·*mos*
elevator ασανσέρ ⓝ a·san·*ser*
email ημέιλ ⓝ i·*me*·il
embarrassed αμήχανος a·*mi*·kha·nos
embassy πρεσβεία ⓕ pre·*zvi*·a
embroidery κέντημα ⓝ *ke*·di·ma
emergency έκτακτη ανάγκη ⓕ *ek*·tak·ti a·*na*·gi
emotional συναισθηματικός si·ne·sthi·ma·ti·*kos*
employee υπάλληλος ⓜ&ⓕ i·*pa*·li·los
employer εργοδότης/εργοδότρια ⓜ/ⓕ er·gho·*tho*·tis/er·gho·*tho*·tri·a
empty a άδειο *a*·thi·o
end τέλος ⓝ *te*·los
endangered species είδη υπό εξαφάνιση ⓝ pl *i*·thi i·*po* ek·sa·*fa*·ni·si
engaged (to marry) αρραβωνιασμένος/αρραβωνιασμένη ⓜ/ⓕ a·ra·vo·niaz·*me*·nos/ a·ra·vo·niaz·*me*·ni
engagement (undertaking) υποχρέωση ⓕ i·po·*khre*·o·si
engine μηχανή ⓕ mi·kha·*ni*
engineer μηχανικός ⓜ&ⓕ mi·kha·ni·*kos*
engineering μηχανική ⓕ mi·kha·ni·*ki*
England Αγγλία ⓕ ang·*gli*·a
English (language) Αγγλικά ⓝ pl ang·gli·*ka*
enjoy oneself απολαμβάνω a·po·lam·*va*·no
enough αρκετά ar·ke·*ta*
enter μπαίνω be·no
entertainment guide οδηγός διασκέδασης ⓜ o·thi·*ghos* thia·ske·tha·sis
entry είσοδος ⓕ *i*·so·thos
envelope φάκελος ⓜ *fa*·ke·los
environment περιβάλλον ⓝ pe·ri·*va*·lon
epilepsy επιληψία ⓕ e·pi·lip·*si*·a
equal opportunity ίσες ευκαιρίες ⓕ pl *i*·ses ef·ke·*ri*·es
equality ισότητα ⓕ i·*so*·ti·ta
equipment εξοπλισμός ⓜ ek·so·pliz·*mos*
escalator κυλιόμενες σκάλες ⓕ pl ki·li·o·me·nes *ska*·les
estate agency κτηματομεσιτικό γραφείο ⓝ kti·ma·to·me·si·ti·ko ghra·*fi*·o
euro ευρώ ⓝ ev·*ro*

Europe Ευρώπη ① ev·ro·pi
European Union Ευρωπαϊκή Ένωση ①
ev·ro·pa·i·ki e·no·si
euthanasia ευθανασία ① ef·tha·na·si·a
evening βράδι ⑩ vra·thi
every κάθε ka·the
everyone καθένας ⑩ ka·the·nas
everything καθετί ⑩ ka·the·ti
exactly ακριβώς a·kri·vos
example παράδειγμα ① pa·ra·thigh·ma
excavation ανασκαφή ① a·na·ska·fi
excellent εξαιρετικός ek·se·re·ti·kos
excess (baggage) υπέρβαρο (φορτίο) ⑩
i·per·va·ro (for·ti·o)
exchange συνάλλαγμα ⑩ si·na·lagh·ma
exchange v ανταλλάσσω a·da·la·so
exchange rate τιμή συναλλάγματος ①
ti·mi si·na·lagh·ma·tos
excluded εξαιρούμενος ek·se·ru·me·nos
exhaust (car) εξάτμιση ① ek·sat·mi·si
exhibition έκθεση ① ek·the·si
exhibit έκθεμα ⑩ ek·the·ma
exit έξοδος ① ek·so·thos
expensive ακριβός a·kri·vos
experience εμπειρία ① e·bi·ri·a
exploitation εκμετάλλευση ①
ek·me·ta·lef·si
export permit άδεια εξαγωγής ①
a·thi·a ek·sa·gho·yis
(by) express mail επείγον (ταχυδρομείο)
⑩ e·pi·ghon (ta·hi·thro·mi·o)
extension (visa) παράταση ① pa·ra·ta·si
eye μάτι ⑩ ma·ti
eye drops σταγόνες ματιών ① pl
sta·gho·nes ma·ti·on
eyes μάτια ⑩ pl ma·tia

F

fabric ύφασμα ⑩ i·faz·ma
face πρόσωπο ⑩ pro·so·po
face cloth πετσέτα προσώπου ①
pet·se·ta pro·so·pu
factory εργοστάσιο ⑩ er·gho·sta·si·o
factory worker εργάτης εργοστασίου ⑩
er·gha·tis er·gho·sta·si·u | εργάτρια εργοστασίου ①
er·gha·tri·a er·gho·sta·si·u
falcon γεράκι ⑩ ye·ra·ki

fall (autumn) φθινόπωρο ⑩ fthi·no·po·ro
fall (down) πτώση ① pto·si
family οικογένεια ① i·ko·ye·ni·a
family name επώνυμο ⑩ e·po·ni·mo
famous α φημισμένος fi·miz·me·nos
fan (machine) ανεμιστήρας ⑩
a·ne·mi·sti·ras
fan (of sport) οπαδός ⑩ o·pa·thos
fanbelt λουρί ⑩ lu·ri
far μακριά ma·kri·a
fare εισιτήριο ① i·si·ti·ri·o
farm φάρμα ① far·ma
farmer γεωργός ⑩&① ye·or·ghos
fashion μόδα ① mo·tha
fast α γρήγορος ghri·gho·ros
fat α παχύς pa·his
father πατέρας ⑩ pa·te·ras
father-in-law πεθερός ⑩ pe·the·ros
faucet βρύση ① vri·si
fault (someone's) λάθος ⑩ la·thos
faulty ελαττωματικός e·la·to·ma·ti·kos
fax machine μηχανή φαξ ① mi·kha·ni faks
February Φεβρουάριος ⑩ fev·ru·a·ri·os
feed v ταΐζω ta·i·zo
feel (touch) v αγγίζω a·gi·zo
feeling (physical) αφή ① a·fi
feelings αισθήματα ⑩ pl es·thi·ma·ta
female α θηλυκός thi·li·kos
fence φράχτης ⑩ frakh·tis
fencing (sport) ξιφομαχία ① ksi·fo·ma·hi·a
ferry φέρυ ⑩ fe·ri
festival φεστιβάλ ⑩ fe·sti·val
fever πυρετός ⑩ pi·re·tos
few λίγοι li·yi
fiancé αρραβωνιαστικός ⑩
a·ra·vo·nia·sti·kos
fiancée αρραβωνιαστικιά ①
a·ra·vo·nia·sti·kia
fiction μυθοπλασία ① mi·tho·pla·si·a
fig σύκο ⑩ si·ko
fight πάλη ① pa·li
filigree (jewellery) φιλιγκράν ⑩ fi·li·gran
fill γεμίζω ye·mi·zo
fillet φιλέτο ⑩ fi·le·to
film (camera/cinema) φιλμ ⑩ film
film speed ταχύτητα φιλμ ① ta·hi·ti·ta film
filtered φιλτραρισμένος fil·tra·riz·me·nos
find βρίσκω vri·sko
fine (penalty) πρόστιμο ⑩ pros·ti·mo
fine (weather) α ωραίος o·re·os

finger δάκτυλο ⓝ *thak*·ti·lo
finish τελείωμα ⓝ te·*li*·o·ma
finish ν τελειώνω te·li·o·no
Finland Φιλανδία ⓕ fi·lan·*thi*·a
fire φωτιά ⓕ fo·*tia*
firewood καυσόξυλα ⓝ pl kaf·*sok*·si·la
first a πρώτος *pro*·tos
first class πρώτη τάξη ⓕ *pro*·ti tak·si
first-aid kit κυτίο πρώτων βοηθειών ⓝ ki·*ti*·o pro·ton vo·i·thi·*on*
first name μικρό όνομα ⓝ mi·*kro* o·no·ma
fish ψάρι ⓝ *psa*·ri
fishing ψάρεμα ⓝ psa·re·ma
fish monger ιχθυοπώλης/ιχθυοπώλισσα ⓜ/ⓕ ikh·thi·o·po·lis/ikh·thi·o·po·li·sa
fish shop ιχθυοπωλείο ⓝ ikh·thi·o·po·*li*·o
flag σημαία ⓕ si·*me*·a
flannel φανέλλα (ύφασμα) ⓕ fa·*ne*·la (i·faz·ma)
flashlight φλας ⓝ flas
flat a επίπεδος e·*pi*·pe·thos
flat (apartment) διαμέρισμα ⓝ thi·a·me·riz·ma
flea ψύλος ⓜ *psi*·los
fleamarket παζάρι ⓝ pa·*za*·ri
flight πτήση ⓕ *pti*·si
flood πλημμύρα ⓕ pli·*mi*·ra
floor πάτωμα ⓝ *pa*·to·ma
floor (storey) όροφος ⓜ *o*·ro·fos
florist ανθοπώλης/ανθοπώλισσα ⓜ/ⓕ an·tho·*po*·lis/an·tho·*po*·li·sa
flour αλεύρι ⓝ a·*lev*·ri
flower λουλούδι ⓝ lu·*lu*·thi
flu γρίππη ⓕ *ghri*·pi
fly πετάω ν pe·*ta*·o
foggy ομιχλώδης o·mi·*khlo*·this
folk (art) a λαϊκός la·i·kos
follow ακολουθώ a·ko·lu·*tho*
food φαγητό ⓝ fa·yi·*to*
food supplies προμήθειες φαγητού ⓕ pl pro·*mi*·thi·es fa·yi·tu
foot πόδι ⓝ *po*·thi
football (soccer) ποδόσφαιρο ⓝ po·*thos*·fe·ro
foreign ξένος kse·nos
forest δάσος ⓝ *tha*·sos
forever πάντα *pa*·da
forget ξεχνώ ksekh·*no*
forgive συγχωρώ sing·kho·*ro*
fork πιρούνι ⓝ pi·*ru*·ni

fortnight δεκαπενθήμερο ⓝ da·ka·pen·*thi*·me·ro
fortune teller μάντης/μάντισσα ⓜ/ⓕ *ma*·dis/*ma*·di·sa
foul φάουλ ⓝ *fa*·ul
foyer φουαγιέ ⓕ fu·a·*ye*
fragile εύθραυστος ef·thraf·stos
France Γαλλία ⓕ gha·*li*·a
free (available) διαθέσιμος thi·a·*the*·si·mos
free (gratis) δωρεάν tho·re·*an*
free (not bound) ελεύθερος e·*lef*·the·ros
freeze παγώνω pa·*gho*·no
fresco φρέσκο ⓝ *fre*·sko
fresh φρέσκος *fre*·skos
Friday Παρασκευή ⓕ pa·ra·ske·*vi*
fridge ψυγείο ⓝ psi·*yi*·o
fried τηγανισμένος ti·gha·niz·*me*·nos
friend φίλος/φίλη ⓜ/ⓕ *fi*·los/*fi*·li
from από a·*po*
frost παγωνιά ⓕ pa·gho·*nia*
frozen παγωμένος pa·gho·*me*·nos
fruit φρούτα ⓝ pl *fru*·ta
fruit picking μάζεμα φρούτων ⓝ *ma*·ze·ma *fru*·ton
fry ν τηγανίζω ti·gha·*ni*·zo
frying pan τηγάνι ⓝ ti·*gha*·ni
full γεμάτο ye·*ma*·to
full-time πλήρους απασχόλησης *pli*·rus a·pa·*skho*·li·sis
fun a διασκεδαστικό thia·ske·tha·sti·*ko*
funeral κηδεία ⓕ ki·*thi*·a
funny αστείος a·*sti*·os
furniture έπιπλα ⓝ pl e·pi·pla
future μέλλον ⓝ *me*·lon

G

game (football) ματς ⓝ mats
game (sport) παινχνίδι ⓝ pegh·*ni*·thi
garage γκαράζ ⓝ ga·*raz*
garbage σκουπίδια ⓝ pl sku·*pi*·thia
garbage can σκουπιδοτενεκές ⓜ sku·pi·tho·te·ne·*kes*
garden κήπος ⓜ *ki*·pos
gardener κηπουρός ⓜ&ⓕ ki·pu·*ros*
gardening κηπουρική ⓕ ki·pu·ri·*ki*
garlic σκόρδο ⓝ *skor*·tho
gas (for cooking) πετρογκάζ ⓝ pe·tro·*gaz*
gas (petrol) βενζίνα ⓕ ven·*zi*·na

gas cartridge μπουκάλα γκαζιού ⓕ
bu·*ka*·la ga·*zi*·u

gastroenteritis γαστρεντερίτιδα ⓕ
gha·stro·e·de·*ri*·ti·tha

gate (airport etc) θύρα ⓕ *thi*·ra

gauze αραχνοΰφαντος ⓕ
a·rakh·no·*i*·fa·dos

gay γκέι *ge*·i

gelatine ζελατίνη ⓕ ze·la·*ti*·ni

Germany Γερμανία ⓕ yer·ma·*ni*·a

get παίρνω *per*·no

get off (transport) κατεβαίνω ka·te·*ve*·no

gift δώρο ⓝ *tho*·ro

gig παράσταση ⓕ pa·*ra*·sta·si

gin τζιν ⓝ dzin

girl κορίτσι ⓝ ko·*rit*·si

girlfriend φιλενάδα ⓕ fi·le·*na*·tha

give δίνω *thi*·no

given name μικρό όνομα ⓝ
mi·*kro* o·no·ma

glandular fever αδενώδης πυρετός ⓜ
a·the·*no*·this pi·re·*tos*

glass (drinking) ποτήρι ⓝ po·*ti*·ri

glasses (spectacles) γιαλιά ⓝ pl yia·*lia*

glove γάντι ⓝ *ghan*·ti

gloves γάντια ⓝ pl *ghan*·tia

glue κόλα ⓕ *ko*·la

go πηγαίνω pi·*ye*·no

go out βγαίνω *vye*·no

go out with (a male) βγαίνω με κάποιον
vye·no me *ka*·pi·on

go out with (a female) βγαίνω με κάποια
vye·no me *ka*·pia

go shopping πάω για ψώνια
pa·o yia *pso*·nia

goal (score/point) γκολ ⓝ gol

goalkeeper τερματοφύλακας ⓜ&ⓕ
ter·ma·to·*fi*·la·kas

goat κατσίκα ⓕ kat·*si*·ka

god (general) θεός ⓜ the·*os*

goddess θεά ⓕ the·*a*

goggles προστατευτικά γιαλιά ⓝ pl
pro·sta·tef·ti·*ka* yia·*lia*

goggles (swimming)
προστατευτικά γιαλιά για κολύμπι
ⓝ pl pro·sta·tef·ti·*ka* yia·*lia* yia ko·*li*·bi

gold χρυσάφι ⓝ khri·*sa*·fi

golf ball μπαλάκι του γκολφ ⓝ
ba·*la*·ki tu golf

golf course γήπεδο του γκολφ ⓝ
yi·pe·tho tu golf

good καλός ka·*los*

government κυβέρνηση ⓕ ki·*ver*·ni·si

gram γραμμάριο ⓝ ghra·*ma*·ri·o

granddaughter εγγονή ⓕ e·go·*ni*

grandfather παπούς ⓜ pa·*pus*

grandmother γιαγιά ⓕ yia·*yia*

grandson εγγονός ⓜ e·go·*nos*

grapefruit γκρέιπ φρούτ ⓝ *gre*·ip frut

grapes σταφύλια ⓝ pl sta·*fi*·lia

grass γρασίδι ⓝ ghra·*si*·thi

grateful ευγνώμων ev·*ghno*·mon

grave τάφος ⓜ *ta*·fos

gray γκρίζος *gri*·zos

great (fantastic) απίθανος a·*pi*·tha·nos

Greece Ελλάδα ⓕ e·*la*·tha

Greek (language) Ελληνικά ⓝ pl
e·li·ni·*ka*

Greek (people) Έλληνες ⓜ pl *e*·li·nes

green πράσινος *pra*·si·nos

greengrocer
οπωροπώλης/οπωροπώλισσα ⓜ/ⓕ
o·po·ro·*po*·lis/o·po·ro·*po*·li·sa

grey γκρίζος *gri*·zos

grilled ψημένο στη σχάρα
psi·*me*·no sti *skha*·ra

grocery οπωροπωλείο ⓝ o·po·ro·po·*li*·o

groundnut φυστίκι ⓝ fi·*sti*·ki

grow μεγαλώνω me·ga·*lo*·no

guaranteed εγγυημένος e·ghi·i·*me*·nos

guess v μαντεύω ma·*de*·vo

guesthouse ξενώνας ⓜ *kse*·no·nas

guide (audio) μαγνητοφωνημένες
οδηγίες ⓕ pl magh·ni·to·fo·ni·*me*·nes
o·dhi·*yi*·es

guide (person) οδηγός ⓜ&ⓕ o·thi·*ghos*

guidebook τουριστικός οδηγός ⓜ
tu·ri·sti·*kos* o·thi·*ghos*

guide dog σκυλί οδηγός ⓝ ski·*li* o·thi·*ghos*

guided tour περιήγηση με οδηγό ⓕ
pe·ri·*i*·yi·si me o·thi·*gho*

guilty a ένοχος *e*·no·khos

guitar κιθάρα ⓕ ki·*tha*·ra

gum μαστίχα ⓕ ma·*sti*·kha

gun όπλο ⓝ *o*·plo

gym (fitness) γυμναστήριο ⓝ
yim·na·*sti*·ri·o

gymnastics γυμναστική ⓕ yim·na·sti·*ki*

gynaecologist γυναικολόγος ⓜ&ⓕ
yi·ne·ko·*lo*·ghos

gyros γύρος ⓜ *yi*·ros

H

hair μαλλιά ⑩ pl ma·*lia*
hairbrush βούρτσα μαλλιών ①
   vur·tsa ma·*lion*
haircut κούρεμα ⑩ *ku*·re·ma
hairdresser κομμωτής/κομμώτρια ⑩/①
   ko·mo·*tis*/ko·*mo*·tri·a
halal χαλάλ kha·*lal*
half μισό mi·*so*
hallucination παραίσθηση ① pa·*res*·thi·si
ham ζαμπόν ⑩ za·*bon*
hammer ⑩ σφυρί sfi·*ri*
hammock αιώρα ① e·o·ra
hand χέρι ⑩ *he*·ri
handbag τσάντα ① *tsa*·da
handball χάντμπολ ⑩ *khand*·bol
handicrafts εργόχειρα ⑩ pl er·*gho*·hi·ra
handkerchief μαντήλι ⑩ ma·*di*·li
handlebars χειρολαβή ① hi·ro·la·*vi*
handmade a χειροποίητο hi·ro·*pi*·i·to
handsome όμορφος *o*·mor·fos
happy ευτυχισμένος ef·ti·hiz·*me*·nos
harassment παρενόχληση ①
   pa·re·*no*·khli·si
harbour λιμάνι ⑩ li·*ma*·ni
hard (not soft) σκληρός skli·*ros*
hard-boiled σφιχτός sfikh·*tos*
hardware store κατάστημα σιδερικών ⑩
   ka·*ta*·sti·ma si·the·ri·*kon*
hash τουρλού ⑩ tur·*lu*
hat καπέλο ⑩ ka·*pe*·lo
have έχω e·kho
have a cold έχω κρύωμα e·kho *kri*·o·ma
have fun διασκεδάζω *thia*·ske·*tha*·zo
hay fever ρινική αλλεργία ①
   ri·ni·ki a·ler·*yi*·a
hazelnut φουντούκι ⑩ fu·*du*·ki
he αυτός af·*tos*
head κεφάλι ⑩ ke·*fa*·li
headache πονοκέφαλος ⑩ po·no·*ke*·fa·los
headlights μεγάλα φώτα αυτοκινήτου
   ⑩ pl me·*gha*·la *fo*·ta af·to·ki·*ni*·tu
health υγεία ① i·*yi*·a
hear ακούω a·*ku*·o
hearing aid ακουστικά ⑩ pl a·ku·sti·*ka*
heart καρδιά ① kar·*thia*
heart attack καρδιακή προσβολή ①
   kar·thi·a·*ki* proz·vo·*li*

heart condition καρδιακή κατάσταση ①
   kar·thi·a·*ki* ka·*ta*·sta·si
heat ζέστη ① *ze*·sti
heated ζεσταμένος ze·sta·*me*·nos
heater σόμπα ① *so*·ba
heating θέρμανση ① *ther*·man·si
heatstroke θερμοπληξία ①
   ther·mo·*plik*·si·a
heatwave καύσωνας ⑩ *kaf*·so·nas
heavy βαρύς va·*ris*
Hellenistic Ελληνιστικός e·li·ni·sti·*kos*
helmet περικεφαλαία ① pe·ri·ke·fa·*le*·a
help βοήθεια ① vo·*i*·thi·a
help v βοηθώ vo·i·*tho*
hepatitis ηπατίτιδα ① i·pa·*ti*·ti·tha
her (ownership/direct object) της tis
herb βότανο ⑩ *vo*·ta·no
herbalist βοτανολόγος ⑩&①
   vo·ta·no·*lo*·ghos
here εδώ e·*tho*
heroin ηρωίνη ① i·ro·*i*·ni
herring ρέγκα ① *re*·ga
high ψηλός psi·*los*
highchair καρέκλα για μωρά ①
   ka·*re*·kla yia mo·*ro*
high school γυμνάσιο ⑩ yim·*na*·si·o
highway δημόσιος δρόμος ⑩
   thi·*mo*·si·os *thro*·mos
hike v πεζοπορώ pe·zo·po·*ro*
hiking πεζοπορία ① pe·zo·po·*ri*·a
hiking boots μπότες πεζοπορίας ① pl
   bo·tes pe·zo·po·*ri*·as
hiking route δρόμος πεζοπορίας ⑩
   thro·mos pe·zo·po·*ri*·as
hill λόφος ⑩ *lo*·fos
Hindu Ινδουιστής/Ινδουίστρια ⑩/①
   in·thu·i·*stis*/in·thu·i·*stri*·a
hire v ενοικιάζω e·ni·ki·*a*·zo
his (ownership/direct object) του tu
historical ιστορικός i·sto·ri·*kos*
history ιστορία ① i·sto·*ri*·a
hitchhike v ταξιδεύω με ωτοστόπ
   tak·si·*the*·vo me o·to·*stop*
HIV έιτς άι βι ⑩ e·idz a·i vi
hockey χόκι ⑩ *kho*·ki
holiday αργεία ① ar·*yi*·a
holidays διακοπές ① pl thi·a·ko·*pes*
home σπίτι ⑩ *spi*·ti
homeless άστεγος a·ste·ghos
homemaker νοικοκύρης/νοικοκυρά
   ⑩/① ni·ko·*ki*·ris/ni·ko·ki·*ra*

homeopathy ομοιοπαθητική ⓕ o·mi·o·pa·thi·ti·*ki*

homosexual ομοφυλόφιλος ⓜ o·mo·fi·*lo*·fi·los

honey μέλι ⓝ *me*·li

honeymoon ταξίδι του μέλιτος ⓝ tak·*si*·thi tu *me*·li·tos

horoscope ωροσκόπιο ⓝ o·ro·*sko*·pi·o

horse άλογο ⓝ *a*·lo·gho

horse riding ιππασία ⓕ i·pa·*si*·a

hospital νοσοκομείο ⓝ no·so·ko·*mi*·o

hospitality φιλοξενία ⓕ fi·lok·se·*ni*·a

hot ζεστός ze·*stos*

hotel ξενοδοχείο ⓝ kse·no·tho·*hi*·o

hot water ζεστό νερό ⓝ ze·*sto* ne·*ro*

hour ώρα ⓕ *o*·ra

house σπίτι ⓝ *spi*·ti

housework νοικοκυριό ⓝ ni·ko·ki·*rio*

how πώς pos

how much πόσο *po*·so

hug ν αγκαλιάζω a·ga·*lia*·zo

huge πελώριος pe·*lo*·ri·os

humanities ανθρωπιστικές σπουδές ⓕ pl an·thro·pi·sti·*kes* spu·*thes*

human resources ανθρώπινο δυναμικό ⓝ an·*thro*·pi·no thi·na·mi·*ko*

human rights ανθρώπινα δικαιώματα ⓝ pl an·*thro*·pi·na thi·ke·o·ma·ta

hundred εκατό e·ka·*to*

hungry (be) ν πεινώ pi·*no*

hunting κυνήγι ⓝ ki·*ni*·yi

hurt ν πληγώνω pli·*gho*·no

husband σύζυγος ⓜ *si*·zi·ghos

hydrofoil ιπτάμενο φελλίνι ⓝ ip·*ta*·me·no thel·fi·ni

I

I εγώ e·*gho*

ice πάγος ⓜ *pa*·ghos

ice cream παγωτό ⓝ pa·gho·*to*

ice-cream parlour παγωτατζίδικο ⓝ pagho·ta·*dzi*·thi·ko

ice hockey άις χόκεϊ ⓝ *a*·is kho·ke·i

icon εικόνα ⓕ i·*ko*·na

identification (ID) ταυτότητα ⓕ taf·*to*·ti·ta

idiot βλάκας ⓜ *vla*·kas

if αν an

ill άρρωστος *a*·ro·stos

immigration μετανάστευση ⓕ ma·ta·*na*·stef·si

important σπουδαίος spu·*the*·os

impossible αδύνατος a·*thi*·na·tos

in μέσα *me*·sa

in a hurry βιαστικός via·sti·*kos*

in front of μπροστά bro·*sta*

included συμπεριλαμβανομένου si·be·ri·lam·va·no·*me*·nu

income tax φόρος εισοδήματος ⓜ *fo*·ros i·so·*thi*·ma·tos

India Ινδίες ⓕ pl in·*thi*·es

indicator δείχτης ⓜ *thikh*·tis

indigestion δυσπεψία ⓕ this·pep·*si*·a

indoor εσωτερικός ⓜ e·so·te·ri·*kos*

industry βιομηχανία ⓕ vi·o·mi·kha·*ni*·a

infection μόλυνση ⓕ *mo*·lin·si

inflammation φλεγμονή ⓕ flegh·mo·*ni*

inflation πληθωρισμός ⓜ pli·tho·riz·*mos*

influenza γρίπη ⓕ *ghri*·pi

information πληροφορία ⓕ pli·ro·fo·*ri*·a

ingredient συστατικό ⓝ si·sta·ti·*ko*

inject ν κάνω ένεση *ka*·no *e*·ne·si

injection ένεση ⓕ *e*·ne·si

injured πληγωμένος pli·gho·*me*·nos

injury πληγή ⓕ pli·*yi*

inner tube (bicycle) εσωτερική σαμπρέλλα ⓕ e·so·te·ri·*ki* sa·*bre*·la

innocent a αθώος a·*tho*·os

insect έντομο ⓝ *e*·do·mo

inside μέσα *me*·sa

instructor δάσκαλος/δασκάλα ⓜ/ⓕ *tha*·ska·los/*tha*·ska·la

insurance ασφάλεια ⓕ as·*fa*·li·a

interest (hobby) ενδιαφέρον ⓝ en·thia·*fe*·ron

interesting ενδιαφέρων en·thia·*fe*·ron

intermission διάλειμμα ⓝ *thia*·li·ma

international διεθνής thi·eth·*nis*

Internet διαδίκτυο ⓝ thi·a·*thik*·ti·o

Internet café καφενείο διαδικτύου ⓝ ka·fe·*ni*·o thi·a·thik·*ti*·u

interpreter διερμηνέας ⓜ&ⓕ thi·er·mi·*ne*·as

interview συνέντευξη ⓕ si·*ne*·def·ksi

invite ν προσκαλώ pros·ka·*lo*

Ioanian Ιωνικός i·o·ni·*kos*

Ireland Ιρλανδία ⓕ ir·lan·*thi*·a

iron (for clothes) σίδερο ⓝ *si*·the·ro

iris (eye) ίρις ⓕ *i*·ris

island νησί ⓝ ni·*si*

Israel Ισραήλ ⓝ iz·ra·*il*
it αυτό af·*to*
IT πληροφορική ① pli·ro·fo·ri·*ki*
Italy Ιταλία ① i·ta·*li*·a
itch φαγούρα ① fa·*ghu*·ra
itemised αναλυτικός a·na·li·ti·*kos*
itinerary κατάλογος ⓜ ka·*ta*·lo·ghos
IUD (contraceptive)
ενδομήτριο αντισυλληπτικό ⓝ
en·tho·*mi*·tri·o a·di·si·lip·ti·*ko*

J

jacket ζακέτα ① za·*ke*·ta
jail φυλακή ① fi·la·*ki*
jam μαρμελάδα ① mar·me·*la*·tha
January Ιανουάριος ⓜ i·a·nu·*a*·ri·os
Japan Ιαπωνία ① i·a·po·*ni*·a
jar βάζο ⓝ *va*·zo
jaw σαγόνι ⓝ sa·*gho*·ni
jealous ζηλιάρης zi·*lia*·ris
jeans τζιν ⓝ dzin
jeep τζιπ ⓝ dzip
jellyfish μέδουσα ① *me*·thu·sa
jet lag τζετ λαγκ ⓝ dzet lag
jewellery κοσμήματα ⓝ pl koz·*mi*·ma·ta
Jewish Ιουδαϊκός/Ιουδαϊκή ⓜ/①
i·u·tha·i·*kos*/i·u·tha·i·*ki*
job δουλειά ① du·*lia*
jogging τρέξιμο ⓝ *trek*·si·mo
joke αστείο a·*sti*·o
journalist δημοσιογράφος ⓜ&①
thi·mo·si·o·*ghra*·fos
journey ταξίδι ⓝ tak·si·thi
judge δικαστής ⓜ&① thi·ka·*stis*
jug κανάτα ① ka·*na*·ta
juice χυμός ⓜ hi·*mos*
July Ιούλιος ⓜ i·u·li·os
junta χούντα ① *khu*·da
jump v πηδώ pi·*tho*
jumper (sweater) πουλόβερ ⓝ pu·*lo*·ver
jumper leads καλώδια μπαταρίας ⓝ pl
ka·*lo*·thi·a ba·ta·*ri*·as
June Ιούνιος ⓜ i·u·ni·os

K

kebab shop σουβλατζίδικο ⓝ
suv·la·*tzi*·thi·ko
ketchup σάλτσα ① *salt*·sa

key κλειδί ⓝ kli·*thi*
keyboard πληκτρολόγιο ⓝ plik·tro·*lo*·yi·o
kick v κλωτσάω klot·*sa*·o
kidney νεφρό ⓝ ne·*fro*
kilo κιλό ⓝ ki·*lo*
kilogram χιλιόγραμμο ⓝ hi·*lio*·gra·mo
kilometre χιλιόμετρο ⓝ hi·*lio*·me·tro
kind (nice) καλός ka·*los*
kindergarten νηπιαγωγείο ⓝ
ni·pi·a·gho·*yi*·o
king βασιλιάς ⓜ va·si·*lias*
kiosk περίπτερο ⓝ pe·*rip*·te·ro
kiss φιλί ⓝ fi·*li*
kiss v φιλώ fi·*lo*
kitchen κουζίνα ① ku·*zi*·na
kiwifruit ακτινίδιο ⓝ ak·ti·*ni*·thi·o
knee γόνατο ⓝ *gho*·na·to
knife μαχαίρι ⓝ ma·*he*·ri
know v ξέρω *kse*·ro
kosher a κόσια *ko*·si·a

L

labourer εργάτης/εργάτρια ⓜ/①
er·*gha*·tis/er·*gha*·tri·a
labyrinth λαβύρινθος ⓜ la·*vi*·rin·thos
lace δαντέλα ① tha·*de*·la
lake λίμνη ① *li*·mni
lamb αρνί ⓝ ar·*ni*
land ξηρά ① ksi·*ra*
landlady νοικοκυρά ① ni·ko·ki·*ra*
landlord ιδιοκτήτης ⓜ i·thi·ok·*ti*·tis
language γλώσσα ① *ghlo*·sa
laptop λάπτοπ ⓝ *lap*·top
large μεγάλος me·*gha*·los
last (previous) προηγούμενος
pro·i·*ghu*·me·nos
last week περασμένη εβδομάδα
pe·raz·*me*·ni ev·tho·*ma*·tha
late καθυστερημένος ka·thi·ste·ri·*me*·nos
later αργότερα ar·*gho*·te·ra
laugh v γελάω ye·*la*·o
launderette πλυντήριο ⓝ pli·*di*·ri·o
laundry (place) πλυντήριο ⓝ pli·*di*·ri·o
law νόμος ⓜ *no*·mos
law (study, profession) νομικά ⓜ no·mi·*ka*
lawyer δικηγόρος ⓜ&① thi·ki·gho·ros
laxative καθαρτικό ⓝ ka·thar·ti·*ko*
lazy τεμπέλης te·*be*·lis

leader αρχηγός ⓜ&ⓕ ar·hi·*ghos*
leaf φύλλο ⓝ *fi*·lo
learn μαθαίνω ma·*the*·no
leather δέρμα ⓝ *ther*·ma
lecturer λέκτορας ⓜ&ⓕ *lek*·to·ras
ledge ξέρες ⓕ pl *kse*·res
left (direction) αριστερός ⓜ a·ri·ste·*ros*
left-luggage (office)
  (γραφείο) φύλαξη αποσκευών ⓝ
  (gra·*fi*·o) *fi*·lak·si a·po·ske·*von*
left-wing αριστερά ⓕ a·ri·ste·*ra*
leg πόδι ⓝ *po*·thi
legal νόμιμος *no*·mi·mos
legislation νομοθεσία ⓕ no·mo·the·*si*·a
legume όσπρια ⓝ pl os·pri·a
lemon λεμόνι ⓝ le·*mo*·ni
lemonade λεμονάδα ⓕ le·mo·*na*·tha
lens φακός ⓜ fa·*kos*
Lent Σαρακοστή ⓕ sa·ra·ko·*sti*
lentil φακές ⓕ pl fa·*kes*
lesbian λεσβία ⓕ les·*vi*·a
less λιγότερο li·*gho*·te·ro
letter (mail) γράμμα ⓝ *ghra*·ma
lettuce μαρούλι ⓝ ma·*ru*·li
liar ψεύτης/ψεύτρα ⓜ/ⓕ *psef*·tis/*psef*·tra
library βιβλιοθήκη ⓕ viv·li·o·*thi*·ki
licence άδεια ⓕ *a*·thi·a
license plate number αριθμός
  κυκλοφορίας ⓜ a·rith·*mos* ki·klo·fo·*ri*·as
lie (not stand) κείτομαι *ki*·to·me
life ζωή ⓕ zo·*i*
life jacket σωσίβιο ⓝ so·*si*·vi·o
lift (elevator) ασανσέρ ⓝ a·san·*ser*
light φως ⓝ fos
light (colour) a ανοιχτός a·nikh·*tos*
light (weight) a ελαφρύς e·la·*fris*
light bulb λάμπα ⓕ *lam*·pa
light meter μετρητής ρεύματος ⓜ
  me·tri·*tis* rev·ma·tos
lighter αναπτήρας ⓜ a·nap·*ti*·ras
like v μου αρέσει mu a·*re*·si
lime (fruit) κιτρολέμονο ⓝ ki·tro·*le*·mo·no
linen (material) λινό ⓝ li·*no*
linen (sheets) σεντόνια ⓝ pl se·*do*·nia
lip balm αλοιφή για τα χείλη ⓕ
  a·li·*fi* yia ta *hi*·li
lips χείλη ⓝ pl *hi*·li
lipstick κραγιόν ⓝ kra·*yion*
liquor store κάβα ⓕ *ka*·va

listen (to) ακούω a·*ku*·o
little (quantity) λίγο *li*·gho
little (size) μικρός mi·*kros*
live (somewhere) v μένω *me*·no
liver συκώτι ⓝ si·*ko*·ti
lizard σαύρα ⓕ *sav*·ra
local a τοπικός to·pi·*kos*
lock κλειδαριά ⓕ kli·tha·*ria*
lock v κλειδώνω kli·*tho*·no
locked κλειδωμένος kli·tho·*me*·nos
lollies καραμέλες ⓕ pl ka·ra·*me*·les
long a μακρύς ma·*kris*
look v κοιτάζω ki·*ta*·zo
look after προσέχω pro·*se*·kho
look for ψάχνω *psakh*·no
lookout παρατηρητήριο ⓝ pa·ra·ti·ri·*ti*·ri·o
loose a χαλαρός kha·la·*ros*
loose change ψιλά ⓝ pl psi·*la*
lose χάνω *kha*·no
lost a χαμένος kha·*me*·nos
lost property office γραφείο
  απωλεσθέντων αντικειμένων ⓝ gra·*fi*·o
  a·po·les·*the*·don a·di·ki·*me*·non
(a) lot πολύ po·*li*
lotion λοσιόν ⓕ lo·*sion*
loud δυνατός θi·na·*tos*
love αγάπη ⓕ a·*gha*·pi
love v αγαπώ a·gha·*po*
lover εραστής/ερωμένη ⓜ/ⓕ
  e·ra·*stis*/e·ro·*me*·ni
low a χαμηλός kha·mi·*los*
lubricant λιπαντικό ⓝ li·pa·di·*ko*
luck τύχη ⓕ *ti*·hi
lucky a τυχερός ti·he·*ros*
luggage αποσκευές ⓕ pl a·po·ske·*ves*
luggage lockers φύλαξη αποσκευών ⓕ
  fi·lak·si a·po·ske·*von*
luggage tag ταμπέλα αποσκευών ⓕ
  ta·*be*·la a·po·ske·*von*
lump εξόγκωμα ⓝ ek·so·gho·ma
lunch μεσημεριανό φαγητό ⓝ
  me·si·me·ria·*no* fa·yi·*to*
lung πνευμόνι ⓝ pnev·*mo*·ni
luxury πολυτέλεια ⓕ po·li·*te*·li·a

M

Macedonia Μακεδονία ⓕ ma·ke·tho·*ni*·a
machine μηχανή ⓕ mi·kha·*ni*
magazine περιοδικό ⓝ pe·ri·o·thi·*ko*

mail (letters) αλληλογραφία ① a·li·lo·ghra·*fi*·a

mail (postal system) ταχυδρομείο ⑩ ta·hi·thro·*mi*·o

mailbox ταχυδρομικό κουτί ⑩ ta·hi·thro·mi·*ko* ku·*ti*

main κύριος *ki*·ri·os

main road κύριος δρόμος ⑩ *ki*·ri·os *thro*·mos

make v κάνω *ka*·no

make-up καλλυντικά ⑩ pl ka·li·di·*ka*

mammogram μαμμογράφημα ⑩ ma·mo·ghra·*fi*·ma

man (male) άντρας ⑩ *a*·dras

manager διευθυντής/διευθύντρια ⑩/① thi·ef·thi·*dis*/thi·ef·*thi*·dri·a

mandarin μανταρίνι ⑩ ma·da·*ri*·ni

mango μάνγκο ⑩ *man*·go

manual work χειρωνακτική εργασία ① hi·ro·nak·ti·*ki* er·gha·*si*·a

many πολλοί po·*li*

map χάρτης ⑩ *khar*·tis

March Μάρτιος ⑩ *mar*·ti·os

margarine μαργαρίνη ① mar·gha·*ri*·ni

marijuana μαριχουάνα ① ma·ri·khu·*a*·na

marine reserve θαλάσσια αποθέματα ① pl tha·*la*·si·a a·po·the·ma·ta

marital status γαμήλια κατάσταση ① gha·*mi*·li·a ka·*ta*·sta·si

market αγορά ① a·gho·*ra*

marmalade μαρμελάδα ① mar·me·*la*·tha

marriage γάμος ⑩ *gha*·mos

married a παντρεμένος/παντρεμένη ⑩/① pa·dre·*me*·nos/pa·dre·*me*·ni

marry παντρεύομαι pa·*dre*·vo·me

martial arts πολεμική τέχνη ① po·le·mi·*ki* tekh·ni

mass (Catholic) λειτουργία ① li·tur·*yi*·a

massage μασάζ ⑩ ma·*saz*

masseur μασέρ ⑩ ma·*ser*

masseuse μασέζ ① ma·*sez*

mat χαλί ⑩ kha·*li*

match (sports) ματς ⑩ mats

matches (for lighting) σπίρτα ⑩ pl *spir*·ta

mattress στρώμα ⑩ *stro*·ma

May Μάιος ⑩ *ma*·i·os

maybe ίσως *i*·sos

mayonnaise μαγιονέζα ① ma·yi·o·*ne*·za

mayor δήμαρχος ⑩&① *thi*·mar·khos

me εγώ e·*gho*

---

meal γεύμα ⑩ *yev*·ma

measles ιλαρά ① i·la·*ra*

meat κρέας ⑩ *kre*·as

mechanic μηχανικός ⑩ mi·kha·ni·*kos*

media μέσα ενημέρωσης ⑩ pl *me*·sa e·ni·*me*·ro·sis

medicine (medication) φάρμακο ⑩ *far*·ma·ko

medicine (study, profession) Ιατρική ① i·a·tri·*ki*

meditation αυτοσυγκέντρωση ① af·to·si·*ge*·dro·si

Mediterranean Μεσογειακός ⑩ me·so·yi·a·*kos*

meet v συναντώ si·na·*do*

melon πεπόνι ⑩ pe·*po*·ni

member μέλος ⑩ *me*·los

menstruation περίοδος ① pe·*ri*·o·thos

menu μενού ⑩ me·*nu*

message μήνυμα ⑩ *mi*·ni·ma

metal μέταλλο ⑩ *me*·ta·lo

metre μέτρο ⑩ *me*·tro

metro (train) μετρό ⑩ me·*tro*

metro station σταθμός μετρό ⑩ stath·*mos* me·*tro*

microwave (oven) φούρνος μικροκυμάτων ⑩ *fur*·nos mi·kro·ki·*ma*·ton

midday (noon) μεσημέρι ⑩ me·si·*me*·ri

midnight μεσάνυχτα ⑩ pl me·*sa*·nikh·ta

migraine ημικρανία ① i·mi·kra·*ni*·a

mild μαλακός ma·la·*kos*

military a στρατιωτικός stra·ti·o·ti·*kos*

military base στρατιωτική βάση ① stra·ti·o·ti·*ki va*·si

military service στρατιωτική θητεία ① stra·ti·o·ti·*ki* thi·*ti*·a

milk γάλα ⑩ *gha*·la

millimetre χιλιοστόμετρο ⑩ hi·li·o·sto·me·tro

million εκατομμύριο ⑩ e·ka·to·*mi*·ri·o

mince κιμάς ⑩ ki·*mas*

mineral water μεταλλικό νερό ⑩ me·ta·li·*ko* ne·*ro*

Minoan Μινωικός mi·no·i·*kos*

minute λεπτό ⑩ lep·*to*

mirror καθρέφτης ⑩ ka·*thref*·tis

miscarriage αποβολή ① a·po·vo·*li*

Miss Δις ① the·spi·*nis*

miss (feel absence of) μου λείπει mu *li*·pi

---

mistake λάθος ⓝ *la*·thos

mix v ανακατώνω a·na·ka·*to*·no

mixed plate ποικιλία ⓕ pi·ki·*li*·a

mobile phone κινητό ⓝ ki·ni·*to*

modem μόντεμ ⓝ *mo*·dem

modern μοντέρνος mo·*der*·nos

moisturiser υγραντική κρέμα ⓕ i·ghra·di·ki *kre*·ma

monarchy μοναρχία ⓕ mo·nar·*hi*·a

monastery μοναστήρι ⓝ mo·na·*sti*·ri

Monday Δευτέρα ⓕ def·*te*·ra

money χρήματα ⓝ pl khri·ma·ta

monk καλόγερος ⓜ ka·*lo*·ye·ros

monk seal φώκια ⓕ *fo*·ki·a

month μήνας ⓜ *mi*·nas

monument μνημείο ⓝ mni·*mi*·o

moon φεγγάρι ⓝ fe·*ga*·ri

more περισσότερος pe·ri·so·te·ros

morning πρωί ⓝ pro·*i*

morning sickness πρωινή αδιαθεσία ⓕ pro·i·ni a·thi·a·the·*si*·a

mosaic μωσαϊκό ⓝ mo·sa·i·*ko*

mosque τζαμί ⓝ dza·*mi*

mosquito κουνούπι ⓝ ku·*nu*·pi

mosquito coil φιδάκι για κουνούπια ⓝ fi·*dha*·ki yia ku·*nu*·pia

mosquito net κουνουπιέρα ⓕ ku·nu·pi·e·ra

motel μοτέλ ⓝ mo·*tel*

mother μητέρα ⓕ mi·*te*·ra

mother-in-law πεθερά ⓕ pe·the·*ra*

motorbike μηχανάκι ⓝ mi·kha·*na*·ki

motorboat βενζινάκατος ⓕ ven·zi·*na*·ka·tos

motorcycle μοτοσυκλέτα ⓕ mo·to·si·*kle*·ta

motorway (tollway) αυτοκινητόδρομος ⓜ af·to·ki·ni·*to*·thro·mos

mountain βουνό ⓝ vu·*no*

mountain bike ποδήλατο για βουνό ⓝ po·*thi*·la·to yia vu·*no*

mountain path μονοπάτι ⓝ mo·no·*pa*·ti

mountain range οροσειρά ⓕ o·ro·si·*ra*

mountaineering ορειβασία ⓕ o·ri·va·si·a

mouse ποντικός ⓜ po·di·*kos*

mouth στόμα ⓝ *sto*·ma

movie φιλμ ⓝ film

Mr Κος ⓜ *khi*·ri·os

Mrs Κα ⓕ khi·*ri*·a

Ms Δις ⓕ the·spi·*nis*

mud λάσπη ⓕ *la*·spi

muesli δημητριακά ⓝ pl thi·mi·tri·a·*ka*

mum μαμά ⓕ ma·*ma*

mumps μαγουλάδες ⓜ pl ma·ghu·*la*·thes

murder δολοφονία ⓕ tho·lo·fo·*ni*·a

murder v δολοφονώ tho·lo·fo·*no*

muscle μυς ⓜ mis

museum μουσείο ⓝ mu·*si*·o

mushroom μανιτάρι ⓝ ma·ni·*ta*·ri

music μουσική ⓕ mu·si·*ki*

music shop κατάστημα μουσικών ειδών ⓝ ka·*ta*·sti·ma mu·si·*kon* i·*thon*

musician μουσικός ⓜ&ⓕ mu·si·*kos*

Muslim Μουσουλμάνος/Μουσουλμάνα ⓜ/ⓕ mu·sul·*ma*·nos/mu·sul·*ma*·na

mussel μύδι ⓝ *mi*·thi

mustard μουστάρδα ⓕ mus·*tar*·tha

mute a βουβός vu·*vos*

my μου mu

Mycenean Μυκηναϊκός mi·ki·na·i·*kos*

mythological μυθολογικός mi·tho·lo·yi·*kos*

N

nail clippers νυχοκόπτης ⓜ ni·kho·*kop*·tis

name όνομα ⓝ o·no·ma

napkin πετσετάκι ⓝ pet·se·*ta*·ki

nappy πάνα ⓕ *pa*·na

nappy rash ερεθισμός από πάνα ⓜ e·re·thiz·mos a·po *pa*·na

national park εθνικό πάρκο ⓝ eth·ni·*ko* par·ko

nationality εθνικότητα ⓕ eth·ni·*ko*·ti·ta

NATO NATO ⓝ *na*·to

nature φύση ⓕ *fi*·si

naturopathy φυσιοθεραπευτική ⓕ fi·si·o·the·ra·pef·ti·*ki*

nausea ναυτία ⓕ naf·*ti*·a

near(by) κοντά ko·*da*

nearest το πιο κοντινό to pio ko·di·*no*

necessary αναγκαίο a·na·ge·o

neck λαιμός ⓜ le·*mos*

necklace κολιέ ⓝ ko·li·e

nectarine νεκταρίνι ⓝ nek·ta·*ri*·ni

need v χρειάζομαι khri·a·zo·me

needle (sewing) βελόνα ⓕ ve·*lo*·na

needle (syringe) σύριγκα ⓕ *si*·ri·ga

negative a αρνητικός ar·ni·ti·*kos*

neither κανένα από τα δύο ka·*ne*·na a·po ta *thi*·o

net δίκτι ⓝ *thik*·ti

Netherlands Ολλανδία ⓕ o·lan·*thi*·a

never ποτέ po·*te*
new νέος *ne*·os
New Year's Day Πρωτοχρονιά ⓕ pro·to·khro·*nia*
New Year's Eve Παραμονή Πρωτοχρονιάς ⓕ pa·ra·mo·*ni* pro·to·khro·*nias*
New Zealand Νέα Ζηλανδία ⓕ *ne*·a zi·lan·*thi*·a
news νέα ⓝ pl *ne*·a
newsagency πρακτορείο εφημερίδων ⓝ prak·to·*ri*·o e·fi·me·*ri*·thon
newspaper εφημερίδα ⓕ e·fi·me·*ri*·tha
newsstand περίπτερο ⓝ pe·*rip*·te·ro
next a επόμενος e·*po*·me·nos
next to δίπλα *thi*·pla
nice ωραίος o·*re*·os
nickname παρατσούκλι ⓝ pa·rat·*su*·kli
night νύχτα ⓕ *nikh*·ta
night out ξενύχτι ⓝ kse·*nikh*·ti
nightclub νάιτ κλαμπ ⓝ *na*·it klab
no όχι o·hi
noisy θορυβώδης tho·ri·*vo*·this
none κανένας ka·*ne*·nas
nonsmoking μη καπνίζοντες mi kap·*ni*·zo·des
noodles λαζάνια ⓝ pl la·*za*·nia
noon μεσημέρι ⓝ me·si·*me*·ri
north βοράς ⓜ vo·*ras*
Norway Νορβηγία ⓕ nor·vi·*yi*·a
nose μύτη ⓕ *mi*·ti
not όχι o·hi
notebook σημειωματάριο ⓝ si·mi·o·ma·*ta*·ri·o
nothing τίποτε *ti*·po·te
November Νοέμβριος ⓜ no·*em*·vri·os
now τώρα *to*·ra
nuclear energy πυρηνική ενέργεια ⓕ pi·ri·ni·*ki* e·*ner*·yi·a
nuclear testing πυρηνικές δοκιμές ⓕ pl pi·ri·ni·*kes* tho·ki·*mes*
nuclear waste πυρηνικά απόβλητα ⓝ pl pi·ri·ni·*ka* a·*pov*·li·ta
number αριθμός ⓜ a·rith·*mos*
numberplate αριθμός κυκλοφορίας ⓜ a·rith·*mos* ki·klo·fo·*ri*·as
nun καλόγρια ⓕ ka·*lo*·ghri·a
nurse νοσοκόμος/νοσοκόμα ⓜ/ⓕ no·so·ko·mos/no·so·*ko*·ma
nut καρύδι ⓝ ka·*ri*·thi

O

oats βρώμη ⓕ *vro*·mi
ocean ωκεανός ⓜ o·ke·a·*nos*
October Οκτώβριος ⓜ ok·*tov*·ri·os
off (food) μπαγιάτικος ba·*yia*·ti·kos
office γραφείο ⓝ ghra·*fi*·o
often συχνά sikh·*na*
oil (cooking) λάδι ⓝ *la*·thi
oil (car) λάδι αυτοκινήτου ⓝ *la*·thi af·to·ki·*ni*·tu
old παλιός pa·*lios*
olive ελιά ⓕ e·*lia*
olive oil λάδι ελιάς ⓝ *la*·thi e·*lias*
Olympic Games Ολυμπιακοί Αγώνες ⓜ o·li·bi·a·*ki* a·*gho*·nes
omelette ομελέττα ⓕ o·me·*le*·ta
on πάνω *pa*·no
on time στην ώρα stin *o*·ra
once μια φορά mia fo·*ra*
one ένα *e*·na
one-way (ticket) απλό εισιτήριο a·*plo* i·si·*ti*·ri·o
onion κρεμύδι ⓝ kre·*mi*·thi
only μόνο *mo*·no
open a ανοιχτός a·nikh·*tos*
open v ανοίγω a·*ni*·gho
opening hours ώρες λειτουργίας ⓕ pl *o*·res li·tur·*yi*·as
opera (house) όπερα ⓕ *o*·pe·ra
operation (medical) εγχείρηση ⓕ eng·*hi*·ri·si
operator χειριστής/χειρίστρια ⓜ/ⓕ hi·ri·*stis*/hi·ri·*stri*·a
opinion γνώμη ⓕ *ghno*·mi
opposite απέναντι a·*pe*·na·di
optometrist οφθαλμίατρος ⓜ&ⓕ of·thal·*mi*·a·tros
or ή i
oracle χρησμός ⓜ khriz·*mos*
orange (fruit) πορτοκάλι ⓝ por·to·*ka*·li
orange (colour) a πορτοκαλής por·to·ka·*lis*
orange juice χυμός πορτοκάλι ⓜ hi·*mos* por·to·*ka*·li
orchestra ορχήστρα ⓕ or·*hi*·stra
orchid ορχιδέα ⓕ or·hi·*the*·a
order σειρά ⓕ si·*ra*
order v διατάζω thia·*ta*·zo

ordinary συνηθισμένος si·ni·thiz·*me*·nos

orgasm οργασμός ⑩ or·ghaz·*mos*

original αρχικός ar·hi·*kos*

Orthodox Ορθόδοξος/Ορθόδοξη ⑩/①
or·*tho*·thok·sos/or·*tho*·thok·si

other άλλος *a*·los

Ottoman a Οθωμανικός o·tho·ma·ni·*kos*

our μας mas

outside έξω *ek*·so

ouzo ούζο ⑩ *u*·zo

ouzeria ουζερί ① u·ze·*ri*

ovarian cyst ωοθηκική κύστη ①
o·o·thi·ti·*ki ki*·sti

ovary ωοθήκη ① o·o·*thi*·ki

oven φούρνος ⑩ *fur*·nos

overcoat πανωφόρι ⑩ pa·no·*fo*·ri

overdose υπερβολική δόση ①
i·per·vo·li·*ki tho*·si

overnight ολονυχτίς o·lo·nikh·*tis*

overseas εξωτερικό ek·so·te·ri·*ko*

owe οφείλω o·*fi*·lo

owner κάτοχος ⑩ *ka*·to·khos

oxygen οξυγόνο ⑩ ok·si·*gho*·no

oyster στρείδι ⑩ *stri*·thi

ozone layer στρώμα όζοντος ①
stro·ma o·zo·dos

P

pacemaker βηματοδότης ⑩
vi·ma·to·*tho*·tis

pacifier (dummy) πιπίλα ① pi·*pi*·la

package πακέτο ⑩ pa·*ke*·to

packet πακέτο ⑩ pa·*ke*·to

padlock κλειδαριά ① kli·*tha*·ria

page σελίδα ① se·*li*·tha

pain πόνος ⑩ *po*·nos

painful οδυνηρός o·thi·ni·*ros*

painkiller παυσίπονο ⑩ paf·*si*·po·no

painter ζωγράφος ⑩&① zo·*ghra*·fos

painting (a work) πίνακας ⑩ *pi*·na·kas

painting (the art) ζωγραφική ①
zo·ghra·fi·*ki*

pair (couple) ζευγάρι ⑩ zev·*gha*·ri

palace παλάτι ⑩ pa·*la*·ti

pan κατσαρόλα ① kat·sa·*ro*·la

pants (trousers) παντελόνι ⑩ pa·de·*lo*·ni

panty liners πετσετάκι υγείας ⑩
pet·se·*ta*·ki i·*yi*·as

pantyhose καλτσόν ⑩ kal·*tson*

paper χαρτί ⑩ khar·*ti*

papers (documents) πιστοποιητικά ⑩ pl
pi·sto·pi·i·ti·*ka*

paperwork προετοιμασία ① εγγράφων
pro·e·ti·ma·*si*·a e·*gra*·fon

paprika πάπρικα ① *pa*·pri·ka

pap smear τεστ παπ ⑩ test pap

paraplegic παραπληγικός ⑩
pa·ra·pli·yi·*kos*

parcel δέμα ⑩ *the*·ma

parents γονείς ⑩ pl gho·*nis*

park πάρκο ⑩ *par*·ko

park (a car) παρκάρω par·*ka*·ro

parliament Βουλή ① vu·*li*

part (component) εξάρτημα ⑩
ek·*sar*·ti·ma

part-time μερική απασχόληση
me·ri·*ki* a·pas·*kho*·li·si

party (night out) πάρτυ ⑩ *par*·ti

party (politics) κόμμα ⑩ *ko*·ma

pass v περνάω per·*na*·o

passenger επιβάτης/επιβάτισσα ⑩/①
e·pi·*va*·tis/e·pi·*va*·ti·sa

passionfruit πάσιον φρουτ ⑩ *pa*·si·on frut

passport διαβατήριο ⑩ thia·va·*ti*·ri·o

passport number αριθμός διαβατηρίου
⑩ a·rith·*mos* thia·va·ti·*ri*·u

past παρελθόν ⑩ pa·rel·*thon*

pasta ζυμαρικά ⑩ pl zi·ma·ri·*ka*

pastry φύλλο ⑩ *fi*·lo

path μονοπάτι ⑩ mo·no·*pa*·ti

patisserie ζαχαροπλαστείο ⑩
za·kha·ro·pla·*sti*·o

pay v πληρώνω pli·*ro*·no

payment πληρωμή ① pli·ro·*mi*

pea αρακάς ⑩ a·ra·*kas*

peace ειρήνη ① i·*ri*·ni

peach ροδάκινο ⑩ ro·*tha*·ki·no

peak (mountain) κορυφή ① ko·ri·*fi*

peanut φυστίκι ⑩ fi·*sti*·ki

pear αχλάδι ⑩ a·*khla*·thi

pedal πετάλι ⑩ pe·*ta*·li

pedestrian πεζός ⑩ pe·*zos*

pelican πελεκάνος ⑩ pe·le·*ka*·nos

pen (ballpoint) στυλό ⑩ sti·*lo*

pencil μολύβι ⑩ mo·*li*·vi

penis πέος ⑩ *pe*·os

penknife σουγιάς ⑩ su·*yias*

pension σύνταξη ① *si*·dak·si

pensioner συνταξιούχος/συνταξιούχα ⓜ/ⓕ si·dak·si·u·khos/si·dak·si·u·kha

people κόσμος ⓜ *koz*·mos

pepper πιπέρι ⓝ pi·*pe*·ri

pepper (bell) πιπεριέρα ⓕ pi·pe·rie·ra

per κάθε *ka*·the

per cent τοις εκατό tis e·ka·*to*

perfect a τέλειος *te*·li·os

performance απόδοση ⓕ a·*po*·tho·si

perfume άρωμα ⓝ *a*·ro·ma

period pain πόνος περιόδου ⓜ *po*·nos pe·ri·o·thu

permission άδεια ⓕ *a*·thi·a

permit άδεια ⓕ *a*·thi·a

person πρόσωπο ⓝ *pro*·so·po

petition συλλογή υπογραφών ⓕ si·lo·*yi* i·po·ghra·fon

petrol πετρέλαιο ⓝ pe·*tre*·le·o

petrol station πρατήριο βενζίνας ⓝ pra·*ti*·ri·o ven·*zi*·nas

pharmacist φαρμακοποιός ⓜ&ⓕ far·ma·ko·pi·*os*

pharmacy φαρμακείο ⓝ far·ma·*ki*·o

phone book τηλεφωνικός κατάλογος ⓜ ti·le·fo·ni·kos ka·*ta*·lo·ghos

phone box δημόσιο τηλέφωνο ⓝ *thi*·mo·si·o ti·*le*·fo·no

phonecard τηλεκάρτα ⓕ ti·le·*kar*·ta

photo φωτογραφία ⓕ fo·to·gra·*fi*·a

photographer φωτογράφος ⓜ&ⓕ fo·to·*ghra*·fos

photography φωτογραφική ⓕ fo·to·ghra·fi·*ki*

phrasebook βιβλίο φράσεων ⓕ viv·*li*·o *fra*·se·on

pickaxe τσεκούρι ⓝ tse·*ku*·ri

pickles τουρσί ⓝ tur·*si*

picnic πίκνικ ⓝ pik·*nik*

pie πίτα ⓕ *pi*·ta

piece κομμάτι ⓝ ko·*ma*·ti

pig γουρούνι ⓝ ghu·*ru*·ni

pill χάπι ⓝ *kha*·pi

the pill το Χάπι ⓝ to *kha*·pi

pillow μαξιλάρι ⓝ mak·si·*la*·ri

pillowcase μαξιλαροθήκη ⓕ mak·si·la·ro·*thi*·ki

pine πεύκο ⓝ *pef*·ko

pineapple ανανάς ⓜ a·na·*nas*

pink ροζ roz

pistachio φυστίκι ⓝ fi·*sti*·ki

place θέση ⓕ *the*·si

place of birth τόπος γεννήσεως ⓜ *to*·pos ye·*ni*·se·os

plane αεροπλάνο ⓝ a·e·ro·*pla*·no

planet πλανήτης ⓜ pla·*ni*·tis

plant φυτό ⓝ fi·*to*

plastic a πλαστικός pla·sti·*kos*

plate πιάτο ⓝ *pia*·to

plateau πλατό ⓝ pla·*to*

platform πλατφόρμα ⓕ plat·*for*·ma

play (theatre) θεατρικό έργο ⓝ the·a·tri·ko *er*·gho

play cards v παίζω χαρτιά *pe*·zo khar·*tia*

play guitar v παίζω κιθάρα *pe*·zo ki·*tha*·ra

plug (bath) βούλωμα ⓝ *vu*·lo·ma

plug (electricity) βύσμα ⓝ *viz*·ma

plum δαμάσκηνο ⓝ tha·*ma*·ski·no

poached ποσέ po·*se*

pocket τσέπη ⓕ *tse*·pi

pocket knife σουγιάς ⓜ su·*yias*

poetry ποίηση ⓕ *pi*·i·si

point σημείο ⓝ si·*mi*·o

point v δείχνω *thi*·khno

poisonous δηλητηριώδης thi·li·ti·ri·*o*·this

police αστυνομία ⓕ a·sti·no·*mi*·a

police officer (in city) αστυφύλακας/αστυφυλακίνα ⓜ/ⓕ a·sti·fi·la·kas/a·sti·fi·la·ki·na

police officer (in country) χωροφύλακας/χωροφυλακίνα ⓜ/ⓕ kho·ro·fi·la·kas/kho·ro·fi·la·*ki*·na

police station αστυνομικός σταθμός ⓜ a·sti·no·mi·kos stath·*mos*

policy πολιτική ⓕ po·li·ti·*ki*

politician πολιτικός ⓜ&ⓕ po·li·ti·*kos*

politics πολιτικά ⓝ pl po·li·ti·*ka*

pollen γύρη ⓕ *yi*·ri

pollution ρύπανση ⓕ *ri*·pan·si

pool (game) μπιλιάρδο ⓝ bi·*liar*·tho

pool (swimming) πισίνα ⓕ pi·*si*·na

poor a φτωχός fto·*khos*

popular δημοφιλής thi·mo·fi·*lis*

pork χοιρινό ⓝ hi·ri·*no*

pork sausage χοιρινό λουκάνικο ⓝ hi·ri·*no* lu·ka·ni·ko

port (sea) λιμάνι ⓝ li·*ma*·ni

positive a θετικός the·ti·*kos*

possible δυνατός thi·na·*tos*

post v ταχυδρομώ ta·hi·thro·*mo*

postage ταχυδρομικά τέλη ⓝ pl ta·hi·thro·mi·*ka* te·li

postcard κάρτα ① *kar*·ta
postcode ταχυδρομικός τομέας ⑩ ta·hi·thro·mi·*kos* to·*me*·as
post office ταχυδρομείο ⑩ ta·hi·thro·*mi*·o
poster πόστερ ⑪ *po*·ster
pot (ceramics) κεραμικό ⑪ ke·ra·mi·*ko*
pot (dope) μαριχουάνα ① ma·ri·khu·*a*·na
potato πατάτα ① pa·*ta*·ta
pottery αγγειοπλαστική ① a·gi·o·pla·sti·*ki*
pound (money) λίρα ① *li*·ra
pound (weight) λίτρα ① *li*·tra
poverty φτώχεια ① *fto*·hia
powder πούδρα ① *pu*·thra
power δύναμη ① *thi*·na·mi
prawn γαρίδα ① gha·*ri*·tha
prayer προσευχή ① pro·sef·*hi*
prayer book βιβλίο προσευχών ⑪ viv·*li*·o pro·sef·*khon*
prefer προτιμώ pro·ti·*mo*
pregnancy test kit τεστ εγκυμοσύνης test e·gi·mo·*si*·nis
pregnant a έγκυος *e*·gi·os
prehistoric προϊστορικός pro·i·sto·ri·*kos*
premenstrual tension ένταση πριν την περίοδο ① *e*·da·si pri tin pe·*ri*·o·tho
prepare προετοιμάζω pro·e·ti·*ma*·zo
prescription συνταγή ① si·da·*yi*
present (gift) δώρο ⑪ *tho*·ro
present (time) παρόν ⑪ pa·*ron*
president πρόεδρος ⑩&① *pro*·e·thros
pressure πίεση ① *pi*·e·si
pretty όμορφος *o*·mor·fos
price τιμή ① ti·*mi*
priest παπάς ⑩ pa·*pas*
prime minister πρωθυπουργός ⑩&① pro·thi·pur·*ghos*
printer (computer) εκτυπωτής ⑩ ek·ti·po·*tis*
prison φυλακή ① fi·la·*ki*
prisoner φυλακισμένος ⑩ fi·la·kiz·*me*·nos
private a ιδιωτικός i·thi·o·ti·*kos*
problem πρόβλημα ⑪ *pro*·vli·ma
produce v παράγω pa·*ra*·gho
profit κέρδος ⑪ *ker*·thos
program πρόγραμμα ⑪ *pro*·gra·ma
projector προβολέας ⑩ pro·vo·*le*·as
promise v υπόσχομαι i·*pos*·kho·me
prostitute πόρνη ① *por*·ni
protect προστατεύω pro·sta·*te*·vo

protected (species) προστατευόμενα (είδη) ⑪ pl pro·sta·te·*vo*·me·na (*i*·thi)
protest διαμαρτυρία ① thi·a·mar·ti·*ri*·a
protest v διαμαρτύρομαι thi·a·mar·*ti*·ro·me
provisions προμήθειες ① pl pro·*mi*·thi·es
prune (dried fruit) ξηρό δαμάσκηνο ⑪ ksi·ro tha·*ma*·ski·no
pub (bar) μπαρ ⑪ bi·ra·*ri*·a
public gardens εθνικός κήπος ⑩ eth·ni·kos *ki*·pos
public relations δημόσιες σχέσεις ① pl thi·*mo*·si·es *she*·sis
public telephone δημόσιο τηλέφωνο ⑪ thi·*mo*·si·o ti·*le*·fo·no
public toilet δημόσια αποχωρητήρια ⑪ pl thi·*mo*·si·a a·po·kho·ri·*ti*·ria
pulse σφυγμός ⑩ sfigh·*mos*
pull v τραβάω tra·*va*·o
pump τρόμπα ① *tro*·ba
pumpkin κολοκύθι ⑪ ko·lo·*ki*·thi
puncture τρύπα ρόδας ① *tri*·pa ro·thas
punch (ticket) v ακυρώνω a·ki·ro·no
pure a καθαρός ka·tha·*ros*
purple μαβής ma·*vis*
purse πορτοφόλι ⑪ por·to·*fo*·li
push v σπρώχνω *sprokh*·no
put βάζω *va*·zo

Q

quadriplegic παραπληγικός ⑩ pa·ra·pli·yi·*kos*
qualifications προσόντα ⑪ pl pro·*so*·da
quality ποιότητα ① pi·*o*·ti·ta
quarantine καραντίνα ① ka·ra·*di*·na
quarter τέταρτο ⑪ *te*·tar·to
queen βασίλισσα ① va·*si*·li·sa
question ερώτηση ① e·*ro*·ti·si
queue ουρά ① u·*ra*
quick a γρήγορος *ghri*·gho·ros
quiet a ήσυχος *i*·si·khos
quit v παραιτούμαι pa·re·*tu*·me

R

rabies λύσσα ① *li*·sa
rabbit κουνέλι ⑪ ku·*ne*·li
race (sport) ιπποδρομία ① i·po·thro·*mi*·a

racetrack ιππόδρομος ⓜ i·po·thro·mos
racing bike ποδήλατο κούρσας ⓝ po·thi·la·to kur·sas
racism ρατσισμός ⓜ rat·sis·mos
racquet ρακέτα ⓕ ra·ke·ta
radiator ψυγείο αυτοκινήτου ⓝ psi·yi·o af·to·ki·ni·tu
radio ράδιο ⓝ ra·thi·o
radish ραπάνι ⓝ ra·pa·ni
railway station σιδηροδρομικός σταθμός ⓜ si·thi·ro·thro·mi·kos stath·mos
rain ⓝ βροχή vro·hi
raincoat αδιάβροχο ⓝ a·thi·av·ro·ho
raisin σταφίδα ⓕ sta·fi·tha
rally ράλι ⓝ ra·li
rape βιασμός ⓜ vi·az·mos
rape v βιάζω vi·a·zo
rare (uncommon) σπάνιος spa·ni·os
rare (food) μισοψημένο mi·so·psi·me·no
rash εξάνθημα ⓝ ek·san·thi·ma
raspberry βατόμουρο ⓝ va·to·mu·ro
rat ποντίκι ⓝ po·di·ki
raw ωμός o·mos
razor ξυριστική μηχανή ⓕ ksi·ri·sti·ki mi·kha·ni
razor blade ξυράφι ⓝ ksi·ra·fi
read v διαβάζω thia·va·zo
reading διάβασμα ⓝ thia·vaz·ma
ready έτοιμος e·ti·mos
real estate agent κτηματομεσίτης/κτηματομεσίτρια ⓜ/ⓕ kti·ma·to·me·si·tis/kti·ma·to·me·si·tri·a
realistic ρεαλιστικός re·a·li·sti·kos
rear (seat etc) οπίσθιος o·pi·sthi·os
reason αιτία ⓕ e·ti·a
receipt απόδειξη ⓕ a·po·thik·si
recently πρόσφατα pros·fa·ta
recommend συνιστώ si·ni·sto
record v καταγράφω ka·ta·ghra·fo
recording καταγραφή ⓕ ka·ta·ghra·fi
recyclable ανακυκλώσιμο a·na·ki·klo·si·mo
recycle ανακυκλώνω a·na·ki·klo·no
red κόκκινο ko·ki·no
referee διαιτητής/διαιτήτρια ⓜ/ⓕ thi·e·ti·tis/thi·e·ti·tri·a
reference (letter) συστατική επιστολή ⓕ si·sta·ti·ki e·pi·sto·li
reflexology αντανακλαστική ⓕ a·da·na·kla·sti·ki
refrigerator ψυγείο ⓝ psi·yi·o

refugee πρόσφυγας ⓜ&ⓕ pros·fi·ghas
refund ⓕ επιστροφή χρημάτων e·pi·stro·fi khri·ma·ton
refuse v αρνούμαι ar·nu·me
regional τοπικός to·pi·kos
(by) registered mail συστημένο sis·ti·me·no
rehydration salts υδρωτικά άλατα ⓝ pl i·thro·ti·ka a·la·ta
relationship σχέση ⓕ she·si
relax v χαλαρώνω kha·la·ro·no
relic κειμήλιο ⓝ ki·mi·li·o
religion θρησκεία ⓕ thri·ski·a
religious a θρήσκος thri·skos
remote a απόμακρος a·po·mak·ros
remote control τηλεκατεύθυνση ⓕ ti·le·ka·tef·thin·si
rent v ενοικιάζω e·ni·ki·a·zo
repair v επισκευάζω e·pi·ske·va·zo
republic δημοκρατία ⓕ thi·mo·kra·ti·a
reservation (booking) κράτηση ⓕ kra·ti·si
residency permit άδεια παραμονής ⓕ a·thi·a pa·ra·mo·nis
rest v ξεκουράζομαι kse·ku·ra·zo·me
restaurant εστιατόριο ⓝ e·sti·a·to·ri·o
restriction περιορισμός ⓜ pe·ri·o·riz·mos
résumé (CV) βιογραφικό σημείωμα ⓝ vi·o·ghra·fi·ko si·mi·o·ma
retired συνταξιούχος si·dak·si·u·khos
retsina (drink) ρετσίνα ⓕ ret·si·na
return (come back) v επιστρέφω e·pi·stre·fo
return (ticket) εισιτήριο μετ' επιστροφής ⓝ i·si·ti·ri·o me·te·pi·stro·fis
review αναθεώρηση ⓕ a·na·the·o·ri·si
rhythm ρυθμός ⓜ rith·mos
rib πλευρό ⓝ plev·ro
rice ρύζι ⓝ ri·zi
rich (wealthy) πλούσιος plu·si·os
ride (horse) ιππασία ⓕ i·pa·si·a
ride (horse) v ιππεύω i·pe·vo
right (correct) a σωστός so·stos
right (direction) δεξιός thek·si·os
right-wing δεξιά ⓕ thek·si·a
ring (jewellery) δαχτυλίδι ⓝ thakh·ti·li·thi
ring (phone) v τηλεφωνώ ti·le·fo·na·o
rip-off γδάρσιμο ⓝ gthar·si·mo
risk ρίσκο ⓝ ri·sko
river ποτάμι ⓝ po·ta·mi
road δρόμος ⓜ thro·mos

road map οδικός χάρτης ⓜ
o·thi·kos khar·tis

roasted ψημένος psi·me·nos

rob ληστεύω li·ste·vo

rock βράχος ⓜ vra·khos

rock climbing αναρρίχηση ⓕ a·na·ri·hi·si

rock music μουσική ροκ ⓕ mu·si·ki rok

rockfalls κατολίσθηση ⓕ ka·to·lis·thi·si

rock group μπάντα ροκ ⓕ ba·da rok

rockmelon πεπόνι ⓝ pe·po·ni

roll (bread) ψωμάκι ⓝ pso·ma·ki

rollerblading τροχοπέδιλο ⓝ
tro·kho·pe·thi·lo

Roman Ρωμαϊκός ro·ma·i·kos

romantic ρομαντικός ro·ma·di·kos

room δωμάτιο ⓝ tho·ma·ti·o

room number αριθμός δωματίου ⓜ
a·rith·mos tho·ma·ti·u

rope σκοινί ⓝ ski·ni

round a στρογγυλός stro·gi·los

roundabout κυκλική διασταύρωση ⓕ
ki·kli·ki thi·a·stav·ro·si

route δρόμος ⓜ thro·mos

rowing κωπηλασία ⓕ ko·pi·la·si·a

rubbish σκουπίδια ⓝ pl sku·pi·thia

rubella ερυθρά ⓕ e·ri·thra

rug χαλί ⓝ kha·li

rugby ράγκμπυ ⓝ rag·bi

ruins ερρίπια ⓝ pl e·ri·pi·a

rule ⓝ κανόνας ka·no·nas

room ρούμι ⓝ ru·mi

run v τρέχω tre·kho

running τρέξιμο ⓝ trek·si·mo

runny nose τρέξιμο μύτης ⓝ
trek·si·mo mi·tis

S

sad λυπημένος li·pi·me·nos

saddle σέλλα ⓕ se·la

safe ασφάλεια ⓕ as·fa·li·a

safe a ασφαλής as·fa·lis

safe sex ασφαλές σεξ ⓝ as·fa·les seks

saint άγιος/αγία ⓜ/ⓕ a·yi·os/a·yi·a

sailing ιστίο ⓝ i·sti·o

salad σαλάτα ⓕ sa·la·ta

salami σαλάμι ⓝ sa·la·mi

salary μισθός ⓜ mis·thos

sale πώληση ⓕ po·li·si

sales tax φόρος πώλησης ⓜ fo·ros po·li·sis

salmon σολομός ⓜ so·lo·mos

salt αλάτι ⓝ a·la·ti

same ίδιος i·thi·os

sand άμμος ⓕ a·mos

sandal σανδάλι ⓝ sa·da·li

sanitary napkin πετσετάκι υγείας ⓝ
pet·se·ta·ki i·yi·as

sardine σαρδέλα ⓕ sar·the·la

Saturday Σάββατο ⓝ sa·va·to

sauce σάλτσα ⓕ sal·tsa

saucepan κατσαρόλα ⓕ kat·sa·ro·la

sauna σάουνα ⓕ sa·u·na

sausage λουκάνικο ⓝ lu·ka·ni·ko

savoury πικάντικος pi·ka·di·kos

say v λέγω le·gho

scalp κρανίο ⓝ kra·ni·o

scarf κασκόλ ⓝ ka·skol

school σχολείο ⓝ skho·li·o

science επιστήμη ⓕ e·pi·sti·mi

scientist επιστήμονας ⓜ&ⓕ
e·pi·sti·mo·nas

scissors ψαλίδι ⓝ psa·li·thi

score v σκοράρω sko·ra·ro

scoreboard πίνακας σκορ ⓜ pi·na·kas skor

Scotland Σκωτία ⓕ sko·ti·a

scrambled χτυπητά (αβγά)
khti·pi·ta (av·gha)

sculpture γλυπτική ⓕ ghlip·ti·ki

sea θάλασσα ⓕ tha·la·sa

seafood θαλασσινά ⓝ pl tha·la·si·na

(be) seasick πάσχει από ναυτία
pa·shi a·po naf·ti·a

seasickness ναυτία ⓕ naf·ti·a

seaside παραλία ⓕ pa·ra·li·a

season εποχή ⓕ e·po·hi

seat (place) θέση ⓕ the·si

seatbelt ζώνη καθίσματος ⓕ
zo·ni ka·thiz·ma·tos

sea turtle θαλάσσια χελώνα ⓕ
tha·la·si·a he·lo·na

sea urchin αχινός ⓜ a·hi·nos

second δευτερόλεπτο ⓝ thef·te·ro·lep·to

second a δεύτερος thef·te·ros

second class δεύτερη τάξη ⓕ
thef·te·ri tak·si

second-hand a μεταχειρισμένος
me·ta·hi·riz·me·nos

second-hand shop παλαιοπωλείο ⓝ
pa·le·o·po·li·o

secretary γραμματέας ⓜ&ⓕ
ghra·ma·*te*·as
see βλέπω *vle*·po
self-employed a ιδιωτικός υπάλληλος
i·thi·o·ti·*kos* i·*pa*·li·los
selfish ατομιστής a·to·mi·*stis*
self-service ⓝ σελφ σέρβις self *ser*·vis
sell v πουλάω pu·*la*·o
seminar σεμινάριο ⓝ se·mi·*na*·ri·o
send στέλνω *stel*·no
sensible συνετός si·ne·*tos*
sensual αισθησιακός e·sthi·si·a·*kos*
separate a χωριστός kho·ri·*stos*
September Σεπτέμβριος ⓜ sep·*tem*·vri·os
serious σοβαρός so·va·*ros*
service υπηρεσία ⓕ i·pi·re·*si*·a
service charge τιμή εξυπηρέτησης ⓕ
ti·*mi* ek·si·pi·*re*·ti·sis
service station βενζινάδικο ⓝ
ven·zi·*na*·thi·ko
serviette πετσέτα φαγητού ⓕ
pet·*se*·ta fa·yi·*tu*
several μερικοί me·ri·*ki*
sew v ράβω *ra*·vo
sex (intercourse) σεξ ⓝ seks
sexism σεξισμός ⓜ sek·siz·*mos*
sexy σέξυ *sek*·si
shade σκιά ⓕ ski·*a*
shadow σκιά ⓕ ski·*a*
shampoo σαμπουάν v sam·pu·*an*
shape σχήμα ⓝ *shi*·ma
share (with) μοιράζομαι mi·*ra*·zo·me
shave v ξυρίζω ksi·*ri*·zo
shaving cream κρέμα ξυρίσματος ⓕ
kre·ma ksi·*riz*·ma·tos
she αυτή af·*ti*
sheep πρόβατο ⓝ *pro*·va·to
sheet (bed) σεντόνι ⓝ se·*do*·ni
shelf ράφι ⓝ *ra*·fi
shiatsu σιάτσου ⓝ si·*at*·su
shield ασπίδα ⓕ as·*pi*·tha
shingles (illness) έρπης ⓜ *er*·pis
ship πλοίο ⓝ *pli*·o
shirt πουκάμισο ⓝ pu·*ka*·mi·so
shoe παπούτσι ⓝ pa·*put*·si
shoes παπούτσια ⓝ pl pa·*put*·si·a
shoe shop υποδηματοποιείο ⓝ
i·po·thi·ma·to·pi·*i*·o
shoot v πυροβολώ pi·ro·vo·*lo*
shop μαγαζί ⓝ ma·gha·*zi*

shop v ψωνίζω pso·*ni*·zo
shopping ψώνια ⓝ pl *pso*·nia
shopping centre αγορά ⓕ a·gho·*ra*
short (height) κοντός ko·*dos*
shortage έλλειψη ⓕ *e*·lip·si
shorts σορτς ⓝ sorts
shoulder ώμος ⓜ *o*·mos
shout v φωνάζω fo·*na*·zo
show v επίδειξη ⓕ e·*pi*·thik·si
show v δείχνω *thikh*·no
shower ντουζ ⓝ duz
shrine βωμός ⓜ vo·*mos*
shut a κλειστός kli·*stos*
shy a ντροπαλός dro·pa·*los*
sick a άρρωστος *a*·ro·stos
side πλευρά ⓕ plev·*ra*
siesta μεσημεριανή ανάπαυση ⓕ
me·si·me·ria·*ni* a·na·paf·si
sign πινακίδα ⓕ pi·na·*ki*·tha
signature υπογραφή ⓕ i·po·ghra·*fi*
silk μετάξι ⓝ me·*tak*·si
silver ασήμι ⓝ a·*si*·mi
similar παρόμοιος pa·*ro*·mi·os
simple απλός a·*plos*
since (May) από (το Μάη) a·*po* (to ma·*i*)
sing v τραγουδώ tra·ghu·*tho*
Singapore Σιγγαπούρη ⓕ sing·ga·*pu*·ri
singer τραγουδιστής/τραγουδίστρια
ⓜ/ⓕ tra·ghu·*thi*·stis/tra·ghu·*thi*·stri·a
single (person) a εργένης/εργένισσα
ⓜ/ⓕ er·*ye*·nis/er·*ye*·ni·sa
single room μονό δωμάτιο ⓝ
mo·*no* tho·*ma*·tio
singlet φανελάκι ⓝ fa·ne·*la*·ki
sister αδερφή ⓕ a·*ther*·fi
sit κάθομαι *ka*·tho·me
size μέγεθος ⓝ *me*·ye·thos
skate v παγοδρομώ pa·gho·thro·*mo*
skateboarding πατίνι ⓝ pa·*ti*·ni
ski v κάνω σκι *ka*·no ski
skiing σκι ⓝ ski
skim milk άπαχο γάλα ⓝ a·pa·kho *gha*·la
skin δέρμα ⓝ *ther*·ma
skirt φούστα ⓕ *fu*·sta
skull κρανίο ⓝ kra·*ni*·o
sky ουρανός ⓜ u·ra·*nos*
sleep v κοιμάμαι ki·*ma*·me
sleeping bag σλίπινγκ μπαγκ ⓝ
sli·ping bag
sleeping berth κρεββατάκι ⓝ
kre·va·*ta*·ki

sleeping car βαγκόν λι ⓝ va·gon li
sleeping pills υπνωτικά χάπια ⓝ pl ip·no·ti·ka kha·pia
sleepy νυσταγμένος nis·tagh·me·nos
slice φέτα ⓕ fe·ta
slide (film) σλάιντ ⓝ sla·id
slow a αργός ar·ghos
slowly αργά ar·gha
small μικρός mi·kros
smaller μικρότερος mi·kro·te·ros
smallest ο μικρότερος o mi·kro·te·ros
smell μυρουδιά ⓕ mi·ru·thia
smile v χαμογελώ kha·mo·ye·lo
smog νέφος ⓝ ne·fos
smoke v καπνίζω kap·ni·zo
snack μικρό γεύμα ⓝ mi·kro ghev·ma
snail σαλιγκάρι ⓝ sa·li·ga·ri
snake φίδι ⓝ fi·dhi
snorkelling υπόγεια κατάδυση ⓕ i·po·yi·a ka·ta·thi·si
snow χιόνι ⓝ hio·ni
snowboarding σκι με χιονοσανίδα ⓝ ski me hio·no·sa·ni·tha
snow pea αρακάς ⓝ a·ra·kas
soap σαπούνι ⓝ sa·pu·ni
soap opera αισθηματικό σίριαλ ⓝ es·thi·ma·ti·ko si·ri·al
soccer ποδόσφαιρο ⓝ po·thos·fe·ro
social welfare κοινωνική πρόνοια ⓕ ki·no·ni·ki pro·ni·a
socialist σοσιαλιστής/σοσιαλίστρια ⓜ/ⓕ so·si·a·li·stis/so·si·a·li·stri·a
sock κάλτσα ⓕ kal·tsa
socks κάλτσες ⓕ pl kal·tses
soft drink αναψυκτικό ⓝ a·nap·sik·ti·ko
soft-boiled μελάτο ⓝ me·la·to
soldier στρατιώτης ⓜ stra·ti·o·tis
some μερικοί me·ri·ki
someone κάποιος ka·pi·os
something κάτι ka·ti
sometimes μερικές φορές me·ri·kes fo·res
son γιος ⓜ yios
song τραγούδι ⓝ tra·ghu·thi
soon σύντομα si·do·ma
sore a πονεμένος po·ne·me·nos
soup σούπα ⓕ su·pa
sour cream ξινή κρέμα ⓕ ksi·ni kre·ma
south νότος ⓜ no·tos
souvenir σουβενίρ ⓝ su·ve·nir
souvenir shop κατάστημα για σουβενίρ ⓝ ka·ta·sti·ma yia su·ve·nir

souvlaki σουβλάκι ⓝ suv·la·ki
soy milk γάλα σόγια ⓝ gha·la so·yi·a
soy sauce σάλτσα σόγια sal·tsa so·yi·a
space διάστημα ⓝ thi·a·sti·ma
Spain Ισπανία ⓕ i·spa·ni·a
sparkling wine σαμπάνια ⓕ sam·pa·ni·a
speak μιλάω mi·la·o
special a ειδικός i·thi·kos
spear καμάκι ⓝ ka·ma·ki
specialist σπεσιαλίστας/σπεσιαλίστρια ⓜ/ⓕ spe·si·a·li·stas/spe·si·a·li·stri·a
speed (velocity) ταχύτητα ⓕ ta·hi·ti·ta
speed limit όριο ταχύτητας ⓝ o·ri·o ta·hi·ti·tas
speedometer ταχύμετρο ⓝ ta·hi·me·tro
spider αράχνη ⓕ a·rakh·ni
spinach σπανάκι ⓝ spa·na·ki
spoiled (food) χαλασμένος kha·laz·me·nos
spoke ακτίνα τροχού ⓕ ak·ti·na tro·khu
spoon κουτάλι ⓝ ku·ta·li
sport σπορ ⓝ spor
sportsman σπόρτσμαν ⓝ sports·man
sportswoman σπορτσγούμαν ⓕ sports·ghu·man
sports store κατάστημα των σπορ ⓝ ka·ta·sti·ma ton spor
sprain στραμπούλισμα ⓝ stra·bu·liz·ma
spring (coil) ελατήριο ⓝ e·la·ti·ri·o
spring (season) άνοιξη ⓕ a·nik·si
square (town) πλατεία ⓕ pla·ti·a
spray σπρέι ⓝ spre·i
stadium στάδιο ⓝ sta·thi·o
stairway σκάλα ⓕ ska·la
stale μπαγιάτικος ba·yia·ti·kos
stamp γραμματόσημο ⓝ ghra·ma·to·si·mo
stand-by ticket εισιτήριο σταντ μπάι ⓝ i·si·ti·ri·o stand ba·i
star (sky) αστέρι ⓝ a·ste·ri
start αρχή ⓕ ar·hi
start v αρχίζω ar·hi·zo
station σταθμός ⓜ stath·mos
stationer's χαρτοπωλείο ⓝ khar·to·po·li·o
statue άγαλμα ⓝ a·ghal·ma
stay μένω me·no
steak (beef) μπριζόλα ⓕ bri·zo·la
steal κλέβω kle·vo
steep απόκρημνος a·po·krim·nos
step βήμα ⓝ vi·ma
stereo στέρεο ⓝ ste·re·o
still water νερό χωρίς ανθρακικό ⓝ ne·ro kho·ris an·thra·ki·ko

sting v τσιμπάω tsi·*ba*·o
stock (food) ζουμί ⓝ zu·*mi*
stockings καλτσόν ⓝ kal·*tson*
stolen κλεμμένο kle·*me*·no
stomach στομάχι ⓝ sto·*ma*·hi
stomachache στομαχόπονος ⓜ
sto·ma·*kho*·po·nos
stone πέτρα ⓕ *pe*·tra
stoned (drugged) μαστουρωμένος
ma·stu·ro·*me*·nos
stop (bus etc) στάση ⓕ *sta*·si
stop (cease) v σταματάω sta·ma·*ta*·o
stop (prevent) v εμποδίζω e·bo·*thi*·zo
storm καταιγίδα ⓕ ka·te·*yi*·tha
story ιστορία ⓕ i·sto·*ri*·a
stove ηλεκτρική κουζίνα ⓕ
i·lek·tri·*ki* ku·*zi*·na
straight ίσιος *i*·si·os
strange παράξενος pa·*rak*·se·nos
stranger (person) ξένος/ξένη ⓜ/ⓕ
kse·nos/*kse*·ni
strawberry φράουλα ⓕ *fra*·u·la
stream ατμός ⓜ at·*mos*
street οδός ⓕ o·*thos*
street market λαϊκή ⓕ la·i·*ki*
strike απεργία ⓕ a·per·*yi*·a
string κλωστή ⓕ klo·*sti*
stroke (health) εγκεφαλικό ⓝ e·ge·fa·li·*ko*
stroller καροτσάκι ⓝ ka·rot·*sa*·ki
strong δυνατός thi·na·*tos*
stubborn ισχυρογνώμων is·hi·rog·no·mon
student σπουδαστής/σπουδάστρια
ⓜ/ⓕ spu·*tha*·stis/spu·*tha*·stri·a
studio στούντιο ⓝ *stu*·di·o
stupid χαζός kha·*zos*
style στυλ ⓝ stil
subtitles υπότιτλοι ⓜ pl i·*po*·ti·tli
suburb προάστειο ⓝ pro·a·*sti*·o
subway η υπόγειος i·*po*·yi·os
subway (train) υπόγειος σιδηρόδρομος
ⓜ i·*po*·yi·os si·thi·*ro*·thro·mos
sugar ζάχαρη ⓕ *za*·kha·ri
suitcase βαλίτσα ⓕ va·*lit*·sa
sultana σταφίδα ⓕ sta·*fi*·tha
summer καλοκαίρι ⓝ ka·lo·*ke*·ri
sun ήλιος ⓜ *i*·li·os
sunblock αντιηλιακό ⓝ a·di·i·li·a·*ko*
sunburn ηλιακό έγκαυμα ⓝ
i·li·a·*ko* e·gav·ma
Sunday Κυριακή ⓕ ki·ria·*ki*

sunglasses γιαλιά ηλίου ⓝ pl yia·*lia* i·*li*·u
sunny ηλιόλουστος i·li·o·lu·stos
sunrise ανατολή ⓕ a·na·to·*li*
sunset δύση ⓕ *thi*·si
sunstroke ηλιοπληξία ⓕ i·li·o·plik·*si*·a
supermarket σουπερμάρκετ ⓝ
su·per·*mar*·ket
superstition πρόληψη ⓕ *pro*·lip·si
supporter (politics, sport) οπαδός
ⓜ&ⓕ o·pa·*thos*
surf σερφ ⓝ serf
surface mail (land) δια ξηράς thi·a ksi·*ras*
surface mail (sea) ατμοπλοϊκώς
at·mo·plo·i·*kos*
surfboard σέρφμπορντ ⓝ serf·bord
surfing σέρφινγκ ⓝ *ser*·fing
surname επώνυμο ⓝ e·po·ni·mo
surprise έκληξη ⓕ *ek*·plik·si
sweater ζακέτα ⓕ za·*ke*·ta
Sweden Σουηδία ⓕ su·i·*thi*·a
sweet a γλυκός ghli·*kos*
sweets γλυκά ⓝ pl ghli·*ka*
swelling πρήξιμο ⓝ *prik*·si·mo
swim v κολυμπώ ko·li·*bo*
swimming (sport) κολύμπι ⓝ ko·*li*·bi
swimming pool πισίνα ⓕ pi·*si*·na
swimsuit μαγιό ⓝ ma·*yio*
Switzerland Ελβετία ⓕ el·ve·*ti*·a
sword σπαθί ⓝ spa·*thi*
synagogue συναγωγή ⓕ si·na·gho·*yi*
synthetic a συνθετικός sin·the·ti·*kos*
syringe σύριγκα ⓕ *si*·ri·ga

T

table τραπέζι ⓝ tra·*pe*·zi
tablecloth τραπεζομάντηλο ⓝ
tra·pe·zo·*ma*·di·lo
table tennis πινγκ πονγκ ⓝ ping pong
tail ουρά ⓕ u·*ra*
tailor ράφτης/ράφτρα ⓜ/ⓕ *raf*·tis/*raf*·tra
take παίρνω *per*·no
take a photo βγάζω φωτογραφία
vga·zo fo·to·gra·*fi*·a
talk v μιλάω mi·*la*·o
tall ψηλός psi·*los*
tampon ταμπόν ⓝ ta·*bon*
tanning lotion λοσιόν για μαύρισμα ⓝ
lo·*sion* yia mav·riz·ma

tap βρύση ① *vri·*si

tap water νερό βρύσης ① ne·ro *vri·*sis

tasty νόστιμος *no·*sti·mos

taverna ταβέρνα ① ta·*ver·*na

tax φόρος ⓜ *fo·*ros

taxi ταξί ⓝ tak·*si*

taxi stand στάση ταξί ① *sta·*si tak·*si*

tea τσάι ⓝ *tsa·*i

teacher δάσκαλος/δασκάλα ⓜ/①
*tha·*ska·los/*tha·*ska·la

team ομάδα ① o·*ma·*tha

teaspoon κουτάλι τσαγιού ⓝ
ku·*ta·*li tsa·*yiu*

technique τεχνική ① tekh·ni·*ki*

teeth δόντια ⓝ *tho·*dia

telegram τηλεγράφημα ⓝ ti·le·*ghra·*fi·ma

telephone τηλέφωνο ⓝ ti·*le·*fo·no

telephone v τηλεφωνώ ti·le·fo·*no*

telephone box δημόσιο τηλέφωνο ⓝ
*thi·*mo·si·o ti·*le·*fo·no

telephone centre τηλεφωνικό κέντρο ⓝ
ti·le·fo·ni·*ko ke·*dro

telescope τηλεσκόπιο ⓝ ti·le·*sko·*pi·o

television τηλεόραση ① ti·le·*o·*ra·si

tell λέγω *le·*gho

temperature (fever) πυρετός ⓜ pi·re·*tos*

temperature (weather) θερμοκρασία ①
ther·mo·kra·*si·*a

temple (church) ναός ⓜ na·*os*

tennis τένις ⓝ *te·*nis

tennis court γήπεδο του τένις ⓝ
*yi·*pe·tho tu *te·*nis

tent τέντα ① *te·*da

tent peg πάσαλος τέντας ⓜ
*pa·*sa·los *te·*das

terracotta pot αγγείο τερακότα ⓝ
a·*gi·*o te·ra·*ko·*ta

terrible τρομερός tro·me·*ros*

test τεστ ⓜ test

thank ευχαριστώ ef·kha·ri·*sto*

that (one) εκείνο e·*ki·*no

theatre θέατρο ⓝ *the·*a·tro

their τους tus

there εκεί e·*ki*

they αυτοί af·*ti*

thick πυκνός pik·*nos*

thin λεπτός lep·*tos*

think νομίζω no·*mi·*zo

third τρίτος *tri·*tos

thirsty διψασμένος thip·saz·*me·*nos

this (one) αυτός ⓜ af·*tos*

thread κλωστή ① klo·*sti*

throat λαιμός ⓜ le·*mos*

thrush (health) μυκητώδης στοματίτις ⓜ
mi·ki·*to·*this sto·ma·*ti·*tis

thunderstorm καταιγίδα ① ka·te·*yi·*tha

Thursday Πέμπτη ① *pem·*ti

tick τσιμπούρι ⓝ tsi·*bu·*ri

ticket εισιτήριο ⓝ i·si·*ti·*ri·o

ticket collector εισπράκτορας ⓜ&①
is·*prak·*to·ras

ticket machine μηχανή εισιτηρίων ①
mi·kha·*ni* i·si·ti·*ri·*on

ticket office γραφείο εισιτηρίων ⓝ
ghra·*fi·*o i·si·ti·*ri·*on

tide παλίρροια ① pa·*li·*ri·a

tight σφιχτός sfikh·*tos*

time ώρα ① *o·*ra

time difference διαφορά ώρας ①
thia·fo·*ra o·*ras

timetable πρόγραμμα ⓝ *pro·*ghra·ma

tin (can) κουτί ⓝ ku·*ti*

tin opener ανοιχτήρι ⓝ a·nikh·*ti·*ri

tiny μικροσκοπικός mi·kro·sko·pi·*kos*

tip (gratuity) φιλοδώρημα ⓝ
fi·lo·*tho·*ri·ma

tire λάστιχο ⓝ *la·*sti·kho

tired κουρασμένος ku·raz·*me·*nos

tissues χαρτομάντηλα ⓝ pl
khar·to·*ma·*di·la

to σε se

toast τοστ ⓝ tost

toaster τοστιέρα ① to·sti·*e·*ra

tobacco καπνός ⓜ kap·*nos*

tobacconist
καπνοπώλης/καπνοπώλισσα ⓜ/①
ka·pno·*po·*lis/ka·pno·*po·*li·sa

today σήμερα *si·*me·ra

toe δάχτυλο ποδιού ⓝ *thakh·*ti·lo po·*thiu*

tofu τόφου ⓝ *to·*fu

together μαζί ma·*zi*

toilet τουαλέτα ① tu·a·*le·*ta

toilet paper χαρτί υγείαςn ⓝ khar·*ti* i·*yi·*as

tomato ντομάτα ① do·*ma·*ta

tomato sauce σάλτσα ① *sal·*tsa

tomb μνήμα ⓝ *mni·*ma

tomorrow αύριο *av·*ri·o

tomorrow afternoon αύριο το απόγευμα
*av·*ri·o to a·*po·*yev·ma

tomorrow evening αύριο το βράδι *av*·ri·o to *vra*·thi

tomorrow morning αύριο το πρωί *av*·ri·o to pro·*i*

tonight απόψε a·*pop*·se

too (excess) πάρα πολύ *pa*·ra po·*li*

tooth δόντι ⓝ *tho*·di

toothache πονόδοντος ⓜ po·*no*·tho·dos

toothbrush οδοντόβουρτσα ⓕ o·tho·*do*·vur·tsa

toothpaste οδοντόπαστα ⓕ o·tho·*do*·pa·sta

toothpick οδοντογλυφίδα ⓕ o·tho·do·*ghli*·fi·tha

torch (flashlight) φακός ⓜ fa·*kos*

touch v αγγίζω a·*gi*·zo

tour περιήγηση ⓕ pe·ri·*i*·yi·si

tourist τουρίστας/τουρίστρια ⓜ/ⓕ tu·*ri*·stas/tu·*ri*·stri·a

tourist office τουριστικό γραφείο ⓝ tu·ri·sti·*ko* ghra·*fi*·o

towards προς pros

towel πετσέτα ⓕ pet·*se*·ta

tower πύργος ⓜ *pir*·ghos

toxic waste τοξικά απόβλητα ⓝ pl tok·si·*ka* a·*pov*·li·ta

toy shop κατάστημα παιγνιδιών ⓝ ka·*ta*·sti·ma pegh·ni·*thion*

track (path) μονοπάτι ⓝ mo·no·*pa*·ti

track (sport) στίβος ⓜ *sti*·vos

trade εμπόριο ⓝ e·*bo*·ri·o

tradesperson έμπορος ⓜ&ⓕ *e*·bo·ros

traffic κυκλοφορία ⓕ ki·klo·fo·*ri*·a

traffic light φανάρι ⓝ fa·*na*·ri

trail μονοπάτι ⓝ mo·no·*pa*·ti

train τρένο ⓝ *tre*·no

train station σταθμός τρένου ⓜ stath·*mos tre*·nu

tram τραμ ⓝ tram

transit lounge αίθουσα τράνζιτ ⓕ *e*·thu·sa *tran*·zit

translate μεταφράζω me·ta·*fra*·zo

transport μεταφορά ⓕ me·ta·fo·*ra*

travel v ταξιδεύω tak·si·*the*·vo

travel agency ταξιδιωτικό γραφείο ⓝ tak·si·thi·o·ti·*ko* ghra·*fi*·o

travel sickness ναυτία ⓕ naf·*ti*·a

travellers cheque ταξιδιωτική επιταγή ⓕ tak·si·thi·o·ti·*ki* e·pi·ta·*yi*

tree δέντρο ⓝ *the*·dro

trip (journey) ταξίδι ⓝ tak·*si*·thi

trolley καροτσάκι ⓝ ka·rot·*sa*·ki

trolley bus τρόλεϊ ⓝ *tro*·le·i

trousers παντελόνι ⓝ pa·de·*lo*·ni

truck φορτηγό ⓝ for·ti·*gho*

trust v εμπιστεύομαι e·bi·*ste*·vo·me

try (attempt) προσπαθώ pros·pa·*tho*

T-shirt μπλουζάκι ⓝ blu·*za*·ki

tube (tyre) σαμπρέλα ⓕ sa·*bre*·la

Tuesday Τρίτη ⓕ *tri*·ti

tumour όγκος ⓜ *o*·gos

tuna τόνος ⓜ *to*·nos

tune σκοπός ⓜ sko·*pos*

tunic χιτώνας ⓜ hi·*to*·nas

Turkey Τουρκία ⓕ tur·*ki*·a

turkey γαλοπούλα ⓕ gha·lo·*pu*·la

Turkish (language) Τουρκικά tur·ki·*ka*

Turkish (people) Τούρκοι ⓜ pl *tur*·ki

turn v γυρίζω yi·*ri*·zo

TV τηλεόραση ⓕ ti·le·o·ra·si

tweezers τσιμπιδάκι ⓝ tsi·bi·*tha*·ki

twice δυο φορές *thio* fo·*res*

twin beds δίκλινο δωμάτιο ⓝ *thi*·kli·no tho·*ma*·ti·o

twins δίδυμα ⓝ pl *thi*·thi·ma

two δύο *thi*·o

type τύπος ⓜ *ti*·pos

typhus τύφος ⓜ *ti*·fos

typical τυπικός ti·pi·*kos*

tyre λάστιχο ⓝ *la*·sti·kho

U

ultrasound υπερηχητικό κύμα ⓝ i·pe·ri·hi·ti·*ko ki*·ma

umbrella ομπρέλα ⓕ o·*bre*·la

uncomfortable άβολος a·vo·los

understand καταλαβαίνω ka·ta·la·*ve*·no

underwear εσώρουχα ⓝ pl e·*so*·ru·kha

unemployed a άνεργος/άνεργη ⓜ/ⓕ a·ner·ghos/a·ner·yi

unfair άδικος a·thi·kos

uniform στολή ⓕ sto·*li*

universe σύμπαν ⓝ *si*·pan [*i*·fi·li·os]

university πανεπιστήμιο ⓝ pa·ne·pi·*sti*·mi·o

unleaded (petrol) αμόλυβδος ⓕ a·*mo*·liv·thos

unsafe ανασφαλής a·nas·fa·*lis*

until μέχρι *me*·khri
unusual ασυνήθιστος a·si·*ni*·thi·stos
UN zone ζώνη των Ηνωμένων Εθνών ①
zo·ni ton i·no·*me*·non e·*thnon*
up πάνω *pa*·no
uphill ανηφορικά a·ni·fo·ri·*ka*
urgent επείγον e·*pi*·ghon
urinary infection ουρική μόλυνση ①
u·ri·*ki* mo·lin·si
USA ΗΠΑ ① *i*·pa
useful χρήσιμος *khri*·si·mos

V

vacancy κενή θέση ① ke·*ni the*·si
vacant ελεύθερος e·*lef*·the·ros
vacation διακοπές ① pl thia·ko·*pes*
vaccination εμβόλιο ⓝ em·*vo*·li·o
vagina κόλπος γυναίκας ⓜ
kol·pos yi·*ne*·kas
validate επικυρώνω e·pi·ki·*ro*·no
valley κοιλάδα ① ki·*la*·tha
valuable πολύτιμος po·*li*·ti·mos
value (price) αξία ① ak·*si*·a
van φορτηγάκι ⓝ for·ti·*gha*·ki
VAT (Value Added Tax) Φ.Π.Α. ⓜ fpa
veal μοσχάρι ⓝ mos·*kha*·ri
vegan βέγκαν ⓜ&① *ve*·gan
vegetable λαχανικά ⓝ pl la·kha·ni·*ka*
vegetarian a χορτοφάγος ⓜ&①
khor·to·*fa*·ghos
vein φλέβα ① *fle*·va
venereal disease αφροδισιακό νόσημα
ⓝ a·fro·thi·si·a·*ko* no·si·ma
venue χώρος ⓜ *kho*·ros
very πολύς po·*lis*
vessel σκάφος ⓝ *ska*·fos
video recorder βίντεο ρεκόρντερ ⓝ
vi·de·o re·*kor*·der
video tape βιντεοταινία ① vi·de·o·te·*ni*·a
view θέα ① *the*·a
village χωριό ⓝ kho·*rio*
vine κλήμα ⓝ *kli*·ma
vinegar ξύδι ⓝ *ksi*·thi
vineyard αμπέλι ⓝ a·*be*·li
virus ιός ⓜ i·*os*
visa βίζα ① *vi*·za
visit επίσκεψη ① e·*pi*·skep·si
visit v επισκέπτομαι e·pi·*ske*·pto·me

vitamins βιταμίνες ① pl vi·ta·*mi*·nes
vodka βότκα ① *vot*·ka
voice φωνή ① fo·*ni*
volleyball ⓝ βόλεϊ vo·le·i
vote v ψηφίζω psi·*fi*·zo

W

wage μισθός ⓜ mis·*thos*
wait (for) περιμένω pe·ri·*me*·no
waiter γκαρσόν ⓝ gar·*son*
waiting room αίθουσα αναμονής ①
e·thu·sa a·na·mo·*nis*
waitress σερβιτόρα ① ser·vi·*to*·ra
wake (someone) up ξυπνάω ksip·*na*·o
walk v περπατάω per·pa·*ta*·o
wall (outer) τείχος ⓝ *ti*·khos
wallet πορτοφόλι ⓝ por·to·*fo*·li
want θέλω *the*·lo
war πόλεμος ⓜ *po*·le·mos
wardrobe ντουλάπα ① du·*la*·pa
warm a ζεστός ze·*stos*
warn ζεσταίνω ze·*ste*·no
wash (oneself) v πλένομαι *ple*·no·me
wash (something) v πλένω *ple*·no
wash cloth (flannel) σφουγγάρι ⓝ sfu·*ga*·ri
washing machine πλυντήριο ⓝ pli·*di*·ri·o
wasp σφήκα ① *sfi*·ka
watch v κοιτάζω ki·*ta*·zo
watch ρολόι ⓝ ro·*lo*·i
water νερό ⓝ ne·*ro*
water bottle μπουκάλι νερού ⓝ
bu·*ka*·li ne·*ru*
water bottle (hot) θερμοφόρα ①
ther·mo·*fo*·ra
waterfall καταράχτης ⓜ ka·ta·*rakh*·tis
watermelon καρπούζι ⓝ kar·*pu*·zi
waterproof a αδιάβροχος
a·thi·*av*·ro·khos
waterskiing θαλάσσιο σκι ⓝ tha·*la*·si·o ski
wave κύμα ⓝ *ki*·ma
way δρόμος ⓜ *thro*·mos
we εμείς e·*mis*
weak a αδύνατος a·*thi*·na·tos
wealthy πλούσιος ⓜ *plu*·si·os
wear v φοράω fo·*ra*·o
weather καιρός ⓜ ke·*ros*
weaving υφαντό ⓝ i·fa·*do*
wedding γάμος ⓜ *gha*·mos

wedding cake γαμήλια τούρτα ① gha·*mi*·li·a *tur*·ta

wedding present γαμήλιο δώρο ⑩ gha·*mi*·li·o *tho*·ro

Wednesday Τετάρτη ① te·*tar*·ti

week εβδομάδα ① ev·tho·*ma*·tha

weekend Σαββατοκύριακο ⑩ sa·va·to·*ki*·ria·ko

weigh ζυγίζω zi·*yi*·zo

weight βάρος ⑩ *va*·ros

weights βάρη ⑩ pl *va*·ri

welcome v καλωσορίζω ka·lo·so·*ri*·zo

welfare πρόνοια ① *pro*·ni·a

well (health) καλά ka·*la*

west δύση ① *thi*·si

wet a βρεγμένος vregh·*me*·nos

what τι ti

wheel τροχός ⑩ tro·*khos*

wheelchair αναπηρική καρέκλα ① a·na·pi·ri·*ki* ka·*re*·kla

when όταν o·tan

where πού pu

which ποιος pios

whisky ουίσκυ ⑩ u·*i*·ski

white άσπρος *as*·pros

who ποιος pios

wholemeal bread ψωμί ολικής αλέσεως ⑩ pso·*mi* o·li·*kis* a·*le*·se·os

why γιατί yia·*ti*

wide πλατύς pla·*tis*

wife σύζυγος ① *si*·zi·ghos

wildflowers αγριολούλουδα ⑩ pl a·ghri·o·*lu*·lu·tha

win v κερδίζω ker·*thi*·zo

wind άνεμος ⑩ *a*·ne·mos

window παράθυρο ⑩ pa·*ra*·thi·ro

windscreen παμπρίζ ⑩ pa·*briz*

windsurfing γουιντσέρφινγκ ⑩ ghu·id·*ser*·fing

wine κρασί ⑩ kra·*si*

wings φτερούγες ① pl fte·*ru*·ghes

winner νικητής ⑩ ni·ki·*tis*

winter χειμώνας ⑩ hi·*mo*·nas

wire καλώδιο ⑩ ka·*lo*·thi·o

wish v εύχομαι *ef*·kho·me

with με me

within (an hour) εντός e·*dos*

without χωρίς kho·*ris*

wok γουόκ ⑩ ghu·*ok*

woman γυναίκα ① yi·*ne*·ka

wonderful θαυμάσιος thav·*ma*·si·os

wood δάσος ⑩ *tha*·sos

wool μαλλί ⑩ ma·*li*

word λέξη ① *lek*·si

work δουλειά ① thu·*lia*

work v δουλεύω thu·*le*·vo

work experience πείρα εργασίας ① *pi*·ra er·gha·*si*·as

workout εξάσκηση ① ek·*sa*·ski·si

work permit άδεια εργασίας ① *a*·thi·a er·gha·*si*·as

workshop εργαστήρι ⑩ er·gha·*sti*·ri

world κόσμος ⑩ *koz*·mos

World Cup Παγκόσμιο Κύπελο ⑩ pa·*goz*·mi·o *ki*·pe·lo

worm σκουλίκι ⑩ sku·*li*·ki

worried ανήσυχος a·*ni*·si·khos

worship v λατρεύω la·*tre*·vo

wrist καρπός ⑩ kar·*pos*

write γράφω *ghra*·fo

writer συγγραφέας ⑩&① si·gra·*fe*·as

wrong a λανθασμένος lan·thaz·*me*·nos

Y

year χρόνος ⑩ *khro*·nos

(this) year (αυτό το) χρόνο (af·to to) *khro*·no

yellow a κίτρινος *ki*·tri·nos

yes ναι ne

yesterday χτες khtes

(not) yet (όχι ακόμη *(o*·hi) a·*ko*·mi

yoga γιόγκα ① *yiog*·ka

yogurt γιαούρτι ⑩ yia·*ur*·ti

you sg inf εσύ e·*si*

you sg pol & pl inf&pol εσείς e·*sis*

young νέος ne·os

your sg pol & pl inf&pol σας sas

your sg inf σου su

youth hostel γιουθ χόστελ ⑩ yuth *kho*·stel

Z

zip/zipper φερμουάρ ⑩ fer·mu·*ar*

zodiac ζωδιακός ⑩ zo·thi·a·*kos*

zoo ζωολογικός κήπος ⑩ zo·o·lo·yi·*kos* *ki*·pos

zucchini κολοκυθάκι ⑩ ko·lo·ki·*tha*·ki

Greek nouns in the **dictionary** have their gender indicated by ⓜ masculine, ⓕ feminine or ⓝ neuter. If it's a plural noun you'll also see pl. When a word that could be either a noun or a verb has no gender indicated, it's a verb. Adjectives are given in the masculine form only – see **adjectives & adverbs** in the **phrasebuilder** for more on how to form feminine and neuter adjectives. Both nouns and adjectives are provided in the nominative case only – refer to the **phrasebuilder** for more information on **case**. You'll also find the English words marked as a adjective and v verb, sg singular, pl plural, inf informal, and pol polite where necessary.

The **greek–english dictionary** has been ordered according to the Greek alphabet:

Αα Ββ Γγ Δδ Εε Ζζ Ηη Θθ Ιι Κκ Λλ Μμ
Νν Ξξ Οο Ππ Ρρ Σσ/ς Ττ Υυ Φφ Χχ Ψψ Ωω

Α α

άβολος a·vo·los *uncomfortable*
αγάπη a·gha·pi ⓕ *love*
αγαπώ a·gha·po *love* ⓥ
Αγγλία ⓕ ang·gli·a *England*
Αγγλικά ⓝ pl ang·gli·ka *English (language)*
αγορά ⓕ a·gho·ra *market • shopping centre*
αγοράζω a·gho·ra·zo *buy* ⓥ
αγόρι ⓝ a·gho·ri *boy*
άδειο a·thi·o *empty* a
αδερφή ⓕ a·ther·fi *sister*
αδερφός ⓜ a·ther·fos *brother*
αδιάβροχο a·thi·av·ro·ho ⓝ *raincoat*
αδύνατος a·thi·na·tos *impossible* a
αερογραμμή ⓕ a·e·ro·ghra·mi *airline*
αεροδρόμιο a·e·ro·thro·mi·o ⓝ *airport*
αεροπλάνο a·e·ro·pla·no ⓝ *airplane*
αίθουσα αναμονής
  e·thu·sa a·na·mo·nis ⓕ *waiting room*
αίθουσα τράνζιτ ⓕ e·thu·sa tran·zit
  transit lounge
αίμα e·ma ⓝ *blood*
ακριβός a·kri·vos *expensive*
ακριβώς a·kri·vos *exactly*
ακυρώνω a·ki·ro·no *cancel*
αλλαγή a·la·yi ⓕ *change*
αλλεργία a·ler·yi·a ⓕ *allergy*
αλληλογραφία a·li·lo·ghra·fi·a ⓕ *mail*
άλλος a·los *other*
άμεσος a·me·sos *direct* a
αναπηρική καρέκλα
  a·na·pi·ri·ki ka·re·kla ⓕ *wheelchair*

ανάπηρος a·na·pi·ros *disabled* a
αναπτήρας ⓜ a·nap·ti·ras *cigarette lighter*
ανατολή ⓕ a·na·to·li *east • sunrise*
αναχώρηση ⓕ a·na·kho·ri·si *departure*
αναχωρώ a·na·kho·ro *depart* ⓥ • *leave* ⓥ
ανεβαίνω a·ne·ve·no *board (transport)* ⓥ
ανεμιστήρας ⓜ a·ne·mi·sti·ras
  fan (machine)
άνετος a·ne·tos *comfortable*
ανθοπώλης ⓜ an·tho·po·lis *florist*
ανθοπώλισσα ⓕ an·tho·po·li·sa *florist*
ανιαρός a·ni·a·ros *boring*
άνοιξη ⓕ a·nik·si *spring (season)*
ανοιχτήρι ⓝ a·nikh·ti·ri *bottle opener •
  can opener • corkscrew*
ανοιχτός a·nikh·tos *light (colour) • open* a
ανταλλάσσω a·da·la·so *exchange* ⓥ
αντιβιοτικά ⓝ pl a·di·vi·o·ti·ka *antibiotics*
αντίγραφο ⓝ a·di·ghra·fo *copy*
αντιηλιακό ⓝ a·di·i·li·a·ko *sunblock*
αντισηπτικό ⓝ a·di·si·lip·ti·ko *antiseptic*
άντρας ⓜ a·dras *man*
απαίσιος a·pe·si·os *awful*
απασχολημένος a·pa·skho·li·me·nos *busy*
απεργία ⓕ a·per·yi·a *strike*
απίθανος a·pi·tha·nos *fantastic • great*
απλό εισιτήριο ⓝ a·plo i·si·ti·ri·o
  one-way (ticket)
απόγευμα ⓝ a·po·yev·ma *afternoon*
απόδειξη ⓕ a·po·thik·si *receipt*
αποσκευές ⓕ pl a·po·ske·ves *baggage*
αποσμητικό ⓝ a·poz·mi·ti·ko *deodorant*
απόψε a·pop·se *tonight*

αργά ar-*gha slowly*
αργότερα ar-*gho*-te-ra *later*
αριθμομηχανή ⓕ a-rith-mo-mi-kha-*ni calculator*
αριθμός ⓜ a-rith-*mos number*
αριθμός διαβατηρίου ⓜ a-rith-*mos* thia-va-ti-*ri*-u *passport number*
αριθμός δωματίου ⓜ a-rith-*mos* tho-ma-*ti*-u *room number*
αριθμός κυκλοφορίας αυτοκινήτου ⓕ a-rith-*mos* ki-klo-fo-*ri*-as af-to-ki-*ni*-tu *car registration*
αριθμός οδήγησης ⓕ a-rith-*mos* o-*thi*-yi-sis *drivers licence*
αριστερός a-ri-ste-*ros left (direction)* a
αρκετά ar-ke-*ta enough*
αρραβωνιασμένη ⓕ a-ra-vo-niaz-*me*-ni *engaged (to marry)*
αρραβωνιασμένος a-ra-vo-niaz-*me*-nos *engaged (to marry)*
αρραβωνιαστικιά ⓕ a-ra-vo-nia-sti-*kia fiancée*
αρραβωνιαστικός ⓜ a-ra-vo-nia-sti-*kos fiancé*
άρρωστος a-ro-stos *ill • sick*
αρχιτέκτονας ⓜ&ⓕ ar-hi-*tek*-to-nas *architect*
αρχιτεκτονική ⓕ ar-hi-tek-to-ni-*ki architecture*
άρωμα ⓝ a-ro-ma *perfume*
ασανσέρ ⓝ a-san-*ser elevator • lift*
ασήμι ⓝ a-*si*-mi *silver*
άσπρος as-pros *white*
αστείος a-*sti*-os *funny*
αστικό λεωφορείο ⓝ a-sti-*ko* le-o-fo-*ri*-o *bus*
αστράγαλος ⓜ a-*stra*-gha-los *ankle*
αστυνομία ⓕ a-sti-no-*mi*-a *police*
αστυνομικός σταθμός ⓜ a-sti-no-mi-*kos* stath-*mos police station*
αστυφύλακας ⓜ a-sti-*fi*-la-kas *police officer*
αστυφυλακίνα ⓕ a-sti-fi-la-*ki*-na *police officer*
ασφάλεια ⓕ as-*fa*-li-a *insurance*
ασφαλές σεξ ⓝ as-fa-*les* seks *safe sex*
ατύχημα ⓝ a-*ti*-hi-ma *accident*
αυγή ⓕ av-*yi dawn*
αύριο av-ri-o *tomorrow*
αυτοκίνητο ⓝ af-to-*ki*-ni-to *car*
αυτοκινητόδρομος ⓜ af-to-ki-ni-*to*-thro-mos *motorway • tollway*
αυτόματη μηχανή χρημάτων ⓕ af-*to*-ma-ti mi-kha-*ni* khri-*ma*-ton *ATM*

αυτός ⓜ af-*tos he • this (one)*
αφή ⓕ a-*fi feeling (physical)*
αφίξεις ⓕ pl a-*fik*-sis *arrivals*
αφτί ⓝ af-*ti ear*

Β β

βαγκόν λι ⓝ va-*gon* li *sleeping car*
βαγόνι φαγητού ⓝ va-*gho*-ni fa-yi-*tu dining car*
βαλίτσα ⓕ va-*lit*-sa *suitcase*
βαμπάκι ⓝ va-*ba*-ki *cotton*
βάρκα ⓕ var-ka *boat*
βαρύς va-*ris heavy*
βγάζω φωτογραφία vga-zo fo-to-gra-*fi*-a *take a photo*
βγαίνω vye-no *go out*
βελόνα ⓕ ve-*lo*-na *needle (sewing)*
βενζίνα ⓕ ven-*zi*-na *gas • petrol*
βενζινάδικο ⓝ ven-zi-*na*-thi-ko *service station*
βήχω vi-kho *cough* ⓥ
βιαστικός via-sti-*kos in a hurry*
βιβλίο viv-*li*-o *book* ⓝ
βιβλιοθήκη ⓕ viv-li-o-*thi*-ki *library*
βιβλιοπωλείο ⓝ viv-li-o-po-*li*-o *bookshop*
βιβλίο φράσεων ⓝ viv-*li*-o *fra*-se-on *phrasebook*
βίζα ⓕ *vi*-za *visa*
βιντεοταινία ⓕ vi-de-o-te-*ni*-a *video tape*
βοήθεια ⓕ vo-*i*-thi-a *help*
βοηθώ vo-*i*-tho *help* ⓥ
βοράς ⓜ vo-*ras north*
βούλωμα ⓝ vu-lo-ma *plug (bath)*
βουνό ⓝ vu-*no mountain*
βούρτσα ⓕ *vur*-tsa *brush*
βράδι ⓝ vra-thi *evening*
βροχή ⓕ vro-*hi rain*
βρύση ⓕ *vri*-si *faucet • tap*
βρώμικος a vro-mi-kos *dirty*
βύσμα ⓝ *viz*-ma *plug (electricity)*

Γ γ

γάλα ⓝ *gha*-la *milk*
γαστροεντερίτιδα ⓕ gha-stro-e-de-*ri*-ti-tha *gastroenteritis*
γεμάτο ye-ma-to *full*
γενέθλια ⓝ pl ye-*ne*-thli-a *birthday*
Γερμανία ⓕ yer-ma-*ni*-a *Germany*
γεύμα ⓝ yev-ma *meal*
γεφύρι ⓝ ye-*fi*-ri *bridge*

Γη ① yi *Earth*
γήπεδο ⑪ *yi·pe·tho court (tennis)*
— **του γκολφ** ⑪ *tu golf golf course*
— **του τένις** ⑪ *tu te·nis tennis court*
γιαγιά ① *yia·yia grandmother*
γιαλιά ⑪ pl *yia·lia glasses • spectacles*
γιαλιά ηλίου ⑪ pl *yia·lia i·li·u sunglasses*
γιατί *yia·ti why*
γιατρός ⑪&① *yia·tros doctor*
γιος ⑪ *yios son*
γιουθ χόστελ ⑪ *yuth kho·stel youth hostel*
γκαρσόν ⑪ *gar·son waiter*
γκέι *ge·i gay* a
γκρίζος *gri·zos gray • grey* a
γλυκός *ghli·kos sweet* a
γλυπτική ① *ghlip·ti·ki sculpture*
γλώσσα ① *ghlo·sa language*
γόνατο ⑪ *gho·na·to knee*
γονείς ⑪ pl *gho·nis parents*
γράμμα ⑪ *ghra·ma letter (mail)*
γραμμάριο ⑪ *ghra·ma·ri·o gram*
γραμματόσημο ⑪ *ghra·ma·to·si·mo stamp*
γραφείο απολεσθέντων αντικειμένων ⑪ *gra·fi·o a·po·le·sthe·thon a·di·ki·me·non left-luggage office*
γραφείο εισιτηρίων ⑪ *ghra·fi·o i·si·ti·ri·on ticket office*
γράφω *ghra·fo write*
γρήγορος a *ghri·gho·ros fast*
γρίπη ① *ghri·pi influenza • flu*
γυμναστήριο ⑪ *yi·mna·sti·ri·o gym (place)*
γυναίκα ① *yi·ne·ka woman*

Δ δ

δάκτυλο ⑪ *thak·ti·lo finger*
δασικός αεροδρομίου ⑪ *thaz·mos a·e·ro·thro·mi·u airport tax*
δάσος ⑪ *tha·sos forest • wood*
δαχτυλίδι ① *thakh·ti·li·thi ring (on finger)*
δείπνο ⑪ *thip·no dinner*
δείχνω *thi·khno point* ⊙ *• show* ⊙
δεκαπενθήμερο ⑪ *tha·ka·pen·thi·me·ro fortnight*
δέμα ⑪ *the·ma parcel*
δεξιός *thek·si·os right (direction)* a
δέρμα ⑪ *ther·ma leather • skin*
δεύτερη τάξη ① *thef·te·ri tak·si second class*
δημόσια αποχωρητήρια ⑪ pl *thi·mo·si·a a·po·kho·ri·ti·ria public toilet*

δημόσιο τηλέφωνο ⑪ *thi·mo·si·o ti·le·fo·no phone box • public telephone*
δημοσιογράφος ⑪&① *thi·mo·si·o·ghra·fos journalist*
δημόσιος δρόμος ⑪ *thi·mo·si·os thro·mos highway*
δια ξηράς *thi·a ksi·ras surface mail*
διαβατήριο ① *thia·va·ti·ri·o passport*
διαδίκτυο ⑪ *thi·a·thik·ti·o Internet*
διάδρομος ⑪ *thi·a·thro·mos aisle*
διαζευγμένη ① *thi·a·zev·ghme·ni divorced* a
διαζευγμένος ⑪ *thi·a·zev·ghme·nos divorced* a
διαθέσιμος *thi·a·the·si·mos free (available)*
διακοπές ① pl *thia·ko·pes vacation*
διάλειμμα ⑪ *thia·li·ma intermission*
διαμέρισμα ⑪ *thi·a·me·riz·ma apartment*
διάρροια ① *thi·a·ri·a diarrhoea*
διαφορά ώρας ① *thia·fo·ra o·ras time difference*
διαφορετικός *thia·fo·re·ti·kos different*
διαχωριστική γραμμή ① *thi·a·kho·ri·sti·ki ghra·mi delineation line*
διερμηνέας ⑪&① *thi·er·mi·ne·as interpreter*
διεύθυνση ① *thi·ef·thin·si address*
δικηγόρος ⑪&① *thi·ki·gho·ros lawyer*
δίκλινο δωμάτιο ⑪ *thi·kli·no tho·ma·ti·o twin beds*
δίπλα *thi·pla beside • next to*
διπλό δωμάτιο ⑪ *thi·plo tho·ma·ti·o double room*
διπλό κρεβάτι ⑪ *thi·plo kre·va·ti double bed*
Δις ① *the·spi·nis Ms • Miss*
δισκέτα ① *thi·ske·ta disk (floppy)*
διψασμένος *thip·saz·me·nos thirsty*
δοκιμάζω *tho·ki·ma·zo try* ⊙
δοκιμαστήριο ρούχων ⑪ *tho·ki·ma·sti·ri·o ru·khon changing room (in shop)*
δολλάριο ⑪ *tho·la·ri·o dollar*
δουλειά ① *thu·lia job • work*
δρόμος ⑪ *thro·mos road • route • way*
δροσερό *thro·se·ro cool (temperature)*
δυνατός *thi·na·tos loud • strong • possible*
δύο *thi·o two*
δύση ① *thi·si sunset • west*
δυσπεψία ① *this·pep·si·a indigestion*
δωμάτιο ⑪ *tho·ma·ti·o room*
δωρεάν *tho·re·an complimentary • free*
δώρο ⑪ *tho·ro gift • present*

E ε

εβδομάδα ⓕ ev-tho-ma-tha *week*
εγγονή ⓕ e-go-ni *granddaughter*
εγγονός ⓜ e-go-nos *grandson*
εγγυημένος e-ghi-i-me-nos *guaranteed*
έγκαυμα ⓝ e-gav-ma *burn*
έγκυος e-gi-os *pregnant*
εγώ e-gho *me*
εδώ e-tho *here*
έθιμο ⓝ e-thi-mo *custom*
εισιτήριο ⓝ i-si-ti-ri-o *fare • ticket*
— **μετ' επιστροφής** ⓜ me-te-pi-stro-fis *return ticket*
— **σταντ μπάι** ⓝ stand ba-i *stand-by ticket*
είσοδος ⓕ i-so-thos *entry*
εκατοστόμετρο ⓝ e-ka-to-sto-me-tro *centimetre*
εκεί e-ki *there*
έκθεμα ⓝ ek-the-ma *exhibit*
έκθεση ⓕ ek-the-si *exhibition*
εκκλησία ⓕ e-kli-si-a *church*
έκπτωση ⓕ ek-pto-si *discount*
έκτακτη ανάγκη ⓕ ek-tak-ti a-na-gi *emergency*
εκτυπωτής ⓜ ek-ti-po-tis *printer (computer)*
ελαττωματικός e-la-to-ma-ti-kos *faulty*
ελαφρύ γεύμα ⓝ e-laf-ri ghev-ma *snack*
ελαφρύς e-la-fris *light (weight)*
ελεύθερος e-lef-the-ros *vacant*
Ελλάδα ⓕ e-la-tha *Greece*
Έλληνες ⓜ pl e-li-nes *Greek (people)*
Ελληνικά ⓝ pl e-li-ni-ka *Greek (language)*
εμβόλιο ⓝ em-vo-li-o *vaccination*
ένα e-na *one*
ένας άλλος e-nas a-los *another*
ένεση ⓕ e-ne-si *injection*
ενοικιάζω e-ni-ki-a-zo *hire* ⓥ • *rent* ⓥ
ενοικίαση αυτοκινήτου ⓕ e-ni-ki-a-si af-to-ki-ni-tu *car hire*
εξαργυρώνω ⓥ ek-sar-yi-ro-no *cash a cheque*
έξοδος ⓕ ek-so-thos *exit*
εξοχή ⓕ ek-so-hi *countryside*
εξπρές eks-pres *express mail* a
έξω ek-so *outside*
εξωτερικό ek-so-te-ri-ko *overseas*
επάνω e-pa-no *aboard*
επείγον e-pi-ghon *urgent*
— **ταχυδρομείο** ⓝ ta-hi-thro-mi-o *by express mail*

επιβάτης ⓜ e-pi-va-tis *passenger*
επιβάτισσα ⓕ e-pi-va-ti-sa *passenger*
επίδειξη ⓕ e-pi-thik-si *show*
επίδεσμος ⓜ e-pi-thez-mos *bandage*
επιδόρπιο ⓝ e-pi-thor-pi-o *dessert*
επικίνδυνος e-pi-kin-thi-nos *dangerous*
επικυρώνω e-pi-ki-ro-no *confirm (booking) • validate*
έπιπλα ⓝ pl e-pi-pla *furniture*
επισκευάζω e-pi-ske-va-zo *repair* ⓥ
επιστήμη ⓕ e-pi-sti-mi *science*
επιστήμονας ⓜ&ⓕ e-pi-sti-mo-nas *scientist*
επιστρέφω e-pi-stre-fo *come back • return* ⓥ
επιστροφή χρημάτων ⓕ e-pi-stro-fi khri-ma-ton *refund*
επιτήρηση παιδιών ⓕ e-pi-ti-ri-si pe-thion *childminding*
επιτρεπόμενες αποσκευές ⓕ pl e-pi-tre-po-me-nes a-po-ske-ves *baggage allowance*
επιχείρηση ⓕ e-pi-hi-ri-si *business*
επόμενος e-po-me-nos *next* a
εποχή ⓕ e-po-hi *season*
επώνυμο ⓝ e-po-ni-mo *surname*
εργόχειρα ⓝ pl er-gho-hi-ra *handicrafts*
ερείπια ⓝ pl e-ri-pi-a *ruins*
εσείς e-sis *you* sg pol & pl
εστιατόριο ⓝ e-sti-a-to-ri-o *restaurant*
εσύ e-si *you* sg inf
εσώρουχα ⓝ pl e-so-ru-kha *underwear*
εταιρεία ⓕ e-te-ri-a *company (firm)*
ευγνώμων ev-ghno-mon *grateful*
εύθραυστος ef-thraf-stos *fragile*
ευτυχισμένος ef-ti-hiz-me-nos *happy*
εφημερίδα ⓕ e-fi-me-ri-tha *newspaper*
έχω e-kho *have*

Z ζ

ζακέτα ⓕ za-ke-ta *jacket • sweater*
ζαχαροπλαστείο ⓝ za-kha-ro-pla-sti-o *cake shop*
ζεστός ze-stos *hot • warm* a
ζωγραφική ⓕ zo-ghra-fi-ki *painting (the art)*
ζωγράφος ⓜ&ⓕ zo-ghra-fos *painter*
ζώνη καθίσματος ⓕ zo-ni ka-thiz-ma-tos *seatbelt*
ζωολογικός κήπος ⓜ zo-o-lo-yi-kos ki-pos *zoo*

Η η

ηθοποιός ⓜ&ⓕ i·tho·pi·os *actor*
ηλεκτρισμός ⓜ i·lek·triz·mos *electricity*
ηλιακό έγκαυμα ⓝ i·li·a·ko e·gav·ma *sunburn*
ήλιος ⓜ *i*·li·os *sun*
ημέρα ⓕ *i*·me·ra *day*
ημερολόγιο ⓝ i·me·ro·lo·yi·o *diary*
ημερομηνία ⓕ i·me·ro·mi·ni·a *date (day)*
— **γεννήσεως** ⓕ ye·ni·se·os *date of birth*
ΗΠΑ ⓕ *i*·pa *USA*
ήσυχος i·si·khos *quiet* a
ήχος κλήσης ⓜ *i*·khos kli·sis *dial tone*

Θ θ

θάλασσα ⓕ tha·la·sa *sea*
θέα ⓕ the·a *view*
θεά ⓕ the·a *goddess*
θεατρικό έργο ⓝ the·a·tri·ko er·gho *play (theatre)*
θέατρο ⓝ the·a·tro *theatre*
θεία ⓕ thi·a *aunt*
θερμοκρασία ⓕ ther·mo·kra·si·a *temperature (weather)*
θερμοπληξία ⓕ ther·mo·plik·si·a *heatstroke*
θερμοφόρα ⓕ ther·mo·fo·ra *(hot) water bottle*
θηλυκός a thi·li·kos *female*
θορυβώδης tho·ri·vo·this *noisy*
Φ.Π.Α. ⓕ fpa *VAT (Value Added Tax)*

Ι ι

ιατρική ⓕ i·a·tri·*ki* *medicine (job, study)*
ιδιωτικός i·thi·o·ti·kos *private* a
ιματιοφυλάκιο ⓝ i·ma·ti·o·fi·la·ki·o *cloakroom*
ινστιτούτο αισθητικής ⓝ in·sti·*tu*·to es·thi·ti·kis *beauty salon*
ιππασία ⓕ i·pa·si·a *horse riding • ride*
ιχθυοπωλείο ⓝ ikh·thi·o·po·*li*·o *fish shop*

Κ κ

κα ⓕ khi·ri·a *Mrs*
καθαρίζω ka·tha·ri·zo *clean* ⓥ
καθάρισμα ⓝ ka·tha·riz·ma *cleaning*

καθαρός ka·tha·ros *clean* a
καθαρτικό ⓝ ka·thar·ti·ko *laxative*
κάθε ka·the *every • per*
καθένας ka·the·nas *each • everyone*
καθετί ⓝ ka·the·ti *everything*
καθημερινός ka·thi·me·ri·nos *daily*
καθρέφτης ⓜ ka·*thref*·tis *mirror*
καθυστερημένος ka·thi·ste·ri·me·nos *late*
καθυστέρηση ka·thi·ste·ri·si *delay* ⓥ
και ke *and*
και οι δύο ke i *thi*·o *both*
κακός ka·kos *bad*
καλλιτέχνης ⓜ ka·li·*tekh*·nis *artist*
καλλιτέχνιδα ⓕ ka·li·*tekh*·ni·tha *artist*
καλλυντικά ⓝ pl ka·li·di·ka *make-up*
καλοκαίρι ⓝ ka·lo·*ke*·ri *summer*
καλός ka·*los* *good* a • *kind* a
κάλτσες ⓕ *kal*·tses *socks*
καλύτερος ka·*li*·te·ros *better*
καλώ ka·lo *call* ⓥ
Καναδάς ⓜ ka·na·*thas* *Canada*
καπέλο ⓝ ka·pe·lo *hat*
καπνίζω kap·ni·zo *smoke* ⓥ
καρδιά ⓕ kar·*thia* *heart*
καρδιακή κατάσταση ⓕ kar·dhi·a·*ki* ka·*ta*·sta·si *heart condition*
καρέκλα ⓕ ka·re·kla *chair*
καροτσάκι ⓝ ka·rot·sa·ki *stroller • trolley*
κάρτα ⓕ *kar*·ta *postcard*
— **επιβίβασης** ⓕ e·pi·*vi*·va·sis *boarding pass*
— **τηλεφώνου** ⓝ ti·le·fo·nu *phonecard*
κασέτα ⓕ ka·se·ta *cassette*
κασκόλ ⓝ ka·skol *scarf*
κάστρο ⓝ *ka*·stro *castle*
κατ' ευθείαν γραμμή ⓕ ka·tef·thi·an gra·*mi* *direct-dial*
κατάθεση ⓕ ka·*ta*·the·si *deposit (bank)*
κατάλογος ⓜ ka·ta·lo·ghos *itinerary*
κατάλυμα ⓝ ka·ta·li·ma *accommodation*
κατάστημα ⓝ ka·ta·sti·ma *department store*
— **για σουβενίρ** ⓝ yia su·ve·nir *souvenir shop*
— **ηλεκτρικών ειδών** ⓝ i·lek·tri·kon i·*thon* *electrical store*
— **μουσικών ειδών** ⓝ mu·si·kon i·*thon* *music shop*
— **ρούχων** ⓝ ruk·hon *clothing store*
— **των σπορ** ⓝ ton spor *sports shop*
κατεβαίνω ka·te·ve·no *get off (train, etc)*
κατεύθυνση ⓕ ka·*tef*·thin·si *direction*

καύσωνας ⓜ *kaf*·so·nas *heatwave*
καφέ ka·*fe* *brown* a
καφενείο ⓝ ka·fe·*ni*·o *coffee shop*
— διαδικτύου ⓝ thi·a·*thik*·*ti*·u *Internet café*
καφές ⓜ ka·*fes* *coffee*
καφεστιατόριο ⓕ ka·fe·sti·a·*to*·ri·o *café*
κενή θέση ⓕ ke·*ni* *the*·si *vacancy*
κέντημα ⓝ *ke*·di·ma *embroidery*
κέντρο ⓝ *ke*·dro *centre*
κέντρο της πόλης ⓝ *ke*·dro tis *po*·lis *city centre*
κέρματα ⓝ pl *ker*·ma·ta *coins*
κεφάλι ⓝ ke·*fa*·li *head*
κήπος ⓜ *ki*·pos *garden*
κινητό ⓝ ki·ni·*to* *mobile phone*
κίτρινος *ki*·tri·nos *yellow* a
κλειδί ⓝ kli·*thi* *key*
κλειδωμένος kli·*tho*·me·nos *locked*
κλειδώνω kli·*tho*·no *lock* ⓥ
κλείνω *kli*·no *close* ⓥ
— θέση the·si *book* ⓥ
κλεισμένος kliz·*me*·nos *closed*
κλειστός kli·*stos* *shut*
κλεμμένο kle·*me*·no *stolen*
κλήση με αντιστροφή της επιβάρυνσης ⓕ *kli*·si me a·dis·tro·*fi* tis e·pi·*va*·rin·sis *collect call*
κλονισμός ⓜ klo·niz·*mos* *concussion*
κόβω *ko*·vo *cut* ⓥ
κοιμάμαι ki·*ma*·me *sleep* ⓥ
κοιμητήριο ⓝ ki·mi·*ti*·ri·o *cemetery*
κόκκινο *ko*·ki·no *red*
κολιέ ⓝ ko·li·*e* *necklace*
κολυμπώ ko·li·*bo* *swim* ⓥ
κολώνα ⓕ ko·*lo*·na *column*
κολόνια ξυρίσματος ⓕ ko·*lo*·ni·a ksi·*riz*·ma·tos *aftershave*
κομμωτής ⓜ ko·mo·*tis* *hairdresser*
κομμώτρια ⓕ ko·mo·*tri*·a *hairdresser*
κοντά ko·*da* *near* • *nearby*
κοντινός ko·di·*nos* *close* a
κοντός ko·*dos* *short (height)*
κόρη ⓕ *ko*·ri *daughter*
κορίτσι ⓝ ko·*rit*·si *girl*
Κος ⓜ *khi*·ri·os *Mr*
κοσμήματα ⓝ pl koz·*mi*·ma·ta *jewellery*
κοστίζω ko·*sti*·zo *cost* ⓥ
κοτόπουλο ⓝ ko·*to*·pu·lo *chicken*
κουβέρτα ⓕ ku·*ver*·ta *blanket*
κουζίνα ⓕ ku·*zi*·na *kitchen*
κουμπί ⓝ ku·*bi* *button*
κουρασμένος ku·raz·*me*·nos *tired*

κούρεμα ⓝ *ku*·re·ma *haircut*
κουτάλι ⓝ ku·*ta*·li *spoon*
— τσαγιού ⓝ tsa·*yiu* *teaspoon*
κουτί ⓝ ku·*ti* *box* • *can* • *tin*
κραγιόν ⓝ pl kra·*yion* *lipstick*
κρασί ⓝ kra·*si* *wine*
κράτηση ⓕ *kra*·ti·si *booking* • *reservation*
κρέας ⓝ *kre*·as *meat*
κρεβάτι ⓝ kre·*va*·ti *bed*
κρέμα ⓕ *kre*·ma *cream*
— ξυρίσματος ⓕ ksi·*riz*·ma·tos *shaving cream*
κρεοπωλείο ⓝ kre·o·po·*li*·o *butcher's shop*
κρυωμένος kri·o·me·nos *cold* a
κτηματομεσιτικό γραφείο ⓝ kti·ma·to·me·si·ti·*ko* ghra·*fi*·o *estate agency*
κτήριο ⓝ *kti*·ri·o *building*
κυλιόμενες σκάλες ⓕ pl ki·li·o·me·nes *ska*·les *escalator*
κυτίο πρώτων βοηθειών ⓝ ki·*ti*·o *pro*·ton vo·i·thi·on *first-aid kit*

Λ λ

λάδι ⓝ *la*·thi *oil*
— αυτοκινήτου ⓝ af·to·ki·*ni*·tu *oil (car)*
λαϊκή ⓕ la·i·*ki* *street market*
λαιμός ⓜ le·*mos* *throat*
λάστιχο ⓝ *la*·sti·kho *tire* • *tyre*
λαχανικά ⓝ pl la·kha·ni·*ka* *vegetable*
λαιμός ⓜ le·*mos* *neck*
λεξικό ⓝ lek·si·*ko* *dictionary*
λεπτό ⓝ lep·*to* *minute*
λεσβία ⓕ lez·*vi*·a *lesbian*
λιγότερο li·*gho*·te·ro *less*
λίμνη ⓕ *lim*·ni *lake*
λινό ⓝ li·*no* *linen (material)*
λιπαντικό ⓝ li·pa·di·ko *lubricant*
λίρα ⓕ *li*·ra *pound (money)*
λίτρα ⓕ *lit*·ra *pound (weight)*
λογαριασμός ⓜ lo·gha·riaz·*mos* *account* • *bill* • *check*
λοσιόν ⓕ lo·sion *lotion*
— για μαύρισμα ⓕ yia *mav*·riz·ma *tanning lotion*

Μ μ

μαβής ma·*vis* *purple*
μαγαζί ⓝ ma·gha·*zi* *shop*
μάγειρας ⓜ *ma*·yi·ras *cook*

μαγείρισσα ① ma·yi·ri·sa *cook*
μαγειρεύω ma·yi·re·vo *cook* ⊙
μαγιό ⑩ ma·yio *swimsuit*
μαζί ma·zi *together*
μαθαίνω ma·the·no *learn*
μακριά ma·kri·a *far*
μακρύς ma·kris *long* a
μαντήλι ⑩ ma·di·li *handkerchief*
μαξιλάρι ⑩ mak·si·la·ri *pillow*
μαξιλαροθήκη ① mak·si·la·ro·thi·ki
  pillowcase
μας mas *our*
μάτι ⑩ ma·ti *eye*
μάτια ⑩ pl ma·tia *eyes*
ματς ⑩ mats *game • match*
μαυρόασπρο (φιλμ) ⑩ mav·ro·a·spro
  (film) *B&W (film)*
μαύρος mav·ros *black*
μαχαίρι ⑩ ma·he·ri *knife*
μαχαιροπήρουνα ⑩ pl ma·he·ro·pi·ru·na
  cutlery
με ερκοντίσιον me er kon·di·si·on
  air-conditioned
μεγάλα φώτα αυτοκινήτου
  ⑩ pl me·gha·la fo·ta af·to·ki·ni·tu
  headlights
μεγάλος me·gha·los *big • large*
μεγαλύτερος me·gha·li·te·ros *bigger*
μέγεθος ⑩ me·ye·thos *size (general)*
μεθαύριο me·thav·ri·o *day after tomorrow*
μεθυσμένος me·thiz·me·nos *drunk*
μενού ⑩ me·nu *menu*
μέσα me·sa *in • inside*
μεσάνυχτα ⑩ pl me·sa·nikh·ta *midnight*
μεσημέρι ⑩ me·si·me·ri *midday • noon*
μεσημεριανό φαγητό ⑩
  me·si·me·ria·no fa·yi·to *lunch*
μετά me·ta *after*
μεταλλικό νερό ⑩ me·ta·li·ko ne·ro
  mineral water
μετάξι ⑩ me·tak·si *silk*
μετασχηματιστής ⑩
  me·ta·shi·ma·ti·stis *adaptor*
μεταφράζω me·ta·fra·zo *translate*
μετρητά ⑩ pl me·tri·ta *cash*
μέχρι me·khri *until*
μη καπνίζοντες mi kap·ni·zo·des
  nonsmoking
μήνας ⑩ mi·nas *month*
μήνυμα ⑩ mi·ni·ma *message*
μητέρα ① mi·te·ra *mother*
μητρόπολη ① mi·tro·po·li *cathedral*

μηχανή ① mi·kha·ni *engine • machine*
  — εισιτηρίων ① i·si·ti·ri·on
  ticket machine
  — φαξ faks *fax machine*
μηχανική ① mi·kha·ni·ki *engineering*
μηχανικός ⑩&① mi·kha·ni·kos
  engineer • mechanic
μικρό όνομα ⑩ mi·kro o·no·ma *first name*
μικρότερος mi·kro·te·ros *smaller*
μιλάω mi·la·o *speak • talk* ⊙
μισό mi·so *half*
μόδα ① mo·tha *fashion*
μοιράζομαι mi·ra·zo·me *share with*
μολύβι ⑩ mo·li·vi *pencil*
μόλυνση ① mo·lin·si *infection*
μονό δωμάτιο ⑩ mo·no tho·ma·tio
  single room
μονοπάτι ⑩ mo·no·pa·ti *path • track • trail*
μόνος mo·nos *alone*
μου mu *my • to me*
μου αρέσει mu a·re·si *like* ⊙
μπαγιάτικος ba·yia·ti·kos *off (spoiled) • stale*
μπαίνω be·no *enter*
μπαλάκια από βαμπάκι ⑩ pl
  ba·la·kia a·po va·ba·ki *cotton balls*
μπάνιο ⑩ ba·nio *bath • bathroom*
μπάντα ① ba·da *band (music)*
μπαρ ⑩ bar *bar*
μπαταρία ① ba·ta·ri·a *battery*
μπέιμπι σίτερ ① be·i·bi si·ter *babysitter*
μπίζνες κλασ biz·nes klas *business class*
μπλε ble *blue* a
μπλοκαρισμένος blo·ka·riz·me·nos
  blocked
μπλουζάκι ⑩ blu·za·ki *T-shirt*
μπότα ① bo·ta *boot (footwear)*
μπουκάλι ⑩ bu·ka·li *bottle*
μπουφές ⑩ bu·fes *buffet*
μπροσούρα ① bro·su·ra *brochure*
μπύρα ① bi·ra *beer*
μπυραρία ① bi·ra·ri·a *bar • pub*
μπωλ ⑩ bol *bowl*
μυρουδιά ① mi·ru·thia *smell*
μύτη ① mi·ti *nose*
μωρό ⑩ mo·ro *baby*

N ν

ναι ne *yes*
ναρκωτικά ⑩ pl nar·ko·ti·ka *illegal drugs*
ναυτία ① naf·ti·a
  nausea • seasickness • travel sickness

νέα ⓝ pl ne·a *news*
Νέα Ζηλανδία ⓕ ne·a zi·lan·*thi*·a *New Zealand*
νέος ne·os *new · young*
νερό ⓝ ne·ro *water*
νοικοκυρά ⓕ ni·ko·ki·*ra* *housewife*
νοικοκύρης ⓜ ni·ko·*ki*·ris *head of the house*
νησί ⓝ ni·*si* *island*
νομικά ⓝ no·mi·*ka* *law (study, profession)*
νοσοκόμος ⓜ no·so·ko·mos *nurse*
νοσοκόμα ⓕ no·so·*ko*·ma *nurse*
νοσοκομειακό ⓝ no·so·ko·mi·a·*ko* *ambulance*
νοσοκομείο ⓝ no·so·ko·*mi*·o *hospital*
νόστιμος no·sti·mos *tasty*
νότος ⓜ no·tos *south*
ντελικατέσεν ⓝ de·li·ka·*te*·sen *delicatessen*
ντους ⓝ duz *shower*
νύχτα ⓕ *nikh*·ta *night*
νωρίς no·*ris* *early*

Ξ ξ

ξενοδοχείο ⓝ kse·no·tho·*hi*·o *hotel*
ξένη ⓕ *kse*·ni *foreign* a · *stranger* ⓝ
ξένος ⓜ *kse*·nos *foreign* a · *stranger* ⓝ
ξενώνας ⓜ kse·*no*·nas *guesthouse*
ξυπνάω ksip·*na*·o *wake · wake (someone) up*
ξυπνητήρι ⓝ ksip·ni·*ti*·ri *alarm clock*
ξυράφι ⓝ ksi·*ra*·fi *razor blade*
ξυρίζω ksi·*ri*·zo *shave*
ξυριστική μηχανή ⓕ ksi·ri·sti·*ki* mi·kha·*ni* *razor*

Ο ο

ο καλύτερος ⓜ o ka·*li*·te·ros *best* a
ο μεγαλύτερος o me·gha·*li*·te·ros *biggest*
ο μικρότερος o mi·*kro*·te·ros *smallest*
οδηγός ⓜ&ⓕ o·thi·*ghos* *driver · guide (person)*
— **διασκέδασης** ⓜ thia·*ske*·tha·sis *entertainment guide*
οδηγώ o·thi·*gho* *drive* ⓥ
οδοντιατρική κλωστή ⓕ o·tho·di·a·tri·*ki* klo·*sti* *dental floss*
οδοντίατρος ⓜ&ⓕ o·tho·*di*·a·tros *dentist*
οδοντόβουρτσα ⓕ o·tho·*do*·vur·tsa *toothbrush*
οδοντόπαστα ⓕ o·tho·*do*·pa·sta *toothpaste*
οδός ⓕ o·*thos* *street*

οδυνηρός o·thi·ni·*ros* *painful*
Οθωμανικός o·tho·ma·ni·*kos* *Ottoman* a
οικογένεια ⓕ i·ko·*ye*·ni·a *family*
Ολλανδία ⓕ o·lan·*thi*·a *Netherlands*
όλοι o·li *all*
ολονυχτίς o·lo·nikh·*tis* *overnight*
ομάδα αίματος ⓕ o·*ma*·tha e·ma·tos *blood group*
όμορφος o·mor·fos *beautiful · handsome*
ομοφυλόφιλος o·mo·*fi*·lo·fi·los *homosexual*
όνομα ⓝ o·no·ma *name*
οπίσθιος o·*pi*·sthi·os *rear (seat etc)*
οπωροπωλείο ⓝ o·po·ro·po·*li*·o *grocery*
όριο ταχύτητας ⓝ o·ri·o ta·*hi*·ti·tas *speed limit*
όροφος ⓜ o·ro·fos *floor (storey)*
όταν o·tan *when*
όχι o·hi *no · not*

Π π

πάγος ⓜ *pa*·ghos *ice*
παγωμένος pa·gho·*me*·nos *frozen*
παγωτό ⓝ pa·gho·*to* *ice cream*
παζάρι ⓝ pa·*za*·ri *fleamarket*
παιδί ⓝ pe·*thi* *child*
παιδιά ⓝ pl pe·*thia* *children*
παιδικό κάθισμα ⓝ pe·thi·*ko* ka·thiz·ma *child seat*
παιδικός σταθμός ⓜ pe·thi·*kos* stath·mos *crèche*
παλάτι ⓝ pa·*la*·ti *palace*
πάλι pa·li *again*
παλιός pa·*lios* *old* a
παλτό ⓝ pal·*to* *coat*
πάνα ⓕ *pa*·na *diaper · nappy*
πανεπιστήμιο ⓝ pa·ne·pi·*sti*·mi·o *university*
παντελόνι ⓝ pa·de·*lo*·ni *pants · trousers*
παντρεμένη ⓕ pa·dre·*me*·ni *married*
παντρεμένος ⓜ pa·dre·*me*·nos *married*
πάνω pa·no *on · up*
παπούς ⓜ pa·*pus* *grandfather*
παπούτσι ⓝ pa·*put*·si *shoe*
πάρα πολύ pa·ra po·*li* *too (expensive etc)*
παραδίνω pa·ra·*thi*·no *deliver*
παράθυρο ⓝ pa·*ra*·thi·ro *window*
παραλαβή αποσκευών ⓕ pa·ra·la·*vi* a·po·ske·*von* *baggage claim*
παραλία ⓕ pa·ra·*li*·a *beach · seaside*
Παραμονή Πρωτοχρονιάς ⓕ pa·ra·mo·*ni* pro·to·khro·*nias* *New Year's Eve*

παράπονο ⓝ pa·ra·po·no *complaint*
παράσταση ⓕ pa·ra·sta·si *gig*
παρκάρω par·ka·ro *park a car*
Πάσχα ⓝ pas·kha *Easter*
πατέρας ⓜ pa·te·ras *father*
παυσίπονο ⓝ paf·si·po·no *painkiller*
παχύς ⓐ pa·his *fat*
πάω για ψώνια pa·o yia pso·nia
— *go shopping*
πεζοδρόμιο ⓝ pe·zo·thro·mi·o *footpath*
πεζοπορία ⓕ pe·zo·po·ri·a *hiking*
πεζοπορώ pe·zo·po·ro *hike*
πεθερά ⓕ pe·the·ra *mother-in-law*
πεθερός ⓜ pe·the·ros *father-in-law*
πεινώ pi·no *(be) hungry*
πελάτης ⓜ pe·la·tis *client*
πελάτισσα ⓕ pe·la·ti·sa *client*
πέος ⓝ pe·os *penis*
περιήγηση ⓕ pe·ri·i·yi·si *tour*
— με οδηγό ⓜ me o·thi·gho *guided tour*
περιμένω pe·ri·me·no *wait*
περίπτερο ⓝ pe·rip·te·ro *kiosk*
περισσότερος pe·ri·so·te·ros *more*
περπατάω per·pa·ta·o *walk*
πετάω pe·ta·o *fly*
πετρέλαιο ⓝ pe·tre·le·o *petrol*
πετρογκάζ ⓝ pe·tro·gaz *gas (for cooking)*
πετσέτα ⓕ pet·se·ta *towel*
πετσετάκι ⓝ pet·se·ta·ki *napkin*
— υγείας i·yi·as ⓕ
panty liners • sanitary napkins
πηγαίνω pi·ye·no *go*
πιάτο ⓝ pia·to *dish • plate*
πικρός pi·kros *bitter* ⓐ
πίνακας ⓜ pi·na·kas *painting (a work)*
πινακοθήκη ⓕ pi·na·ko·thi·ki *art gallery*
πίνω pi·no *drink*
πιπίλα ⓕ pi·pi·la *dummy • pacifier*
πιρούνι ⓝ pi·ru·ni *fork*
πισίνα ⓕ pi·si·na *swimming pool*
πίστωση ⓕ pi·sto·si *credit*
πιστωτική κάρτα ⓕ pi·sto·ti·ki kar·ta
credit card
πλατεία ⓕ pla·ti·a *square (town)*
πλάτη ⓕ pla·ti *back (body)*
πλατφόρμα ⓕ plat·for·ma *platform*
πλένω ple·no *wash* ⓥ
πληγή ⓕ pli·yi *injury*
πληγωμένος pli·gho·me·nos *injured* ⓐ
πληροφορία ⓕ pli·ro·fo·ri·a *information*
πληροφορική ⓕ pli·ro·fo·ri·ki *IT*
πληρωμή ⓕ pli·ro·mi *payment*
πλυντήριο ⓝ pli·di·ri·o *launderette •*
laundry • washing machine

ποδήλατο ⓝ po·thi·la·to *bicycle • bike*
πόδι ⓝ po·thi *foot • leg*
ποδόσφαιρο ⓝ po·thos·fe·ro *football*
ποιος pios *which • who*
πόλη ⓕ po·li *city*
πολυτέλεια ⓕ po·li·te·li·a *luxury*
πολύτιμος po·li·ti·mos *valuable*
πονόδοντος ⓜ po·no·tho·dos *toothache*
πονοκέφαλος ⓜ po·no·ke·fa·los *headache*
πόνος ⓜ po·nos *pain*
πόρνη ⓕ por·ni *prostitute*
πορτοκαλής por·to·ka·lis *orange (colour)*
πορτοφόλι ⓝ por·to·fo·li *purse*
ποτάμι ⓝ po·ta·mi *river*
ποτήρι ⓝ po·ti·ri *drinking glass*
ποτό ⓝ po·to *drink*
πού pu *where*
πουκάμισο ⓝ pu·ka·mi·so *shirt*
πουλόβερ ⓝ pu·lo·ver *jumper • sweater*
πούρο ⓝ pu·ro *cigar*
πρακτορείο εφημερίδων ⓝ
prak·to·ri·o e·fi·me·ri·thon *newsagency*
πράσινος pra·si·nos *green*
πρατήριο βενζίνας ⓝ pra·ti·ri·o ven·zi·nas
petrol station
πρεσβεία ⓕ prez·vi·a *embassy*
πριν prin *before*
πρόγευμα ⓝ pro·yev·ma *breakfast*
πρόγραμμα ⓝ pro·ghra·ma *timetable*
προετοιμασία εγγράφων ⓝ
pro·e·ti·ma·si·a e·gra·fon *paperwork*
προηγούμενος pro·i·ghu·me·nos
last • previous
προκαταβολή ⓕ pro·ka·ta·vo·li
deposit (on house etc)
προμήθεια ⓕ pro·mi·thi·a *commission*
προμήθειες φαγητού ⓕ pl
pro·mi·thi·es fa·yi·tu *food supplies*
προξενείο ⓝ prok·se·ni·o *consulate*
προορισμός ⓜ pro·o·riz·mos *destination*
προσαύξηση τιμής ⓕ pro·saf·ksi·si
ti·mis *cover charge*
πρόστιμο ⓝ pros·ti·mo *fine (penalty)*
προσωπική επιταγή ⓕ pro·so·pi·ki
e·pi·ta·yi *check (banking) • cheque*
πρόσωπο ⓝ pro·so·po *face*
προϋπολογισμός ⓜ pro·i·po·lo·yiz·mos
budget
προφυλακτικό ⓝ pro·fi·lak·ti·ko *condom*
προχθές prokh·tes *day before yesterday*
πρωί ⓝ pro·i *morning*
πρώτη τάξη ⓕ pro·ti tak·si *first class*
Πρωτοχρονιά ⓕ pro·to·khro·nia
New Year's Day

πτήση ⓕ *pti·si flight*
πυρετός ⓜ *pi·re·tos fever*

Ρ ρ

ράδιο ⓝ *ra·thi·o radio*
ραντεβού ⓝ *ra·de·vu appointment • date*
ράφτης ⓜ *raf·tis tailor*
ράφτρα ⓕ *raf·tra tailor*
ρεσεψιόν ⓕ *re·sep·sion check-in (desk)*
ρέστα ⓝ pl *re·sta change (money)*
ρεύμα ⓝ *rev·ma current (electricity)*
ρινική αλλεργία ⓕ *ri·ni·ki a·ler·yi·a hay fever*
ροζ *roz pink*
ρούχα ⓝ pl *ru·kha clothing*

Σ σ

Σαββατοκύριακο ⓝ *sa·va·to·ki·ria·ko weekend*
σακίδιο ⓝ *sa·ki·thi·o backpack*
σάκος ⓜ *sa·kos bag*
σαμπάνια ⓕ *sam·pa·nia champagne*
σαπούνι ⓝ *sa·pu·ni soap*
σε *se at • to*
σεισμός ⓜ *siz·mos earthquake*
σελφ σέρβις ⓝ *self ser·vis self-service*
σεμινάριο ⓝ *se·mi·na·ri·o conference (small) • seminar*
σεντόνι ⓝ *se·do·ni sheet (bed)*
σεντόνια ⓝ pl *se·do·nia bed linen*
σερβιτόρα ⓕ *ser·vi·to·ra waitress*
σεξ ⓝ *seks sex*
σεφ ⓜ *sef chef • cook*
σημειωματάριο ⓝ *si·mi·o·ma·ta·ri·o notebook*
σήμερα *si·me·ra today*
σι ντι ⓝ *si di CD*
σι ντι ρομ ⓝ *si di rom disk (CD-ROM)*
σίδερο ⓝ *si·the·ro iron (for clothes)*
σιδηροδρομικός σταθμός ⓜ *si·thi·ro·thro·mi·kos stath·mos railway station*
σκάλα ⓕ *ska·la stairway*
σκιά ⓕ *ski·a shade*
σκληρός *skli·ros hard (not soft)*
σκοτεινός *sko·ti·nos dark* a
σκουλαρίκια ⓝ pl *sku·la·ri·kia earrings*
σκουπιδοτενεκές ⓜ *sku·pi·tho·te·ne·kes garbage can*
σκούρος *sku·ros dark (colour)* a

σκυλί ⓝ *ski·li dog*
Σκωτία ⓕ *sko·ti·a Scotland*
σλάιντ ⓝ *sla·id slide (film)*
σοκολάτα ⓕ *so·ko·la·ta chocolate*
σορτς *sorts shorts*
σουβενίρ ⓝ *su·ve·nir souvenir*
σουγιάς ⓜ *su·yias penknife*
σουτιέν ⓝ *su·ti·en bra*
σπασμένος *spaz·me·nos broken*
σπίρτα ⓝ pl *spir·ta matches (for lighting)*
σπίτι ⓝ *spi·ti home*
σπουδαίος *spu·the·os important*
σπουδαστής ⓜ *spu·tha·stis student*
σπουδάστρια ⓕ *spu·tha·stri·a student*
σπρέι ⓝ *spre·i spray*
σταθμός ⓜ *stath·mos station*
σταθμός λεωφορείου ⓜ *stath·mos le·o·fo·ri·u bus station*
σταθμός μετρό ⓜ *stath·mos me·tro metro station*
σταθμός τρένου ⓜ *stath·mos tre·nu train station*
στάση ⓕ *sta·si stop (bus, tram, etc)*
  — λεωφορείου ⓕ *le·o·fo·ri·u bus stop*
  — ταξί ⓕ *tak·si taxi stand*
σταχτοθήκη ⓕ *stakh·to·thi·ki ashtray*
στεγνός *stegh·nos dry* a
στήθος ⓝ *sti·thos chest (body)*
στην ώρα *stin o·ra on time*
στόμα ⓝ *sto·ma mouth*
στομάχι ⓝ *sto·ma·hi stomach*
στομαχόπονος ⓜ *sto·ma·kho·po·nos stomachache*
στραμπούλισμα ⓝ *stra·bu·liz·ma sprain*
στρώμα ⓝ *stro·ma mattress*
στυλό ⓝ *sti·lo pen (ballpoint)*
σύζυγος ⓜ&ⓕ *si·zi·ghos husband • wife*
συμπεριλαμβανομένου *si·be·ri·lam·va·no·me·nu included*
συνάδελφος ⓜ *si·na·thel·fos colleague*
συναδέλφισσα ⓕ *si·na·thel·fi·sa colleague*
συνάλλαγμα ⓝ *si·na·lagh·ma exchange*
σύνδεσμος ⓜ *sin·thez·mos connection*
συνέδριο ⓝ *si·ne·thri·o conference (big)*
συνεισφέρω *si·nis·fe·ro contribute*
συνιστώ *si·ni·sto recommend*
σύνορο ⓝ *si·no·ro border*
συνταγή ⓕ *si·da·yi prescription*
σύνταξη ⓕ *si·dak·si pension*
συνταξιούχα ⓕ *si·dak·si·u·kha pensioner*
συνταξιούχος ⓜ *si·dak·si·u·khos pensioner*
σύντομα *si·do·ma soon*
συντροφιά ⓕ *si·dro·fia company (friends)*

σύντροφος ⓜ si·dro·fos *companion*
συντρόφισσα ⓕ si·dro·fi·sa *companion*
συστημένο sis·ti·me·no *by registered mail*
σωσίβιο ⓝ so·si·vi·o *life jacket*

Τ τ

ταμείο ⓝ ta·mi·o *cash register*
ταμίας ⓜ&ⓕ ta·mi·as *cashier*
ταμπόν ⓝ ta·bon *tampon*
ταξίδι ⓝ tak·si·thi *journey • trip*
 — **εργασίας** ⓝ er·gha·si·as *business trip*
 — **του μέλιτος** ⓝ tu me·li·tos
 honeymoon
ταξίδι με ωτοστόπ tak·si·thi me o·to·stop
 hitchhike ⓥ
ταξιδιωτική επιταγή ⓕ tak·si·thi·o·ti·ki
 e·pi·ta·yi *travellers cheque*
ταξιδιωτικό γραφείο ⓝ tak·si·thi·o·ti·ko
 ghra·fi·o *travel agency*
ταυτότητα ⓕ taf·to·ti·ta
 identification • identification card
ταχυδρομείο ⓝ ta·hi·thro·mi·o
 mail • post office
ταχυδρομικό κουτί ⓝ ta·hi·thro·mi·ko
 ku·ti *mailbox*
ταχυδρομικός τομέας ⓜ
 ta·hi·thro·mi·kos to·me·as *postcode*
ταχυδρομώ ta·hi·thro·mo *post* ⓥ
ταχύτητα φιλμ ⓕ ta·hi·ti·ta film *film speed*
τελεφερίκ ⓝ te·le·fe·rik *chairlift (skiing)*
τέλος ⓝ te·los *end*
τελωνείο ⓝ te·lo·ni·o *customs*
τένις ⓝ te·nis *tennis*
τέχνη ⓕ tekh·ni *craft • art*
τηγάνι ⓝ ti·gha·ni *frying pan*
τηγανίζω ti·gha·ni·zo *fry* ⓥ
τηλεγράφημα ⓝ ti·le·ghra·fi·ma *telegram*
τηλεκατεύθυνση ⓕ ti·le·ka·tef·thin·si
 remote control
τηλεόραση ⓕ ti·le·o·ra·si *television • TV*
τηλεφωνικός κατάλογος ⓜ
 ti·le·fo·ni·kos ka·ta·lo·ghos *phone book*
τηλέφωνο ⓝ ti·le·fo·no *telephone*
τηλεφωνώ ti·le·fo·no *telephone* ⓥ
της tis *her (ownership/direct object)*
τιμή ⓕ ti·mi *price*
 — **εισόδου** ⓕ i·so·thu *admission (price)*
 — **εξυπηρέτησης** ⓕ ek·si·pi·re·ti·sis
 service charge
 — **συναλλάγματος** ⓝ si·na·lagh·ma·tos
 currency exchange • exchange rate

τίποτε ti·po·te *nothing*
τίτλος κατόχου αυτοκινήτου ⓜ tit·los
 ka·to·khu af·to·ki·ni·tu *car owner's title*
το πιο κοντινό to pio ko·di·no *nearest*
τοπικός to·pi·kos *local* a
τοστ ⓝ tost *toast*
τοστιέρα ⓕ to·stie·ra *toaster*
του tu *his (ownership/direct object)*
τουαλέτα ⓕ tu·a·le·ta *toilet*
τουριστική θέση ⓕ tu·ri·sti·ki the·si
 economy class
τουριστικό γραφείο ⓝ tu·ri·sti·ko ghra·fi·o
 tourist office
τουριστικός οδηγός ⓜ
 tu·ri·sti·kos o·thi·ghos *guidebook*
τράπεζα ⓕ tra·pe·za *bank*
τραπεζικός λογαριασμός ⓜ tra·pe·zi·kos
 lo·gha·riaz·mos *bank account*
τρένο ⓝ tre·no *train*
τρόλεϊ ⓝ tro·le·i *trolley bus*
τρώγω tro·gho *eat* ⓥ
τσάντα ⓕ tsa·da *handbag*
τσιγάρο ⓝ tsi·gha·ro *cigarette*
τσιμιδάκι ⓝ tsi·bi·tha·ki *tweezers*
τσίρκο ⓝ tsir·ko *circus*
τσιρότο ⓝ tsi·ro·to *Band-Aid*
τυρί ⓝ ti·ri *cheese*
τώρα to·ra *now*

Υ υ

υπεραστικό λεωφορείο ⓝ
 i·pe·ra·sti·ko le·o·fo·ri·o *intercity bus*
υπέρβαρο φορτίο ⓝ i·per·va·ro for·ti·o
 excess baggage
υπηρεσία ⓕ i·pi·re·si·a *service*
υπνοδωμάτιο ⓝ ip·no·tho·ma·ti·o
 bedroom
υπόγειος i·po·yi·os *subway* a
 — **σιδηρόδρομος** ⓜ
 si·thi·ro·thro·mos *subway train*
υποδηματοποιείο ⓝ i·po·thi·ma·to·pi·i·o
 shoe shop
υπότιτλοι ⓜ pl i·po·ti·tli *subtitles*
υποχρέωση ⓕ i·po·khre·o·si
 engagement • obligation

Φ φ

φαγητό ⓝ fa·yi·to *food*
 — **για μωρά** ⓝ yia mo·ra *baby food*
φαγούρα ⓕ fa·ghu·ra *itch*

φάκελος ⑩ *fa*·ke·los *envelope*
φακοί επαφής ⑩ pl fa·*ki* e·pa·*fis* *contact lenses*
φακός ⑩ fa·*kos lens* • *flashlight* • *torch*
φαρμακείο ⑪ far·ma·*ki*·o *pharmacy*
φάρμακο ⑪ *far*·ma·ko *medicine*
— **για το βήχα** ⑪ yia to *vi*·kha *cough medicine*
φαρμακοποιός ⑩&⑪ far·ma·ko·pi·*os pharmacist*
φερμουάρ ⑩ fer·mu·*ar zip* • *zipper*
φέρι ⑪ *fe*·ri *ferry*
φέτα ⑪ *fe*·ta *slice*
φθινόπωρο ⑪ fthi·*no*·po·ro *autumn* • *fall*
φιλενάδα ⑪ fi·le·*na*·tha *girlfriend*
φίλη ⑪ *fi*·li *friend*
φιλμ ⑪ film *film* • *movie*
φιλοδώρημα ⑪ fi·lo·*tho*·ri·ma *gratuity* • *tip*
φίλος ⑩ *fi*·los *boyfriend* • *friend*
φλας ⑩ flas *flashlight*
φλιτζάνι ⑪ fli·*dza*·ni *cup*
φόρεμα ⑪ *fo*·re·ma *dress*
φούρνος ⑩ *fur*·nos *bakery* • *oven*
— **μικροκυμάτων** ⑩ mi·kro·ki·*ma*·ton *microwave oven*
φουσκάλα ⑪ fu·*ska*·la *blister*
φούστα ⑪ *fu*·sta *skirt*
φρένα ⑪ pl *fre*·na *brakes*
φρέσκος *fre*·skos *fresh*
φρούτα ⑪ pl *fru*·ta *fruit*
φτηνός fti·*nos cheap* a
φύλαξη αποσκευών ⑪ *fi*·lak·si a·po·ske·*von luggage lockers*
φως ⑪ fos *light*
φωτογραφία ⑪ fo·to·gra·*fi*·a *photo*
φωτογραφική ⑪ fo·to·ghra·fi·*ki photography*
φωτογραφική μηχανή ⑪ fo·to·ghra·fi·*ki* mi·kha·*ni camera*
φωτογράφος ⑩&⑪ fo·to·*ghra*·fos *photographer*

χαλασμένος kha·laz·*me*·nos *broken down* • *out of order* • *spoiled (food)*
χαλκός ⑩ khal·*kos copper*
χαμένος kha·*me*·nos *lost* a
χάπι ⑪ *kha*·pi *pill*
χάρτης ⑩ *khar*·tis *map (of country/town)*
χαρτί ⑪ khar·*ti paper*
— **υγείας** ⑪ i·*yi*·as *toilet paper*

χαρτομάντηλα ⑪ pl khar·to·*ma*·di·la *tissues*
χαρτονόμισμα ⑪ khar·to·no·*miz*·ma *banknote*
χαρτοπωλείο ⑪ khar·to·po·*li*·o *stationer's shop*
χαρτοφύλακας ⑩ khar·to·*fi*·la·kas *briefcase*
χειμώνας ⑩ hi·*mo*·nas *winter*
χειροποίητο hi·ro·*pi*·i·to *handmade* a
χέρι ⑪ *he*·ri *arm* • *hand*
χιλιόγραμμο ⑪ hi·*lio*·gra·mo *kilogram*
χιλιόμετρο ⑪ hi·*lio*·me·tro *kilometre*
χιόνι ⑪ *hio*·ni *snow*
χορεύω kho·*re*·vo *dance* ⓥ
χορός ⑩ kho·*ros dancing*
χορτοφάγος ⑩&⑪ khor·to·*fa*·ghos *vegetarian* a
χρήματα ⑪ pl *khri*·ma·ta *money*
Χριστούγεννα ⑪ pl khri·*stu*·ye·na *Christmas*
χρόνος ⑩ *khro*·nos *year*
χρυσάφι ⑪ khri·*sa*·fi *gold*
χρώμα ⑪ *khro*·ma *colour*
χτένα ⑪ *khte*·na *comb*
χτες khtes *yesterday*
χωρίς kho·*ris without*
χώρος ⑩ *kho*·ros *venue* • *place*
— **για κάμπινγκ** ⑩ yia *kam*·ping *camping ground* • *campsite*
χωροφύλακας ⑩ kho·ro·*fi*·la·kas *police officer*
χωροφυλακίνα ⑪ kho·ro·fi·la·*ki*·na *police officer*

Ψ ψ

ψαλίδι ⑪ psa·*li*·thi *scissors*
ψάρεμα ⑪ *psa*·re·ma *fishing*
ψηφιακός psi·fi·a·*kos digital* a
ψηλός psi·*los high* • *tall*
ψιλά ⑪ pl psi·*la change (money)*
ψιχάλα ⑪ psi·*kha*·la *drizzle*
ψυγείο ⑪ psi·*yi*·o *fridge* • *refrigerator*
ψωμί ⑪ pso·*mi bread*
ψωνίζω pso·*ni*·zo *shop* ⓥ

Ω ω

ώμος ⑩ *o*·mos *shoulder*
ώρα ⑪ *o*·ra *hour* • *time*
ώρες λειτουργίας ⑪ pl *o*·res li·tur·*yi*·as *opening hours*

A

abbreviations 10
accents 13
accidents 58, 191
accommodation 65
addresses 63, 66, 98, 116
addressing people 109
adjectives (grammar) 17
adverbs (grammar) 17
age 105, 112
air conditioning 48, 55, 70
alcoholic drinks 167
allergies 174, 202
alphabet 34
alternative treatments 204
ambulance 191
amounts 35, 37, 171
animals 113, 155
apologising 204
appointments 97
architecture 94
arranging to meet 129
art 139
articles (grammar) 17
asking someone out 131
ATMs 43, 91, 92

B

babysitter 103
bag (shopping) 171
baggage 49
ballet 119, 128
banking 91, 100
bargaining 77
bars 128, 169
basics (food) 157
basics (meeting people) 107
battery (camera) 81
beach 153
beer 168

beliefs 137
be (verb) 18
bicycle 59
bill (restaurant) 161
birthday 105
boat 45, 52
body parts (diagram) 203
booking (accommodation) 66
books 78
border crossing 61
breast-feeding 105
bus 45, 50, 64
business 97
business card 97

C

calendar 40
camping 65, 72, 152
car (general) 55
car (diagram) 58
cardinal numbers 35
car & motorbike hire 55
case (grammar) 19
cell phone 89
changing money 44, 68, 91
changing room (babies) 103
changing room (gym) 145
checking in (accommodation) 66
checking out (accommodation) 71
chemist 104, 195, 204
cheque (banking) 44, 91
children 103
children (discounts) 43, 61, 96, 103
children's menu 159
cinema 117, 119, 127
clothes 79, 95
coach (bus) 50
coffee 166
communications 85, 98
compass points 51, 63
complaints (accommodation) 70

complaints (bills) 44, 71, 164
complaints (shopping) 76, 83
compliments (food)...............................165
computer facilities 90, 98
conditions (health)..............................198
conference 97
consonant sounds...................................12
contact details 87, 89, 97, 98, 116
contraception 134, 201, 202
cost (accommodation) 67
cost (admission) 95
cost (banking)..91
cost (beach)...153
cost (camping)...72
cost (internet)...90
cost (phone) 88, 89
cost (restaurant)...................................161
cost (shopping)......................................171
cost (sport)...145
cost (transport)......................................56
credit cards 43, 67, 77, 92
culinary reader 175
cultural differences.....................137, 138
currency...44
customs (border crossing) 61
customs (local/national) 138
Cyprus..9

D

dancing 118, 131
dates (calendar) 39, 40, 66
days of the week......................................40
deaf travellers.......................................101
debit cards 43, 77
declaration (customs) 62
delays (travel)..45
demonstratives (grammar)...................20
dentist 195, 206
dentist (children)..................................105
department store 75
diagram (body parts)............................203
diagram (car)..58
diagram (room) 68
diagram (street) 64
diagram (table)......................................164
dictionary (English–Greek)..................207
dictionary (Greek–English)..................239
dictionary (shopping) 78

directions...56, 63
disabled travellers...............................101
discounts 47, 96, 103
diving...150
doctor 191, 195
doctor (children)...................................105
doctor (women)....................................195
drinking.....................128, 167, 170, 197
drugs (illicit)...130
duty-free...50, 79
DVDs...81

E

eateries 159, 168
eating out..157
electronic goods.....................................79
elevator..69
email..98, 116
embassies...194
emergencies...191
emergency department.......................195
emotions 60
endearments...135
entertainment guide..............................78
environment..125
etiquette tips.............................107, 159
exchange rate................................44, 91

F

family...114
family ticket..103
farewells.......................108, 115, 136
fauna...155
feelings...121
ferry 45, 52, 56
film (camera)...128
film (cinema)...................117, 119, 127
finding a place to eat...........................158
fines (punishment)................................194
fishing..146
flora..155
food & drink..157
food (preparation) 165, 172
food (takeaway) 163
football (soccer).........................142, 144
foreign exchange office.................43, 91

formality 109
fractions 37
future (time) 42

G

galleries 139
garage (petrol station) 57
gas (fuel) 57
gay travellers 127, 192
gender (grammar) 21, 35, 36, 79
glossary (grammar) 32
going out 127
goodbyes 107, 108
grammar 15
greetings 107
guides 93, 96, 151

H

hairdressing 80
halal food 173
have (verb) 21
health 195
hiking 141, 151
hire (bicycle) 59
hire (car & motorbike) 55
hire (sports) 145
hobbies 117
horse riding 147
hospital 195
hotel 61, 65
hot water 69

I

identification 61, 92
idioms 60, 74
illnesses 53, 198
immigration 61
insurance (car hire) 56
insurance (road) 57
insurance (travel) 192, 196
insurance (work) 99
interests 117
Internet 86, 90, 98
intonation (pronunciation) 13
introductions (meeting people) 108
invitations 98, 128, 131, 169

J

jewellery 84
jobs 99, 113

K

keys 58, 69
kosher food 173

L

language difficulties 33
language map 8
lawyer 194
lift 101
local drinks 167
local specialties 158, 162, 171
lost 192
love 135
luggage 49, 55

M

making conversation 110
maps 51, 56, 60, 63, 93, 151
map (language) 8
market 75
meals 157
measures (amounts) 35, 37, 171
mechanic 58
medication 62, 194, 195, 196, 199
meeting (business) 97
meeting people 107
menu 159, 162
menu (child's) 103
menu reader 162, 175
messages (accommodation) 69
messages (phone) 89
metro 51
mobile phone 89
money 194
months 40
motorbike 55
museums 139
music 81, 117, 118

N

names 38, 105, 106
nationalities 111
negatives (grammar) 22
newspapers 78
nonalcoholic drinks 166
nonsmoking (section) 47, 159
numbers 35

O

occupations 113
older people 96
opening hours 95
opinions 121, 122
optometrist 195
ordering food 173
ordinal numbers 36
outdoors 151

P

paperwork 99
park (playground) 104
parking (car) 57, 72, 101, 193
parts of the body 203
party (entertainment) 128
party (politics) 123
passport 61, 66, 194
passport photos 82
past (time) 41
pensioners 96
personal pronouns (grammar) 23
petrol 57
pharmacist 104, 195, 204
phone 87, 98, 194
phone number 87, 116
photos 94, 111
photography 81
pick-up lines 131
PIN 92
plane 45, 50
plants 155
playing sport 143
plurals (grammar) 24
police 52, 191, 192
politeness 109

politics 118, 123
possessives (grammar) 25
post office 85
preparing food 165, 172
prepositions (grammar) 26
prescriptions (medical) 196, 204
present (time) 41
problems (car & motorbike) 58
problems (romance) 136
pronunciation 11
public phone 87

Q

quantities 35, 37, 171
queries (accommodation) 68
queries (restaurant) 160
questions (grammar) 27

R

reading (books) 78
reading Greek 13
receipts 69, 196
recommendations
  (accommodation) 66, 71
recommendations (books) 78
recommendations (eating out) 158
recommendations (food) 160
recommendations (music) 81
refunds 44, 77
rejections (romance) 132
religion 137
renting (accommodation) 73
repairs (bicycle) 59
repairs (general) 83
requests (accommodation) 68
requests (grammar) 29
requests (shopping) 76
reservations (accommodation) 66, 158
reservations (taxi) 54
reservations (travel) 46, 48
residency permit 100
responding to invitations 129
résumé 100
reverse charges (phone) 87
romance 131
room (diagram) 68